Y0-CDJ-791

高中英语
词汇精选

俞敏洪 ○ 编著

西安交通大学出版社
XI`AN JIAOTONG UNIVERSITY PRESS

图书在版编目(CIP)数据

高中英语词汇精选 / 俞敏洪编著. —西安：西安
交通大学出版社，2012.11
ISBN 978-7-5605-4287-4

Ⅰ．①高…　Ⅱ．①俞…　Ⅲ．①英语—词汇—高中—教
学参考资料　Ⅳ．①G634.413

中国版本图书馆 CIP 数据核字(2012)第 073529 号

书　　　名	高中英语词汇精选	
编　　著	俞敏洪	
责任编辑	董云梅　孙　岩	
封面设计	大愚设计	
出版发行	西安交通大学出版社	
地　　址	西安市兴庆南路 10 号(邮编:710049)	
电　　话	(010)62605588　62605019(发行部)	
	(029)82668315(总编室)	
读者信箱	bj62605588@163.com	
印　　刷	北京四季青印刷厂	
字　　数	400 千	
开　　本	880mm×1230mm　1/32	
印　　张	10.5	
版　　次	2012 年 11 月第 1 版　2012 年 11 月第 1 次印刷	
书　　号	ISBN 978-7-5605-4287-4/G・444	
定　　价	25.00 元	

寻找生命的榜样 (代序)

我并不是一个很聪明的人，从小学到大学几乎从没得过第一名。不是我不努力，而是我努力了也成不了第一名。惟一的一次第一名是我连续两年落榜之后在 1980 年的高考中考出了全县外语类总分第一名，正是这次第一名把我送进了北京大学。也许是因为天资愚笨，我总是羡慕那些比我优秀的人，追随在他们后面，还热心地为他们做事。我的优点就是从来不妒嫉比我优秀的人，我总是努力模仿他们，把他们作为我学习的榜样。正是这一优点成就了我的今天。

父母是最接近我们的学习榜样。我的父母都是淳朴的农民，他们虽无力教我读书，但却用他们的勤劳和善良教会我做人的基本道理和是非标准，他们对我的影响无法用文字来描述，是我一生都受用不尽的。我生命中第一个榜样是雷锋同志。在我开始懂事时正是全国学习雷锋的高潮。记得有一次为了学习雷锋，我和另一个小朋友为一户人家担水，结果那个小朋友被父母骂了一顿，因为他自己家里的水还没有担满。而我母亲却夸奖了我。这样的事情在我小时候时常发生。父母的鼓励养成了我喜欢帮助别人的习惯。这一习惯使我在后来的工作和生活中受益良多。

我高中毕业时正值恢复全国高考，我的一个同学考上了一所大专师范学院。他是当时我们班惟一考上大学的人，这在全校引起了轰动。同学们在羡慕一番后都回家变成了地道的农民。我却一直想着这件事，下决心第二年再考，结果又失败了。想放弃的我看到他暑假回来春风得意的样子，心里就不服气，来年又考了一次。这一次轮到他羡慕我了，因为我进了中国最好的大学之一。后来我一直对他心存感激，到现在我们仍是好朋友。

　　进了大学后我发现同学都比我优秀，自己真是一穷二白。穷是经济上的，白是知识上的。经济上的穷不可怕，知识上的空白却让我陷入了极度的自卑。好在我的自卑不是心胸狭隘，最后自卑反而成了我学习的动力。在北大读书的几年，尽管从没谈过恋爱，但却追随了不少优秀人物，公开或偷偷地从他们身上吸取精华。现在在新东方共事的很多优秀人物都是我过去二十多年学习的榜样。王强特别喜欢买书读书，我几乎每星期都追随他逛书店，自己也买书来读。王强迄今已有藏书逾万册，我的藏书虽不及他，却学到了和他相近的读书习惯。徐小平当年在北大是著名的活跃分子，思想敏锐，口若悬河，我经常听他侃大山，听到激动人心处就赶紧记下，回去暗暗模仿。今天我上课风格里有一部分就来自徐小平。另外还有我上铺的包凡一，他独到的批判精神和自嘲精神，对我后来的做事方式和判断力也产生了很深的影响。

　　我读过不少名人传记，也仰慕过毛泽东的天才、富兰克林的智慧、林肯的信念、卢梭的坦诚，甚至羡慕过毕加索的九次婚姻。但这些伟大人物离我们的生活太远，他们远不如那些与我们朝夕相处的人们对我们的影响力大。所以，我们要善于从生活中寻找榜样，诚心诚意地向他们学习，这样，即使你不能超越他们，你也会变得更加优秀！

新东方教育科技集团董事长兼总裁

本书特点

本书以教育部制订的最新版《普通高中英语课程标准(实验)》为依据，涵盖最新版《普通高等学校招生全国统一考试大纲》所要求的全部重要词汇，并按照单词难易程度和考试要求的不同，将单词分为简单单词和核心单词。其中核心单词为高中英语学习的重点，读者除了要掌握其拼写和发音外，还要熟练掌握其用法和搭配。因此，我们在核心单词部分，除了给出音标和中文释义外，还设有以下项目：

【记】通过谐音、串连、图形、联想等多种生动有趣的方法帮助读者记忆单词的词形和词义。

【用】通过分析历年高考真题，本书将真题中考查的语法内容提炼总结后放到对应的单词下面，使读者在记忆单词时能及时了解该单词的语法功能和使用方法。需要指出的是此部分总结的内容全部来自高考真题，对读者备考有很强的指导性。

【例】将对应的单词放到一个句子或短语中，辅助读者记忆单词的同时又使读者掌握了该单词的正确用法。

【考】该部分内容为真题中经常考查的惯用短语和习语，熟练掌握这部分内容不但可以提高读者的阅读和写作能力，而且可以加强语感，进而提高整体英文水平。

【衍】我们将主词的派生词、同义词和反义词进行总结后统一放在该栏目下，这些单词之间联系紧密，"打包"记忆既不增加读者的负担，又扩大了读者的词汇数量。

【辨】英语中有许多单词或短语，它们的意思相近或用法相似，既是考试中的常客，也是最让考生头痛的难点。为帮助读者解决这一难题，我们将易混单词或词组进行归纳，以最简单的语言进行阐释，确保内容翔实、语言简练。

另外，本书用"*"标记出了对于高中生较为生僻的词汇，读者对于这类词汇不必强求拼写，在阅读中遇到时能够识别词义即可。

在每个 List 后面，附有 15 道词汇练习。此部分习题以历年高考真题为主，使读者在平时的学习中就能熟悉高考的命题特点，进而了解高考命题规律。不仅能有效地巩固读者的记忆成果，对每个 List 也进行了重点提炼，所以该部分习题也可作为复习重点用于考前突破。

"读书可以益智"，好的图书更要反复认真阅读。希望读者能够静下心来细心阅读本书，使它能够发挥最大的功效，帮助读者在英语学习上迅速进步。

目 录

简单单词

accent ['æksənt] *n.* 口音，音调

act [ækt] *n.* 法令，条例 *vt.* 行动 *vi.* 演戏

ad [æd] (=advertisement) *n.* 广告

AD *n.* 公元

address [ə'dres; 'ædres] *n.* 地址

adult ['ædʌlt] *n.* 成年人

Africa ['æfrikə] *n.* 非洲

against [ə'geinst] *prep.* 对着，反对

aid [eid] *n.* 援助，救护；辅助器具 *v.* 帮助

aircraft ['ɛəkrɑ:ft] *n.* (单复数同) 飞机

airline ['ɛəlain] *n.* 航空公司，航空系统

airspace ['ɛəspeis] *n.* 领空

arrow ['ærəu] *n.* 箭，箭头记号

astronaut ['æstrəˌnɔ:t] *n.* 宇航员

Atlantic [ət'læntik] *adj.* 大西洋的

atom ['ætəm] *n.* 原子，微粒

author ['ɔ:θə] *n.* 作者，作家

avenue ['ævəˌnju:] *n.* 大道

award [ə'wɔ:d] *n.* 奖品，奖励

baggage ['bægidʒ] *n.* 行李

bamboo [ˌbæm'bu:] *n.* 竹

bandage ['bændidʒ] *n.* 绷带

basin ['beisn] *n.* 水盆，脸盆

bat [bæt] *n.* 球棒；蝙蝠

1

bathroom ['bɑ:θˌru:m] n. 浴室，洗手间

bathtub ['bɑ:θˌtʌb] n. 澡盆，浴缸

battery ['bætəri] n. 电池

bay [bei] n. 湾，海湾

BC n. 公元前

beach [bi:tʃ] n. 海滨，海滩

bean [bi:n] n. 豆，豆科植物

beast [bi:st] n. 野兽，牲畜

*beddings ['bediŋz] n. 被褥

bell [bel] n. 钟，铃；钟形物

belt [belt] n. (皮)带

biology [bai'ɔlədʒi] n. 生物(学)

bomb [bɔm] n. 炸弹 vt. 轰炸

boot [bu:t] n. 长筒靴，靴子

bowl [bəul] n. 碗

bowling ['bəuliŋ] n. 保龄球

boxing ['bɔksiŋ] n. 拳击(运动)

brush [brʌʃ] n. 刷子 vt. 刷；擦

button ['bʌtn] n. 纽扣；(电铃等的)按钮 v. 扣(纽扣)

*cab [kæb] n. (英 taxi)出租车

cabbage ['kæbidʒ] n. 卷心菜，洋白菜

cafe ['kæfei; kæ'fei] n. 咖啡馆，餐馆

cage [keidʒ] n. 笼，鸟笼

camel ['kæml] n. 骆驼

candle ['kændl] n. 蜡烛

candy ['kændi] n. 糖果

cap [kæp] n. 帽子；(瓶子)盖；笔套

capital ['kæpitl] n. 首都，省会；大写；资本

captain ['kæptin] n. (海军)上校；船长；队长

carpet ['kɑ:pit] n. 地毯

carrot ['kærət] n. 胡萝卜

castle ［ˈkɑːsl; ˈkæsl］ n. 城堡

cave ［keiv］ n. 洞，穴，地窖

CD （=compact disk） n. 光盘

ceiling ［ˈsiːliŋ］ n. 天花板，顶棚

cent ［sent］ n. 美分（100 cents = 1 dollar）

cheek ［tʃiːk］ n. 面颊，脸蛋

cheese ［tʃiːz］ n. 奶酪

chemist ［ˈkemist］ n. 药剂师；化学家

chess ［tʃes］ n. 棋，国际象棋

Christmas ［ˈkrisməs］ n. 圣诞节（12月25日）

church ［tʃəːtʃ］ n. 教堂，教会

concert ［ˈkɔnsət］ n. 音乐会，演奏会

cook ［kuk］ n. 炊事员，厨师 v. 烹调，做饭

cooker ［ˈkukə］ n. 炊具（锅、炉灶等）

cookie ［ˈkuki］ n. 小甜饼

cotton ［ˈkɔtn］ n. 棉花 adj. 棉花的

cough ［kɔf］ n./v. 咳嗽

cow ［kau］ n. 母牛，奶牛

curtain ［ˈkəːtn］ n. 窗帘

*cushion ［ˈkuʃn］ n. 垫子

dam ［dæm］ n. 水坝，堰堤

disk ［disk］（=disc） n. 磁盘

eagle ［ˈiːgl］ n. 鹰

essay ［ˈesei］ n. 散文，随笔

feather ［ˈfeðə］ n. 羽毛

fever ［ˈfiːvə］ n. 发烧，发热

fist ［fist］ n. 拳头

fox ［fɔks］ n. 狐狸

fur ［fəː］ n. 毛皮，皮

glove ［glʌv］ n. 手套

glue ［gluː］ n. 胶水

goat [gəut] n. 山羊

god [gɔd] n. 神（God 上帝）

grammar ['græmə] n. 语法

grey/gray [grei] adj. 灰色的，灰白的

ham [hæm] n. 火腿

handkerchief ['hæŋkətʃiːf] n. 手帕

handsome ['hænsəm] adj. 英俊的

highway ['haiwei] n. 公路，大路

hobby ['hɔbi] n. 爱好，嗜好

hole [həul] n. 洞，坑

hotdog ['hɔtdɔg] n. 热狗（红肠面包）

huge [hjuːdʒ] adj. 巨大的，庞大的

hunger ['hʌŋgə] n. 饥饿 v. 饥饿；渴望

jar [dʒɑː] n. 罐子，坛子

jaw [dʒɔː] n. 下巴；钳子

jeans [dʒiːnz] n. 牛仔裤

kitchen ['kitʃin] n. 厨房

lab [læb]（= laboratory）n. 实验室

lead [liːd] v.（led, led, leading）领导，带领 n. 铅

lemon ['lemən] n. 柠檬 adj. 柠檬色（味）的

lemonade [ˌlemə'neid] n. 柠檬水

lend [lend] vt.（lent, lent, lending）借（出），把…借给

lid [lid] n. 盖子

lip [lip] n. 嘴唇

liquid ['likwid] n. 液体 adj. 液体的

lorry ['lɔri; 'lɔːri] n.（美truck）运货汽车，卡车

lung [lʌŋ] n. 肺

madam(e) ['mædəm] n. 夫人，女士

*maid [meid] n. 女仆，少女

mailbox ['meilbɔks] n. 邮箱，邮筒

*maple ['meipl] n. 枫树

*marble [ˈmɑːbl] n. 大理石；玻璃球

march [mɑːtʃ] n. 游行，行进

mat [mæt] n. 垫子

mathematics [ˌmæθəˈmætiks] n. 数学

merry [ˈmeri] adj. 高兴的，愉快的

metre [ˈmiːtə] n. (美meter) 米，公尺

mild [maild] adj. 温和的；轻微的

millionaire [ˌmiljəˈnɛə] n. 百万富翁

missile [ˈmisail; ˈmisl] n. 导弹

*mist [mist] n. 雾

model [ˈmɔdl] n. 模型，样式；范例；模范

Mom [mɔm] n. (英Mum)妈妈

monitor [ˈmɔnitə] n. 班长；监视器 vi. 监视，监听

*monument [ˈmɔnjumənt] n. 纪念碑，纪念物

*mop [mɔp] v. (mopped, mopped, mopping) 用拖把拖地
n. 拖把

mosquito [məˈskiːtəu] n. 蚊子

motorcycle [ˈməutəˌsaikl] n. 摩托车

moustache [məˈstɑːʃ] n. 小胡子

mud [mʌd] n. 泥，泥浆

mushroom [ˈmʌʃruːm] n. 蘑菇

*mustard [ˈmʌstəd] n. 芥末，芥子粉

*mutton [ˈmʌtn] n. 羊肉

*navy [ˈneivi] n. 海军

neat [niːt] adj. 整洁的，灵巧的

needle [ˈniːdl] n. 针

nephew [ˈnefjuː] n. 侄子，外甥

nest [nest] n. 巢，窝

network [ˈnetwəːk] n. 网络，网状系统

niece [niːs] n. 侄女，甥女

noodle [ˈnuːdl] n. 面条

*novelist ['nɔvəlist] n. 小说家

nowadays ['nauədeiz] adv. 当今，现在

nuclear ['nju:kliə(r)] adj. 原子核的，原子能的，核动力的

nursery ['nə:səri] n. 托儿所

Olympic(s) [əu'limpik(s)] n./adj. 奥林匹克(的)

overcoat ['əuvəkəut] n. 大衣

ox [ɔks] n. (pl. oxen)牛，公牛

paint [peint] n. 油漆 v. 油漆；绘画

part-time ['pɑ:t 'taim] adj./adv. 兼职的(地)，部分时间的(地)

path [pɑ:θ] n. 小道，小径

*pause [pɔ:z] n./vi. 暂停，停止

PC (=personal computer) n. 个人电脑

peach [pi:tʃ] n. 桃子

pear [pεə] n. 梨子，梨树

*pension ['penʃən] n. 养老金

*pill [pil] n. 药丸，药片

pillow ['piləu] n. 枕头

pilot ['pailət] n. 飞行员

pine [pain] n. 松树

pineapple ['pain,æpl] n. 菠萝

ping-pong ['piŋpɔŋ] n. 乒乓球

*pint [paint] n. (液量单位)品脱

pioneer [ˌpaiə'niə] n. 先锋，开拓者

pipe [paip] n. 管子，输送管

planet ['plænit] n. 行星

plastic ['plæstik] adj. 塑料的

platform ['plæt,fɔ:m] n. 讲台,(车站的)月台

pocket ['pɔkit] n. (衣服的)口袋

poem ['pəuim] n. 诗

poet ['pəuit] n. 诗人

*pole [pəul] n. 杆，电线杆；极

policy ['pɔləsi] n. 政策，方针

*polish ['pɔliʃ] v. 擦亮，磨光

pond [pɔnd] n. 池塘

pool [puːl] n. 水塘，水池

popcorn ['pɔpˌkɔːn] n. 爆米花

port [pɔːt] n. 港口，码头

postage ['pəustidʒ] n. 邮费

postcode ['pəustkəud] n. (美 zip code)邮政编码

*poster ['pəustə] n. 海报，广告(画)

pot [pɔt] n. 锅，罐

powder ['paudə] n. 粉，粉末

*premier ['premiə; 'priːmiə] n. 总理

president ['prezidənt] n. 总统；主席

pub [pʌb] n. 酒店，酒吧

*pulse [pʌls] n. 脉搏；脉冲 v. 搏动，跳动

purse [pəːs] n. 钱包

push [puʃ] n./v. 推，推动

*quilt [kwilt] n. 被子

*racial ['reiʃəl] adj. 种族的

*radiation [ˌreidi'eiʃən] n. 放射，放射物

*radioactive [ˌreidiəu'æktiv] adj. 放射性的

*radium ['reidiəm] n. 镭

*rag [ræg] n. 破布，抹布

*rainbow ['reinbəu] n. 彩虹；幻想

*random ['rændəm] adj. 随意的，任意的

rank [ræŋk] n. 职衔，军衔

rapid ['ræpid] adj. 快的，迅速的

rat [ræt] n. 老鼠

*raw [rɔː] adj. 生的，未加工的

*ray [rei] n. 光辉，光线

*razor ['reizə] n. 剃须刀

reality [riˈæliti] *n.* 现实

receipt [riˈsiːt] *n.* 收据

receiver [riˈsiːvə] *n.* 电话听筒

recent [ˈriːsnt] *adj.* 近来的，最近的

*reception [riˈsepʃn] *n.* 接待

*receptionist [riˈsepʃənist] *n.* 接待员

*recipe [ˈresəpi] *n.* 食谱

recite [riˈsait] *v.* 背诵

record [ˈrekɔːd] *n.* 记录；唱片

[riˈkɔːd] *v.* 录制，记录

reform [riˈfɔːm] *n.* 改革，改善 *v.* 改革，革新

refrigerator [riˈfridʒəˌreitə] *n.* 冰箱

*regulation [ˌregjuˈleiʃn] *n.* 规则，规章

*reject [riˈdʒekt] *vt.* 拒绝

relationship [riˈleiʃənʃip] *n.* 关系

*relative [ˈrelətiv] *n.* 亲属，亲戚

*relevant [ˈreləvənt] *adj.* 有关的

reliable [riˈlaiəbl] *adj.* 可靠的

relief [riˈliːf] *n.* 缓解(疼痛)；轻松

*religion [riˈlidʒən] *n.* 宗教

*religious [riˈlidʒəs] *adj.* 宗教的

*remark [riˈmɑːk] *n./v.* 陈述，评论

remote [riˈməut] *adj.* 遥远的

*represent [ˌropriˈzent] *vt.* 代表，表现

*reputation [ˌrepjuˈteiʃn] *n.* 名誉，名声

retire [riˈtaiə] *vi.* 退休

riddle [ˈridl] *n.* 谜，神秘的事

*rooster [ˈruːstə] *n.* (英cock)公鸡

*rugby [ˈrʌgbi] *n.* 英式橄榄球

salary [ˈsæləri] *n.* 薪水

*salute [səˈluːt] *n./v.* 敬礼，问候

satellite ['sætəlait] n. 卫星

*saucer ['sɔ:sə] n. 茶碟, 小圆盘

sausage ['sɔsidʒ; 'sɔ:sidʒ] n. 香肠, 腊肠

saying ['seiiŋ] n. 俗话, 谚语

*scar [skɑ:] n. 伤疤

scarf [skɑ:f] n. 领巾, 围巾

scenery ['si:nəri] n. 风景, 景色

scholar ['skɔlə] n. 学者

scholarship ['skɔləʃip] n. 奖学金

scientific [ˌsaiən'tifik] adj. 科学的

*seagull ['si:gʌl] n. 海鸥

seat [si:t] n. 座位, 座 vt. 使就座, 可容纳

*seaweed ['si:wi:d] n. 海草, 海藻

*semicircle ['semiˌsə:kl] n. 半圆

*severe [si'viə] adj. 严重的

sew [səu] v. (sewed, sewed/sewn, sewing) 缝, 缝补, 缝纫

*shabby ['ʃæbi] adj. 破旧的, 衣衫褴褛的

shallow ['ʃæləu] adj. 浅的, 不深的, 肤浅的

shave [ʃeiv] vt. 刮(脸, 胡子)

*shaver ['ʃeivə] n. 电动剃须刀

sheet [ʃi:t] n. 薄片, 薄板

shelf [ʃelf] n. (pl. shelves) 架子, 搁板; 暗礁

shore [ʃɔ:] n. 滨, 岸

shorts [ʃɔ:ts] n. 短裤, 运动短裤

shoulder ['ʃəuldə] n. 肩膀 v. 肩负, 担当

shower ['ʃauə] n. 阵雨; 淋浴

*sideways ['saidweiz] adj. 斜向一边的

sigh [sai] vi./n. 叹息, 叹气

sightseeing ['saitˌsi:iŋ] n. 游览, 观光

signal ['signəl] n. 信号, 暗号

*signature ['signitʃə] n. 签名

silver ['silvə] n. 银

simplify ['simplifai] vt. 简单化, 单一化

*sincerely [sin'siəli] adv. 真诚地

skateboard ['skeitbɔ:d] n. 冰鞋, 滑板

ski [ski:] n. 滑雪板 v. 滑雪

skyscraper ['skai₁skreipə] n. 摩天楼

slavery ['sleivəri] n. 奴隶制度

sleeve [sli:v] n. 袖子, 袖套

*slice [slais] n. 片, 切面(薄)片

*smog [smɔg] n. (= smoke + fog)烟雾

smooth [smu:ð] adj. 光滑的, 平坦的

*sneaker ['sni:kə] n. (pl.)轻便运动鞋

*sneeze [sni:z] n./vi. 打喷嚏

snowy ['snəui] adj. 雪(白)的; 下雪的; 多(积)雪的

*sob [sɔb] n./v. (sobbed, sobbed, sobbing)抽泣, 呜咽地说

*socialism ['səuʃəlizəm] n. 社会主义

*socialist ['səuʃəlist] n. 社会主义者 adj. 社会主义的

sparrow ['spærəu] n. 麻雀, 雀型鸟类

spokesman ['spəuksmən] n. (pl. spokesmen)(男)发言人

spokeswoman ['spəuks₁wumən] n. (pl. spokeswomen) 女发言人

*spoonful ['spu:nful] n. 一匙(的量)

squirrel ['skwirəl; 'skwə:rəl] n. 松鼠

stage [steidʒ] n. 舞台; 阶段

stair [stɛə] n. 楼梯

steak [steik] n. 牛排

steal [sti:l] vt. (stole, stolen, stealing)偷, 窃取

steam [sti:m] n. 蒸汽, 水蒸气

steel [sti:l] n. 钢, 钢铁

*steward [stju:əd; 'stu:əd] n. (火车、飞机、轮船等)男乘务员

*stewardess [₁stju:ə'des; 'stu:ədəs] n. 女乘务员, 空中小姐

*stocking ['stɔkiŋ] n. 长筒袜

*storage [ˈstɔːridʒ] n. 贮藏，储存

stove [stəuv] n. (供烹饪用的)火炉，煤炉，电炉

*strait [streit] n. 海峡

*string [striŋ] n. 细绳，线，带

studio [ˈstjuːdiəu; ˈstuːdiəu] n. 工作室，演播室

*suite [swiːt] n. (一)套，(一)组

*sunburnt [ˈsʌnbəːnt] (=sunburned) adj. 晒黑的，晒伤的

sweat [swet] n. 汗，汗水

*tablet [ˈtæblit] n. 药片

*tailor [ˈteilə] n. 裁缝

tank [tæŋk] n. 储水箱；坦克

tap [tæp] n. (自来水、煤气等的)龙头

task [tɑːsk; tæsk] n. 任务，工作

*tasteless [ˈteistlis] adj. 无滋味的

*taxpayer [ˈtæksˌpeiə] n. 纳税人

*telescope [ˈteliskəup] n. 望远镜

*temple [ˈtempl] n. 庙宇，寺院

thread [θred] n. 线

throat [θrəut] n. 喉咙

thunder [ˈθʌndə] n./vi. 雷声，打雷

*thunderstorm [ˈθʌndəstɔːm] n. 雷暴雨，大雷雨

tidy [ˈtaidi] adj. 整洁的，干净的 v. 弄整洁，弄干净

*tin [tin] n. (美 can)罐头

tiny [ˈtaini] adj. 极小的，微小的

*tip [tip] vt. (tipped, tipped, tipping) 告诫，提示；给小费 n. 顶端；小费；提示

*tiresome [ˈtaiəsəm] adj. 令人厌倦的

tomb [tuːm] n. 坟墓

toothache [ˈtuːθeik] n. 牙痛

toothbrush [ˈtuːθbrʌʃ] n. 牙刷

toothpaste [ˈtuːθpeist] n. 牙膏

*tortoise ['tɔ:təs] *n.* 乌龟

towel ['tauəl] *n.* 毛巾

tower ['tauə(r)] *n.* 塔

*track [træk] *n.* 轨道，路线；田径

treasure ['treʒə] *n.* 金银财宝，财富

troop [tru:p] *n.* 部队

trousers ['trauzəz] *n.* (*pl.*)裤子，长裤

truck [trʌk] *n.* 卡车，运货车 *v.* 装车，用货车运

*trunk [trʌŋk] *n.* 树干；大箱子

*turkey ['tə:ki] *n.* 火鸡

*turning ['tə:niŋ] *n.* 拐弯处，拐角处

tutor ['tju:tə; 'tu:tə] *n.* 家庭教师，指导教师

typewriter ['taipˌraitə] *n.* 打字机

typist ['taipist] *n.* 打字员

tyre ['taiə] *n.* (美 tire) 轮胎

umbrella [ʌm'brelə] *n.* 雨伞

underground ['ʌndəgraund] *adj.* 地下的 *n.* (美 subway)地铁

vase [vɑ:z; veis] *n.* (花)瓶；瓶饰

vast [vɑ:st; væst] *adj.* 巨大的，广阔的

violin [ˌvaiə'lin] *n.* 小提琴

wallet ['wɔlit] *n.* 皮夹子

worm [wə:m] *n.* 蠕虫，蚯蚓

核心单词

Word List 1 4.17 ✓

*abandon [əˈbændən] *vt.* 放弃
【记】联想记忆：a+band(乐队)+on → 乐队表演时，抛开一切杂念→放弃
【例】He *abandoned* his wife and went away with all their money. 他抛弃了他的妻子并带走了他们所有的钱。

abandon

ability [əˈbiliti] *n.* 能力，才能
【记】来自able(*adj.* 能够的)
【考】**ability to do...** 有做…的能力：I don't doubt your ability to do the work. 我不怀疑你有承担这项工作的能力。
【衍】disability (*n.* 残疾；无能)

*abnormal [æbˈnɔːml] *adj.* 反常的，变态的
【记】词根记忆：ab(反)+normal(正常的)→反常的
【例】The warm December weather in northern Canada was *abnormal*. 十二月份，加拿大北部气候温暖是不正常的。

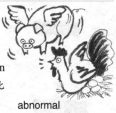
abnormal

aboard [əˈbɔːd] *prep./adv.* 在船上，上船
【记】联想记忆：a+board(木板，甲板)→在甲板上→在船上
【例】She went *aboard* the ship. 她上了船。

*abolish [əˈbɔliʃ] *vt.* 废止，废除
【例】Bad customs should be *abolished*. 应当废除不良习俗。

*abortion [əˈbɔːʃn] *n.* 流产，堕胎
【例】*Abortion* is sometimes used to save the mother's life. 流产有时可以挽救母亲的生命。

about [əˈbaut] *adv.* 大约；到处，周围 *prep.* 关于；在附近，在周围

13

A

【用】1. **be about to do...** 将要（正打算）做某事：I was just about to leave when the phone rang. 我刚要走，电话铃响了。注意：be about to do不能与表示将来的具体时间状语连用。2. **How/What about...?** …怎么样?（表示建议）：What about getting a pet? 养只宠物好吗？

【例】He lives somewhere *about* here. 他住在这附近。

【考】1. **talk about** 谈论，议论 2. **think about** 考虑 3. **hear about** 听说 4. **know about** 了解，知道 5. **look about** 四处观看

abroad [əˈbrɔːd] *adv.* 到（在）国外

【记】联想记忆：ab+road（道路）→上路→出国，到国外

【用】**abroad** 表示到（在）国外，是一个副词，前面不加介词。但可以说from abroad，表示从国外回来。

【考】**be/go abroad** 在/去国外：Emily usually goes abroad to travel in the summer. 艾米莉常在夏天出国旅行。

***abrupt** [əˈbrʌpt] *adj.* 突然的，意外的

【例】an *abrupt* change in the weather 天气的突然变化

***absence** [ˈæbsəns] *n.* 不在，缺席，没有

【例】The decision was made in my *absence*. 这个决定是我不在的时候做出的。

absent [ˈæbsənt] *adj.* 缺席的，不在的

【考】**be absent from** 缺席：He had been absent 95 times from class and had six failing grades for the year. 今年他逃了95次课，6门功课不及格。

***absolute** [ˈæbsəluːt] *adj.* 完全的，绝对的

【例】The Prime Minister had *absolute* control of his cabinet. 首相对他的内阁有绝对的控制权。

absorb [əbˈsɔːb] *vt.* 吸收；吸引

【记】词根记忆：ab（离去）+sorb（吸收）→吸收掉→吸收

【用】**be absorbed in doing...** 专心做某事：He is absorbed in reading. 他在全神贯注地读书。

【例】I used a sponge to *absorb* the spilled milk. 我用海绵吸干了溢出来的牛奶。

***abstract** [ˈæbstrækt] *n.* 抽象，概要 *adj.* 抽象的

【例】an *abstract* idea 抽象概念

*abundant [əˈbʌndənt] *adj.* 丰富的，充裕的

【例】*Abundant* rainfall made the land fertile. 丰沛的雨水使得土地肥沃。

*abuse [əˈbjuːz] *vt.* 滥用

[əˈbjuːs] *n.* 辱骂，粗话

【记】词根记忆：ab(变坏)+use(使用)→使用不当→滥用

【例】Don't *abuse* your authority! 不要滥用你的权力！//A stream of *abuse* came from his lips.他说了一些粗话。

*academy [əˈkædəmi] *n.* 学院

【例】an *academy* of music 音乐学院

【衍】academic(*adj.* 学院的，学术的；理论的)

*accelerate [əkˈseləreit] *vt.* 加速，促进

【记】词根记忆：ac(加强)+celer(速度)+ate(使…)→加速

【例】Too much sunshine *accelerates* the aging process of your skin. 过量的阳光会加快你皮肤衰老的进程。

accept [əkˈsept] *v.* 接受

【记】词根记忆：ac+cept(拿，抓)→拿住→接受；同根词有：except (*v.* 除外)；conception(*n.* 概念)

【例】Please *accept* my apologies. 请接受我的歉意。

【衍】acceptable (*adj.* 可接受的)

【辨】**accept, receive**

accept表示主观上"接受"，而**receive**表示客观上"收到"，如：She received a birthday present from a boy but did not accept it. 她收到一个男孩送来的生日礼物，但没有接受。

*access [ˈækses] *n.* 入门，通路 *vt.* 接近；存取

【考】**have access to...** 有(使用/接近)…的权利：The students have free access to these books. 学生可以自由使用这些图书。

*accessible [əkˈsesəbl] *adj.* 可使用的，可进入的，易接近的

【例】The tower is not *accessible* to the public. 这座塔不对公众开放。

【衍】inaccessible (*adj.* 无法进入的，无法使用的)

accident

accident [ˈæksidənt] *n.* 事故，意外的事

【例】traffic *accident* 交通事故

accommodation [əˌkɔməˈdeiʃn] *n.* (*pl.*) 膳宿

【例】Our *accommodations* in the expensive hotel were not very good. 我们下榻的那家奢侈的饭店食宿并不好。

accompany [əˈkʌmpəni] *vt.* 陪伴，伴随；伴奏

【例】Can you *accompany* me to the hospital? 你能陪我去医院吗?

accomplish [əˈkʌmpliʃ;əˈkɔmpliʃ] *vt.* 完成，达到

【例】I was not able to *accomplish* all I set out to do. 我不能完成所有我事先计划要做的事情。

【衍】accomplishment(*n.* 成就)

account [əˈkaunt] *n.* 账目；描述 *v.* 总计有，认为

【记】ac+count(计算)→账目

【考】**account for** (在数量、比例方面)占: Travel and tourism account for 11.4 percent of employment in the United States. 旅游业中的就业机会占美国全部就业机会的11.4%。

accountant [əˈkauntənt] *n.* 会计，会计师

【记】account(账目)+ant(…的人)→管账目的人→会计

【例】My *accountant* will prepare my taxes. 我的会计师会给我准备好税金的。

accumulate [əˈkjuːmjuleit] *vt.* 堆积，积累

【例】You will *accumulate* a good small library, if you buy 10 books every month. 每个月买十本书，你就能积累一个丰富的小图书馆。

accurate [ˈækjurit] *adj.* 正确的，准确的

【例】Your statements about the cost of the house were not *accurate*. 你对这房子造价方面的说明不够准确。

【衍】inaccurate(*adj.* 不正确的); accuracy*(*n.* 准确性)

【辨】**accurate, correct, right**
accurate 强调"准确的，精准的"(肯定正确但更强调其准确性); **correct** 强调"正确的"; **right** 则可表示"恰当的"(同义词为 suitable)或"正确的"(同义词为correct)。

accuse [əˈkjuːz] *vt.* 控告，谴责

【用】**accuse sb. of doing sth.** 控告某人做某事: The police accused him of stealing. 警方控告他偷窃。

【例】He was *accused* of incompetence. 他被指责为不称职。

*accustomed [əˈkʌstəmd] *adj.* 通常的，习惯的

【记】ac(加强)+custom(习惯)+ed→习惯的

【用】**be accustomed to...** 习惯于…: He has been accustomed to the customs here. 他已经习惯了这里的风俗。

ache [eik] *vi.* 疼痛 *n.* 痛，疼痛

【例】My head begins to *ache* when I read too much. 看书太多的话，我的头就开始疼。

ache

achieve [əˈtʃiːv] *vt.* 达到，取得

【例】The team *achieved* victory after lots of hard work. 经过艰苦的训练后，这支队伍取得了胜利。// *achieve* great success 取得巨大成功

【衍】achievement(*n.* 成就，功绩)

*acid [ˈæsid] *adj.* 酸的

【例】*acid* rain 酸雨

*acknowledge [əkˈnɔlidʒ] *vt.* 答谢；承认

【例】I *acknowledged* Tom for all of his help with the project. 我非常感谢汤姆在这个项目上对我的帮助。// He is *acknowledged* as the best tennis-player in the world.他被公认为是世界最佳网球选手。

*acquaintance [əˈkweintəns] *n.* 相识，熟人

【例】I met an *acquaintance* of yours at the train station. 我在火车站碰到了你的一个熟人。

【衍】acquaint(*vt.* 通知，使认识)

*acquire [əˈkwaiə] *vt.* 获得，学到

【例】Tom *acquired* a famous painting from an art dealer. 汤姆从一个艺术品经销商那里得到一幅名画。

*acquisition [ˌækwiˈziʃn] *n.* 获得，获得物

【例】Tom's newest *acquisition* is a sports car. 汤姆的最新添置是一辆跑车。

acre [ˈeikə] *n.* 英亩；田地

【例】*acres* of land 广阔的土地

across [əˈkrɔs;əˈkrɔːs] *prep.* 横过，穿过

【记】a(加强)+cross(横过)→横过

【考】**come across** 偶遇，不期而遇

【例】We swam *across* the river. 我们游到河对岸。

A

action [ˈækʃn] *n.* 行动

【记】词根记忆：act(行动)+ion(名词后缀)→行动

【考】**take action**(**against...**) 采取行动(对抗…)：Immediate action should be taken to stop the spreading of the fire. 必须采取紧急措施以阻止火势蔓延。

active [ˈæktiv] *adj.* 积极的，主动的

【记】词根记忆：act(行动)+ive(形容词后缀)→积极的

【例】You are not *active* enough in putting forward your suggestions. 在提出自己建议的方面你不够积极。

activity [ækˈtiviti] *n.* 活动

【记】词根记忆：act(活动)+ivity(名词后缀)→活动

【例】social *activities* 社会活动

actress [ˈæktris] *n.* 女演员

【记】来自act(扮演)+ress(女性)→女演员；actor(*n.* 男演员)
类比记忆：waiter(*n.* 男服务生)，waitress(*n.* 女服务生)

【例】Many *actresses* attended the party. 许多女演员出席了那个聚会。

actual [ˈæktʃuəl] *adj.* 实际的，现实的

【例】in *actual* life 在现实生活中

****adapt** [əˈdæpt] *v.* (使)适应；改编

【考】**adapt to...** 适应…：Many plants and animals have adapted to life in the desert. 许多动植物已经适应了在沙漠里生存。

【衍】adaptation*(*n.* 改编；适应)

add [æd] *v.* 添加，增加

【考】1. **add...to...** 把…加到…：Many words are added to the new edition of the dictionary. 这个新版本的词典里加了许多词语。2. **add to...** 增加某物：The bad weather added to our difficulties. 坏天气增加了我们的困难。3. **add up** 把…加起来：Please add up all the money I should pay. 请把我要付的钱加起来。4. **add up to...** 总计达到…：The income adds up to 10,000 dollars. 收入达到一万美元。

****addicted** [əˈdiktid] *adj.* 入迷的，上瘾的

【例】He is *addicted* to smoking. 他吸烟上瘾了。

****addition** [əˈdiʃn] *n.* 增加，加法

【记】联想记忆：add(加)+ition→增加

【考】1. **in addition** 另外　2. **in addition to** 除…之外

*adequate [ˈædikwit] *adj.* 足够的，适当的

【例】We took *adequate* food for the holiday. 我们为假期带足食品。

【衍】inadequate(*adj.* 不充分的)

*adjust [əˈdʒʌst] *v.* 适应；调整，调节

【例】John *adjusted* himself very quickly to the weather of France. 约翰很快使自己适应了法国的天气。

【衍】adjustable(*adj.* 可调节的)；adjustment*(*n.* 调整，调节)

*administration [ədˌminisˈtreiʃn] *n.* 管理；行政部门

【例】business *administration* 工商管理

admire [ədˈmaiə] *vt.* 钦佩，羡慕

【考】**admire sb. for sth.** 因某事而佩服某人：I *admire* Anne for her courage. 我佩服安妮的勇气。

【衍】admirable*(*adj.* 令人钦佩的，绝妙的)

*admission n.准入，接纳；承认；入场费

单元自测

1. Bill was doing a lot of physical exercises to build up his _____.
   A. ability　　　　B. force　　　　C. strength　　　　D. mind

2. The news that Lindbergh intended to fly the Atlantic alone was _____ with disbelief.
   A. received　　　　B. accepted　　　　C. taken　　　　D. met

3. _____ is known to all, good friends _____ happiness and value to life.
   A. It; add　　　　B. As; add　　　　C. It; add up　　　　D. As; add to

4. One of the consequences of our planet's being warming up is a(n) _____ in the number of natural disasters.
   A. result　　　　B. account　　　　C. reason　　　　D. increase

5. After the accident, she had _____ all over.
   A. pains　　　　B. pain　　　　C. ache　　　　D. aches

6. —Did your uncle fly to Paris directly?
   —No, he travelled from Hong Kong _____ London.
   A. through　　　　B. by way of　　　　C. across　　　　D. on way of

7. We all know that _____ speak louder than words.
   A. movement　　　　B. performances　　　　C. operations　　　　D. actions

8. While a person is asleep, a part of his brain is still _____.

A. active   B. alive   C. awake   D. aware

9. _____ for his bravery, William was asked to give a speech.

 A. Admired B. Admiring C. Having admired D. Being admired

10. _____ its beautiful scenery, it has a pronounced musical atmosphere and is known as "the city of music".

 A. In spite of B. In addition to C. In relation to D. In place of

11. The reasons for our decision are _____ in my report.

 A. set off   B. set in   C. set out   D. set about

12. So many directors _____, the board meeting had to be put off.

 A. were absent B. been absent C. had been absent D. being absent

13. The writer was _____ in his novel that he forgot to flick the ashes from his cigarette.

 A. absorbed B. lost   C. devoted   D. interested

14. It is not easy for such a young boy to understand such a(n) _____ concept.

 A. easy   B. big   C. huge   D. abstract

15. The sunlight came in _____ the windows in the roof and lit up the whole room.

 A. through B. across   C. on   D. over

答案：CCBDA BDCAB CDADA

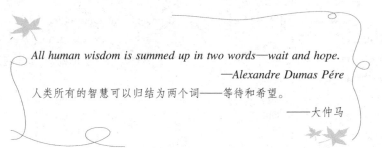

All human wisdom is summed up in two words—wait and hope.

—Alexandre Dumas Pére

人类所有的智慧可以归结为两个词——等待和希望。

——大仲马

Word List 2 4.18 √

admit [əd'mit] *v.* (admitted, admitted, admitting) 承认；准许（入场，入学等）

【用】1. **admit doing...** 承认做过某事：Luz admitted stealing clothes from the shop. 露兹承认从商店偷了衣服。2. **admit...into/to...** 让…进入…：More middle school graduates will be admitted into universities. 将有更多的中学毕业生进入大学。

【衍】admission（*n.* 准入，接纳）

adolescence ['ædəu'lesəns] *n.* 青春期

【例】*Adolescence* can be a confusing time. 青春期是一个充满疑惑的时期。

【衍】adolescent*（*n.* 青年 *adj.* 青春期的，青春的）

adopt [ə'dɔpt] *vt.* 采用；收养

【记】词根记忆：ad+opt（选择）→选择→采用

【例】We should *adopt* the consumers' suggestion. 我们应该接受用户的建议。//As they had no children of their own, they *adopted* an orphan. 他们没有亲生儿女，就收养了一个孤儿。

adore [ə'dɔ:] *vt.* 爱慕，崇拜

【记】谐音记忆："我倒"→ adore

【例】Grandpa *adored* Grandma from the day they first met. 从相遇的那一天起，爷爷就喜欢上了奶奶。

adore

advance [əd'vɑ:ns；əd'væns] *v./n.* 推进，前进

【考】**in advance** 预先，提前：We will have to book our tickets in advance. 我们得提前订票。

【衍】advanced（*adj.* 高级的，先进的）

advantage [əd'vɑ:ntidʒ；əd'væntidʒ] *n.* 优点，好处

A

【考】**take advantage of** 利用：Let's take advantage of the long vacation and make a trip to Hong Kong. 我们利用这个长假去香港旅行吧!

【例】Her rich experience gave her an *advantage* over other applicants for the job. 她丰富的经验使她比其他求职者更具优势。

【衍】disadvantage（*n.* 缺点，坏处）

adventure [əd'ventʃə] *n.* 冒险；奇遇

【例】The spy's work was filled with *adventures*. 间谍的工作中充满了冒险。

advertise ['ædvətaiz] *vt.* 为…做广告

【例】We *advertised* our sale in the local paper. 我们在当地报纸上进行广告促销。

【衍】advertisement（*n.* 广告）

advice [əd'vais] *n.* 忠告，劝告，建议

【考】1. **ask for advice** 征求意见 2. **give/offer some advice** 提建议 3. **take/follow one's advice** 采纳/接受某人的意见 4. **two pieces of advice** 两条建议

advise [əd'vaiz] *vt.* 忠告，劝告，建议

【用】1. advise后接宾语从句时，从句谓语用虚拟语气，即：**should+ do**，其中should可以省略：I advised that you（should）get a haircut before your interview. 我建议过你面试前该先理个发。具有相同用法的动词还有：insist, demand, desire, request, require, order, command, prefer, propose, ask, suggest等。2. **advise** 后接动名词作宾语，即：**advise doing...** 建议做某事：I advise starting early. 我建议早点出发。3. **advise**后接动词不定式作宾语补足语，即：**advise sb.（not）to do sth.** 建议某人（不）做某事：The teacher advised his students to choose proper major. 那位老师建议学生们选择适合的专业。

advocate ['ædvəkeit] *vt.* 提倡，鼓吹

【例】The social activist *advocated* change. 社会行动主义者提倡变革。

affair [ə'fɛə] *n.* 事，事情

【例】I have a few *affairs* to take care of this week. 我这周有很多事要处理。

affect [ə'fekt] *vt.* 影响

【记】词根记忆：af+fect（做）→影响，同根词有：effect（*n.* 影响）；infect（*v.* 感染）；perfect（*adj.* 完美的）

【例】The bad climate *affected* her health. 恶劣的气候影响了她的健康。

affection [əˈfekʃən] *n.* 友爱，爱情

【例】Bill completely ignored Lisa's *affections*, and that hurt her feelings. 比尔完全无视丽莎的爱意，这使她很伤心。

afford [əˈfɔːd] *vt.* 负担得起（费用/时间）；提供

【用】**afford** 常接动词不定式作其宾语。注意：afford一词常用于be able to或can之后：You can't afford to miss another piano lesson. 你不能再缺钢琴课了。

【例】They cannot *afford* the medical fee. 他们负担不起医药费。

afraid [əˈfreid] *adj.* 害怕的，恐惧的

【用】1. **be afraid of（doing）sth.** 害怕…（忧虑某事可能导致的后果）：Are you afraid of dogs? 你怕狗吗？ 2. **be afraid to do sth.** 因害怕而不敢做某事：Billy was afraid to go into the cave. 比利怕进山洞。3. **be afraid +从句** 害怕…，恐怕…：

afraid

I'm afraid I might get hurt. 我担心会受到伤害。4. **I'm afraid so/not.** 恐怕（不）是这样：—Is he badly hurt? —I'm afraid so. —他伤得很重吗？ —恐怕是的。

【衍】frightened（*adj.* 害怕的，受惊的）；scared（*adj.* 恐惧的）

after [ˈɑːftə; ˈæftə] *prep./conj./adv.* 在…之后，后来

【例】*After* you, sir! 先生，请您先走! // I'll call you back *after* I've spoken to David. 跟大卫说完我就给你回电话。// *after* five days（=five days later）五天后

【考】1. **after all** 毕竟，终究：I think you should help him. After all, he is your friend. 我认为你应该帮他。毕竟，他是你的朋友。2. **be after** 追逐，想得到：I think he is after my job. 我觉得他想得到我的工作。3. **soon after** 不久以后

afterward(s) [ˈɑːftəwəd(z); ˈæftəwəd(z)] *adv.* 后来

【例】Mary went to work, and *afterward* she went to dinner. 玛丽去上班，然后再去吃饭。

A

*agency [ˈeidʒənsi] *n.* 代理处，行销处

【例】My father operates an insurance *agency*. 我父亲开了一家保险代理公司。

*agenda [əˈdʒendə] *n.* 议程

【例】How many items are on the *agenda*? 这份议程有多少项？

*agent [ˈeidʒənt] *n.* 代理商

【例】David served as an *agent* for the shipping company. 大卫给航运公司作代理。

*aggressive [əˈgresiv] *adj.* 侵略的，咄咄逼人的

【例】The country made an *aggressive* attack on a neighboring land. 那个国家对邻邦发起了侵略袭击。

agree [əˈgriː] *v.* 同意；应允

【衍】agreement（*n.* 同意；协议）；disagreement（*n.* 不符；争论）

【辨】**agree with, agree to, agree on**
三者都表"同意"的意思，但介词后所接内容不一样，**agree with**后面常接人，表同意某人的观点或适应某地的气候或饮食；**agree to**中的to可能是介词也可能是动词不定式，作介词时后面接物，表批准/赞同某计划或提议，作不定式时后面接动词原形，即agree to do... 表同意做某事；**agree on**后面常接物或动名词，agree on... / doing... 表就某方面意见达成一致。

*agriculture [ˈægrikʌltʃə] *n.* 农业，农学

【衍】agricultural*（*adj.* 农业的）

ahead [əˈhed] *adj./adv.* 在前，向前

【例】Our company is *ahead* of other makers of spare parts for the airplane. 我们公司在飞机零部件制造上比别的公司强。//go *ahead* 向前走

AIDS 艾滋病

aim [eim] *n.* 目的 *v.* 计划；瞄准，针对

【用】1. **aim(sth.) at...** 瞄准，以…为目标：The archer aimed the arrow at the target. 射手将箭瞄准靶子。//We aim at quality rather than quantity. 我们以质量而不是数量为目标。2. **aim to do...** 打算做…：Mary aimed to earn her college tuition during the summer. 玛丽打算暑假期间挣回自己的大学学费。

*alarm [əˈlɑːm] *n.* 警报

【例】*alarm* clock 闹钟

*album [ˈælbəm] *n.* 照相簿，集邮本，签名纪念册

alcohol

*alcohol [ˈælkəhɔl; ˈælkəhɔːl] *n.* 酒精，酒

【例】drink *alcohol* 喝酒

【衍】alcoholic* (*adj.* 含酒精的；*n.* 酒鬼）

alike [əˈlaik] *adj.* 相同的，相似的 *adv.* 类似于，以同样的方式

【例】The twins look *alike*, but they don't act alike. 这对双胞胎长得很像，举止却不像。//Big people, little people, black people, white people— we treat them all *alike*. 大人物、小人物、黑人、白人——我们都一视同仁。

alive [əˈlaiv] *adj.* 活着的，存在的

【用】alive 是典型的表语形容词，很少用作定语。作定语时，应置于所修饰词之后。

【例】Won't new anti-aging techniques keep us *alive* for centuries? 新的抗衰老技术会让我们长生不老吗？

all [ɔːl] *adj./pron./adv.* （三者以上）全部

【用】1. all 与not 连用表示部分否定：Not all the students could pass the exams.（=All the student couldn't pass the exams.）并不是所有的同学都能及格。此类词语还有both, every等。2. 在定语从句中，all 作先行词时，关系代词必须用that（或省略）：This is all that I have. 这就是我的所有。3.主语中有all, 谓语的单复数要由all所修饰或指代的名词的单复数决定。即：如果指代人或物，谓语用复数：All are silent. 所有的人都不作声。如果代表一个整体，用单数：All is silent on the island now. 此时此刻，岛上万籁俱寂。

【考】1. **after all** 毕竟，终究 2. **above all** 首先，最重要的 3. **in all** 总共 4. **all over** 遍及 5. **all through** 一直，始终 6. **not at all** 一点也不 7. **all day/night/week/month/year** 整日/夜/周/月/年

*allergic
adj.过敏的

allow [əˈlau] *vt.* 允许，准许

【用】1. **allow (doing) sth.** 允许（做）某事：Smoking is not allowed in public. 公共场所不许吸烟。2. **allow sb. to do sth.** 允许某人做某事，注意其被动形式：sb. be allowed to do sth.：The government servants aren't allowed to accept rewards.公务员不得接受酬谢。

*allowance [əˈlauəns] *n.* 津贴，补贴

【例】Bill's *allowance* is twenty dollars a week. 比尔每周有20美元的

A

补贴。

almost [ˈɔːlməust] *adv.* 几乎，差不多

【用】almost 常与 **no, none, nothing, never** 等表否定的词连用：
Almost no one believed him. 几乎没有人相信他。

【辨】**almost, nearly**
两词都有"几乎；差不多"的意思，有时可以互换，但 **almost** 可与 no, none, nothing, never 等否定词连用，**nearly** 却不可以；而 **nearly** 在句中可与 not 连用，**almost** 不可以。

alone [əˈləun] *adj.* 单独的，孤独的

【例】He was *alone* in the house. 他独自一人待在家里。

【考】**let alone** 更不用说：He hasn't enough money for food, let alone going to cinema. 他连吃饭钱都不够，就更不用说去看电影了。

【辨】**alone, lonely**
两词意思相近，**alone** 表示"独自一人"，是一种客观的状态；而 **lonely** 表示"孤独寂寞"，是一种主观的感受。如：He is alone in the house, but he doesn't feel lonely. 他独自一人在家，但他并不感到孤独。

alongside [əˌlɒŋˈsaid] *adv./prep.* 在旁边，沿着

【记】along（沿着）+side（边）→沿着

【例】The car drew up *alongside* the road. 小汽车在路边停下来。

alphabet [ˈælfəbet] *n.* 字母表

already [ɔːlˈredi] *adv.* 已经

【例】She had *already* gone when I arrived. 我到的时候她已经走了。

also [ˈɔːlsəu] *adv.* 也

【用】**also** 与 **too, as well** 一样只能用于肯定句，否定句中用 either。

【例】If you will jump, I will *also*. 如果你要跳，我也要跳。

alternative [ɔːlˈtəːnətiv] *adj.* 选择性的，二者择一的

【例】I have an *alternative* plan in case it rains during the picnic. 万一野餐时下雨，我还有一个备选的计划。

although [ɔːlˈðəu] *conj.* 虽然，尽管

altitude [ˈæltitjuːd; ˈæltituːd] *n.* 高度，高处

【例】The pilot announced that our *altitude* was 30,000 feet. 飞行员宣

布我们的海拔为30,000英尺。

altogether [ˌɔːltəˈgeðə] *adv.* 总共

always [ˈɔːlweiz] *adv.* 总是，一直，永远

【用】注意：**always**常与现在进行时连用，表示反复性、一贯性的动作，常带有赞扬或厌恶的感情色彩：He is always thinking of how he can do more for the people. 他总是在考虑如何为人们多做点事。

【例】The child is *always* biting his nails. 那个孩子老是咬指甲。

*** amateur** [ˈæmətə] *adj.* 业余爱好的 *n.* 业余爱好者

【例】The band was made up of *amateur* musicians. 乐队由一些音乐业余爱好者组成。

amaze [əˈmeiz] *vt.* 惊奇，惊叹，震惊

【例】The magician *amazed* the children with interesting tricks. 魔术师有趣的戏法令孩子们惊叹不已。

【衍】amazing（*adj.* 令人惊异的）；amazed（*adj.* 吃惊的，感到惊奇的）

*** ambassador** [æmˈbæsədə] *n.* 大使

【衍】ambassadress（*n.* 女大使；大使夫人）

*** ambiguous** [æmˈbigjuəs] *adj.* 暧昧的，不明确的

【例】The professor gave an *ambiguous* answer to Jane's question. 教授就简的问题给了一个含糊的答复。

*** ambition** [æmˈbiʃn] *n.* 雄心，野心

【例】Mary has a lot of *ambition*, but she often changes her goals. 玛丽雄心勃勃，但却总是改变目标。

ambulance [ˈæmbjuləns] *n.* 救护车

ambulance

单元自测

1. Sandy could do nothing but _____ to his teacher that he was wrong.
   A. admit   B. admitted   C. admitting   D. to admit

2. The rubber plantation _____ as far as the river.
   A. advances   B. extends   C. lies   D. develops

3. _____ Mr Brown's anger, it was his own son who didn't agree _____ him.
   A. To; with   B. Because of; to   C. With; of   D. For; on

4. Every new _____ has the possibility of making or losing money.　（2002上海）
   A. event   B. venture   C. adventure   D. expectation

5. Please give me _____ on how to learn English.
   A. some suggestion   B. some advice
   C. some advices   D. a little suggestion

6. I should like to rent a house, comfortable and _____ in a quiet neighborhood.
   A. over all   B. above all   C. all in all   D. after all

7. Though the long-term _____ cannot be predicted, the project has been approved（批准）by the committee.
   A. affect   B. effort   C. effect   D. afford

8. —Can you _____ to travel this summer?
   —No, I haven't got enough money and ____now seems to be impossible.
   A. afford, save money   B. afford, to save money
   C. intend, it   D. want, saving money

9. —Go for a picnic this weekend, OK?
   — _____. I love getting close to nature.   （2004福建）
   A. I couldn't agree more   B. I'm afraid not
   C. I believe not   D. I don't think so

10. A good storyteller must be able to hold his listeners' curiosity _____ he reaches the end of the story.   （2003上海）
    A. when   B. unless   C. after   D. until

11. _____ she wondered if she had made a mistake.
    A. Not until long afterwards that
    B. It was not until long afterwards that
    C. Not long until afterwards
    D. It was long afterwards until

12. There are forty-five students in our class, and they are _____ interested in football.
    A. most   B. almost   C. nearly   D. mostly

13. Forgive him, please. I don't think he broke your mirror _____.
    A. with care   B. on purpose   C. for fun   D. with aim

14. He is the most famous musician _____.
    A. live   B. alive   C. lively   D. likely

15. The manager said that he wouldn't _____ anyone to smoke in the office.
    A. allow   B. agree   C. hope   D. see

答案：ABABB BCBAD BDBBA

Word List 3 4.19

amount [əˈmaunt] *vi.* (+to) 总计；等于 *n.* 数量

【记】联想记忆：a+mount (看作mountain山)→到达顶峰→总计

【例】The damage after the fire *amounted* to $500,000. 火灾造成的损失共计50万美元。

【考】1. **a large amount of** 大量 2. **the total amount of** 总额

*ample [ˈæmpl] *adj.* 充足的，丰富的

【考】**be ample for** 对…来说足够的：My income is small, but it is ample for my needs. 我收入虽然不高，但足够我自己花了。

*amuse [əˈmjuːz] *vt.* 使快乐，逗乐

【例】The playful kitten always *amuses* Grandma. 顽皮的小猫总能把奶奶逗乐。

【衍】amusing (*adj.* 有趣的，逗乐的)；

amused (*adj.* 愉快的，开心的)；

amusement (*n.* 娱乐，消遣)

amuse

analyse [ˈænəlaiz] *vt.* 分析，分解

【例】People do not *analyse* every problem they meet. 人们不会对遇到的每一个问题都进行分析。

【衍】analysis (*n.* 分析，分解)

ancestor [ˈænsestə] *n.* 祖宗，祖先

【例】Her *ancestors* came from Italy. 她的祖先来自意大利。

*anchor [ˈæŋkə] *v.* 抛锚，停泊 *n.* 锚

【例】John *anchored* the boat just off shore. 约翰就把船停泊在岸边了。

ancient [ˈeinʃənt] *adj.* 古代的，古老的

【例】an *ancient* city 古城

anger [ˈæŋgə] *n.* 愤怒

【例】Joe's *anger* erupted when he learn

that his car had been stolen. 乔得知自己的车被盗后，怒火中烧。

【考】1. **be filled with anger** 满腔怒火 2. **in anger** 愤怒地

angle [ˈæŋgl] *n.* 角度

【例】The reporter wrote the story from the political *angle*. 记者从政治角度写了这篇报道。

angry [ˈæŋgri] *adj.* 生气的，愤怒的

【考】1. **be angry with sb.** 生某人的气 2. **be angry at/about** 因…而生气

ankle [ˈæŋkl] *n.* 踝

【例】There is something wrong with my *ankle*. 我的脚踝有点儿毛病。

*anniversary [ˌæniˈvɜːsəri] *n.* 周年纪念

【例】My parents were in Europe on their fiftieth wedding *anniversary*. 我父母在欧洲度过了他们结婚50周年纪念日。

announce [əˈnauns] *v.* 宣布，宣告

【例】John and Mary *announced* their engagement last night. 昨天晚上约翰和玛丽宣布了他们订婚的消息。

【衍】announcement (*n.* 通告，声明)

annoy [əˈnɔi] *v.* 使烦恼，使生气；骚扰

【例】John's little brother *annoyed* him by changing the TV channels. 约翰的弟弟总是换台，弄得他很烦。

【衍】annoyance (*n.* 烦恼); annoying (*adj.* 烦人的); annoyingly (*adv.* 烦人地)

annoy

*annual [ˈænjuəl] *adj.* 一年一次的，每年的

【例】The *annual* company barbecue was a success. 公司一年一度的烧烤野餐很成功。

another [əˈnʌðə] *adj.* 另一；别的 *pron.* 另一个

【用】**another** + 数词 + 名词复数：另外的…，再…：We waited for another ten minutes, and then left. 我们又等了十分钟就离开了。//If you want to change for a double room you'll have to pay another $15. 如果你们要换双人间，就得再付15美元。

【例】Can I have *another* cookie? 我能再吃一块小甜饼吗？//I took the dress back and exchanged it for *another*. 我把衣服拿了回去，另换了一件。

【考】1. **one after another** 一个接一个地 2. **one another** 彼此

answer [ˈɑːnsə; ˈænsər] *n.* 答案 *v.* 回答，应答，接电话

【考】1. **in answer to** 回答；响应 2. **answer for** 负责

***antique** [ænˈtiːk] *n.* 古董

anxiety [æŋˈzaiəti] *n.* 忧虑，焦急

【例】Mary's *anxieties* prevented her from starting a new job. 玛丽焦虑不安，这使她无法开展新工作。

antique

anxious [ˈæŋkʃəs] *adj.* 忧虑的，焦急的

【用】1. **be anxious about...** 担忧…：The host was anxious about how the party would go. 主人对派对如何进行有点担忧。2. **be anxious for...** 渴望…：Mr. Lee is anxious for a new car. 李先生非常想拥有一辆新车。3. **be anxious to do sth.** 急于做某事：Jane was anxious to read the book she had just bought. 简迫不及待地想看她刚买的书。

anxious

【衍】anxiously（*adv.* 忧虑地）; eager（*adj.* 热切的，渴望的）

any [ˈeni] *pron./adj.* 任何的；一些，什么

【用】any 表示"一些"时，常用于疑问句、否定句、条件句中，后接不可数名词或可数名词复数。当any用于肯定句中，后接可数名词单数时，意为"任一"：Take any book you like. 你喜欢哪本书就拿哪本。

【例】This room hasn't *any* chair. 这间房子里连把椅子都没有。

anybody [ˈenibɔdi] *pron.* 任何人，无论谁

【例】I haven't seen *anybody*. 我什么人也没看见。

anyhow [ˈenihau] *adv.* 不管怎样

【例】It may rain, but *anyhow* I shall go out. 天可能要下雨，但无论如何我都要出门。

anything [ˈeniθiŋ] *pron.* 某事（物）；任何事（物）

【用】1. **anything**表示某事（物），用于疑问句和否定句中，相当于肯定句中的**something**：Was there anything interesting in the mail? 邮件里面有什么有趣的事情吗？注意：修饰anything, something,

A

nothing等不定代词的形容词要后置：anything else其他的事。2. **anything** 表示任何事(物)，可以用于肯定句、疑问句或否定句中：You can do anything you like. 你爱做什么就做什么。

【考】**anything but** 绝对不：The house is anything but safe. 这房子绝对不安全。

anyway ['eniwei] *adv.* 不管怎样

【例】I'm sorry about that. *Anyway*, I think I'll be able to get in to work tomorrow. 对此我感到抱歉，但不管怎样，我想明天我会去上班。

***apart** [ə'pɑːt] *adv.* 分离，分别地 *adj.* 分开的

【例】The plants are about one meter *apart*. 这些植物的间隔大约在一米左右。

apartment [ə'pɑːtmənt] *n.* (英 flat) 公寓，房间

【例】a row of high-rise *apartments* 一排公寓大楼

apologize [ə'pɒlədʒaiz] *vi.* 道歉，谢罪

【考】**apologize to sb. for sth.** 因某事向某人道歉：Martin apologized to us for hurting our feelings. 马丁因伤害了我们的感情而道歉。

【衍】apology (*n.* 道歉，歉意)

***apparent** [ə'pærənt] *adj.* 明显的，清楚的

【记】联想记忆：ap+parent （父母）→父母对我们的爱很清楚→清楚的

【例】It was *apparent* that he knew nothing about how to repair cars. 很明显，他一点儿也不知道怎样修理小汽车。

【衍】apparently (*adv.* 明显地)

***appeal** [ə'piːl] *n./v.* 呼吁，请求

【考】**appeal to** 恳求，呼吁：He appealed to his neighbors for help. 他向邻居们求助。

appear [ə'piə] *vi.* 出现；看来，似乎

【用】注意：appear是不及物动词，因此不能用被动语态。作系动词时，与seem同义。

【例】The sun *appeared* on the horizon at five o'clock this morning. 今天清晨5点，太阳出现在了地平线上。//The lost dog *appears* to be lonely. 迷路的小狗看起来很孤独。

appearance [ə'piərəns] *n.* 出现，露面；容貌

【例】With the *appearance* of the president, everyone rose. 总统出现

了，人们全体起立。

*appendix [ə'pendiks] n. 附录，附属品；阑尾

*appetite ['æpitait] n. 食欲，胃口

【例】The children's *appetite* was ruined by too much candy. （摄入）太多的糖破坏了孩子的食欲。

*applaud [ə'plɔ:d] v. 鼓掌，喝彩

applaud

【例】At the end of the performance, the audience *applauded* loudly. 演出结束的时候，观众掌声雷动。

apply [ə'plai] v.申请；应用

applicant
n.申请人
application
n.请求,申请

【例】How many jobs did Ben *apply* for? 本申请了多少份工作?

【考】**apply oneself to** 致力于：After a short holiday, he applied himself once more to his studies. 短暂的假期过后，他再次投入到学习中。

【衍】applied (*adj.* 应用的); applicant* (*n.* 申请者); application (*n.* 申请); applicable (*adj.* 适用的)

*appoint [ə'pɔint] vt. 指定，任命

【例】I *appointed* Joe to be my assistant. 我指定乔为我的助理。

appointment [ə'pɔintmənt] n. 约会

【考】**make an appointment** 约会，约定

appreciate [ə'pri:ʃieit] vt. 欣赏，感激

【例】When I reread his poems recently, I began to *appreciate* their beauty. 当我最近重读他的诗时，我才开始欣赏到它们的美。//We *appreciated* the help of our friends. 我们感激朋友们给予的帮助。

approach [ə'prəutʃ] n. 方式，方法 v. 接近，靠近

【考】**the approach to** …的方法

*appropriate [ə'prəupriət] adj. 适当的

【例】The spoken language is not *appropriate* in the workplace. 这种口语不适合在工作场所出现。

*approve [ə'pru:v] vt. 批准，通过 vi. 赞成，满意

【记】和prove (*vt.* 证明) 一起记

【例】The author *approved* the editor's changes. 作者认同了编辑的修改。

A

【衍】approval*（n. 赞成，承认）

approximately [ə'prɒksimətli] adv. 近似地，大约

【例】*Approximately* how long does it take to arrive at the city? 去城里大约要多久?

*apron
n. 围裙

***arbitrary** ['ɑːbitrəri; 'ɑːrbitreri] adj. 武断的，任意的

【例】Buying a home should not be an *arbitrary* decision. 买房子决不能武断决定。

***arch** [ɑːtʃ] n. 拱门，拱形

* **architecture** ['ɑːkitektʃə] n. 建筑，建筑学

* architect
n. 建筑师

【记】联想记忆: arch（拱门）+itec+ture→拱门也是建筑

【例】classical *architecture* 古典建筑

Arctic ['ɑːktik] n. 北极

【例】the *Arctic* Circle 北极圈

【衍】Antarctic（n. 南极）

单元自测

1. The book contains a large _____ of information.

   A. deal   B. amount   C. number   D. sum

2. —You don't mind me smoking here, do you?

   — _____.

   A. No, I really hate smoking   B. I'd appreciate it if you didn't

   C. No, you can't smoke here   D. You'd better give up smoking

3. He _____ to all his friends that he was getting married.

   A. told   B. spoke   C. announced   D. replied

4. She had long been expecting a chance to study abroad, and at last she got _____.

   A. it   B. that   C. another   D. one

5. "I'm looking for a doctor," the voice replied and then _____ the reason.

   A. explained   B. answered   C. showed   D. told

6. I'm _____ to get the tickets for the show, as there are hardly any left.

   A. worried   B. anxious   C. after   D. troubled

7. —When shall we meet again?

   —Make it _____ day you like; it's all the same to me.   （1996全国）

   A. one   B. any   C. another   D. some

8. We haven't enough books for _____; some of you will have to share.（2005全国1）

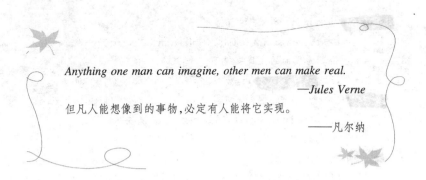
A. somebody   B. anybody   C. everybody   D. nobody

9. I can't tell the exact time when I'll get there. _____, I'll be there as early as I can.

    A. Anyhow   B. In case   C. No matter   D. Therefore

10. _____ breaks the law should be punished without any exception.

    A. Anyone   B. Who   C. Whoever   D. Those who

11. —One week's time has been wasted.

    —I can't believe we did all that work for _____.   （2004重庆）

    A. something   B. nothing   C. everything   D. anything

12. —Where have you been?

    —I got caught in the traffic; _____ I would have been here sooner.

    A. however   B. although   C. anyway   D. otherwise

13. Help will come from UN, but the aid will be _____ near what is needed.

    A. everywhere   B. somewhere   C. anywhere   D. nowhere

14. He _____ to me for the mistake he had made.

    A. excused   B. apologized   C. pardoned   D. regretted

15. She _____ much younger than she really is.

    A. turns   B. becomes   C. grows   D. appears

答案：BBCDD BBCAC BDDBD

Anything one man can imagine, other men can make real.

　　　　　　　　　　　　　　　　　—*Jules Verne*

但凡人能想像到的事物，必定有人能将它实现。

　　　　　　　　　　　　　　　——凡尔纳

Word List 4

4.20

argue [ˈɑːgjuː] *v.* 争论，说服

【例】Susan and her brother *argued* over which television program to watch. 苏珊和弟弟为看哪个电视节目而争论。

【衍】argument (*n.* 争论，辩论)

arise [əˈraiz] *vi.* (arose, arisen, arising) 起来，升起；出现

【例】When the actors appeared, the audience *arose* and applauded. 当演员出现时，观众起身鼓掌喝彩。//Here's my phone number and call me if trouble *arises*. 这是我的电话号码，有问题给我打电话。

arithmetic [əˈriθmətik] *n.* 算术

arm [ɑːm] *n.* 手臂；支架 *v.* 以…装备，武装起来

【例】He held her in his *arms*. 他把她抱在怀里。

【考】1. **arm in arm** 手挽手 2. **arm sb. with sth.** 以…武装某人：The army was armed with the most advanced weapons. 该部队配备了最先进的武器。

armchair
n. 扶手椅

arrange [əˈreindʒ] *vt.* 安排，布置

【考】**arrange...for...** 安排：Bob arranged a party for Mary's birthday. 鲍勃为玛丽的生日安排了一个派对。

army
n. 军队；大批

【衍】arrangement (*n.* 安排，布置)

arrest

arrest [əˈrest] *vt./n.* 逮捕，拘留

【例】The police *arrested* the thief. 警察逮捕了那名小偷。

arrive [əˈraiv] *vi.* 到达，达到

【用】arrive是不及物动词，后接表示地点的名词时需要用at（小地方）或in（大地方）：We arrived at the airport at six. 我们6点钟到达了机场。// She arrived in Rome just now. 她刚刚到达罗马。

【衍】arrival (*n.* 到来，到达)

arrow
n. 箭

artificial *adj.* 人造的，不自然的，做作的 artist *n.* 画家；美术家

article ['ɑːtikl] *n.* 文章；东西；冠词

【例】This *article* mainly tells about the story of a beauty. 这篇文章主要讲述了一个美丽女人的故事。

as [æz] *conj.* 当…时；正如…一样；因为 *prep.* 作为，以…身份 *adv.* 一样…

【用】1. **as**+*adj./adv.*+**as...** 像…一样…：This is not as easy as we imagined. 这不像我们想像的那么简单。//He came as soon as he could. 他尽可能快地赶来了。注意：这个结构中的形容词或副词应为原级。2. 否定句中多用 **not so**+ *adj./adv.* +**as...** 结构：This is not so easy as we imagined. 这不像我们想像的那么简单。

【考】1. **as if/ though** 好像 2. **as a matter of fact** 事实上，实际上 3. **as to/for** 关于，至于 4. **as well** 也，又，同样 5. **so as to** 以便 6. **so long as/as long as** 既然，只要 7. **as a result** 因此

ash *n.* 灰；灰烬

ashamed [ə'ʃeimd] *adj.* 惭愧的，害臊的，羞耻的

【考】**be/feel ashamed for...** 为…而感到惭愧：Are you ashamed for having lied?你撒了谎感到害臊吗？

ask [ɑːsk] *v.* 询问；要求

aside *adv.* 在旁边

【用】1. **ask sb. to do sth.** 要求某人做某事：Jane asked me to do her a favor. 简要我帮她个忙。2. **ask** 后接宾语从句时，从句谓语动词应使用虚拟语气（should）do 的形式。

【考】1. **ask for sth.** 要求，请求 2. **ask（sb.）about sth.**（向某人）打听某事

asleep [ə'sliːp] *adj.* 睡着的，熟睡的

【记】词根记忆：a（…的）+sleep（睡觉）→睡着的

【用】**asleep** 常作表语，用作定语时需置于被修饰词之后。此类表语形容词还有alone, alike, awake等。

【考】**fall asleep** 睡着：Alcohol makes you exited and prevents you from falling asleep. 酒精使你兴奋，让你睡不着觉。

【衍】sleepy（*adj.* 瞌睡的）；sleeping（*adj.* 睡着的，睡觉用的）

✱aspect ['æspekt] *n.* 方面；外表

【例】The students try to look at all *aspects* of the situation. 学生们试着全面看待这种情况。

✱assess [ə'ses] *vt.* 估定，评定

【例】It took a while to *assess* the damage from the tornado. 评估龙卷风所造成的损失需要一段时间。

37

A

【衍】assessment（*n.* 估价）

*assist [əˈsist] *v.* 帮助，协助

assistance
n.援助，帮助，协助

【例】A nurse *assisted* the surgeon during the operation. 手术过程中，有一名护士协助外科医生。

【衍】assistant*（*n.* 助手，助理）

*associate [əˈsəuʃieit] *v.* 结合，结交

【例】Judy always *associates* happiness with money. 朱迪总是把幸福和钱联系在一起。

【衍】association（*n.* 协会；联系，关系）

*assume [əˈsjuːm; əˈsuːm] *vt.* 假定，设想

【例】Mary mistakenly *assumed* that she would get the job. 玛丽错认为她会得到那份工作。

【衍】assumption（*n.* 假定，设想）

*astonish [əˈstɔniʃ] *vt.* 使惊讶

astronaut
n. 宇航员

【例】The ending of the book will *astonish* you. 这本书的结局会让你很惊讶。

*astronomy [əˈstrɔnəmi] *n.* 天文学

【衍】astronomer（*n.* 天文学家）

at [æt] *prep.* 在…；以…

【考】1. **at once** 立刻 2. **at a time** 一次 3. **at times** 有时 4. **at table** 在吃饭 5. **at the age of...** 在…岁时 6. **be good at...** 擅长做…

athlete [ˈæθliːt] *n.* 运动员

【例】An *athlete* must eat well and exercise often. 运动员必须营养饮食，经常锻炼。

*Atlantic
n.&a. 大西洋

【衍】athletic*（*adj.* 运动的）

atmosphere [ˈætməsfiə] *n.* 气氛；大气

【例】We live in an *atmosphere* of freedom. 我们生活在自由的环境中。

attach [əˈtætʃ] *vt.* 系上，贴上

【例】The girl *attached* a big bow to the birthday present. 女孩在生日礼物上系了一个大蝴蝶结。

*attack [əˈtæk] *v./n.* 攻击，袭击

【例】Our dog *attacked* the neighbor's cat. 我们的狗攻击了邻居家的猫。// The police are launching a major attack on drug dealers. 警方对毒品贩子发动了大规模的攻击。

A

*attain [əˈtein] vt. 获得，达到

【例】Tim finally *attained* the degree. 提姆最终获得了学位。

attempt [əˈtempt] vt./n. 试图，尝试

【例】The teacher suggested that the student make an *attempt* at writing the essay. 老师建议同学们尝试写论文。

*attend [əˈtend] v. 出席，参加；专心，考虑；看护，照料

【例】*attend* the meeting 参加会议 // Tom was ready to *attend* to everybody's business but his own. 汤姆乐于助人却忽略了自己。

attend

attention [əˈtenʃn] n. 注意，关心

【考】1. **have one's attention** 让某人注意 2. **pay attention to** 注意 3. **draw/catch one's attention** 引起某人注意

attitude [ˈætitjuːd; ˈætituːd] n. 态度，看法

【考】**one's attitude to/toward(s)...** 某人对某事的态度

attract [əˈtrækt] v. 吸引，引起

【例】He tried to *attract* the attention of the beauty. 他试图引起这个美女的注意。

【衍】attraction (n. 吸引，吸引力)；attractive (adj. 迷人的，有吸引力的)

audience [ˈɔːdiəns] n. 观众，听众

【例】Thousands of *audience* crowded the concert hall. 数千名听众挤满了音乐大厅。

*authentic [ɔːˈθentik] adj. 真的，可信的

【例】Is that an *authentic* painting from Van Gogh, or a copy? 那幅油画是凡高的真迹还是复制品？

*authority [ɔːˈθɔriti] n. 权威；当局

【例】Tom thinks he is an *authority* on baseball statistics, but he isn't. 汤姆觉得自己是棒球统计的权威，可是他不是。// I have to report this to the *authorities*. 我得向官方报告此事。

*automatic [ɔːtəˈmætik] adj. 自动的，机械的

【记】词根记忆：auto（自己）+matic→自己动→自动的

【例】The Smiths bought an *automatic* dishwasher. 史密斯家买了台自动洗碗机。

A

autonomous [ɔːˈtɔnəməs] *adj.* 自治的

【记】词根记忆：auto（自己）+nom（名字）+ous→自己给自己起名字→自治的

【例】The colony wished to become an *autonomous* state. 殖民地希望能变为自治的国家。

autumn n. 秋天

available [əˈveiləbl] *adj.* 有空的；可得到的，可用的

【例】Is Dr. Black *available*? I'd like to talk to him. 布莱克医生有空吗？我想跟他谈一谈。//I'm afraid there are no seats *available* on that flight. 那次航班恐怕已经没有空座了。

average [ˈævəridʒ] *adj.* 平均的；普通的 *n.* 平均数

【考】**on average** 平均：The companies spend, on average, 70 per cent of the total cost of the product itself on packaging. 那些企业平均花费产品总成本的70%用于包装。

avoid [əˈvɔid] *vt.* 避免，躲开，逃避

【用】**avoid doing sth.** 避免某事发生：These measures can avoid people suffering road accidents. 这些措施可以让人避免遭遇交通事故。

awake [əˈweik] *v.* (awoke, awoken, awaking) 唤醒 *adj.* 醒着的

【考】**keep sb. awake** 让某人醒着：Smoking before bedtime keeps you awake. 睡前抽烟会让你睡不着。

aware [əˈwɛə] *adj.* 知道的，意识到的

【考】**be aware of/that...** 意识到…：You can be aware that people judge you by your table manners. 你会意识到人们会根据你饭桌上的仪态来评价你。

award n. 奖励，奖品

away [əˈwei] *adv.* 离开，远离

【考】1. **right away** 立刻 2. **run away** 跑开 3. **break away from** 脱离

awesome [ˈɔːsəm] *adj.* 可怕的，引起敬畏的

【记】awe（敬畏）+some（…的）→引起敬畏的

【例】An *awesome* storm overtook the small ship. 一场可怕的风暴掀翻了小船。

awful [ˈɔːfl] *adj.* 糟糕的，可怕的

【记】来自awe（敬畏）+ful→令人敬畏的→可怕的

【例】The food at that restaurant was *awful*. 那家餐馆的饭菜太难吃了。

awful

B

【衍】awkwardly（*adv.* 笨拙的）；awkwardness（*n.* 笨拙）

awkward ['ɔːkwəd] *adj.* 笨拙的；难使用的

【例】The tools may be *awkward* for someone with a very small hand. 这些工具对于那些手很小的人来说可能不太好用。

【衍】awkwardly（*adv.* 笨拙地）；awkwardness（*n.* 笨拙）

bachelor ['bætʃələ] *n.* 学士；单身汉

【例】*Bachelor* of Education 教育学学士

【衍】master（*n.* 硕士）；doctor（*n.* 博士）

back [bæk] *adv.* 回（原处），向后 *adj.* 后面的

n. 背后，后部；背

bachelor

【考】1. **get back to** 回到，恢复 2. **take back** 收回 3. **at the back of** 在…的后面

4. **back and forth** 来回，往返 5. **back up** 后退；支持；备份

background ['bækɡraund] *n.* 背景

【记】back（背）+ground（地面）→背后的环境→背景

【例】*background* information 背景知识

backward(s) ['bækwəd(z)] *adj./adv.* 向后地

【例】It is not easy to walk *backwards*. 倒着走路不容易。

✗ **bacon** ['beikən] *n.* 熏肉；Bacon 培根（姓氏）

【例】*Bacon* and eggs are Bill's favorite breakfast food. 熏肉和鸡蛋是比尔最喜欢的早餐食品。

bacterium [bæk'tiəriəm] *n.* (*pl.* bacteria）细菌

【例】A single *bacterium* is unlikely to cause a disease. 单独的一个细菌是不太可能诱发疾病的。

✗ **badminton** ['bædmintən] *n.* 羽毛球

baggage
n. 行李

【例】*Badminton* is a relaxing sport. 羽毛球是种休闲运动。

bakery ['beikəri] *n.* 面包店

【记】来自bake（烘烤）+ry→面包店

【例】It is very busy at the *bakery* before sunrise. 日出前，面包房里很繁忙。

badminton

balance ['bæləns] *n.* 平衡 *v.* 使平衡，权衡

【考】**keep balance** 保持平衡

【例】The girl lost her *balance* and fell off the *balance* beam. 小女孩

B

失去了平衡，从平衡木上摔了下来。

【衍】balanced（*adj.* 平稳的，和谐的）

*balcony [ˈbælkəni] *n.* 阳台；包厢

【例】We ate breakfast on the *balcony* at the ski lodge. 我们在滑雪场小屋的阳台上吃早餐。

balcony

*ballet [ˈbælei] *n.* 芭蕾舞，芭蕾舞剧

【记】发音记忆

【例】*Swan Lake* is the name of a famous *ballet*. 《天鹅湖》是一出著名芭蕾舞剧的剧名。

balloon [bəˈluːn] *n.* 气球

【例】The party room was decorated with colorful *balloons*. 晚会现场装饰着五颜六色的气球。

ban [bæn] *vt.*（banned, banned, banning）禁止，取缔 *n.* 禁令

【例】The college *banned* alcohol from parties on campus. 这所大学禁止在校园内的聚会上饮酒。

band [bænd] *n.* 乐队；带子，镶边

【例】a jazz *band* 一支爵士乐队

单元自测

1. When he _____ with his sister, he suddenly _____ into tears.
   A. was arguing; burst
   B. argued; burst
   C. had argued; was bursting
   D. was arguing; was burst

2. The train will _____ London at 5:30.
   A. arrive
   B. come
   C. get
   D. reach

3. _____ I know the money is safe, I shall not worry about it.　　（2003北京）
   A. Even though
   B. Unless
   C. As long as
   D. While

4. The boy was _____ of his _____ conduct.
   A. ashamed; shameful
   B. shameful; ashamed
   C. shameful; shamed
   D. shameless; ashamed

5. I felt it an honor _____ to speak here.
   A. to ask
   B. asking
   C. to be asked
   D. having asked

6. She felt so _____ that she could hardly open her eyes.
   A. sleepy
   B. asleep
   C. sleeping
   D. sleep

7. The book, which he has worked _____ for three years, hasn't been _____ yet.

   A. for; reported   B. at; published   C. on; published   D. as; printed

8. _____ the enemy for two months, our soldiers _____ the city on a cold day.

   A. Surrounded; set out to attack   B. Having surrounded; set out to attack

   C. Surrounding; set about attacking   D. Having surrounded; set about attacking

9. Believing these people have their special _____, the police have been keeping a _____ watch on them.

   A. ideas; good   B. attempts; close

   C. ways; tight   D. minds; serious

10. The line before the cinema is so long, but I have to _____ it.

   A. attend   B. join   C. take   D. connect

11. Though I spoke to him many times, he never took any _____ of what I said.

   A. notice   B. remark   C. observation   D. attention

12. The company is starting a new advertising campaign to _____ new customers to its stores.   （2005上海）

   A. join   B. attract   C. stick   D. transfer

13. Do you have an afternoon _____ this week to meet the President?

   A. probable   B. feasible   C. possible   D. available

14. Free medical treatment in this country covers sickness of mind as well as _____ sickness.

   A. normal   B. average   C. regular   D. ordinary

15. They were not yet _____ of the hopelessness of their situation.

   A. aware   B. awake   C. sensitive   D. recognize

答案：ADCAC ABBBB ABDDA

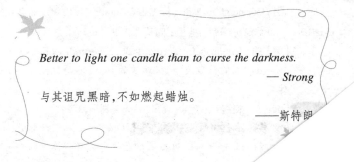

Better to light one candle than to curse the darkness.

— *Strong*

与其诅咒黑暗,不如燃起蜡烛。

——斯特朗

Word List 5 4.22

bar [bɑ:] n. 酒吧；条，横木；栅栏

【例】a coffee *bar* 咖啡馆

barbecue [ˈbɑ:bikju:] n. 烤肉野餐

【记】就是我们常说的"巴比Q"

【例】Let's have our friends over for a *barbecue* Saturday! 周六把朋友们全都叫过来烧烤吧！

barber [ˈbɑ:bə] n. 理发师

【例】I hope I remember to ask the *barber* not to cut my hair too short. 我希望我记得要要求理发师不要把我的头发理得太短。

【衍】barbershop (n. 理发店)

bare [beə] vt. 使赤裸，露出 a. 赤裸的

【例】The dog *bared* its teeth and growled. 狗龇着牙咆哮着。

bargain [ˈbɑ:gin] n. (经讨价还价之后) 廉价货 v. 讨价还价

【用】**bargain with sb. (about/over sth.)** 与某人 (就…) 讲价：We bargained with the car salesman. 我们同汽车销售商讨价还价。

【例】This jacket is a real *bargain* at such a low price. 这件夹克衫价格这么低，真是便宜。

bark [bɑ:k] v. 狗叫 n. 狗叫声

【例】Our neighbor's dog *barks* constantly. 我们邻居的狗叫个不停。

barrier [ˈbæriə] n. 栅栏，挡板；障碍 (物)

【例】The *barrier* between the desks gave both workers some privacy. 办公桌中间的挡板使 (挡板两边的) 职员不受打扰。// social *barrier* 社交障碍

base [beis] n. 根据地，底部 vt. 以…为基础，基于…

【考】**be based on...** 以…为基础：One's success is based on how hard he has tried. 一个人成功的基础是他努力的程度。

44

【例】*base* station 基点，基地 // a wooden *base* 木制底

【衍】basis（*n.* 基础，根据）

basement [ˈbeismənt] *n.* 地下室

【例】We stored all our old things in the *basement*. 我们把所有的旧物都存放在地下室里。

basic [ˈbeisik] *adj.* 基本的 *n.* 要素，基础

【例】*basic* requirements 基本要求 // *basics* of a subject 学科的基础知识

【衍】basically（*adv.* 基本上，主要地）; basis（*n.* 根据；基础；原理）

bathe [beið] *v.* 洗澡，沐浴，浸洗

【例】I *bathed* and changed my clothes. 我洗了澡，换了衣服。

【衍】bathing（*n.* 游泳，洗海水澡）; bather（*n.* 入浴者）

bean curd *n.* 豆腐

【例】Would you like another piece of *bean curd*? 你要再吃一块豆腐吗?

bear [bɛə] *v.*（bore, borne/born, bearing）承担；忍受 *n.* 熊

【例】Who will *bear* the losses caused by pollution? 谁将承担污染所造成的损失? //I can't *bear* sad music. 我受不了悲伤的音乐。

beard [biəd] *n.*（下巴上的）胡须

【例】Chris decided to grow a *beard*. 克里斯决定留胡子。

beat [biːt] *v.*（beat, beaten, beating）打赢；跳动；敲打 *n.*（音乐）节拍

【例】Do you think the Rockets will *beat* the Bulls? 你认为火箭队会战胜公牛队吗? //My heart missed a *beat*. 我的心跳停了一下。

beauty [ˈbjuːti] *n.* 美，美丽；美人

【记】*Beauty and the Beast*（迪斯尼出品的经典动画片《美女与野兽》）

【例】Mary has a natural *beauty* and needs no makeup. 玛丽天生丽质，不需要化妆。

because [biˈkɔz; biˈkɔːz] *conj.* 因为

【考】**because of** 由于，因为

【辨】**because, because of**
because, because of 都表示"因为"。because为连词，后跟表原因的状语从句；because of为介词短语，后跟名词、代词或动名词。如：I didn't go out for a walk because it was raining (=because of rain).

45

become [bi'kʌm] *vt.* (became, become, becoming) 变得，成为

【例】Helen *became* an electronic engineer. 海伦成了一名电子工程师。

【考】**become of...** 遭遇，发生：What has become of your uncle?

【辨】**become, turn**

become和**turn**都可用作连系动词，表示"成为，变为"。**become**后跟单数名词时需用不定冠词，并可后接形容词的比较级形式。而**turn**后接名词时不带冠词，后接形容词时一般不接比较级形式。

before [bi'fɔː] *prep.* 在…以前，在…前面 *adv.* 以前 *conj.* 在…之前

【用】**before**作连词，引导时间状语从句，表示主句动作在从句所指时间之前发生：My husband rarely comes to bed before 2 a.m. 我丈夫很少在凌晨2点之前上床睡觉。也可以表示主句动作在从句所指时间之前持续：It will be years before we meet again. 我们要过好多年才会再见面。

【辨】**1. long before, before long**

long before意为"很久以前"，常与一般过去时或过去完成时连用，跟从句时也可用在现在进行时的句子里。**before long**意为"不久之后，很快"，在句中常作状语，多与动词一般过去时和一般将来时连用。

2. before, ago

before, ago都指"以前，…之前"。**before**一般指过去的一个时间点之前，多用过去完成时；**ago**指从现在起的以前，通常用一般过去时。

beg [beg] *v.* (begged, begged, begging) 请求，乞求

【用】**beg sb. to do sth.** 恳求某人做某事

【考】**1. beg one's pardon** 请求某人的原谅 **2. beg for sth.** 乞求某物

【衍】beggar (*n.* 乞丐)

begin [bi'gin] *v.* (began, begun, beginning) 开始，着手

【考】**1. begin with...** 以…开始：He began his speech with a joke. 他以一个笑话作为演讲的开头。**2. begin to do**与**begin doing**经常可以互换使用，但是当主语是物或begin本身为进行时态时，多用**to do**：It began to rain. 天开始下雨了。

【衍】beginning (*n.* 开始，开端)

*****behalf** [bi'hɑːf; bi'hæf] *n.* 利益，为

B

【用】1. **on behalf of** ... 代表···，为了··· 2. **on someone's behalf** 代表某人，为了某人

behave ［bi ˈheiv］*v.* 举止，表现，行为得体

【例】Sonia has been *behaving* strangely lately. 索尼亚近来表现有点奇怪。//You can come if you promise to *behave* yourself. 只要你答应听话，就可以来。

【衍】behavio(u)r（*n.* 行为，举止）; well-behaved（*adj.* 彬彬有礼的，行为端正的）

*belief
n. 信任、
信仰*

***being** ［ˈbiːiŋ］*n.* 生物，人；存在

【例】She believes she has talked to *beings* from other planets. 她认为自己跟外星人说过话。

believe ［bi ˈliːv］*vt.* 相信；认为

【用】1. **I believe so/not.** 我认为(不)是这样。如：—Do you think it's going to rain over the weekend?—I believe not. —你认为周末会下雨吗？—我认为不会。2. **believe+sb./sth.+to do（be）** ...认为···：I believed him to be right. 我认为他是正确的。注意：这种句型的被动表达比较常用，即 **... be believed to be（do）** ... 据认为···：He was believed to be right. 他被认为是正确的。//Two prisoners are believed to have escaped. 两个犯人被认定逃跑了。

【考】1. **believe in** 信仰，崇尚 2. **believe it or not** 信不信由你

【衍】belief（*n.* 信条，信念）

*bell
n. 铃声*

【辨】**believe, believe in**

believe 和 **believe in** 都有相信的意思，但程度上有所不同。**believe in** 意为信任，信奉：We must believe in ourselves. 我们必须对自己有信心。当宾语是"人"时，二者在意思上区别很大：I believe him. 我相信他（所说的话）。I believe in him. 我信任他（为人可靠）。

***belly** ［ˈbeli］*n.* 肚子

【例】Lie down on your *belly*. 趴下。

belong ［bi ˈlɔŋ；bi ˈlɔːŋ］*vi.* 属，附属

【用】**belong to** 属于···：The earth belongs to the living. 地球属于一切生物。注意：此结构中的to是介词，因此后接名词。

【衍】belongings（*n.* 财产，所有物）

below ［bi ˈləu］*prep.* 在···下面 *adv.* 在下面

belt

B n.

【例】The temperature is *below* zero. 温度在零度以下。//See Paragraph nine *below* for more details. 详情请见下面第九段。

bench [bentʃ] *n.* 长凳；工作台

【例】He spent hours sitting on a *bench* in the park. 他在公园的长椅上坐了几个小时。

bend [bend] *v.* (bent, bent, bending) 弯曲，弯腰，屈身

【例】*Bend* your arms and touch your shoulders. 曲臂触摸双肩。//He *bent* over the sink to do the dishes. 他伏在水槽上面刷碟子。

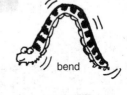
bend

【衍】bent (*adj.* 弯的)

beneath [bi'ni:θ] *prep.* 在…下方(面)

【例】They rested *beneath* the trees. 他们在树下休息。

beneficial [ˌbeni'fiʃl] *adj.* 有益的，受益的

【用】(be) **beneficial to...** 对…有益：A temperate climate is beneficial to the health. 温和的气候有利于健康。

benefit ['benifit] *n.* 利益，好处 *vt.* 使受益

【例】Many people find that regular physical activity gives them an unexpected *benefit*. 许多人发现定期运动给他们带来了意外的好处。

besides [bi'saidz] *prep.* 除…以外(还有) *adv.* 另外，再说

【例】I have other people to consider *besides* you. 除了你之外，我还要考虑其他人。//Rachel wouldn't enjoy the show. *Besides*, it's too expensive. 雷切尔不喜欢这场演出。再说，也太贵了。

【衍】beside (*prep.* 在…旁边)

【辨】besides, except, except for

besides 意思是"除…之外，另外还有…"。如：He received a sum of money besides the honors. 除了荣誉之外，他还得到了一笔钱。**except** 意思是"除去，除了"，如：Everyone went to the meeting except Tom. 除了汤姆，所有人都去参加了会议。而 **except for** 意思为"除去…一点之外"，有"美中不足"之意，因此 **except for** 前后的内容也是不同类的。如：Your composition is well written except for a few spelling mistakes. 你的作文写得很好，就是有一点拼写错误。另外，只有 **except** 的后面可以接 that 从句。

B

*betray [biˈtrei] *vt.* 出卖，背叛

【例】I would rather die than *betray* my country. 我宁死也不会背叛我的祖国。

beyond [biˈjɔnd] *prep.* 超过；(表示位置)在…的那边

【记】香港著名乐队的名字：Beyond

【例】He was driving *beyond* the speed limit. 他超速行驶。// *Beyond* the river was a great forest. 河那边是一大片森林。

【考】1. **beyond doubt** 毋庸置疑 2. **beyond sb.** 为某人所不能理解

★bid [bid] *v./n.* (bid/bade, bid/bidden, bidding) 出价，投标

【例】He *bid* $50 for a piece of stamp. 他为一张邮票出价50美元。

bill [bil] *n.* 钞票；账单；法案，议案

【考】**pay one's bill** 买单：He paid his bill and went out of the restaurant. 他买完单后，走出了那家饭店。

【例】a ten-dollar *bill* 一张十美元的钞票 // The *bill* was carried by the Senate. 这项法案在参议院获得通过。

*bingo [ˈbiŋgəu] *n.* 宾果(一种赌博游戏)

【例】a *bingo* hall 宾果游戏厅

*biochemistry [ˌbaiəuˈkemistri] *n.* 生物化学

【记】bio(生命，生物)+chemistry(化学)→生物化学

【例】experiment in *biochemistry* 生化实验

*biography [baiˈɔgrəfi] *n.* 传记

biology
n.

【记】词根记忆：bio(生命，生物)+graph(写)+y→写……一生→传记

birthplace [ˈbəːθˌpleis] *n.* 出生地，故乡

【记】组合词：birth(出生)+place(地方)→出生地，故乡

【例】This town is my *birthplace*. 这个小镇是我出生的地方。

*biscuit [ˈbiskit] *n.* 饼干

【例】cream *biscuits* 奶油饼干

*bishop [ˈbiʃəp] *n.* 主教

bit [bit] *n.* 一点，一些，少量

【用】1. **a bit**可以用作副词，用来修饰形容词、副词以及动词：The box is a bit heavy. 这个箱子有点重。2. **a bit** 可用来修饰形容词、副

B

词的比较级，并可和too连用：This coat is a bit too big. 这件衣服太大了点。 3. **a bit**不能直接修饰名词，须用**a bit of**：I have a bit of money with me. 我随身只带了一点钱。

【考】1. **a bit of** 一点，一些（修饰不可数名词）2. **bit by bit** 一点点地 3. **not a bit** 一点也不

【辨】**a bit, a little**

后面接形容词时，二者在肯定句中可以互换，但在否定句中意思则相反，即not a bit=not at all，而not a little=very much；**a little**后可接不可数名词，而**a bit**不可以，但a bit of后面可接不可数名词。

bite [bait] v. (bit, bitten, biting) 咬，叮 n. 咬；一口

【例】Their dog *bit* a hole in my trousers. 他们的狗把我的裤子咬了一个窟窿。//He ate the bread at one *bite*. 他一口吃掉了那块面包。

bitter [ˈbitə] adj. 有苦味的；痛苦的；严酷的

【例】The medicine is too *bitter* to take. 这种药太苦了根本没法吃。

【衍】bitterly (adv. 苦苦地，惨痛地)

blame [bleim] n./vt. 责备，责怪

blackboard
n.

【用】1. **be to blame (for...)** 应（为…）受到责备：Tom is to blame for his carelessness. 汤姆应该为他的粗心大意受到责备。 2. **blame sb. for sth.** 为某事责怪某人：Dad blamed Sam for the accident. 爸爸为这次事故责备了萨姆。 3. **blame sth. on sb.** 把某事归咎于某人

blank [blæŋk] adj. 空的；茫然的 n. 空格，空白（处）

【例】a *blank* tape 空白磁带// During the exam my mind was a *blank*. 考试的时候，我的脑子里一片空白。

blanket [ˈblæŋkit] n. 毛毯，毯子

【例】a piece of *blanket* 一块毯子

blanket

单元自测

1. —Has she had much _____ in teaching English?

　—No. She is just a new hand.

　A. base　　　　　B. future　　　　　C. energy　　　　　D. experience

2. With her name _____, her heart _____ faster.

　A. called; was knocking　　　　　B. called; knocked

　C. being called; was beaten　　　　D. being called; beat

3. Parents should take seriously their children's requests for sunglasses _____ eye protection is necessary in sunny weather. （2004上海）

   A. because   B. though   C. unless   D. if

4. Now computers _____ an important part in our life.

   A. do   B. play   C. take   D. become

5. How long do you suppose it is _____ he arrived there?

   A. when   B. before   C. after   D. since

6. When I arrived, the meeting _____ for ten minutes.

   A. had begun   B. began   C. had been on   D. have been on

7. The country is still struggling to meet the _____ needs of its people.

   A. common   B. ordinary   C. basic   D. usual

8. —Do you think it's going to rain over the weekend?

   — _____.   （1994全国）

   A. I don't believe   B. I don't believe it

   C. I believe not so   D. I believe not

9. Dalian is _____ the most beautiful cities of China.

   A. belonged to   B. belonging to   C. among   D. considered as

10. Keep the medicine out of the reach of children _____ the age of ten.

    A. less than   B. younger than   C. at   D. below

11. We are interested in the weather because it _____ us so directly—what we do and even how we feel.

    A. benefits   B. guides   C. affects   D. limits

12. I don't mind picking up your things from the store. _____, the walk will do me good.（2004全国）

    A. Sooner or later   B. Still   C. In time   D. Besides

13. His best-known work that is _____ all praise can be seen in the museum.

    A. without   B. beyond   C. with   D. within

14. —Is John a little tired?

    —No, he's not a _____ tired but he is not a _____ hungry.

    A. little; little   B. bit; bit   C. little; bit   D. bit; little

15. The medicine tastes _____, but works _____.

    A. bitter; well   B. bitter; good   C. bitterly; well D. bitterly; good

Word List 6

bleed [bli:d] *v.* (bled, bled, bleeding) 出血，流血
【例】The cut on my arm *bled* for a long time. 我胳膊上的伤口流了好长时间的血。

blood n. 血

*bless [bles] *vt.* 保佑，降福
【例】*Bless* all those who are hungry, lonely or sick. 求神赐福于那些饥饿、孤独或患病的人。

blind adj. 瞎的

block [blɔk] *n.* （木、石等）大块；街区 *v.* 阻塞，阻挡
【记】联想记忆：b+lock（锁）→封锁→阻塞，阻挡
【考】1. **a block of** 一块：a block of wood 一块木头 2. **block sth.** (**up**) 阻碍，堵塞：The drain was blocked up by mud. 下水道被污泥堵了。

blouse [blauz;blaus] *n.* 宽罩衫，（妇女、儿童穿的）短上衣
【例】How much is this *blouse*? 这件短上衣多少钱？

blow [bləu] *n.* 击，打击 *v.* (blew, blown, blowing) 吹（气）；刮风
【考】1. **blow away** 吹走 2. **blow about** 炫耀 3. **blow down** 刮倒 4. **blow out** 吹灭 5. **blow up** 使充气；爆炸

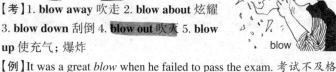
blow

【例】It was a great *blow* when he failed to pass the exam. 考试不及格给他带来了沉重的打击。

boat n. 小船

board [bɔːd] *n.* 木板；布告牌；委员会 *vt.* 上（船、火车、飞机）
【考】1. **on board** 在船/火车/飞机上 2. **get on board** 登船/机/火车

body building *n.* 健美
【例】*body building* exercise 健身操

boil [bɔil] *v.* 沸腾，烧开；煮
【例】*boiling* water 沸水 // *boiled* water 开水 // *boiling* point 沸点

bomb
n.f.v.炸弹轰炸

【考】boil down to 等于；归结为：Most of the crimes may boil down to a question of money. 大多数犯罪都可归结为金钱问题。

bone
n.骨联结；连接

bond [bɒnd] n. 联结，联结物 v. 粘合，结合

【例】the *bonds* of friendship 友谊的联结//These two substances won't *bond* together. 无法将这两种物质粘在一起。

bonus ['bəunəs] n. 奖金，红利

【例】The workers got a Christmas *bonus*. 工人得到了圣诞节奖金。

book
n.&v.预定

boom [buːm] n. 繁荣；隆隆声 v. 发出隆隆声；兴隆，使繁荣

【例】The oil market is enjoying a *boom*. 石油市场欣欣向荣。// Business is *booming*. 生意日益繁荣。

boot
n.靴子

booth [buːð;buːθ] n. 岗；（为某种用途而设的）亭或小隔间

【记】和tooth（n. 牙齿）一起记

【例】a voting *booth* 投票站

border ['bɔːdə] n. 边缘；边境，国界

【考】on the border of 在…的边缘：She sat on the border of the desk. 她坐在桌边。

bored [bɔːd] adj. 无聊的，厌烦的

【考】be bored with 厌倦：She was bored with her job. 她对自己的工作感到厌倦。

【衍】boring（adj. 乏味的）

born [bɔːn] adj. 出生的

【例】He was *born* in Beijing. 他出生在北京。

botany ['bɒtəni] n. 植物学；植物

borrow
v.借

【例】I think *botany* is a very interesting subject. 我觉得植物学是一门很有意思的学科。

【衍】botanical*（adj. 植物学的）

both [bəuθ] adj. 双方的 pron. 两者，双方

【用】1. **both**意为**one and the other**，用作形容词时，一般放在定冠词、指示代词、所有格及其他形容词之前：both my parents 2. **both** 在句中作同位语：The boys both did well in the exam. 两个男孩都考的不错。//These children are both hers. 这些孩子都是她的。3. **both...and...** …和…（连接两个并列句子成分，连接两个主语时谓语用复数）：Both he and I are music lovers. 他和我都是音乐爱好者。

bother [ˈbɔðə] *vt.* 烦扰，打扰

【考】**bother sb. with/about**… 因…打扰、麻烦某人：Don't bother yourself about me. 别为我烦心了。

*bounce [ˈbauns] *v.* 使反弹，跳跃

bounce

【例】The children were *bouncing* a ball. 孩子们在拍球。

*bound [baund] *adj.* 被束缚的；有义务的 *v.* 跳跃

【考】**be bound to do sth.** 有义务做某事：I'm bound to do this work. 我有义务做这项工作。

*boundary [ˈbaundəri] *n.* 边界，分界线

【例】the *boundaries* of the country 国界

*bow [bau] *v./n.* 鞠躬，弯腰

【例】He *bowed* to us. 他向我们鞠躬。

*boycott [ˈbɔikɔt] *n./vt.* 联合抵制

【例】They're *boycotting* the shop. 他们联合抵制那家商店。

brake [breik] *n.* 闸 *v.* 刹车

【例】a hand *brake* 手闸//The Car *braked* to a stop. 车刹住不走了。

branch [brɑ:ntʃ;bræntʃ] *n.* 树枝；分支；分公司

【例】a *branch* of a tree 树枝//a Party *branch* 党支部

brand [brænd] *n.* 商标，牌子

【例】Do you like this *brand* of coffee? 你喜欢这个牌子的咖啡吗?

*bravery [ˈbreivəri] *n.* 勇敢，勇气

【记】来自 brave（*adj.* 勇敢的）

【例】He was given a medal for *bravery*. 他因勇敢而被授予了一枚奖章。

break [breik] *v.*（broke, broken, breaking）打破（断，碎），撕开 *n.* 间隙

【考】1. **break away from** 从…脱离，打破 2. **break down** 出故障，坏掉 3. **break in** 插嘴，破门而入 4. **break into** 强行进入；渗进：Sunlight broke into the room. 阳光照射进房间。5. **break off** 中止，中断 6. **break out** 爆发 Fighting broke out in the bar. 酒吧里发生了斗殴。7. **have/take a break** 休息一下

*breakthrough [ˈbreikθru:] *n.* 突破

【记】break（打破）+through（通过）→突破

【例】a scientific *breakthrough* 科学突破

B

breast [brest] *n.* 胸部；胸怀

【例】Joy filled his *breast*. 他满心欢喜。

breath [breθ] *n.* 气息，呼吸

【考】1. **take a breath** 吸气 2. **hold/catch one's breath** 屏住呼吸

3. **out of breath** 上气不接下气

【衍】breath-taking（*adj.* 惊人的）

breathe [briːð] *v.* 呼吸

【考】1. **breathe in** 吸入 2. **breathe out** 呼出

【衍】breathless（*adj.* 呼吸急促的，喘不过气来的；无呼吸的）

*brick** [brik] *n.* 砖；砖块

【记】砖（brick）墙被打破（break）

【例】ice-cream *brick* 冰砖

break
brick

bride [braid] *n.* 新娘

bridge
n. 桥

【例】Venice is compared to be the *bride* of the sea. 威尼斯被比作大海的新娘。

【衍】bridegroom（*n.* 新郎）

brief [briːf] *adj.* 简洁的

bright
a. 明亮的，愉快的

【考】**in brief** 简而言之：In brief, you did a good job! 总而言之，你干得不错！

*brilliant** [ˈbriliənt] *adj.* 闪耀的；有才气的

【例】a *brilliant* color 亮丽的色彩//a *brilliant* scientist 才华横溢的科学家

【衍】brilliance（*n.* 光辉，显赫）

bring [briŋ] *vt.* (brought, brought, bringing) 拿来，带来，取来

【考】1. **bring about** 引起 2. **bring in** 赚钱，带进来 3. **bring along** 带来 4. **bring back** 归还

broadcast [ˈbrɔːdkɑːst] *v.* (broadcast / broadcasted, broadcast / broadcasted, broadcasting) 广播 *n.* 广播节目

broad
a. 宽的

【记】联想记忆：broad（宽，广）+cast（投，射）→传播的范围很广→广播

【例】The station begins *broadcasting* at 6 a.m. 电台清晨6点开始播音。

*brochure** [ˈbrəʊʃə; brəʊˈʃʊər] *n.* 小册子

【例】a holiday *brochure* 度假指南

broken [ˈbrəʊkən] *adj.* 弄坏了的，破碎的

brother
B n. 兄弟

【记】break的过去分词

【例】a *broken* window 一扇碎了的窗户

broom [bru:m] *n.* 扫帚

【例】A new *broom* sweeps clean. 新官上任三把火。

broom

*brunch [brʌntʃ] *n.* 早午饭

【记】该词由breakfast（早餐）的首部和 lunch（午餐）的尾部缩合而成。

【例】I don't think *brunch* is good for our health. 我认为早午饭不利于身体健康。

brown
n.& a. 棕色的，棕色

单元自测

1. The presentation of the president was ended with "May God _____ America!"
   A. come to   B. help   C. bless   D. glorify

2. —Did you come to the museum by bike yesterday?
   —No. Two metres of snow fell during the night. As a result, several main roads _____.

   A. piled snow   B. had been closed
   C. were blocked   D. covered with snow

3. The glass of water is too hot. I prefer some cold _____ water.
   A. boiling   B. boiled   C. having boiled   D. to boil

4. I had to buy _____ these books because I didn't know which one was the best.
   A. both   B. none   C. neither   D. all   （2004上海）

5. The boy threw a stone into the river which _____ the smooth surface of the water.
   A. broke   B. disturbed   C. bothered   D. interrupted

6. If you carry on working like this, you will _____ sooner or later.
   A. give off   B. get down   C. break down   D. hold on

7. His death will be _____ to his family.
   A. a terrible blow   B. blow   C. blowing   D. blown

8. The business can _____ in between 200 and 400 million dollars _____ year.
   A. bring; a   B. make; each   C. get; one   D. earn; every

9. The advertisement has been heard _____ three times today.
   A. to broadcast   B. have broadcast   C. broadcasting   D. broadcast

10. Our car got _____ in the mud, which delayed our journey.
    A. broken   B. stopped   C. stuck   D. lost

11. Those who work hard will receive a _____ at the end of the year.

    A. money   B. salary   C. bonus   D. compensation

12. The students are _____ with their math class.

    A. good   B. bad   C. boring   D. bored

13. The _____ of the bike is broken so I have to ride slowly in case of emergency.

    A. tire   B. brake   C. handle   D. chain

14. The big company has _____ all over the country.

    A. branches   B. places   C. organizations   D. groups

15. The doctor told him to _____ deeply in order to check his lungs.

    A. sleep   B. breath   C. breathe   D. think

答案：CCBDB CAAAC CDBAC

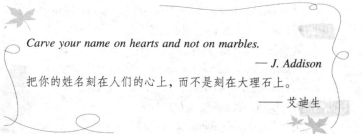

Carve your name on hearts and not on marbles.

— *J. Addison*

把你的姓名刻在人们的心上，而不是刻在大理石上。

—— 艾迪生

Word List 7

4.24

brush v & n. 刷；刷子；画笔

bucket ['bʌkit] *n.* 桶；铲斗
【例】One *bucket* of paint will be enough for the ceiling. 刷天花板一桶油漆就够用了。

***Buddhism** ['budizəm] *n.* 佛教
【例】*Buddhism* is an ancient religion. 佛教是种古老的宗教。

★ budget ['bʌdʒit] *n.* 预算
【例】a family *budget* 家庭预算

buffet ['bʌfit] *n.* 打击，伤害
【例】suffer the *buffets* of a cruel fate 遭受悲惨命运的打击

build [bild] *v.* (built, built, building) 建造 *n.* 构造
【考】1. **build up** 建设，增进，树立：Bill was doing a lot of physical exercise to build up his strength. 比尔为增强体力做了大量运动。
2. **build on /upon...** 建立在…的基础上

building ['bildiŋ] *n.* 建筑物，房屋，大楼
【例】an office *building* 办公大楼

bun [bʌn] *n.* 馒头，小甜面包
【例】I don't like *bun* at all. 我一点都不喜欢小甜面包。

bunch [bʌntʃ] *n.* 串，束
【考】**a bunch of** 一束，一串，一群：a bunch of flowers 一束花

***burden** ['bə:dn] *n.* 担子，负担
【例】A donkey can carry a heavy *burden*. 驴子能驮重担。

***bureaucratic** [ˌbjuərə'krætik] *adj.* 官僚政治的
【例】a *bureaucratic* government 官僚政府

★ burglar ['bə:glə] *n.* 盗贼，窃贼
【例】The *burglar* got into the house through the bedroom window. 窃贼从卧室的窗户潜入这所房子。

burglar

58

B

【衍】burglarious（*adj.* 夜盗的，犯夜盗罪的）

*burst [bəːst] *v.*（burst, burst, bursting）突然发生；爆炸
【考】1. **burst into (laughter/tears/cheers...)** 突然（大笑/哭/欢呼…）起来 2. **burst out doing** 突然…起来：They burst out laughing. 他们突然大笑起来。

bury ['beri] *vt.*（buried, buried, burying）埋，葬
【考】**bury (oneself) in** 埋头于，专心于：He buried himself in reading. 他埋头苦读。

bush [buʃ] *n.* 灌木丛，矮树丛

business ['biznis] *n.* 商业，生意；职业，事业
【例】*Business* is always brisk before New Year. 新年前夕生意总是很兴隆。// Mind your own *business*. 少管闲事。
【考】1. **have business with** 与（某人、某事）有关 2. **on business** 因公，有事 3. **get down to business** 言归正传，开始干正事

businessman ['biznismæn] *n.*（男）商人
【例】He is a successful *businessman*. 他是位成功的商人。
【衍】businesswoman（*n.* 女商人；女企业家）

busy ['bizi] *adj.* 忙碌的
【考】1. **be busy with...** 忙于… 2. **be busy (in) doing...** 忙于做…

but [bʌt] *conj.* 但是，可是 *prep.* 除了，除…外
【考】1. **not only... but (also) ...** 不但…而且…：She is not only beautiful but bright. 她不仅漂亮而且聪明。2. **not...but...** 不是…而是… 3. **but for** 要不是：But for my brother's help, I would not have finished. 要不是我弟弟帮忙，我是无法完成的。

*butcher ['butʃə] *vt.* 屠宰（动物），残杀（人）*n.* 肉店；屠夫
【例】They *butchered* the prisoners. 他们残杀囚犯。

butter
n. 黄油；奶油

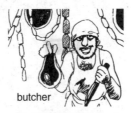
butcher

*butterfly ['bʌtəflai] *n.* 蝴蝶

by [bai] *prep.* 靠近，到…时；被；由；以…的标准
【例】a rocking-chair *by* the window 窗边的摇椅 // We have learned more than

button
n.&v.纽扣

butterfly

* cabbage
n. 洋白菜
cage
n. 笼

2,000 words *by* now. 到现在我们已经学了两千多个单词了。// The boys were rescued *by* firemen. 孩子们被消防队员救了出来。// I would like to pay *by* cheque. 我想用支票付帐。

【考】1. **by oneself** 独自，独力：No one helped me. I did it all by myself. 没有人帮我，我自己做的。 2. **by the way** 顺便 3. **by and by** 不久以后 4. **by the end of** 到…结束时 5. **by means of** 通过，依靠 6. **by way of** 经由 7. **by accident** 偶然 8. **by chance** 偶然，意外地

*cafeteria	[ˌkæfi'tiəriə] *n.* 自助餐厅

calculate ['kælkjuleit] *v.* 计算，核算

【例】a *calculating* machine 一台计算机

【衍】calculator (*n.* 计算机，计算器)

call [kɔːl] *n.* 叫；电话 *vt.* 称呼；呼唤；叫

【例】contact *call* 联系电话// *call* the public's attention 唤起公众的注意

【考】1. **call sb.** 给…打电话 2. **call sb. sth.** 称呼…为…：Don't call me "Joe". 别叫我乔！

【衍】recall (*vt.* 回忆，记起)

calm [kɑːm; kɑ:lm] *adj.* 镇静的，沉着的 *v.* 镇静；沉着

【记】接到求救电话（call）一定要镇静（calm）

【考】**calm down** （使）平静下来，（使）镇定下来：It was difficult to calm down the movie fans. 让影迷们平静下来真是不容易。

【衍】calmly (*adv.* 平静地，冷静地)

camel
n. 骆驼

camera ['kæmərə] *n.* 照相机，摄像机

【例】a digital *camera* 数码相机 // *camera* crew 摄制组

【衍】cameraman (*n.* 摄影师，摄像师)

camp [kæmp] *n./ vi.* 野营，宿营

【例】summer *camp* 夏令营

【考】**go camping** 宿营

【衍】campsite (*n.* 宿营地)；campfire (*n.* 营火)

campaign [kæm'pein] *n.* 战役；竞选活动 *vi.* 参加活动；作战

【例】an advertising *campaign* 广告活动

can [kæn] *modal v.* 可能；能够；可以

【用】情态动词的特点是不能单独作谓语，必须和后面的动词连用共同构成谓语，没有人称和数的变化。can是最常用的情态动词之一：1. 表示能力，有"会，能够"的意思，主要用在一般现在时中：

Can you drive a car? 你会开车吗？2.表示可能，常用于否定句或疑问句：Can it be true? 这是真的吗？//Today is Sunday. He can't be at school today. 今天是星期天，他不可能去上学了。3.表示允许，口语中代替may，有"可以"的意思：You can use my car. 你可以用我的车。

【辨】**can, be able to**

can表示能力时，可以用**be able to**代替；**can**只有can和could两种时态，而**be able to**可用于其他时态；**be able to**强调"通过努力有能力做到"，如果表示"某事已经成功"应用**be able to**，而不用**could**：He was able to leave Europe before the war began. 他在战争开始前就能离开欧洲了。

can [kæn] *n.* (英tin) 罐头；铁罐；垃圾桶
【例】I ate a *can* of beans for supper. 晚饭我吃了一罐青豆。

canal [kə'næl] *n.* 运河；水道
cancer
n. 癌
【例】Do you think swimming is allowed in the *canal*? 你觉得可以在这个运河里游泳吗？

cancel ['kænsəl] *vt.* 取消
【例】*cancel* membership 取消会员资格

candidate ['kændidit; 'kændideit] *n.* 候选人
【例】The reporter asked the *candidate* some tough questions. 记者问了候选人一些棘手的问题。

canteen [kæn'ti:n] *n.* 餐厅，食堂
candle
n. 蜡烛
【记】联想记忆：can + tee (看作tea茶) + n →能喝茶、聊天的地方→餐厅。
candy
n. 糖果
【例】We ate lunch at the *canteen*. 我们在食堂吃了午饭。
【衍】restaurant (*n.* 饭店)；inn (*n.* 旅馆)；hotel (*n.* 酒店)；dining-hall (*n.* 餐厅)；pub (*n.* 酒吧)；bar (*n.* 酒吧)

canteen

capsule ['kæpsju:l; 'kæpsl] *n.* 胶囊；太空舱
【例】The doctor gave Tom some *capsules* for his fever. 医生给汤姆开了一些治发烧的胶囊。

caption ['kæpʃən] *n.* 标题，字幕
capital
n. 首都

【例】The editor wrote *captions* for the pictures. 编辑为这些图片附上了标题。

【例】The editor wrote *captions* for the pictures. 编辑为这些图片附上了标题。

*carbon [ˈkɑːbən] *n.* 碳

【记】联想记忆：car+bon（看作born）→汽车产生的废气→二氧化碳→碳

【例】*carbon* atoms 碳原子 // *carbon* dioxide 二氧化碳

【衍】carbonate（*n.* 碳酸盐）

carbon *dioxide*

care [kɛə] *v.* 介意…，在乎；在意；关心 *n.* 照料，保护；小心

【考】1. **take care of** 照顾，照料：I don't think Peter is too young to take care of the pet dog. 彼得虽小，但我认为他能照顾好小狗。2. **take care** 当心：Take care and don't eat any more fish. 当心，别再吃鱼了。3. **care for** 喜欢，照料 4. **care about** 关心，在乎

【衍】careful（*adj.* 小心的，谨慎的）；carefully（*adv.* 仔细地）；careless（*adj.* 粗心的；草率的）

*carpenter [ˈkɑːpəntə] *n.* 木匠

【记】美国著名兄妹组合"木匠合唱团"，又名卡朋特（Carpenter）

【例】employ a *carpenter* 雇用一名木匠

carriage [ˈkæridʒ] *n.* 四轮马车；（火车）客车厢

*carrier [ˈkæriə] *n.* 搬运者；（车的）置物架

【例】aircraft *carrier* 航空母舰

carry [ˈkæri] *v.* 携带，搬运，背

【考】1. **carry on** 坚持，继续 2. **carry out** 执行，完成

【辨】**take, bring, get, carry**

这几个动词都有"带，拿"的意思，但它们在意义和用法上不一样。**take** 意为"带去，拿走"，指从说话人所在的地方把某人或某物拿去、拿走，可以和 away 等副词连用。"随身带去"用 take sth.（sb.）with sb.：Take more clothes with you. It's going to snow. 多带些衣服，要下雪了。**bring** 意为"带来，拿来"，指从别处把某人或某物拿/带到说话人所在的地方，可以和 along, down 等副词连用。"随身带来"可用 bring sth.（sb.）with sb.：Why don't you bring your son along? 为何不把你的儿子带来？**get** 表示到别处去把某人或某物"叫来，拿来"，较口语化，运用较广泛：I'll go back to get my dictionary. 我回去拿词典。**carry** 意为"搬运，扛，背"，着重指

carpet
n.地毯

carrot
n.胡萝卜

cartoon
n.卡通片

62

以车船、肩、手等把人或重物从一处带到另一处去。有时也指随身携带，但不表示带到什么地方。如：Can you carry the box? 这箱子你扛得动吗？

C

*carve [kɑːv] v. 刻；雕刻

【考】be carved with 刻有…：The stone was carved with some words. 石头上刻有一些文字。

case [keis] n. 情况；病例；案件；容器

【用】1. in case 万一，如果：In case you don't have my phone number, it's 87654321. 如果你没有我的电话号码，那我告诉你：87654321。在in case引导的从句中，谓语动词可用虚拟语气，即(should) do。但不用虚拟语气也可以：Take your coat in case it rains/should rain. 2. in the case of 在…的情况：It's a number to call in case of emergency. 这个号码在发生意外时可以拨打。

【衍】showcase (n. 陈列窗)；suitcase (n. 手提包)；staircase (n. 楼梯)

cash [kæʃ] n. 现金，现钞 vt. 兑现

*cassette n. 金d

【例】He said he was out of cash. 他说他没有现金了。

【衍】cashier (n. 出纳员)

*cast [kɑːst; kæst] vt. (cast, cast, casting) 扔，抛 n. 演员表

castle n. 城堡

【考】cast away (船) 遭遇海难，失事

【例】The fishermen cast their nets into the sea. 渔民在海上撒网。

*casual ['kæʒuəl] adj. 偶然的，不经意的；非正式的

【例】a casual interest 暂时的兴趣//The Smiths dropped in yesterday for a casual visit. 史密斯一家昨天突然来访。

【衍】casually (adv. 随便地，临时地)

*catalogue ['kætələg; 'kætəlɔːg] n. 目录

【例】When you want to see if a library has the book you want, you can use the catalogue in the library. 要想知道图书馆是否有你要找的那本书，可以查看那里的书籍目录。

单元自测

1. To _____ fit, we must take plenty of exercise.
   A. keep   B. do   C. make   D. build

2. She was late for class because her bike _____ on the way.

A. broke down   B. fell off   C. turned over   D. burst out

3. The World Wide Web is sometimes jokingly called the World Wide Wait because it
_____ be very slow.

    A. should   B. must   C. will   D. can

4. —Would you like to come to dinner tonight?

    —I'd like to, _____ I'm too busy.   （1994全国）

    A. and   B. so   C. as   D. but

5. There is an apple garden near my house. The apples are measured _____ kilos and
the workers who pick apples are paid _____ the hour.

    A. in; in   B. by; on   C. in; by   D. in; on

6. We _____ our middle school teacher yesterday.

    A. paid a visit   B. called on   C. called at   D. called in

7. _____ reading is faster than reading aloud.

    A. Silent   B. Still   C. Quiet   D. Calm

8. It's nearly seven o'clock. Jack _____ be here at any moment.   （1995全国）

    A. must   B. need   C. should   D. can

9. Bill doesn't _____ what people say about him.

    A. care   B. matter   C. want   D. interest

10. —I always look out when crossing the street.

    —You're right. You cannot be too _____.

    A. nervous   B. careless   C. hurried   D. careful

11. The driver drove _____ hit a big tree and the car came to a stop.

    A. too carelessly to   B. carelessly enough to

    C. so carelessly that he   D. so careless that he

12. He had to _____ his father's business after his death, though he didn't really want
to continue it.

    A. carry out   B. pick up   C. set up   D. carry on

13. I always take something to read when I go to the doctor's _____ I have to wait.

    A. in case   B. so that   C. in order   D. as if（2005全国卷2）

14. He _____ his research work _____ I went to see him.

    A. was busy in; for the first time   B. was busy to do; whenever

    C. was busy with; the last time   D. devoted to; each time

15. Mary likes to _____ herself in reading when she is not happy.

    A. devote   B. devoting   C. bury   D. burying

答案：AADDC BACAD CDACC

Word List 8

catch [kætʃ] *vt.* (caught, caught, catching)接住；捉住；赶上；染上（疾病）

【例】*catch* the criminal 抓住罪犯//*catch* one's plane 赶上飞机

【考】1. **catch on** 受欢迎：Animals here seem to be catching on. 动物们在这看起来是受欢迎的。2. **catch up with** 赶上 3. **catch sight of** 看到 4. **catch fire** 着火 5. **catch（a）cold** 感冒

*category [ˈkætigəri] *n.* 种类

【例】Which literary *category* would this book go in? 这本书属于哪一类文学书籍？

*cater [ˈkeitə] *v.* 投合；备办食物

【考】**cater to** 满足；迎合：Will the restaurant cater to our special requests? 饭店会满足我们特别的要求吗？

cater

【衍】self-catering（*adj.* 自助的，自给的）

*catholic [ˈkæθəlik] *adj.* 天主教的

cattle [ˈkætl] *n.* 牛（总称）；家畜

【用】**cattle** 是集合名词，谓语动词永远用复数形式。表示一头牛可以用 a head of cattle。

【例】They have long been known for the fine breeds（品种）of *cattle*. 这种牛品种优秀，闻名已久。

cause [kɔːz] *n.* 原因，起因 *vt.* 促使，引起

【记】和because（*conj./adv.* 因为）一起记

【例】The public have known a great deal about the *causes* of heart disease. 人们对于导致心脏病的原因已大有了解。//This disease may *cause* memory loss. 这种病会导致记忆丧失。

*caution [ˈkɔːʃən] *n.* 小心，谨慎

【例】The hunter approached the lion with *caution*. 猎人小心地向狮子走去。

【衍】cautious（*adj.* 小心的，谨慎的）

celebrate ['selibreit] *v.* 庆祝

【例】When did people begin to *celebrate* the New Year? 人们什么时候开始庆祝新年？

【衍】celebration*（*n.* 庆祝，庆祝会）

C ceiling
n. 天花板, 顶棚

cent
n. 美分

***cell** [sel] *n.* 细胞；蜂房；电池

【例】cancer *cells* 癌细胞 // The queen lays one egg in each *cell*. 蜂后在每个蜂房里都产下一枚卵。 // a dry *cell* 干电池

centigrade ['sentigreid] *adj.* 摄氏的；百分度的

【记】词根记忆：cent（百）+i+grade（等级，级别）→百分度的

【例】In this summer, the temperature is sometimes forty degrees *centigrade*. 今年夏天，气温有时高达40摄氏度。

centimetre ['sentimi:tə]（美centimeter）*n.* 公分，厘米

【记】词根记忆：centi（百分之一）+metre（米）→百分之一米→公分，厘米

【例】This pencil is around 15 *centimetres* long. 这支铅笔大概有15厘米长。

century
n. 世纪

central ['sentrəl] *adj.* 中心的，中央的；主要的

【记】来自centre（*n.* 中心）

【例】the *central* government 中央政府//a *central* figure 主要人物

ceremony ['serimeni; 'serimeuni] *n.* 典礼，仪式

【例】a wedding *ceremony* 结婚典礼

certain ['sə:tən] *adj.*（未指明真实名称的）某…；确定的，无疑的；一定会…

【用】1. **be certain to do sth.** 肯定会，无疑：He is certain to agree. 他肯定会同意。2. **be certain of/about sth.** 确信，肯定：I'm not certain of/about what she wants. 我不确信她想要什么。3. **be certain that+从句**：确信，无疑：I'm certain that he saw me. 我肯定他看见我了。

***certificate** [sə'tifikit] *n.* 证明，证明书

【例】a *certificate* of birth 出生证明

【辨】**certificate, license**

certificate和**license**都有"证书"的意思，但**certificate**侧重于"证明书"：a birth/marriage/death certificate 出生/结婚/死亡证；**license**侧重于"许可证，执照"：a driving/business license 驾驶/营业执照

chain store(s) *n.* 连锁店

【例】He owned many *chain stores*. 他拥有多家连锁店。

chain [tʃein] *n.* 链，链条

【考】**a chain of** 一系列的：a chain of misfortunes 一连串的灾难

chairman [ˈtʃɛəmən] *n.* (*pl.* chairmen) 男主席，男会长

【例】*chairman* of the board/directors 董事长

【衍】chairwoman (*n.* 女主席，女会长)

challenge [ˈtʃælindʒ] *n.* 挑战(性) *vt.* 挑战…

【用】1. **challenge sb. to do sth.** 挑战某人做…，邀请比赛：He challenged me to play another tennis game. 他向我挑战，邀我跟他再打一场网球。2. **challenge sb. to sth.** 挑战某人做…：Their school challenged ours to a football match. 他们学校向我们学校发起了足球挑战赛。

【例】issue/give a *challenge* 发出挑战//accept/take a *challenge* 接受挑战 // He challenged me to a game of chess. 他向我挑战下棋。

【考】**beyond challenge** 无与伦比，不可比拟

【衍】challenging (*adj.* 具有挑战性的)

champion [ˈtʃæmpiən] *n.* 冠军，优胜者

【例】the boxing *champion* of the world 世界拳击冠军

champion

chance [tʃɑːns；tʃæns] *n.* 机会，可能性

【考】1. **by chance** 偶然，凑巧 2. **by any chance** 万一，也许 3. **take one's chance** 碰运气，冒险

change [tʃeindʒ] *vt.* 改变；更换；兑换 *n.* 零钱；变化

【考】1. **change sth. with sb.** 和…交换… 2. **change sth. into sth.** 变成；兑换(把钱换成零票或外币)

【衍】changeable* (*adj.* 易变的，变化无常的)

channel [ˈtʃænəl] *n.* 海峡；频道；通道

【记】卫视音乐台就是Channel V

【例】the English *Channel* 英吉利海峡 // the History *Channel* 历史频道

chant [tʃɑːnt] *v.* 唱，歌颂 *n.* 圣歌，赞美诗

【记】发音记忆："唱"→唱圣歌

【例】*chant* a hero's deeds 歌颂英雄事迹

C

chant
v.n. 吟诵，颂歌

*chaos [ˈkeiɔs] *n.* 混乱

【例】The desk was a *chaos* of papers and unopened letters. 桌上杂乱地堆放着纸和未开封的信件。

chapter [ˈtʃæptə] *n.* 章

【例】Open your books to *Chapter* 3. 把你们的书翻到第三章。

character [ˈkæriktə] *n.* 字符；性格

【例】a Chinese *character* 一个汉字 // He has a strong but gentle *character*. 他坚强而又温柔。

【衍】characteristic* (*adj.* 特有的，典型的)

charge [tʃɑːdʒ] *v.* 收费；指控；索价；充电 *n.* 费用，价钱

【考】1. **in charge of** 支配，负责: My mom was in charge of the baby. 我妈妈负责照顾那个婴儿。2. **in the charge of** 受…的支配，由…负责: The baby was in the charge of my mom. 那个婴儿由我妈妈负责照顾。3. **take charge** (**of sth.**) 控制，掌管 4. **free of charge** 免费 5. **charge sb. some money** 向某人要价 (收费)

【衍】overcharge (*v.* 要价过高)

cheap
adj. 便宜的

chart [tʃɑːt] *n.* 图表；航海图

【例】climatic *chart* 气候图

cheat [tʃiːt] *v.* 哄骗，欺骗，骗取 *n.* 骗子；诈骗

【例】Some students *cheated* in examinations. 有些学生考试作弊。

check [tʃek] *v.* 核对，检查，批改 *n.* 检查，批改

【例】Only when your identity has been *checked*, will you be allowed in. 核实身份后你才可以进入。

cheek
n. 面颊，脸蛋

【考】1. **check in (at)** 登记，报道 2. **check out (of)** 结帐退房 (宾馆等) 3. **check (up) on** 检查 4. **in check** 受控制的

cheer [tʃiə] *n./v.* 欢呼，喝彩

【例】The spectators are *cheering* for the winner. 观众们正为冠军喝彩。

【考】1. **cheer sb. on** 为…鼓气，加油 2. **cheer sb. up** 使…高兴，振作起来

【衍】cheerful (*adj.* 兴高采烈的，快活的)

*cheers [tʃiəz] *int.* 干杯；(英口语) 谢谢，再见

*chef [ʃef] *n.* 厨师

cheese
n. 奶酪

【例】My cousin is a *chef*. 我的堂兄是位厨师。

chemical [ˈkemikl] *adj.* 化学的 *n.* 化学制品

chemist n.代药

【例】a *chemical* reaction 化学反应

【衍】chemistry (*n.* 化学)

C

cheque [tʃek] (美check) *n.* 支票

【例】a blank *cheque* 空白支票

chest [tʃest] *n.* 箱子; 胸部

chess n.象棋

【例】a tool *chest* 一个工具箱 //Chris was paralyzed from the *chest* down. 克里斯胸部以下全部瘫痪。

【衍】breast (*n.* 胸部)

✱ **chew** [tʃuː] *v.* 咀嚼

【记】发音记忆:"刍"→一些动物能够反刍→咀嚼

【例】a piece of *chewing* gum 口香糖

chew

chief [tʃiːf] *adj.* 主要的,首要的 *n.* 领导

chicken n.鸡肉

【记】发音记忆:"欺负"→位高权重的人才能欺负人→领导

【考】1. **chief of all** 最主要的是… 2. **in chief** 主要地,尤其

【例】Rice is the *chief* crop in most southern provinces. 水稻是南方大多数省份的主要作物。// the *chief* of police 警察局长

childhood [ˈtʃaildhud] *n.* 幼年时代,童年

【记】来自child (儿童) +hood (名词后缀)→童年

【例】She had an unhappy *childhood*. 她有一个不幸的童年。

choice [tʃɔis] *n.* 选择,抉择

chocolate n.巧克力

【考】**have no choice but to do sth.** 别无选择,只能…: At that time the taxi driver had no choice but to turn to the tourist. 当时,那位出租车司机别无选择,只能求助于游客。

✱**choir** [ˈkwaiə] *n.* 唱诗班

【例】a church *choir* 教堂唱诗班

✱**choke** [tʃəuk] *n./v.* 窒息

【例】A coin went down his throat and he started to *choke*. 一块硬币卡在他的喉咙里,他开始透不过气来。

单元自测

1. In order to _____ with the advanced countries, we must keep learning.

    A. catch up   B. get along   C. put up   D. go on

2. Careless driving _____ a lot of accidents.
   A. affects   B. makes   C. causes   D. results

3. Wait till you are more _____. It's better to be sure than sorry.
   A. inspired   B. satisfied   C. calm   D. certain

4. I'll try as hard as I can, but I don't have much _____ of winning the game.
   A. lock   B. opportunity   C. chance   D. fate

5. "How wide is the Atlantic Ocean?" "That _____. From where to where?"
   A. changes   B. depends   C. remains   D. refers

6. —The manager is away.
   —Who is taking _____ of the company?
   A. charge   B. place   C. part   D. position

7. You look pale. You'd better go to hospital to have a blood _____.
   A. look   B. check   C. test   D. measure

8. —Victor looks unhappy.
   —Yes. He always _____ our success.
   A. cheers   B. envies   C. admires   D. stops

9. —I've at last passed the driving test!
   — _____!
   A. Cheers   B. Good luck   C. Come on   D. Congratulations

10. We've missed the last bus. I'm afraid we have no _____ but to take a taxi.
    A. way   B. choice   C. possibility   D. selection

11. He changed a 5-dollar bill _____ 5 single.
    A. for   B. with   C. into   D. on

12. The driver was fined by the police for his expired _____.
    A. certificate   B. certification   C. permission   D. license

13. The football team of No. 1 middle school invited us to a match and we decided to accept the _____.
    A. chance   B. challenge   C. match   D. opportunity

14. Bill changed the _____ of the TV without asking for permission of his family.
    A. program   B. contents   C. channel   D. color

15. In the past few years, Jane's child is her _____ pleasure.
    A. chief   B. principle   C. best   D. most

Word List 9

4.26

choose [tʃuːz] *vt.* (chose, chosen, choosing) 选择

【用】1. **choose between A and B** 在A和B中挑选 2. **choose sth. from sth.** 从…挑选… 3. **cannot choose but do sth.** 别无选择，只好做…: She can't choose but take the awful job. 她别无选择，只能干那份糟糕的工作。

【例】He *chose* to play basketball. 他决定打篮球。

chopsticks [ˈtʃɒpˌstiks] *n.* 筷子

【记】联想记忆: chop (砍) +sticks (棍) →砍成两半的棍子→筷子

【例】When you go to a Chinese restaurant you have to use *chopsticks*. 到中国餐馆用餐就得用筷子。

chorus [ˈkɔːrəs] *n.* 合唱

【例】a mixed *chorus* 男女合唱

Christian [ˈkristʃən] *n.* 基督教徒和天主教徒的总称

【例】a *Christian* country 信奉基督教的国家

Christmas
n.圣诞节
church
n.教堂

cigarette [ˌsigəˈret] *n.* 纸烟，香烟

【例】a pack of *cigarettes* 一包香烟

circle [ˈsəːkl] *n.* 圆圈 *v.* 围起来，环绕

【例】They sat in a *circle* round the fire. 他们围着炉火坐成一圈。// The birds *circled* around in the air. 鸟儿在空中盘旋。

circuit [ˈsəːkit] *n.* 电路

【例】a television *circuit* 电视线路

circulate [ˈsəːkjuleit] *vt.* 使流通，使运行

【例】Please *circulate* these fliers. 请发放这些传单。

circumstance [ˈsəːkəmstəns] *n.* 环境，情况

【例】The *circumstances* forced me to accept it. 迫于环境的压力不得不接受。

circus [ˈsəːkəs] *n.* 马戏团

【例】a traveling *circus* 流动马戏团

71

citizen [ˈsitizn] *n.* 公民，市民

【记】联想记忆：citi（看作city城市）+zen（人）→市民，公民

【例】an American *citizen* 一个美国公民

civil [ˈsivl] *adj.* 国内的；平民（非军人）的；民用的

【例】a *civil* war 内战//a *civil* court 民事诉讼法庭

【衍】civilian*（*adj.* 民间的，民用的；*n.* 平民）

civilization [ˌsivəlaiˈzeiʃn;ˌsivəliˈzeiʃn] *n.* 文明，文化

【例】the *civilization* of ancient Egypt 古埃及文化

【衍】civilize（*v.* 使开化，使文明）

clap [klæp] *v.*（clapped, clapped, clapping）拍手，鼓掌

【例】They *clap* their hands in time to the music. 他们随着音乐的节拍拍起手来。

*clarify [ˈklærifai] *v.* 澄清，阐明

【例】I hope what I say could *clarify* the situation. 我希望我所说的能澄清这一情况。

classic [ˈklæsik] *adj.* 经典的，一流的

【例】modern *classic* writers 当代一流的作家

【辨】classic, classical

classic和classical词形相像，词义也接近。classic "经典的，最优秀的"：a classic novel 最佳的小说；而 classical "古典的"，是指艺术上的一个流派：classical music古典音乐。

*classify [ˈklæsifai] *vt.* 分类

【记】词根记忆：class（种类）+ify（使）→分出级别→分类

【例】They *classified* these books by subject. 他们按学科将这些图书进行分类。

classmate [ˈklɑːsmeit] *n.* 同班同学

【例】Tom and Jerry are *classmates*, but they don't get along well with each other. 汤姆和杰尔是同班同学，但他们相处得并不好。

claw [klɔː] *n.* 爪

【例】The eagle held a mouse in its *claws*. 老鹰的爪子里抓着一只老鼠。

*clay [klei] *n.* 粘土，泥土

【例】a *clay* pot 一个陶罐

clerk [klɑːk;kləːk] *n.* 书记员，办事员，职员
【例】a bank *clerk* 银行职员

*click** [klik] *v.* 点击 (计算机用语)；发出滴答声 *n.* 滴答声
【记】联想记忆：钟表 (clock) 发出滴答声 (click)
【例】*click* the mouse 点击鼠标

climate [ˈklaimət] *n.* 气候；风气，趋势 ~~climb v.爬~~
【例】a mild *climate* 温和的气候//a *climate* of unrest 不安的气氛

clone [kləun] *n./v.* 克隆，无性繁殖
~~clinic n.诊所~~
【记】发音记忆
【例】*clone* technology 克隆技术

close [kləus] *adj.* 近的；亲密的 *adv.* 近，靠近
~~cloth n.布~~
[kləuz] *v.* 关，关闭
【考】**close to** 接近：I live close to the shops. 我住得离商店很近。

clothing [ˈkləuðiŋ] *n.* (总称) 衣服
~~clothes n.衣服~~
【例】a piece of *clothing* 一件衣服

【辨】clothing, clothes
clothing 和 **clothes** 都有"衣服"的意思。**clothing** 是集合名词，为衣服
~~cloud n.云~~
的总称，既包括各类衣服，也包括鞋、帽等身上穿的一切，可用量
词表示件数，如：an article of/a piece of clothing 一件衣服。**clothes**
统指各种衣服(上衣，裤子，内衣等)，谓语动词永远用复数形式。

cloudy [ˈklaudi] *adj.* 多云的，阴天的
【例】*Cloudy* mornings give way to clear evenings. 早晨云遮日，晚上
星满天。

*clumsy** [ˈklʌmzi] *adj.* 笨拙的
【例】It's not easy walking in these *clumsy* shoes. 穿着这双笨重的鞋
走路真是难受。

coach [kəutʃ] *v.* 指导，训练 *n.* 教练；马车，长途车
~~coal n.煤~~
【例】He *coaches* me to swim. 他教我游泳。// head *coach* 主教练 //
by *coach* 乘长途汽车

coast [kəust] *n.* 海岸，海滨
【例】a town on the *coast* 海滨城镇 // off the *coast* 在海岸附近的海上

*cocoa** [ˈkəukəu] *n.* 可可粉
【例】*Cocoa* is a kind of powder made from cacao seeds. 可可粉是一

coin
n.硬币

*coke n.可乐

C

一种由可可豆加工而成的粉状物。

*coincidence [kəuˈinsidəns] n. 一致，巧合

【例】What a *coincidence*! 太巧了！

collar [ˈkɔlə] n. 衣领

【记】和dollar（n. 美元）一起记

【例】a white *collar* worker 白领工作者

*colleague [ˈkɔliːg] n. 同事

【记】联想记忆：col（共同）+league（联盟）→工作于同一个联盟→同事

【例】David and I are *colleagues*. 我和大卫是同事。

collect [kəˈlekt] v. 收集，搜集

【例】I used to *collect* stamps when I was a kid. 小时候我曾经集邮。

【衍】collection*（n. 收藏品，收集物）

college [ˈkɔlidʒ] n. 学院；专科学校

【考】1. **go to college** 上大学 2. **be in college** 在上大学

*collision [kəˈliʒn] n. 碰撞，冲突

【例】a *collision* between two trains 两列火车相撞

come [kʌm] vi. (came, come, coming) 来，来到 *link. v.* 变成

colour
n & v.颜色 & 给…涂色

【用】**come to**（like, realize, know, understand...）逐渐开始（喜欢、认识到、知道、理解等）：She told the lie so many times that she came to believe it. 她说那个谎言的次数多得她自己都开始相信了。

【考】1. **come about** 发生 2. **come across** 偶然遇到：I came across my college roommate in the street. 今天我在大街上遇到了大学时的室友。3. **come along** 进展；一起 4. **come from** 来自 5. **come in** 进来，到达 6. **come on** 进行；快点 7. **come out** 出来，出版 8. **come to** 到达，总计 9. **come true** 实现 10. **come up** 上来，上升，走过来

comb [kəum] v. 梳 n. 梳子

【例】Have you *combed* your hair? 你梳头了吗？

*combine [kəmˈbain] v. (使)联合，(使)结合

【用】**combine sth. with/and sth.** 把…和…结合、混合起来：Combine the egg with a little flour and heat the mixture gently. 把鸡蛋和少量面粉调匀，用小火加热。

*comedy [ˈkɔmidi] n. 喜剧

【例】a comedy writer 喜剧作家

comfort ['kʌmfət] *v.* 安慰，（使痛苦）缓和 *n.* 安慰，慰问

【例】I tried my best to *comfort* Tom after his mother's death. 汤姆的母亲去逝后我尽力安慰他。

【衍】comfortable (*adj.* 舒服的，安逸的)

*command [kə'mɑːnd;kə'mænd] *n./v.* 命令

【用】1. **command sb. to do sth.** 命令某人做某事 2. **command+从句**，从句谓语用虚拟语气，即：**should+do**，其中should可以省略：My father commands that I (should) set out right now. 父亲命令我立即出发。宾语从句需要用这种虚拟语气的动词还有：insist, demand, desire, request, require, order, command, prefer, propose, ask, advise, suggest等。

【考】**have a command of sth.** 控制/掌握：He had a good command of English. 他精通英语。

comment ['kɔment] *n.* 评论 *v.* 评论；注释

【例】ask for *comment* 征求意见 // He refused to *comment* on the election results. 他拒绝评论选举的结果。

【考】**make comments on/upon sth.** 评论某事

*commercial [kə'məːʃəl] *adj.* 商业的，贸易的

【例】a *commercial* company 贸易公司

*commit [kə'mit] *v.* (committed, committed, committing) 犯 (错误)，干 (坏事)

Committee
n. 委员会

【例】If you *commit* a crime, you can never escape being punished. 你要是犯了罪，就必定会受到惩罚。

【衍】commitment* (*n.* 许诺，承担义务)；committee (*n.* 委员会)

common ['kɔmən] *adj.* 普通的；公共的；共有的

【考】1. **have... in common** 共同，共有…：We have our differences, but we have a lot in common. 我们有所不同，但也有许多相同之处。2. **common sense** 常识

单元自测

1. —I'd like to buy an FM radio.

　　—Well. We've got several models _____.

　　A. to choose　　B. chosen from　　C. to be chosen　　D. to choose from

2. The plane _____ over the landing field for twenty minutes when the pilot was told that he should use the Eastside Field.

A. had been circling   B. is circling

C. was circling   D. had circled

3. These trees can't be grown in such a cold _____ as ours.

  A. weather   B. climate   C. season   D. space

4. It is bad _____ to stand too _____ to another person when speaking to him.

  A. manner; close   B. manner; nearly

  C. manners; nearly   D. manners; close

5. I don't want to go into the sea. I'd rather lie on the _____.

  A. coast   B. bank   C. beach   D. seaside

6. He went from door to door, _____ waste paper and magazines.

  A. receiving   B. achieving   C. accepting   D. collecting

7. It is more important for them to _____ what they learned in books _____ practice than just _____ what they are taught in class.

  A. put; to; do   B. put; into; doing

  C. combine; with; to do   D. combine; and; doing

8. —I heard Jack _____ back from London.

  —Really? Let's go and see him tonight.

  A. had come   B. has returned   C. is   D. come

9. I bought a shirt because it was good in quality and _____ in price.

  A. reasonable   B. valuable   C. comfortable   D. enjoyable

10. We can hardly imagine what his _____ to the news would be.

  A. opinion   B. impression   C. reaction   D. comment

11. On no _____ will I accept these items.

  A. condition   B. circumstance   C. conditions   D. circumstances

12. The news of the president's visit _____ quickly throughout the city.

  A. extended   B. scattered   C. circulated   D. broadcast

13. Sarah, hurry up. I'm afraid you can't have time to _____ before the party.

  A. get changed   B. get change

  C. get changing   D. get to change   (2004全国)

14. Bill likes all kinds of _____ music, especially symphonies.

  A. classic   B. classical   C. pop   D. light

15. It's quite strange that the man sleeps with his mouth _____ and his eyes _____.

  A. closed; open   B. closed; opened

  C. closing; open   D. closing; opening

Word List 10 4.27

communicate [kə'mju:nikeit] v. 交际，传达（感情，信息等），通信

communicate

【记】联想记忆：commun（看作common公共的）+ic+ate→公共传播→交际

【考】**communicate with sb.** 交流情况，交换信息：The police communicate with each other by radio. 警察通过无线电互相联络。

【衍】communication（n. 交际，交往；通讯）

*communism ['kɔmjunizəm] n. 共产主义

【记】联想记忆：commun（看作common共有的）+ism（表主义的名词后缀）→财产共有→共产主义

【例】the Principles of *Communism* 共产主义原理

*communist ['kɔmjunist] n. 共产主义者 adj. 共产党的，共产主义的

【记】联想记忆：commun（看作common共有的）+ist（表人的名词后缀）→支持共产主义的人→共产主义者

【例】a *communist* country 共产主义国家

companion [kəm'pænɪən] n. 同伴，同事

【记】联想记忆：compani（看作company陪伴）+on→同伴

【例】A dog is a faithful *companion*. 狗是忠实的伙伴。

compare [kəm'pɛə] vt. 比较，对照

【记】联想记忆：com（一起）+pare（看作pair对）→把这对一起比较→对照

【用】1. **compared with/to** 和…比较起来：Compared with/to the whole human history, our own lives seem so short. 与整个人类历史相比，我们自己的生命是如此短暂。2. **compare...to...** 把…比作喻成…：Poets often compare death to sleep. 诗人常把死亡比作睡眠。3. **compare...with...** 把…与…相比较：I am c

77

notes with mine. 我正在比较我们的笔记。

【衍】comparable（*adj.* 可比较的，比得上的）

> 【辨】**compare... with... , compare... to... , compared with/to**
> 这些结构都有比较的含义。compare是及物动词，compare... with...
> 是把两者进行对比；compare... to ... 是把某事物比喻成另外一种
> 事物：He compared her to rose. 他把她比作玫瑰。而compared with/
> to相当于介词短语，表示"与…相比"，此时to和with可以互换：
> Living in a town can't compare with living in the country in many
> respects. 在许多方面，城市生活比不上乡村生活。

*compass [ˈkʌmpəs] *v.* 包围 *n.* 指南针

【例】Suddenly we *compassed* the enemies on all sides. 我们以迅雷不
及掩耳之势将敌人团团包围。

*compensate [ˈkɔmpenseit] *v.* 补偿，赔偿

【考】**compensate for**：The insurance company will compensate you
for your losses. 保险公司会赔偿你的损失。

compete [kəmˈpiːt] *vi.* 比赛，竞赛

【记】比赛（compete）有终结（complete），竞争无止境

【考】1. **compete with/against sb. in sth.** 在某方面与某人竞争 2. **compete with/against sb. for sth.** 为了某物与某人竞争

【衍】competition（*n.* 比赛，竞赛）

*competence [ˈkɔmpitəns] *n.* 能力

【记】联想记忆：compete（竞争）+nce→竞争需要能力

【例】No one doubts his *competence* as a teacher. 大家都相信他能胜
任老师的工作。

complete [kəmˈpliːt] *vt.* 完成，结束 *adj.* 完成的，完整的

【例】She has *completed* her studies. 她完成了学业。//This is a
complete story. 这是一个完整的故事。

*complex [kəmˈpleks; ˈkɔmpleks] *adj.* 复杂的；联合的 *n.* 联合体

【例】Life is getting more and more *complex*. 生活变得越来越复杂。

*component [kəmˈpəunənt] *n.* 成分；零部件

【例】This factory manufactured *components* for the car industry. 该工
厂为汽车制造业生产零部件。

composition [ˌkɔmpəˈziʃn] *n.* 作文；作曲

【例】You've made several grammatical mistakes in the *composition*.

你的作文中犯了几处语法错误。

comprehension [ˌkɔmpriˈhenʃən] *n.* 理解

【例】The problem is beyond my *comprehension*. 这个问题我无法理解。

*****compromise** [ˈkɔmprəmaiz] *v.* 妥协，折中

【记】联想记忆：com+promise（保证）→相互保证→妥协

【例】I would rather die than *compromise*. 我宁死不屈。

*****compulsory** [kəmˈpʌlsəri] *adj.* 必修的；义务的

【例】A composition class is *compulsory* for all college students. 写作课是所有大学生的必修课。// *compulsory* education 义务教育

concentrate [ˈkɔnsəntreit] *v.* 集中，聚集

【记】词根记忆：con（共同）+centr（中心）+ate（使…）→使…都到一个中心→集中

【考】**concentrate（sth.）on/upon sth.**（把某事物）集中在…：We must concentrate our efforts on improving education. 我们必须致力于改进教育工作。

concept [ˈkɔnsept] *n.* 概念，观念

【例】the basic *concepts* of mathematics 数学的基本概念

【衍】conceptual（*adj.* 观念的，概念的）

concern [kənˈsəːn] *n.* 关系，关心 *vt.* 涉及，关系到

【例】Obesity is a major public health *concern*. 肥胖是大众健康的主要关注点。

【考】1. **be concerned about/for sth.** 担心，忧虑，关心 2. **be concerned with...** 与…有关

conclude [kənˈkluːd] *v.* 推论，总结；完成，结束

【例】Let's *conclude* this meeting before 5:00. 让我们在5点前结束这个会议吧。// He *concluded* that the theory was invalid. 经推断他认为该理论不成立。

【衍】conclusion（*n.* 结论；结束）

*****concrete** [ˈkɔnkriːt] *adj.* 具体的，有形的

【例】The scientist had no *concrete* data to support his theory. 这位科学家没有具体的数据来支持自己的理论。

*****condemn** [kənˈdem] *vt.* 谴责，声讨

【例】We *condemned* him for his bad conduct. 我们谴责他行为不

检点。

condition [kənˈdiʃən] *n.* 条件，状况

【例】working *conditions* 工作条件 // living *conditions* 生活状况

【考】1. **on condition that** 只要，如果 2. **under/in...condition** 在…的状况下

【衍】conditional (*adj.* 有条件的，受制约的)

conduct [kənˈdʌkt] *vt.* 引导；管理

【记】安全管理(conduct)生产，保证产品(product)质量

【例】The guider *conducted* the hikers along the trail. 导游带着徒步旅行者们沿小路前行。

【衍】conductor (*n.* 管理人；售票员；乐队指挥)

conference [ˈkɔnfərəns] *n.* (正式的) 会议

【例】a *conference* room 会议室 // You will see her at the press *conference*. 你会在记者招待会上见到她。

confident [ˈkɔnfidənt] *adj.* 自信的，确信的

【考】**be confident in** 对…自信：The man was confident in his looks. 那个男人对自己的长相很自信。

【例】He was very *confident*. 他很自信。

【衍】confidently (*adv.* 自信地)；confidential (*adj.* 秘密的，机密的)

confirm [kənˈfəːm] *vt.* 确定，批准

【记】联想记忆：con+firm (坚定)→十分坚定→确定，批准

【例】Please *confirm* our reservations at the restaurant. 请确认一下我们旅店的预定情况。

*conflict [ˈkɔnflikt] *n.* 斗争，冲突

【例】an armed *conflict* 武装冲突

confuse [kənˈfjuːz] *vt.* 使糊涂，搞乱

【记】女孩子喜欢欲拒(refuse)还迎，男生都被搞糊涂(confuse)了

【例】She spoke so fast that she completely *confused* me. 她讲话太快，我都被她搞糊涂了。

【衍】confusing (*adj.* 混乱的，让人糊涂的)；confused (*adj.* 困惑的，糊涂的)

congratulation [kənˌɡrætjuˈleiʃn] *n.* (*pl.*) 祝贺

C

【例】—I have passed the exam! —*Congratulations*!
—我考试及格了！—祝贺你！
【衍】congratulate（*vt.* 祝贺）

connect ［kə'nekt］*vt.* 连接，把…联系起来
【例】A USB port is a place where you can *connect* other machines to a computer. 你可以通过USB接口将其他设备与电脑连接起来。
【考】**connect A to/with B** 把A和B联系（连接）起来
【衍】connection（*n.* 联系；关系）; connector（*n.* 连接器）;
　　　disconnect（*vt.* 使分离）; reconnect（*vt.* 重新连接）

*conscience ［'kɔnʃəns］*n.* 道德心，良心
【例】My *conscience* made me tell the truth. 在良心的驱使下我说了实话。

*consensus ［kən'sensəs］*n.* 一致意见，合意
【例】The students were all in *consensus* about where to go swimming. 学生们就去哪儿游泳达成了一致。

consequence ［'kɔnsiˌkwəns］*n.* 结果，后果
【例】You must be responsible for the *consequences* of your actions. 你必须为自己的所作所为负责。

conservative ［kən'sə:vətiv］*adj.* 守旧的，保守主义的；谨慎的
【例】Old people are often more *conservative* than young people. 老年人通常要比年轻人保守。// the *Conservative* Party 保守党
【衍】conservation（*n.* 保存，保护）

conservative

consider ［kən'sidə］*vt.* 考虑；认为
【用】1. **consider doing sth.** 考虑做某事：Have you considered going abroad? 你考虑过出国吗? 2. **consider sb./sth.（as）+n.** 认为…：We consider him our top problem solver. 我们把他看作是最顶级的问题解决专家。3. **consider sb./sth.（to be）+n./adj.** 认为…：This TV contest is considered the most successful in this summer. 这个电视竞赛节目被认为是这个暑假最成功的节目。
【衍】consideration（*n.* 考虑；关心）; considerate（*adj.* 体贴的；考虑周到的）

consist ［kən'sist］*vi.* 由…组成
【考】**consist of** 由…组成：The final examination report consisted of

ten lines. 期末测试报告共有10行文字。

【衍】consistent*（*adj.* 一致的，调和的）

constant ['kɔnstənt] *adj.* 经常的，不断的

【例】The *constant* noise from the road gave Bill a headache. 公路上持续不断的噪音让比尔头疼。

*constitution [ˌkɔnsti'tju:ʃən; ˌkɔnsti'tu:ʃən] *n.* 宪法，章程

单元自测

1. It is _____ knowledge that animals like snakes and frogs are cold blooded.

   A. usual   B. ordinary   C. normal   D. common

2. _____ with the size of the whole earth, the biggest ocean does not seem big at all.

   A. Compare   B. When comparing

   C. Comparing   D. When compared   （2004湖北）

3. To gain honor for our country, we will try our best _____ the game.

   A. competing in   B. competing against

   C. to compete with   D. to compete in

4. All the preparations for the task _____, and we're ready to start.

   A. completed   B. complete

   C. had been completed   D. have been completed

5. I'd get it for you _____ I could remember who last borrowed it.

   A. except that   B. if only

   C. on condition that   D. considering whether

6. Tom, _____ yourself. Did you forget the school rules?

   A. behave   B. believe   C. perform   D. conduct

7. We are considering _____ a birthday party for her that day.

   A. to have   B. having   C. for   D. how to have

8. —Mum, I've passed the college entrance examination.

   — _____.

   A. Congratulations on your success   B. That's all right

   C. What a pleasure   D. I hope so

9. I'm planning to hold a party in the open air, but I can make no guarantee because it _____ the weather.

   A. links with   B. depends on   C. connects to   D. decides on

10. Scientists have discovered a close _____ between smoking and several serious diseases.

    A. action   B. union   C. connection   D. combination

11. Lincoln was _____ as one of the greatest presidents.

   Which one can't be used?

   A. considered   B. regarded   C. thought   D. looked on

12. This committee _____ three personnel appointed by the owner and five appointed

   by the contractor.

   A. is composed of   B. consists in   C. makes up   D. sets out

13. They use smells, sounds and movements to _____ with other animals.

   A. talk   B. speak   C. communicate   D. say

14. To _____ for his unpleasant experiences in the company, the man drank a little

   more than was good for him.

   A. pay   B. compensate   C. balance   D. equalize

15. As far as I'm _____, I agree that Shanghai isn't a romantic place.

   A. concerned   B. related   C. involved   D. linked

答案: ABABC CACDB DDDDB A

Great men are rarely isolated mountain peaks; they are the summits of ranges.   —*Higginson*

伟人很少是突兀的山，他们是众山中的最高峰。

—— 希金森

Word List 11

construct [kən'strʌkt] *vt.* 构筑；建造

【例】The workers *constructed* a fountain in the town square. 工人们在小镇的广场上建造了一座喷泉。

construction [kən'strʌkʃən] *n.* 建造，建设；建筑物

【例】the *construction* industry 建筑业

【考】**be under construction** 修建中

consult [kən'sʌlt] *v.* 请教，商议；查询

【例】I *consulted* with a lawyer about what to do next. 我和律师商讨下一步该怎么做。// *consult* a guidebook 查询旅游指南

【衍】consultant* (*n.* 顾问，咨询者)

consume [kən'sjuːm;kən'suːm] *vt.* 消耗，消费

consume

【例】They say children are *consuming* more meat and soft drinks than before. 他们说和从前相比，孩子们肉吃得更多，软饮料也喝得更多了。

【衍】consumer (*n.* 消费者); consumption (*n.* 消费)

contain [kən'tein] *vt.* 包含；包括

【例】The bag *contained* a book. 包里装着一本书。

【衍】container* (*n.* 容器，集装箱)

contemporary [kən'temprəri;kən'tempəreri] *adj.* 当代的

【例】*contemporary* painters 当代画家 // *contemporary* literature 当代文学

content [kən'tent] *adj.* 满意的

['kɔntent] *n.* 内容；含量

【记】词根记忆：con+tent (伸展)→全身舒展→满意的

【例】After a good meal, we were all *content*. 美餐一顿之后，我们都心满意足了。// This dessert has a high fat *content*. 这种甜点脂肪含

量很高。

【考】1. **be content with...** 对…满意 2. **be content to do...** 乐于做…

continent ['kɔntinənt] *n.* 大陆，大洲

continue [kən'tinjuː] *v.* 延伸；继续

【考】1. **continue to do/doing** 继续做…: I'll continue to study. 我会继续学习。2. **continue with sth.** 继续做…: The woman continued with her sports after she got back home. 这位女士回到家后继续做运动。

【衍】continuing (*adj.* 持续的，连续的); continuous (*adj.* 持续的，连续的)

*****contradict** [ˌkɔntrə'dikt] *v.* 同…矛盾，同…抵触

【记】词根记忆: contra (反)+dict (说话，断言)→反说→同…抵触

【例】The facts *contradict* his theory. 事实与他的理论相悖。

【衍】contradictory* (*adj.* 反驳的，反对的)

contrary ['kɔntrəri; 'kɔntreri] *n.* 反面 *adj.* 相反的

【记】来自contra (相反)+ry (性质)→相反的

【考】**on the contrary** 相反: I'm not ill. On the contrary, I'm very healthy. 我没生病，相反，我很健康。

*****contribute** [kən'tribjuːt] *v.* 捐款，捐献

【考】**contribute to** 有助于，是…的部分原因: Lack of exercises may contribute more to juvenile obesity. 缺乏锻炼会使青少年更容易患上肥胖症。

【衍】contribution (*n.* 贡献)

control [kən'trəul] *vt./n.* (controlled, controlled, controlling) 控制

【例】The Romans used to *control* a vast empire. 罗马人曾经统治着一个庞大的帝国。// Passport *Control* 出入境关卡 // remote *control* 遥控器

【考】1. **lose control over sth.** 对…失去控制 2. **have control over/ take control of** 控制… 3. **out of control** 失控 4. **self-control** 自控

*****controversial** [ˌkɔntrə'vəːʃəl] *adj.* 争论的，争议的

【例】a *controversial* issue 有争议的问题

convenient [kən'viːniənt] *adj.* 便利的，方便的

【考】1. **be convenient to sb.** 对…来说方便: Come and see me whenever it is convenient to you. 只要方便，你可以随时来看我。

2. **convenient to do sth.** 便于…: The mobile phone is fashionable in

style and convenient to carry. 该手机外形时尚且便于携带。

【衍】convenience（n. 便利）

*conventional [kən'venʃənl] adj. 惯例的，传统的；常规的

【例】a *conventional* design 传统样式 // *conventional* weapons 常规武器

conversation [ˌkɔnvə'seiʃən] n. 谈话，交谈

【例】an international *conversation* 国际间的对话

【考】**have a conversation with** 和…交谈

*convey [kən'vei] vt. 搬运；传播，传达

【例】His words *conveyed* a sense of anger. 他的话表明他很气愤。

*convince [kən'vins] vt. 使确信，使信服

【例】What can I do to *convince* you of the truth? 我要怎么做才能让你相信这是事实？

corporation [ˌkɔːpə'reiʃən] n. 公司，企业

【例】Mary works for a *corporation* that produces computers. 玛丽为一家生产计算机的公司工作。

correction [kə'rekʃən] n. 改正

【记】来自correct（改正）+ion（名词后缀）→改正

【例】*corrections* of the errors 改错

*correspond [ˌkɔri'spɔnd;ˌkɔːri'spɔnd] vi. 通信；一致；相当；协调

【记】词根记忆：cor（共同）+respond（做出反应）→做出相同的反应→一致

【例】The two poets *corresponded* for many years. 这两位诗人相互通信已有多年。

*corrupt [kə'rʌpt] adj. 腐败的，贪污的 v. 腐烂，腐蚀

【例】the *corrupt* politicians 腐败的政客 // Greed *corrupted* the mayor. 贪婪让这位市长走向腐败。

cost [kɔst;kɔːst] n. 成本；代价 vt.（cost, cost, costing）花费；使付出（代价）

【用】cost的主语是事或物，常接双宾语，即**cost sb. sth.** 花费某人多少钱；使某人付出什么代价：The cell-phone cost me $215. 这部手机花了我215美元。//That operation cost him his sight. 那次手术使他付出了失明的代价。

【考】1. **at the cost of** 以…的代价 2. **at all cost** 不惜一切代价

【衍】costly（*adj.* 昂贵的，贵重的）

cosy [ˈkəuzi] *adj.* 舒适的，安逸的

【例】a *cosy* room 舒适的房间

cottage [ˈkɔtidʒ] *n.* （郊外的）小屋，村舍；别墅

【记】棉花（cotton）地里的小屋（cottage）；
其他表建筑的单词：block（大楼，大厦）；
building（建筑物）；flat（公寓）；apartment
（公寓）；house（房子）；room（房间）；villa
（别墅）；dormitory（宿舍）

cottage

【例】farmer's *cottage* 村舍

could [kud]（can的过去式）*modal v.* 表示能力、许可、请求、可能等

【用】1. 表示可能，只能用于肯定句：表示现在或将来的可能用
could+do/be...：It could be a trap. 这可能是个陷阱。表示过去的可
能用**could+have+done/been**：They could have forgotten to phone. 他
们可能忘了打电话。注意：may和might以及can都有类似用法。
2. 用于否定句，表示否定推测：对现在或将来的否定推测用
couldn't+do/be...：You couldn't talk to the dead. 你不可能和死人谈
话。对过去的否定推测用**couldn't+have+done/been**：They couldn't
have gone skiing in the mountains last winter because there was little
snow there. 去年冬天他们不可能去山里滑雪，因为那儿根本没有
什么雪。注意区别：could和can用于否定句可以表示"不可能"，而
may或might用于否定句表示"可能不…"，如：He may/might not
know the truth. 他可能不知道真相。//He can/could not know the
truth. 他不可能知道真相。

【例】He *could* read when he was three. 他三岁时就能认字。// *Could
you give me a ride to school?* 我能搭你的车去学校吗？

count [kaunt] *v.* 数，计算；有价值

【例】*Count* your steps so that you know how far you have gone. 数着
自己的步子你就知道已经走了多远了。

【考】1. **counted on sb.** 依靠，指望 2. **count up** 共计

【衍】countless（*adj.* 无数的）；counter*（*n.* 计数器；柜台）

countryside [ˈkʌntrisaid] *n.* 乡下，农村

【记】联想记忆：country（国家）+side（边）→位于国家的周边→
乡下

【例】I will spend this summer holiday in the *countryside*. 我将在乡下度过这个暑假。

C

couple [ˈkʌpl] *n.* 夫妇；(一)对, (一)双

【考】**a couple of** 几个：a couple of times/weeks / hundred dollars 几次/几星期/几百美金

couple

courage [ˈkʌridʒ] *n.* 勇气, 胆略

【考】1. **get courage** 获得勇气 2. **lose courage** 失去勇气

course [kɔːs] *n.* 过程, 经过；课程

【例】science *courses* 理科课程

【考】**of course** 当然

court [kɔːt] *n.* 法庭, 法院；球场

【例】football *courts* 足球场

【考】**go to court** 上法庭

【衍】*courtyard* (*n.* 庭院, 院子)

cousin [ˈkʌzn] *n.* 堂(表)兄弟, 堂(表)姐妹

*****crash** [kræʃ] *v./n.* 碰撞, 坠毁

 cover
n. & v. 覆盖；盖上

【例】Tom lost control of his car at the first bend and *crashed*. 在第一个转弯处, 汤姆的车失去控制撞坏了。

crash

*****crayon** [ˈkreiən] *n.* 蜡笔, 蜡笔画

*****cream** [kriːm] *n.* 奶油, 乳脂

【例】ice-*cream* 冰激凌

create [kriːˈeit] *vt.* 创造；造成

COW
n. 奶牛

crazy
a. 疯狂的

【例】Most waves are *created* when winds blow across the ocean. 大多数的海浪是风吹过海洋时形成的。

【衍】*creation* (*n.* 创造；创造物); *creative* (*adj.* 创造性的); *creativity* (*n.* 创造性); *creature* (*n.* 人；动物；创造物)

credit [ˈkredit] *n.* 信用；信赖；贷方

【例】*credit* card 信用卡

【考】1. **offer sb. credit** 赊账 2. **give credit** 信任, 信赖

*****crew** [kruː] *n.* 全体人员

【例】The director ordered his *crew* to stop filming. 导演命令全体工作人员停止拍摄。

crime [kraim] *n.* (法律上的) 罪，犯罪

【记】联想记忆：cri (看作 cry 哭) +me (我) →你犯了罪，我为你流泪

【例】campus *crime* 校园犯罪

【衍】criminal (*n.* 罪犯)

*criterion [krai'tiəriən] *n.* (*pl.* criteria) 标准，规则

【例】What were the *criteria* for hiring the new employees? 招聘新员工的标准是什么？

单元自测

1. —Mum, I dislike the vegetables.

—Help yourself to them. They _____ a lot of vitamin C.

A. include　　　B. hold　　　C. take　　　D. contain

2. The firemen told us the difficulty they had _____ the fire _____.

A. to get; under control　　　B. getting; controlled

C. got; controlled　　　D. getting; to control

3. If it is quite _____ to you, I will visit you next Tuesday.　　（2005年天津卷）

A. convenient　　　B. fair

C. easy　　　D. comfortable

4. My sister met him at the Grand Theatre yesterday afternoon, so he _____ your lecture.　　（2000上海）

A. couldn't have attended　　　B. needn't have attended

C. mustn't have attended　　　D. shouldn't have attended

5. —Mum, I'm going to visit my aunt. What about a week?

—A week is too long. Try to be back in a _____ of days.

A. number　　　B. dozen　　　C. couple　　　D. score

6. —It is cold here. Would you mind my closing the window?

— _____.

A. Yes, please　　　B. No, of course not

C. Yes, close it please　　　D. No, you can close it

7. —Have you moved into the new house?

—No, the building is _____ construction.

A. at　　　B. under　　　C. for　　　D. in

8. This is not an economical (节约的) way to get more water; _____, it is very expensive.

A. or else　　　B. on the contrary　　　C. in short　　　D. on the other hand

9. According to the weather report, the weather will _____ to be fine till this weekend.

A. continue B. become C. go D. change

10. The private enterprise manager _____ a generous sum to the relief of the physically disabled.

A. assigned B. contributed C. furnished D. administered

11. People will always remember him _____ his contributions _____ the country.

A. to; to B. for; for C. for; to D. to; for

12. Many Beijingers have already learned enough English to _____ a conversation with an English speaker.

A. go on B. carry on C. keep on D. hold on

13. We've _____ a beautiful new house from an old ruin.

A. invented B. produced C. created D. made

14. You should learn to be independent, and don't always _____ others' help.

A. count for B. count on C. look for D. look on

15. He saved his daughter at the _____ of his life.

A. value B. spending C. cost D. price

答案：DBVAC BBBAB CBCBC

Have no fear of perfection—you'll never reach it.

—S. Dali

不要为十全十美担心——你永远也做不到十全十美。

——达里

Word List 12

4.29

CROP n.庄稼,收成 CROSS n.&v. 十字架 越过

*crossing [ˈkrɔsiŋ; ˈkrɔːsiŋ] n. 十字路口, 人行横道

crossroads [ˈkrɔsrəudz; ˈkrɔːsrəuds] n. 交叉路口
【记】组合词: cross (交叉) +roads (道路)→交叉路口

crowd [kraud] n. 人群; 堆 v. 拥挤, 群聚
【用】1. crowd意为"人群"时可作可数名词: in the crowd 在人群中;
the crowds 人群 2. 作动词的时候, 一般考查其派生词的意思:
crowded (adj. 拥挤的): a crowded bus 拥挤的汽车; the crowded
streets 拥挤的街道
【衍】crowdness (n. 拥挤); overcrowded (adj. 过度拥挤的)

cruel [kruəl] adj. 残忍的, 残酷的, 无情的

CRY n.&v.哭

【例】a *cruel* stepmother 无情的继母 // It seems *cruel* not to give some
money to beggars. 不给乞丐钱显得没有人情味。
【考】be cruel to sb. 对某人残忍
【衍】cruelty (n. 残酷, 无情)

*cube [kjuːb] n. 立方体, 立方
【衍】cubic* (adj. 立方体的)

*cuisine [kwiˈziːn] n. 烹饪 (术)

culture [ˈkʌltʃə] n. 文化
【考】traditional Chinese culture 中国传统文化

*cupboard [ˈkʌbəd] n. 碗柜, 橱柜
【记】组合词: cup (杯子) +board (木板)→用木板做的放杯子的地
方→橱柜

*cure [kjuə] n./v. 治疗, 医好
【例】Modern medicine has *cured* many diseases. 现代医学
多疾病。

91

【辨】cure, heal, treat

cure多指治愈疾病，使人恢复健康：This new medicine soon cured my cold. 这种新药很快治好了我的感冒。heal多指治愈伤口或创伤，使之复原：His wounds are healing over. 他的伤正在复原。// She won't be sad too long; time will heal most trouble. 她不会伤心太久的，时间会抚平大部分的伤痛。treat强调治疗的过程，指通过药物、特别的食品或运动治疗病人或治病，不强调结果：Which doctor is going to treat him for his illness? 他的病会由哪位医生来治疗呢？

*curious ['kjuəriəs] *adj.* 好奇的，奇异的

【用】1. **be curious about+sth.** /从句 对…好奇：be curious about life 对生命的好奇//She is curious about how people and wildlife can coexist peacefully in an area. 她对人类和野生动植物怎样在一个地区和平共处很好奇。2. **be curious +that从句** 奇特，不寻常：It was curious that she didn't tell anyone. 她没有告诉任何人，这很反常。3. **be curious to do sth.** 好奇去做…：We are curious to know what you do in your spare time. 我们很好奇您闲暇时都做些什么。

【衍】curiously（*adv.* 好奇地）

*currency ['kʌrənsi] *n.* 货币

【例】We exchanged our *currency* at a bank in the airport. 我们在机场的一家银行兑换了货币。

curtain
n. 帘, 幕

*curriculum [kə'rikjuləm] *n.* 课程

【例】My high school has a good mathematics *curriculum*. 我所在的高中开设的数学课很不错。

custom ['kʌstəm] *n.* 习惯，习俗

【例】Eating roast turkey is a Thanksgiving *custom*. 过感恩节吃烤火鸡是一种习俗。

customer ['kʌstəmə] *n.* （商店等的）顾客，主顾

【例】The angry *customer* asked to see the manager. 怒气冲冲的顾客要求见经理。

*customs ['kʌstəmz] *n.* 海关，关税

【例】*customs* station 海关// pass through *Customs* 通关

cycle ['saikl] *n.* 周期；循环 *vi.* 骑自行车，循环 *vt.* 使循环

【例】a wave *cycle* 波动周期 // I cannot *cycle* to school today because my bike is broken. 今天我不能骑车上学，因为我的车坏了。

cyclist
n. 骑自行车的人

daily a.&adv.& n.每日的

【衍】bicycle（*n.* 自行车）；recycle（*v.* 回收）；tricycle（*n.* 三轮车）；cyclist（*n.* 骑自行车的人）

damage ['dæmidʒ] *n./v.* 毁坏，损害

*dam
水坝

【用】**damage**作名词，含义为"损害"时不可数，其复数形式damages意为"赔偿费"。

【例】brain *damage* 大脑损伤 // Will this shampoo *damage* the hair? 这种洗发水会损害头发吗？

【考】**damage to...** 对…造成损害，伤害：They are doing damage to our houses. 他们正在毁坏我们的房子。

【衍】damaging（*adj.* 破坏性的）

damp [dæmp] *adj.* 潮湿的 *n.* 潮湿

【例】The climate here is warm and *damp*. 这里是暖湿气候。

danger ['deindʒə] *n.* 危险

【考】**be in danger** 处于危险中

【衍】endanger（*vt.* 危及）；endangered（*adj.* 濒危的）

dangerous ['deindʒrəs] *adj.* 危险的

【例】*dangerous* condition/situation 危险的情况

【考】**be dangerous to** 对…是危险的

【衍】dangerously（*adv.* 危险地）

dare [dɛə] *v.* 敢，敢于

*dark
n.&a.黑暗的
darkness
n. 黑暗

【用】dare的用法与need用法相似，既可作情态动词，又可作实义动词。当dare作情态动词时，没有人称和数的变化：He dare express his views boldly. 他敢于大胆发表意见。当dare作实义动词时，需有人称和数的变化：He dares to go alone. 他敢一个人去。在疑问句、否定句或条件句中常省略dare后接的不定式符号to：He doesn't dare（to）go alone. 他不敢一个人去。

*dash** [dæʃ] *n./v.* 快跑，猛撞 *n.* 少量

【例】Tom made a *dash* for the train. 汤姆向火车猛冲过去。//a *dash* of good luck 一点好运气

data ['deitə] *n.* 资料，数据

【例】climate *data* 气候数据

【考】1. **send the data** 传送数据 2. **get the data** 获得资料

【衍】database*（*n.* 资料库，数据库）

daughter ['dɔːtə] *n.* 女儿

【衍】step-daughter（*n.* 继女）；granddaughter（*n.* 孙女，外孙女）；daughter-in-law（*n.* 儿媳）

*dawn [dɔːn] *n.* 黎明，拂晓

【考】**at dawn** 在黎明时分

*deadline [ˈdedlain] *n.* 最后期限，截止日期

【记】联想记忆：dead（死）+line（线）→
死期→最后期限

【考】**meet the deadline** 在最后期限之前
完成：Professor Smith is working on the
project day and night to meet the deadline.
史密斯教授夜以继日地工作，希望能在最后期限内完成这一项目。

deadline

deaf [def] *adj.* 聋的

【例】a *deaf*-and-dumb man 聋哑人

【衍】blind（*adj.* 瞎的）；lame（*adj.* 瘸的）；deaf（*adj.* 聋的）；dumb
（*adj.* 哑的）

deal [diːl] *v.*（dealt, dealt, dealing）处理 *n.* 量，数额；交易

【用】1. **a great deal of...** 大量（修饰不可数名词）2. **make a deal** 成
交 3. **deal with** 处理，解决：I don't know how to deal with it.（= I
don't know what to do with it.）我不知道该如何解决这个问题。

【衍】dealer（*n.* 商人）

*debate [diˈbeit] *n./v.* 讨论，辩论

【考】**debate on sth.** 有关…的讨论

【例】political *debate* 政治辩论

debate

debt [det] *n.* 债务，欠款

【例】in *debt* 欠债，欠情

*decade [ˈdekeid] *n.* 十年

【例】several *decades* 几十年

decide [diˈsaid] *v.* 决定，下决心

【用】1. **decide+**（**not**）**to do...** 决定（不）做…：We decided not to
climb the mountains because it was raining heavily. 我们决定不爬山
了，因为雨下得很大。2. **decide sth.** 决定某事：decide the rent 决
定房租 3. **decide+**（**that**）**...** 决定…：He's decided that he's not going
to play computer games. 他决定不再玩电脑游戏了。

decision [diˈsiʒn] *n.* 决定，决议

【考】1. **make a decision** 做决定 2. **reach a decision** 达成决议

D

*declare [diˈklɛə] v. 宣布，声明；（向海关等）申报

【例】If you have nothing to *declare*, go through the Green Channel. 如果你无需申报，请走绿色通道。

*decline [diˈklain] v. 衰败；倾斜；谢绝

【例】The quality of the restaurant's food *declined* over the years. 这家饭店饭菜的质量近年来有所下降。

decorate [ˈdekəreit] v. 装饰，修饰

【例】Every Christmas, we *decorate* a pine tree. 每年圣诞节，我们都装饰一棵松树。

【衍】decoration* (n. 装饰，修饰)

decrease [diˈkriːs] n./v. 减小，减少

【记】和increase (v. 增加) 一起记

【例】The birthrate in Europe has been in a steady *decrease* since the 1960s. 20世纪60年代以来，欧洲的人口出生率持续下降。

deed [diːd] n. 行为，事迹

【例】moral *deeds* 道德行为

deep [diːp] adj. 深的，深厚的 adv. 深深地；至深处

deer
n. 鹿

【例】*deep* sleep 熟睡 // *deep* breath 深呼吸 // *deep* knowledge 渊博的知识

【衍】deeply (adv. 深深地)

defeat [diˈfiːt] vt. 击败；战胜

【例】The Rockets *defeated* the Bulls by 92 to 87. 火箭队以92比87战胜了公牛队。

【衍】undefeated (adj. 不可战胜的)

defend [diˈfend] vt. 保护，防御

【记】父母的过分保护 (defend) 会增加孩子的依赖 (depend) 性

【考】**defend oneself** 自我保护：Plants can defend themselves by using both physical and chemical means. 植物可以通过物理和化学方法来进行自我保护。

【衍】defence (n. 保护，防御)

degree [diˈɡriː] n. 程度，度数；文凭

【例】thirty *degrees* centigrade 30摄氏度 // bachelor's *degrees* 学士学位

*delay [diˈlei] n./v. 拖延

【考】1. **delay one's payment** 延迟付款 2. **call for a delay on sth.** 要求推迟某事

*delete [diˈliːt] *vt.* 删除

【例】I *deleted* her name from the guest list. 我把她的名字从客人名单上删掉了。

*deliberately [diˈlibərətli] *adv.* 故意地

【例】Tom *deliberately* spilled his coffee on my shirt. 汤姆故意将咖啡洒到我的衬衫上。

*delicate [ˈdelikət] *adj.* 精巧的，精致的

【例】a *delicate* vase 一个精致的花瓶

delicious   a. 美味的

单元自测

1. We were _____ by his speech.

   A. deep moving   B. deep moved   C. deeply moving   D. deeply moved

2. —Didn't you go to the concert?

   —I was to go, but then _____.

   A. I didn't decide   B. I didn't decide to

   C. I decide not   D. I decided not to

3. They have been _____ with that company for many years.

   A. comparing   B. dealing   C. keeping   D. combining

4. She _____ out alone at night.

   A. dare not to go   B. dares not go

   C. doesn't dare to go   D. dares not to go

5. According to recent reports, one of the rare animals, _____ crocodile, is in _____ danger of dying out.

   A. a; the   B. /; a   C. /; the   D. the; /

6. The bookcase _____ when we were moving.

   A. damaged   B. has damaged

   C. was being damaged   D. got damaged

7. _____ and no way to reduce her pain and suffering from the terrible disease, the patient sought her doctor's help to end her life.

   A. Having given up hope of cure   B. With no hope for cure

   C. There being hope for cure   D. In the hope of cure

8. My grandpa has three sons. So I have two _____.

   A. aunts   B. uncles   C. daughters   D. parents

9. It is said that the company in _____ charge of him is in _____ debt now.

    A. the; the   B. /; /   C. /; the   D. the; /

10. The decision _____, the next problem was how to make a good plan.

    A. having made   B. had been made

    C. having been made   D. was made

11. A kind of glass dish that _____ heat is useful.

    A. resists   B. rejects   C. defends   D. keeps

12. —How do you find the soup in my restaurant?

    — _____.

    A. The waiter sent it to me

    B. It was on the table already when I came

    C. I ordered it ahead of time

    D. I have never had such delicious soup before

13. It is the _____ in China to eat dumplings during the Spring Festival.

    A. habit   B. rule   C. requirement   D. custom

14. According to the research, the birthrate in Europe has been in a steady _____ since the 1960s.

    A. decrease   B. grow   C. reduce   D. rise

15. Little Tom _____ tell a lie to his father.

    A. dare not   B. dare to   C. dares not to   D. dares

答案：AADDA CDBBD DBCDD

Ideas are like the stars—we never reach them, but like mariners, we chart our course by them.   —C. Schurs

理想就像是星星——我们永远无法到达，但是我们像水手一样，用它们指引航程。   ——舒尔茨

Word List 13 430

*delight [diˈlait] *n.* 快乐，乐事 *vt.* 使高兴，使快乐

【考】1. **delight sb.** 让…快乐、高兴 2. **with delight** 高兴地

【衍】delighted (*adj.* 高兴的，快乐的)

*deliver [diˈlivə] *vt.* 投递 (信件，邮包等)；交付，给

【考】**deliver sth./sb. to sb.** 把…交给某人：We delivered the criminal to the police. 我们把罪犯交给了警察。

demand [diˈmɑːnd;diˈmænd] *n./v.* 要求，需要

【用】**demand** 后接宾语从句时，从句谓语动词应使用虚拟语气，即**demand that sb. (should) do** 形式：They have demanded that all the facts (should) be made public. 他们要求把全部事实公之于众。

【考】1. **in great/high demand** 急需 2. **meet the demand** 满足需要 3. **demand for sth.** 需要…

【衍】demanding (*adj.* 苛求的)

dentist [ˈdentist] *n.* 牙科医生

department [diˈpɑːtmənt] (缩为 Dept.) *n.* 部门，(大学的) 系

【记】联想记忆：de+part (部分)+ment→部门

【例】department store 百货商店 // He worked in community welfare *department.* 他在社会福利部工作。

dentist

departure [diˈpɑːtʃə] *n.* 离开；背离

【用】**departure from** 背离：That is a thorough departure from the traditional diet of vegetables, rice and little meat. 这与吃蔬菜、米饭和少量肉类的传统饮食完全背道而驰。

depend [diˈpend] *vi.* 依靠，指望；取决于

【考】**depend on** 依靠，指望：Some animals and plants depend on each other for existence. 一些动物和植物相互依存。

98

D

*deposit [di'pɔzit] n./v. 存 (款); 堆积

【例】She *deposited* her money in the bank. 她把钱存入了银行。

*depth [depθ] n. 深, 深度

【记】联想记忆: dep (看作deep深的) +th→深度

【例】a 3,000-meter *depth* of ice 3,000米厚的冰层

describe [di'skraib] vt. 描写, 叙述

【例】The poem *describes* the moonlight on the lake. 这首诗描写的是湖光月色。

【衍】description (n. 描述, 描写)

desert [di'zə:t] v. 舍弃, 遗弃

['dezət] n. 沙漠

【例】The mother dog *deserted* the puppy. 母狗遗弃了小狗。

【衍】dessert (n. 甜点); deserted (adj. 无人的; 荒废的)

deserve [di'zə:v] vt. 应受, 值得

【记】联想记忆: de+serve (服务) →提供了服务就应受待遇

【例】The naughty child *deserved* the punishment. 这个淘气的孩子应该受到惩罚。

design [di'zain] v. 设计, 制定计划 n. 样式

【记】联想记忆: de+sign (标记) →做标记→设计

【例】Artists were invited to *design* clothes and settings for operas and ballets. 艺术家被邀请来为歌剧和芭蕾设计服装和舞台背景。// special *design* 特殊的设计

desire [di'zaiə] n./v. 渴望, 期望

【例】The people all over the world *desire* peace. 全世界的人们都渴望和平。

【考】1. **have desire for sth.** 渴望… 2. **have desire to do sth.** 渴望做…: has no desire to eat 不想吃饭

*desperate ['despərit] adj. 令人绝望的, 不顾一切的

【例】a *desperate* soldier 一名绝望的士兵

*destination [,desti'neiʃən] n. 目的地

【例】It took us all day to reach our *destination*. 我们花了整整一天的时间才到达目的地。

destroy [di'strɔi] v. 破坏, 毁坏

【例】*destroy* forests 破坏森林 // *destroy* trust 破坏信任

99

detective [diˈtektiv] *n.* 侦探

【记】detect（发现，察觉）+ive→侦探

detective

determine [diˈtə:min] *v.* 决定；测定；确定

【例】Our social positions *determine* the way we are dressed. 我们的社会地位决定我们的穿着方式。// I was very grateful and *determined* to repay him one day. 我非常感激他，决定以后报答他。

【衍】determined（*adj.* 决定的）；determination（*n.* 决定，决心）

develop(e) [diˈveləp] *v.* (使)发展；(使)发育；开发；冲洗(照片)

【例】*develop* the economy 发展经济//*develop* children's problem-solving abilities 开发儿童解决问题的能力//Special chemicals are needed to *develop* film. 冲胶卷需要用特殊的化学品。

【衍】developed（*adj.* 发达的）；developing（*adj.* 发展中的）；development（*n.* 发展，发育）

devote [diˈvəut] *vt.* 把…奉献，把…专用（于）

【记】联想记忆：de+vote（投票）→把票投给他→把…奉献

【用】1. **devote oneself to** 专心于…：Energy engineers will devote themselves to modern technology. 能源工程师将全心投入现代技术的研发。2. **be devoted to** 专心于，致力于：Tom is not devoted to the job. 汤姆并没有专心工作。3. **devote sth. to sth.** 把…专用…：They want me to devote all my time to my studies. 他们希望我把所有的时间都用在学习上。注意：与devote搭配的to是介词，后接名词或动名词。

【衍】devotion（*n.* 奉献，奉献精神）

***diagram** [ˈdaiəgræm] *n.* 图表，图样

【例】The *diagram* helped me assemble the bike. 这张图样帮助我组装了这辆自行车。

dial [ˈdaiəl] *v.* 拨（电话号码）

【例】I *dialed* several times, but I got a busy sign each time. 我拨了好几次电话，但每次都是忙音。

dialogue [ˈdaiələg; ˈdaiəlɔ:g] *n.* （美dialog）对话

【例】the political *dialogue* 政治对话

diamond [ˈdaiəmənd] *n.* 钻石，金刚石；菱形

【记】发音记忆："戴梦得"→著名的珠宝品牌→钻石

diary
n. 日记

dictionary n.字典

dictation [dik'teiʃən] *n.* 听写

【例】The teacher uses *dictation* to teach listening skills. 老师通过听写来教授听力技巧。

die [dai] *v.* (died, died, dying) 死亡；消失；熄灭

【用】1. **die of sth.** 因…而死（原因是来自内部），多指死于某种疾病，后常接下列名词：hunger, cold, poison, illness, old age, a disease, cancer, thirst, sorrow, disappointed love（失恋）, a fever, heat... 2. **die from sth.** 由于…而死（原因常来自外部），多指死于疾病以外，后常接下列名词：accident, overwork, carelessness, drinking, smoking, some unknown cause等。注意：die为瞬间动词，不能与表示时间段的状语连用。

【考】**die out** 灭绝，熄灭：The fire became weak and finally died out. 火变得微弱，最终熄灭了。

diet ['daiət] *n.* 饮食；节食 *v.* 节食

【记】联想记忆：过度节食（diet）会死（die）人的

【例】the traditional *diet* 传统饮食 // Both the *diet* and the exercise will help me to lose weight. 节食和锻炼将有助于我减肥。

differ ['difə] *vi.* 不一致，有区别

【考】1. **differ on sth.** 关于…观点不一致 2. **differ from...** 和…不同，相异

【衍】difference (*n.* 不同，区别)

different ['difrənt] *adj.* 不同的，有差异的

【考】**be different from sth.** 与…不同：Allow children the space to voice their opinions, even if they are different from your own. 允许孩子表达自己的观点，即使他们和你的观点不同。

【衍】differently (*adv.* 不同地)

difficulty ['difikəlti] *n.* 困难，费力；异议

【考】1. **have difficulty (in) doing sth.** 做…有困难 2. **have difficulty with sth.** 做…有困难 3. **without difficulty** 容易地，毫不费力地

【衍】difficult (*adj.* 困难的，艰难的)

dig [dig] *v.* (dug, dug, digging) 挖（洞、沟等），掘

【例】*dig* a hole 挖坑

***digest** [di'dʒest] *v.* 消化；领会

['daidʒest] *n.* 摘要，概要；文摘

【记】联想记忆：dig（挖）+est→不断地挖，刨根问底→领会

D

【例】*digest* the food 消化食物 // Tom *digested* the difficult article slowly. 汤姆慢慢地领会了这篇难懂的文章。

【衍】digestion（*n.* 消化）

*digital ［'didʒitl］*adj.* 数字的，数码的

【记】Olympus 广告语：My digital story! 我的数码故事！

【例】*digital* camera 数码相机

✱dignity ［'digniti］*n.* 尊严，高贵

【例】The black robes of a judge give a look of *dignity*. 法官的黑色长袍给人威严的感觉。

dilemma ［di'lemə］*n.* 进退两难的局面

【例】The boss was in a *dilemma*. 老板进退维谷。

✱dimension ［di'menʃn］*n.* 尺寸，尺度

【例】What are the *dimensions* of the painting? 这幅画多大？

✱dinosaur ［'dainəsɔ:］*n.* 恐龙

【例】The *dinosaurs* were on the earth for over 160 million years. 恐龙在地球上生存了一亿六千多万年。

*dioxide ［dai'ɔksaid］*n.* 二氧化物

【例】carbon *dioxide* 二氧化碳

dip ［dip］*v.*（dipped, dipped, dipping）浸，蘸

【例】Mary *dipped* her toe in the cold water. 玛丽将脚趾头放到冷水中。

*diploma ［di'pləumə］*n.* 毕业文凭，学位证书

【例】college *diploma* 大学文凭

direct ［di'rekt］*adj.* 直接的，直达的 *v.* 指挥，指导

【例】a *direct* cause 直接原因 // The teacher *directed* kids to build solar collectors. 老师指导孩子们做太阳能收集器。

【衍】indirect（*adj.* 间接的）；directly（*adv.* 直接地）；director（*n.* 主管；导演）

direction ［di'rekʃn］*n.* 方向；说明（书）；指导

【例】a sense of *direction* 方向感 // Do you always understand the *directions* on a bottle of medicine? 你都明白药瓶上的服用说明吗？

*directory ［di'rektəri］*n.* 姓名地址录；公司名录

director n. 指挥者，让长，主任，导演等

单元自测

1. Everybody in the little town knew my first teacher, so we had no _____ finding his home.
   A. difficulties in   B. difficulty with   C. difficulty   D. difficulty to

2. This city seems to be quite different _____ it used to be.
   A. from what   B. from that   C. to what   D. to that

3. It _____ no difference whether he will come or not.
   A. has   B. causes   C. makes   D. gets

4. —How is the old man now?
   —Sorry, he _____ though they did all they could to save him.
   A. was dead   B. had died   C. has been dead   D. died

5. Her son, to whom she was so _____, went abroad ten years ago.
   A. loved   B. cared   C. devoted   D. affected

6. —Why do these photographs look so black?
   —The film was not _____ in the right way.
   A. washed   B. developed   C. printed   D. worked

7. We _____ to get the work done before May Day.
   A. are decided   B. are determined   C. are offered   D. are made up our mind

8. The house that _____ by the fire belongs to _____.
   A. was destroyed; mine   B. destroyed; mine
   C. was destroyed; me   D. destroyed; me

9. —The education system rather than the teachers _____ to answer for the heavy burden on the students.
   —I agree. I hope the reform being carried out in our country at present will bring about the _____ results.
   A. are; desired   B. is; desired
   C. are; desiring   D. is; desiring

10. His _____ of the plane was correct and could really fly.
    A. shape   B. pattern   C. design   D. model

11. —How long are you staying?
    —I don't know. _____.   （2004江苏）
    A. That's OK   B. Never mind
    C. It depends   D. It doesn't matter

12. The teacher demanded that our examination paper _____ handed in at once.
    A. be   B. must be   C. would be   D. had to be

13. The shop owner will get all these ordered TV sets _____ to the customers today.

    A. be delivered   B. delivered   C. delivering   D. to deliver

14. —How can I use this washing machine?

    —Well, just refer to the _____.

    A. explanations   B. expressions   C. introductions   D. directions

15. The temple was _____ and _____ to pieces.

    A. deserted; fell   B. deserted; falling

    C. deserting; falling   D. deserting; fell

答案：CACDC BBCBD CABDA

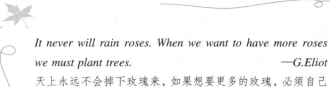

*It never will rain roses. When we want to have more roses
we must plant trees.*   —*G.Eliot*

天上永远不会掉下玫瑰来，如果想要更多的玫瑰，必须自己
种植。   —— 艾略特

Word List 14

dirt [dəːt] *n.* 污物，脏物
【记】联想记忆：拍拍衬衫（shirt）上的灰尘（dirt）
【衍】dirty（*adj.* 脏的，肮脏的）

disabled [dis'eibld] *adj.* 残疾的
【记】dis+able（能干的）+d→不能干的→残疾的
【衍】disable（*vt.* 使失去能力，使不起作用）；disability（*n.* 残疾）

disadvantage [ˌdisəd'vɑːntidʒ; ˌdisəd'væntidʒ] *n.* 不利条件，弱点
【记】dis+advantage（有利条件）→不利条件
【例】the advantages and *disadvantages* 利弊

disagree [ˌdisə'griː] *vi.* 意见不一致，持不同意见
【记】dis+agree（同意）→不同意→意见不一致
【考】1. **disagree with sb.** 与…意见不一：The woman disagrees with him. 这名女子和他意见不一。2. **disagree on/about sth.** 在…上意见不一：They disagree about the suggestion. 他们对这条建议意见不一。
【衍】disagreement（*n.* 意见不一致，争端）

disappear [ˌdisə'piə] *vi.* 消失
【记】dis+appear（出现）→消失
【例】Wildlife is *disappearing* because of shooting and the loss of wildland habitat. 狩猎以及野生栖息地的减少是导致野生物种逐渐消失的原因。
【衍】disappearance（*n.* 消失）

disappoint [ˌdisə'point] *v.* （使）失望
【记】dis+appoint（委任）→没有受到委任→使失望
【例】Tom did not want to *disappoint* his parents. 汤姆不想母失望。

105

【衍】 disappointment（n. 失望）; disappointed（adj. 失望的）; disappointing（adj. 令人失望的）

disaster [di'zɑːstə; di'zæstə] n. 灾难，祸患

【例】 a natural disaster 自然灾害

discount ['diskaunt] n. 折扣

【记】 联想记忆：dis+count（数）→不按原来的价格计算→折扣

【例】 People get an discount at the department store at Christmas. 圣诞节期间人们在百货商店买东西享受折扣。

discount

*discourage [dis'kʌridʒ] vt. 使气馁，打消（念头）

【记】 dis+courage（勇气）→使失去勇气→使气馁

【例】 The loss of the game discouraged the whole team. 比赛的失败使整支队伍垂头丧气。

【衍】 discouraged（adj. 沮丧的，气馁的）; discouraging（adj. 令人气馁的）

discover [dis'kʌvə] vt. 发现，找到

【记】 联想记忆：dis（去掉）+cover（盖子）→拿掉盖子→发现，找到

【例】 We discovered a new restaurant in the city. 我们在城里发现了一家新开的餐馆。

【衍】 discovery（n. 发现）; rediscover（vt. 再次发现）; undiscovered（adj. 未发现的）

*discrimination [dis,krimi'neiʃn] n. 歧视

【例】 Certain kinds of discrimination are illegal. 某些歧视是违法的。

discrimination

discuss [dis'kʌs] v. 讨论，议论

【考】 discuss the problem with sb. 与…一起讨论问题

【衍】 discussion（n. 讨论，辩论）

disease [di'ziːz] n. 病，疾病

【例】 a disease of the eyes 眼疾

*disgusting [dis'gʌstiŋ] adj. 令人讨厌的

【例】 disgusting food 令人厌恶的食物

dislike [dis'laik] *n./vt.* 不喜欢，嫌恶
【记】dis+like（喜爱）→不喜爱
【例】The books in the shop gave him a *dislike*. 他不喜欢商店里的书。//They *disliked* the idea. 他们不喜欢这个主意。

dismiss [dis'mis] *v.* 解雇；解散
【记】联想记忆：dis+miss（想念）→不想我，我就走→让…离开
【例】He was so irresponsible that I decided to *dismiss* him. 他太不负责了，我决定解雇他。

dismiss

distance ['distəns] *n.* 距离
distant
a. 远的
【记】来自distant（*adj.* 在远处的）
【例】a *distance* of 20 kilometers 20公里的距离// The *distance* between bus stops is too long. 公交车站之间的距离太远了。
【考】1. **at a distance** 隔一段距离 2. **in the distance** 在远处

distinction [dis'tiŋkʃn] *n.* 区别，差别
【例】class *distinctions* 等级差别 // social *distinctions* 社会差别

✶ **distinguish** [dis'tiŋgwiʃ] *v.* 区分，辨别
【例】People could not *distinguish* the twins. 人们分不清这对双胞胎谁是谁。

* **distribute** [dis'tribjuːt] *v.* 分布，分配
【例】Fat on human beings is *distributed* in different ways. 脂肪以不同方式分布于人体内。

district ['distrikt] *n.* 区，地区
【例】the *district* sports meet 地区运动会

disturb [dis'təːb] *v.* 打扰，扰乱
【例】I'm really sorry to have *disturbed* you. 很抱歉打扰你了。
【衍】disturbing（*adj.* 烦扰的）；disturbed（*adj.* 扰乱的）

dive [daiv] *vi.* 跳水
【例】*dive* into the water 跳入水中

* **diverse** [dai'vəːs] *adj.* 不同的，多种多样的
【例】*diverse* flowers 不同的花

divide [di'vaid] *v.* 分，划分；除以
【例】This river *divides* at its mouth. 这条河在河口处分岔。// *Divide*

15 by 3 you get 5. 15除以3得5。

【考】**divide...into...** 把…划分为几份: This country was divided into three parts. 这个国家被划分为三个部分。

【衍】divided (*adj.* 分开的，不同的); division (*n.* 分开，区分)

【辨】**divide, separate**

divide, separate 都有"分开"之意。 **divide** 表示把一个整体分成若干部分，如: Divide the class into two groups. 把全班分成两组。 **separate** 侧重指把原来连在一起的或靠近的人或物分开，也指"离别，分居"，如: He went over and separated the two boys who are fighting. 他走过去把两个打架的男孩分开。

divorce [diˈvɔːs] *n.* 离婚 *vt.* 使离婚

【例】Their marriage finally ended up in *divorce.* 他们的婚姻最终以离婚而结束。

*****dizzy** [ˈdizi] *adj.* 头晕目眩的

【例】The room was so hot that he felt *dizzy.* 房间里热得让他感到头晕目眩。

do [duː] *vt.* (did, done, doing) 做，干 *aux. v.* 用以构成疑问句及否定句

【考】1. **do away with** 摆脱，废除 2. **do well in** 在…做得好 3. **do sb. a favour** 帮某人忙 4. **have something to do with...** 和…有关

document [ˈdɔkjumənt] *n.* 文件，文献

【例】a business *document* 商务文件

doll [dɔl;dɔːl] *n.* 玩偶，玩具娃娃

【例】Barbie *doll* 芭比娃娃

*****donate** [dəuˈneit; ˈdəuneit] *v.* 捐赠，赠送

【例】The school calls on the students to *donate* their blood voluntarily. 学校号召学生义务献血。

dormitory [ˈdɔːmitri; ˈdɔːmitəri] (缩为dorm) *n.* 学生宿舍

【记】词根记忆: dorm (睡眠) +itory→睡觉的地方→宿舍

*****dot** [dɔt] *n.* 点，圆点

【记】和pot (*n.* 壶) 一起记

double [ˈdʌbl] *adj.* 两倍的；双重的 *n.* 两个；双打 *v.* 加倍

【例】*double* room 双人间 // men's *doubles* 男子双打 // They hope the average human life span can be *doubled.* 他们希望人均寿命可以

翻倍。

doubt [daut] *n./v.* 怀疑，疑惑

【考】1. **no doubt** 毫无疑问 2. **without doubt** 毫无疑问 3. **beyond doubt** 勿庸置疑的

【例】People *doubt* the outcome of his experiments. 人们怀疑他的实验结果。

*download** [ˌdaunˈləud] *n./vt.* 下载（计算机用语）

【例】*download* the game 下载游戏

downstairs [ˌdaunˈstɛəz] *adv.* 在楼下，到楼下

【例】go *downstairs* 下楼

downtown [ˌdaunˈtaun] *n./adj.* 市区（的），闹市区（的）

【例】*downtown* Manhattan 曼哈顿商业区

dozen [ˈdʌzn] *n.* 十二个；许多

【考】1. **a dozen** 一打 2. **dozens of** 几十个，很多

*draft** [drɑːft; dræft] *vt.* 起草 *n.* 草稿

【例】The secretary was *drafting* a speech for the minister. 秘书正在为部长起草演讲稿。

drag [dræg] *v.* (dragged, dragged, dragging) 拖，拽

drag

【例】Tom *dragged* the toy duck behind him. 汤姆拽着身后的玩具鸭。

draw [drɔː] *v.* (drew, drawn, drawing) 绘画；拉，吸引；提取（金钱）

【考】1. **draw a conclusion** 得出结论 2. **draw one's attention** 吸引…的注意

【衍】drawing（*n.* 图画，素描）

*drawback** [ˈdrɔːbæk] *n.* 缺点，障碍

【记】draw（拉）+back（向后）→拖后腿→缺点

【例】Everything has its *drawbacks*. 凡事都有不足之处。

drawer [drɔː] *n.* 抽屉

【记】来自draw（拉）+er→可抽拉的东西→抽屉

dream [driːm] *v.* (dreamed/dreamt, dreamed/dreamt, dreaming) 做梦，梦想 *n.* 梦，梦想

【考】**dream of sth./doing sth.** 梦想（做）…：I often dream of becoming a teacher. 我常梦想成为一名教师。

dress [dres] *v.* 穿衣，打扮 *n.* 女服，连衣裙；服装

【用】1.（be）**dressed in...** 穿着…：Dressed in a white uniform, he looks more like a cook than a doctor. 穿着白色制服的他看起来更像个厨师而不是医生。2. **dress sb.** 给某人穿衣服：She dressed herself neatly for work. 为了工作她穿得很整洁。注意：dress的宾语只能是人，不能是衣服。

【例】She had to *dress* like a man. 她不得不穿得像个男人。

【考】**dress up** 打扮，伪装：Some people dress up to pretend to be beggars. 一些人装扮成乞丐。

【衍】undress（*v.* 脱衣服）

单元自测

1. Happy boys and girls are dressed _____ on Sunday, coming to the square.
   A. up   B. in   C. on   D. with

2. The carriage was _____ by four horses.
   A. rolled   B. pushed   C. driven   D. drawn

3. —Peter is very clever and he studies hard as well.
   —No _____ he always wins first in the examinations.
   A. doubt   B. question   C. wonder   D. problem

4. He went on to do a part time job after work _____ his income.
   A. for raise   B. to double   C. to rise   D. to reduce

5. —Will $ 200 _____?
   —I'm afraid not. We need at least 50 more dollars.   （2004湖北）
   A. count   B. satisfy   C. fit   D. do

6. The professor divided his spare time _____ walking and writing.
   A. between   B. into   C. to   D. among

7. John was late for the business meeting because his flight had been _____ by a heavy storm.   （2004辽宁）
   A. kept   B. stopped   C. slowed   D. delayed

8. Tom never works hard at his lessons, so it's not _____ to see a _____ look on his face after the exam.
   A. surprised; disappointing   B. surprised; disappointed
   C. surprising; disappointing   D. surprising; disappointed

9. While building a tunnel through the mountain, _____.

    A. an underground lake was discovered.

    B. there was an underground lake discovered.

    C. a lake was discovered underground

    D. the workers discovered an underground lake

10. "We must keep a secret of the things _____ here," the general said _____ at the man in charge of information office.

    A. having been discussed; and seriously staring

    B. to be discussed; seriously stared

    C. discussed; and stared seriously

    D. being discussed; seriously staring

11. From the top of _____ Empire State Building, you could see up to _____ distance of 130 kilometers on a clear day.

    A. a; the   B. /;a   C. an; the   D. the; a

12. They disagreed _____ each other _____ whose pronunciation was better.

    A. about; on   B. with; on   C. with; in   D. on; to

13. I dislike _____ hot coffee before going to bed, but tonight I'd like _____ a try.

    A. drinking; having   B. to drink; to have

    C. drinking; to have   D. to drink; having

14. The twins look almost alike, so many people could not _____ them.

    A. notice   B. recognize   C. distinguish   D. classify

15. _____ on-going division between English-speaking Canadians and French-speaking Canadians is _____ major concern of the country.

    A. The; /   B. The; a   C. An; the   D. An; the

答案：ADCBD BDDDC DBCCB

111

Word List 15

drier ['draiə] (=dryer) *n.* 烘干机，吹风机

【记】来自 dry (*v.* 干燥)

drill [dril] *v.* 钻（孔）；重复训练 *n.* 钻头；（反复的）训练

【例】*drill* a hole in the ice 在冰上钻个孔

drier

drink [driŋk] *v.* (drank, drunk, drinking) 喝 *n.* 饮酒

【例】a cool *drink* 冷饮//You're *drinking* too much. 你喝得太多了。

drive v.驾驶

drop [drɔp] *v.* (dropped, dropped, dropping) 掉下，落下 *n.* 滴，下降

【例】A few *drops* of rain landed on the roof. 几滴雨落在了屋顶上。

driver n.驾驶

【考】1. **drop in/by** 顺便拜访 2. **drop off** 脱落；打盹 3. **drop out** 放弃

drug [drʌg] *n.* 药，药物；毒品

drop 滴落 落下

【例】*drug* store 药店 // take *drugs* 服药；吸毒

drug

drum [drʌm] *n.* 鼓

【例】beat *drums* 打鼓

drunk [drʌŋk] *adj.* 醉的

dry v2a.干的 干燥

【记】联想记忆：喝（drink）多了自然会醉（drunk）

【例】*drunk* driving 酒后驾车 // He is slightly *drunk*. 他有点醉了。

duck [dʌk] *n.* 鸭子 *v.* 躲避，浸入水中

【例】a cooked *duck* 煮熟的鸭子//*duck* into a subway 躲进地铁

***due** [dju:] *adj.* 预期的，约定的

【例】It was the night before the composition was *due*. 过了今晚就要交作文了。

【考】**due to** 由于，应归于：Your eating habits will be broken due to lack of sleep. 你的饮食习惯会因为缺乏睡眠而打破。

*dull [dʌl] *adj.* 单调无味的；阴暗的；迟钝的

【例】They think science is difficult and *dull*. 他们认为理科难学而且枯燥无味。//a *dull* child 反应迟钝的孩子

dumpling [ˈdʌmpliŋ] *n.* 饺子

during [ˈdjuəriŋ; ˈduriŋ] *prep.* 在…期间，在…过程中

【例】What did the man do *during* these weeks? 那个人在这几个星期里都做了什么？//*during* the operation 在手术过程中

dusk [dʌsk] *n.* 黄昏

【考】**at dusk** 在黄昏

dust [dʌst] *n.* 灰尘，尘土

【例】*Dust* blew into my eyes. 灰尘吹进我眼睛里了。

【衍】dustman (*n.* 清洁工)；dusty (*adj.* 积满灰尘的)；dustbin (*n.* 垃圾箱)

duty [ˈdjuːti; ˈduːti] *n.* 责任，义务；税

【考】1. **on duty** 值班，值日 2. **off duty** 下班 3. **a sense of duty** 责任感 4. **duty free** 免税

【衍】dutiful (*adj.* 顺从的)

*dynamic [daiˈnæmik] *adj.* 有活力的；动力的，动力学的

【记】词根记忆：dynam (力量)+ic→有活力的

【例】He is a *dynamic* person. 他充满活力。

*dynasty [ˈdinəsti; ˈdainəsti] *n.* 朝代，王朝

each [iːtʃ] *adj./pron.* 每人，每个，每件

【例】Give an apple to *each* child. 给每个孩子一个苹果。

【辨】**each, every**

each 可用作代词和形容词，**every** 只能用作形容词；二者都用作形容词时意义相同，**each** 指两个或两个以上中的每一个具体的人或物，着重个别的含义，如：Each book on this shelf is worth reading. 这个书架上的每本书都值得一读。**every** 指三个或三个以上中的每一个，着重于整体、共性的含义，如：I've read every book on that shelf. 我读了那个书架上的所有书。

*eager [ˈiːgə] *adj.* 渴望的，热切的

【考】**be/feel eager to do sth.** 渴望做…：She is eager to see this film. 她特别想看这部电影。

【衍】eagerly (*adv.* 渴望地，热切地)；eagerness (*n.* 渴望，热切)

*eagle
n. 鹰

113

earn [ə:n] *vt.* 挣得，赚得

【例】*earn* money 赚钱 // *earn* profit 获得利润

【考】**earn one's living** 谋生

earthquake ['ə:θkweik] *n.* 地震

【记】组合词：earth（地球）+quake（震动）→地震

【例】The city was completely destroyed by *earthquakes*. 城市在地震中化为乌有。

Easter ['i:stə] *n.* 复活节

【例】*Easter* Island 复活节岛

eastern ['i:stən] *adj.* 东方的，东部的

【例】*Eastern* and Western Europeans 东欧人和西欧人

eastward(s) ['i:stwəd(z)] *adv.* 向东

【例】We traveled *eastwards* for several days. 我们向东走了几天。

*ecology [i:'kɔlədʒi] *n.* 生态学

【记】词根记忆：eco（生态）+logy（…学）→生态学

edge [edʒ] *n.* 边缘

【考】**on the edge of** 在…的边缘

*edition [i'diʃn] *n.* （发行物的）版，版本

【例】A new *edition* of the dictionary is coming out soon. 这本字典的新版本马上就要面世了。

editor ['editə] *n.* 编辑

【记】来自edit（*v.* 编辑）

【例】Her mother is an *editor*. 她母亲是编辑。

educate ['edjukeit] *v.* (educated, educated, educating) 教育，培养

【例】He was once *educated* at a local grammar school. 他曾在当地的一所语法学校学习过。//This has helped *educate* people about the prevention of heart disease. 这有助于培养人们预防心脏病的意识。

【衍】educator（*n.* 教育家）; educated（*adj.* 受过教育的）

education [,edju'keiʃən] *n.* 教育，培养

【例】higher *education* 高等教育//He got a good *education*. 他受过良好的教育。

【考】**further education** 进修，继续教育

【衍】educational（*adj.* 教育的）; co-educational（*adj.* 联合教育的）

*effect [i'fekt] *n.* 效果；作用，影响

【记】词根记忆：ef（出）+fect（做）→做出效果

【例】side *effect* 副作用//the greenhouse *effect* 温室效应//the snow-balling *effect* 雪球效应

【考】1. **have effect(s) on sth.** 对…有影响，起作用：That game can have an important effect on children. 那种游戏对孩子影响重大。

2. **take effect** 生效 3. **put into effect** 使生效

effort [ˈefət] *n.* 努力，艰难的尝试

【例】individual/personal *efforts* 个人的努力

【考】**make an effort to do sth.** 努力做…：My cousin made an effort to learn swimming. 我表弟努力学习游泳。

【衍】effortlessly（*adv.* 容易地）

✶eggplant [ˈeɡplɑːnt] *n.* 茄子

【记】联想记忆：egg（蛋）+plant（植物）→蛋形的植物→茄子

either [ˈaɪðə] *adj./pron.* (两者之中)任一 *conj.* 或者，要么… *adv.* 也

【用】1. **either...or...** 或者…或者…：Dr. Black comes from either Oxford or Cambridge; I can't remember which. 布莱克博士不是来自牛津就是剑桥，我记不清了。注意：连接两个并列主语时，谓语动词与邻近主语一致：Either you or I am wrong. 不是你错了，就是我错了。2. 用于否定句或短语后，表"也"：She asked no questions, and she didn't scold us either. 她没有问什么，也没有批评我们。

elder [ˈeldə] *adj.* 年长的 *n.* 长者，前辈

【例】*elder* brother 哥哥

【衍】elderly（*adj.* 过了中年的，稍老的）

✶elect [iˈlekt] *vt.* (投票)选举

【例】Tom was *elected* chairman of the Student Union. 汤姆被选为学生会主席。

【衍】elected（*adj.* 当选的）

electric [iˈlektrik] *adj.* 电的

【记】词根记忆：electr（电）+ic→电的

【例】an *electric* clock 电子钟

electrical [iˈlektrikəl] *adj.* 与电有关的，电气的

【记】词根记忆：electr（电）+ical→电的

【例】an *electrical* engineer 电气工程师

electricity [iˌlekˈtrisiti] *n.* 电；电流

【记】词根记忆：electr（电）+icity→电

【例】produce/make *electricity* 发电 //provide electricity

DANGEROUS KEEP OUT

the *electricity* 供电

*electronic [iˌlek'trɔnik] *adj.* 电子的

【记】来自electric (*adj.* 电的)

【例】an *electronic* scanner 电子扫描仪

【衍】electronically (*adv.* 电子地)

*elegant ['eligənt] *adj.* 文雅的, 雅致的

【例】This *elegant* luggage is manufactured by LV. 这个精巧的旅行箱由LV公司制造。

else [els] *adv.* 别的, 其他的

【用】用于不定代词或疑问词之后, 表示其他的…, 别的…: Get someone else to do it. 找别人做。//What else did you do? 你还做了什么?

embarrass [im'bærəs] *vt.* 使困窘, 使局促不安

【衍】embarrassing (*adj.* 令人尴尬的);

embarrassed (*adj.* 尴尬的)

embassy ['embəsi] *n.* 大使馆

emergency [i'mə:dʒənsi] *n.* 紧急情况或状态

【记】联想记忆: 紧急情况 (emergency) 出现 (emerge)

【例】an *emergency* measure 紧急措施//an *emergency* operation 急诊手术; 应急运转 // You should only use this door in an *emergency*. 在紧急情况下才能使用这扇门。

*emperor ['empərə] *n.* 皇帝

employ [im'plɔi] *vt.* 雇用

【例】It is now expensive to *employ* a carpenter. 现在请木匠很贵。

【衍】employee (*n.* 雇员); employer (*n.* 雇主); employment (*n.* 雇用); unemployed (*adj.* 失业的)

单元自测

1. Why not trust and use David? He is still as strong as _____ in the team.

　　A. somebody else　B. everybody else　C. anybody else　　D. nobody else

2. —Do you enjoy these two novels?

　　—I should if _____ of them were written lively.

　　A. either　　　　B. each　　　　　C. every　　　　　D. all

3. Now and then they would _____ our house and have a talk with us.

A. drop in on   B. drop in   C. call on   D. drop in at

4. When you call on a French man, you may chat for an hour or so, _____ not even a coffee or water is offered.

    A. during this time   B. by this time

    C. during which time   D. by which time

5. The _____ a teacher has on children is usually greater than that of their parents.

    A. use   B. effect   C. effort   D. energy

6. I invited him to have _____ drink with me but he said he was in such _____ hurry that he had no time to spare.

    A. the; /   B. a; /   C. a; a   D. /; a

7. During National Day, they stood _____ duty every 1.5 miles along the road.

    A. in   B. off   C. at   D. on

8. _____ I _____ some difficulties, my friend, Mr. Robert always gives me a hand.

    A. Whenever; happen to   B. If, find

    C. Each time; meet with   D. Every time; came to

9. The public should be _____ in how to use energy more effectively.

    A. educated   B. taught   C. told   D. studied

10. In dealing with public relations, we should make every _____ to prevent the conflict in personality.

    A. effect   B. power   C. energy   D. effort

11. Tom is Lily's _____ bother, who is 3 years _____ than her.

    A. older; older   B. older; elder   C. elder; older   D. elder; elder

12. _____ in her most beautiful skirt, the girl tried to make herself _____ at the party.

    A. Dressed; noticed   B. Dressing; noticed

    C. Dressed; noticing   D. Dressing; being noticing

13. Merlin was very proud of his invention and _____ arriving at the party on wheels while playing the violin.

    A. would like   B. preferred   C. dreamed of   D. dreamed in

14. The saleswoman in the shop is always _____ to please everybody.

    A. unexpected   B. eager   C. shocked   D. proud

15. The water isn't fit _____.

    A. drinking   B. drunk

    C. to drink   D. to be drunk

CDDAD CACBC

Word List 16

empty [ˈempti] *vt.* 倒空 *adj.* 空的

【例】Will you please go and *empty* that drawer? 你能去倒一下抽屉吗？// The street was *empty*. 大街上空无一人。

encourage [inˈkʌridʒ] *vt.* 鼓励，激励

【记】词根记忆：en（使…）+courage（精神）→使有精神→鼓励

【考】**encourage sb. to do sth.** 鼓励某人做某事：His parents have encouraged him to overcome difficulties in life. 父母鼓励他克服生活中的困难。

【衍】encouragement（*n.* 鼓励）；encouraging（*adj.* 鼓励的，鼓舞的）

end [end] *v.* 结束，终止 *n.* 终点；结束

【例】*end* one's marriage 结束婚姻 // I'm at the *end* of my rope. 我现在山穷水尽。

【考】1. **in the end** 最后 2. **at the end of sth.** 在…的末尾：at the end of this year 今年年终 3. **by the end of sth.** 到…结束的时候 4. **come to an end** 停止 5. **end up** 结束；死 6. **on end** 连续地

【衍】endless（*adj.* 无尽的）；ending（*n.* 结尾，最后）

energetic [ˌenəˈdʒetik] *adj.* 精力旺盛的

【记】来自energy（*n.* 精力）

【例】I felt *energetic*. 我感到精力充沛。

【衍】energetically（*adv.* 积极地）

energy [ˈenədʒi] *n.* 精力；能量

【记】词根记忆：en+erg（活动，能量）+y→精力；能量

【例】*energy* sources 能源 // *energy* conservation 节能

engine [ˈendʒin] *n.* 发动机，引擎

【记】发音记忆

【例】turn off the *engine* 关掉引擎

enemy
n.敌人

118

engineer [ˌendʒiˈniə] *n.* 工程师；技师

【记】engine（引擎）+er→修理发动机的人→工程师

【例】computer *engineer* 电脑工程师 // motor *engineers* 汽车技师

enjoy [inˈdʒɔi] *v.* 欣赏，享受…之乐趣，喜欢

【记】en（使…进入状态）+joy（欢乐，喜悦）→享受…之乐趣

【考】1. **enjoy oneself** 玩得高兴 2. **enjoy sth.** 喜欢…：He didn't enjoy the meal. 他不喜欢这顿饭。3. **enjoy doing sth.** 喜欢做…：They enjoy watching television before going to bed. 他们喜欢睡觉前看会儿电视。

【衍】enjoyable（*adj.* 愉快的，有趣的）；enjoyment（*n.* 快乐，喜欢）

*****enlarge** [inˈlɑːdʒ] *v.* 扩大

【记】词根记忆：en（使…）+large（大的）→扩大

【例】The photographer *enlarged* my photograph. 摄影师放大了我的照片。

enough [iˈnʌf] *n./adj./adv.* 足够（的/地）；充足（的/地）

【用】1.enough作副词时，应置于它所修饰的形容词、副词或动词的后面：If I had a long enough holiday, I'd visit Europe. 如果我有一个足够长的假期，我就去欧洲玩。2. *adj.*+**enough**+**to do sth.** 足够…去做…：I was old enough to move out on my own. 我年纪已经够大的了，可以搬出去自己住。

【例】I think I have said *enough*. 我想我已经说得够多了。//There is *enough* time to go shopping. 有足够的时间去购物。

*****enquiry** [inˈkwaiəri] *n.* 询问

【记】来自enquire（*v.* 询问）

【例】Please direct your *enquiry* to the information desk. 请到咨询台询问。

enter [ˈentə] *v.* 进入

【例】Susan *entered* the advertising business after college. 苏珊大学毕业后从事广告行业。

【考】1. **enter a school** 入学 2. **enter a country** 进入一个国家 3. **enter into** 进入 4. **enter for** 报名参加(考试、比赛等)

【衍】entry*（*n.* 进入；入口）

*****enterprise** [ˈentəpraiz] *n.* 企业，事业

【例】Monica manages a publishing *enterprise*. 莫妮卡经营一家出版社。

119

*entertainment [ˌentə'teinmənt] n. 娱乐，娱乐表演

【例】Zoos use animals as a means of *entertainment*. 动物园将动物当作娱乐手段。

enthusiastic a. 热情的

E

entire [in'taiə] adj. 整个的，全部的

【记】联想记忆：en+tire（累的）→身心俱惫→全部的

【衍】entirely（adv. 完全地）

entrance ['entrəns] n. 入口；入场；入学许可

* entry n. 进入

【例】*entrance* at a party 晚会的入口 // *entrance* fees 入场费 // an *entrance* examination 入学考试

envelope ['enveləup] n. 信封

【例】I put a stamp on the *envelope* and mailed it. 我把邮票贴在信封上，然后把信寄了出去。

envelope

environment [in'vaiərənmənt] n. 环境

【例】living *environment* 生存环境//protect the *environment* 保护环境

envy ['envi] vt./n. 忌妒，羡慕

【例】His success made the others *envy* him. 他的成功让他人忌妒。

equal ['i:kwəl] adj. 平等的，相等的 vt. 等于，比得上

eraser n. 橡皮

【例】Men and women should enjoy *equal* rights. 男女应该享有平等权利。//Few pleasures can *equal* that of a cool drink on a hot day. 没有比在大热天喝一杯冷饮更让人高兴的了。

envy

【考】**equal to...** 等于…，与…平等

【衍】equally（adv. 同样地，相同地）；equality*（n. 平等，同等）

*equip [i'kwip] vt. (equipped, equipped, equipping)装备；训练

【考】**be equipped for** 准备好，为…训练好

【衍】equipment（n. 装备，设备）

error ['erə] n. 错误

【例】They try to find a solution by trial and *error*. 他们反复试验以寻求解决方案。

error

*erupt [i'rʌpt] v. (火山等) 喷发，爆发

【例】No people expected the volcano to *erupt* again. 没有人盼着这座火山再次喷发。

error

【衍】eruption（*n.* 喷发）

escape [iˈskeip] *v./n.* 逃跑，逃脱，避开

【例】Three prisoners *escaped*. 有三个囚犯逃跑了。//The two officers were extremely lucky to *escape* serious injury. 那两个官员没受重伤简直太幸运了。//He had a very narrow *escape*. 他死里逃生。

【辨】escape, avoid

escape和avoid都有逃避、避免的意思。avoid是指避开某种有害的或不愿接近的东西，如：I avoided him as much as possible. 我尽可能避开他。escape往往指在已经遇到危险的时候，平安地逃避过去，如：He escaped punishment by the death of the only witness. 惟一证人的死亡让他逃过了惩罚。

especially [iˈspeʃəli] *adv.* 特别，尤其

essay
n.散文

【记】来自especial（*adj.* 特别的）

【例】You should improve your English, *especially* your spoken English. 你应该提高你的英语水平，尤其是口语。

European [ˌjuərəˈpiən] *adj.* 欧洲的，欧洲人的 *n.* 欧洲人

Europe
n.欧洲

【例】*European* football 欧式足球//the *European* Union 欧盟//Do the *Europeans* shake hands wherever they go and with whomever they meet? 欧洲人是不是无论到哪、不管碰到什么人都和对方握手呢？

*****evaluate** [iˈvæljueit] *vt.* 评价，估计

【例】We *evaluated* the students' skills on the basis of test results. 我们根据测试的结果来评估学生的技术水平。

even [ˈiːvn] *adv.* 甚至，更加，还要 *adj.* 平坦的

【用】even作副词，用于修饰名词、动词、比较级和状语，表示强调：Even my cat liked him. 甚至连我的猫都喜欢他。//Even more people now watch the show. 现在看这个节目的人更多了。

【考】1. **even if/though** 即使 2. **even so** 即使这样

【衍】uneven（*adj.* 不平坦的）

event [iˈvent] *n.* 事件，大事；竞赛

【例】people, places and *events* of stories 故事的人物、地点和事件//sports *event* 体育比赛

【考】**event by event** 逐渐地

*****eventually** [iˈventʃuəli] *adv.* 最终地

【例】Our flight *eventually* left five hours late. 我们的班机最终晚了五小时起飞。

ever [ˈevə] *adv.* 曾经；无论何时

【例】I would never *ever* come to this restaurant again. The food is terrible! 我以后再也不会来这家饭店了，饭菜太难吃！

【衍】however (*adv.* 无论如何); whatever (*pron.* 无论怎样); whenever (*conj./adv.* 无论什么时候); whichever (*pron.* 无论哪一个); whoever (*pron.* 无论谁); whomever (*pron.* 无论谁)

every [ˈevri] *adj.* 每一，每个的；每…

【例】Take this pill *every* four hours. 每四小时吃一次药。

everyday [ˈevridei] *adj.* 日常的

【例】*everyday* problems 日常问题 // *everyday* interests 平时的兴趣爱好

【辨】**everyday, every day**
everyday是形容词，在句中作定语，意思为"日常的"，同义词为daily，如：everyday life 日常生活；而词组**every day**在句中作时间状语，意为"每天"，如：I go to school by bike every day. 我每天骑车上学。

everywhere [ˈevriwɛə] *adv.* 到处

【例】He follows her *everywhere*. 她到哪他都跟着。

evidence [ˈevidəns] *n.* 证据

【记】词根记忆：e+vid（看见）+ence（名词后缀）→眼见为实→证据

【例】This *evidence* does not prove the defendant's guilt. 这一证据不能证明被告有罪。

* **evident** [ˈevidənt] *adj.* 明显的，显然的

【记】词根记忆：e+vid（看见）+ent（…的）→能看得见的→明显的

【例】It is *evident* that you are not telling me the truth. 很明显，你没和我说实话。

* **evolution** [ˌiːvəˈluːʃn; ˌevəˈluːʃn] *n.* 进展，演变，进化

【例】Darwin's Theory of *Evolution* 达尔文的进化论

evolution

exact [igˈzækt] *adj.* 精确的，准确的，确切的

【例】There is no *exact* answer up to present. 到

目前为止还没有准确答案。//the *exact* age 确切的年龄

【衍】exactly（*adv.* 准确地，确切地）

exam [ig'zæm]（=examination）*n.* 考试，测试；检查

【例】prepare for an *exam* 准备考试//pass an *exam* 通过考试//have an *exam* 考试//cheat in an *exam* 考试作弊//physical *exam* 体育考试// final/last *exam* 期末考试

【衍】reexamination（*n.* 复试）

examine [ig'zæmin] *v.* 检查，诊察

【例】*examine* the audio system 检查音响系统//The doctor *examined* the pregnant woman. 医生给那名孕妇做了检查。

example [ig'zɑːmpl;ig'zæmpl] *n.* 例子，范例

【例】The teacher wrote an *example* on the blackboard. 老师在黑板上写了一个例子。

【考】1. **for example** 例如 2. **give an example** 举例 3. **take...for example** 以…为例

excellent ['eksələnt] *adj.* 极好的，优秀的

【例】*excellent* English 极好的英文//*excellent* students 优秀学生

【衍】excellently（*adv.* 优良地，极好地）

except [ik'sept] *prep.* 除…之外

【用】1. **except ...** 除了…：Nobody will know except you. 除了你没人会知道。2. **except for...** 除了：The room is empty except for a table. 房间里除了一张桌子外什么也没有。3. **except that...** 除了…，后面接从句：She remembered nothing except that his hair was black. 她什么都不记得了，只记得他的头发是黑的。

【衍】exception（*n.* 例外）

exchange [iks'tʃeindʒ] *n./v.* 交换，交流；兑换

【记】联想记忆：ex+change（变换）→双方相互交换→交换，交流

【例】*exchange* of gifts 交换礼物 // We *exchanged* our opinions about the project at the meeting. 在会上，我们就这个项目交换了意见。

exchange

【考】1. **exchange a few words** 说话 2. **in exchange** 作为交换

单元自测

1. I know nothing about the young lady _____ she is from Beijing. （2000上海）

    A. except   B. except for   C. except that   D. besides

2. —Let me examine you, boy.

    —I don't want _____.

    A. to examine   B. examined   C. being examined   D. to be examined

3. —Is _____ finished?

    —Not yet. My dirty clothes are still soaking in the washing machine.

    A. something   B. anything   C. nothing   D. everything

4. —The exam was very easy, wasn't it?

    —Yes, but I don't think _____ could pass it.

    A. somebody   B. anybody   C. everybody   D. nobody

5. _____ athletes from the world _____ the Olympic Games.

    A. Every four years; take part in   B. Each four years; take part in

    C. Every fourth year; join   D. Each four years; join in

6. —Are you feeling better?

    —I'm all right today. But I couldn't feel _____ yesterday.

    A. any better   B. even worse   C. still fine   D. very bad

7. It's always difficult being in a foreign country, _____ if you don't speak the language.

    A. extremely   B. naturally   C. basically   D. especially

8. Over 500 people were trapped above the fire, for the building was built without any _____.

    A. escape   B. safe   C. water   D. care

9. Five multiplied _____ six _____ thirty.

    A. by; equals   B. by; are   C. with; is   D. with; equals

10. If I had _____, I'd visit Europe, stopping at all the small interesting places.

    A. a long enough holiday   B. an enough long holiday

    C. a holiday enough long   D. a long holiday enough

11. The child is so full of _____ that he cannot keep still.

    A. force   B. energy   C. power   D. strength

12. My grandfather is as _____ as a young man and hates sitting around doing nothing all day. （2003上海）

    A. enthusiastic   B. energetic   C. talkative   D. sensitive

13. _____ the end of last month was he set free from the prison.

    A. At   B. By   C. Not until   D. Not until at

14. —Did he decide to take part in the competition?

    —Yes, of course. He _____ to.

    A. had encouraged   B. had been encouraged

    C. has been encouraged   D. was to be encouraged

15. Which do you enjoy _____ your weekends, fishing or watching TV?

    A. spending   B. to spend   C. being spent   D. spend

答案：CDDCA BDAAA BBCBB

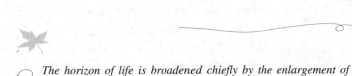

The horizon of life is broadened chiefly by the enlargement of the heart.　　　　　　　　　　　　　　　　　　　*—Black*

生活的地平线是随着心灵的开阔而变得宽广的。

——布莱克

Word List 17

excite [ik'sait] *vt.* 刺激；使兴奋，使激动

【例】The thought of a trip to the mountains *excited* him. 一想到要去山里玩，他就无比兴奋。

【衍】excited（*adj.* 兴奋的）；exciting（*adj.* 令人兴奋的）；excitement（*n.* 激动，兴奋）

excuse [iks'kju:z] *n.* 借口，理由 *vt.* 原谅，宽恕

【例】— I didn't know this was a one-way street, officer.
  —Sorry, but that's no *excuse*.
  —长官，我不知道这是单行道。
  —很遗憾，但这不是理由。

【考】**Excuse me.** 对不起。/借光。/打扰一下。

exercise ['eksəsaiz] *n.* [C] 练习；[U] 锻炼 *v.* 锻炼

【考】**do/take some exercise** 锻炼

【例】physical *exercise* 体育锻炼 // His back hurt so much that he could not *exercise* all week. 他的背伤得很厉害，整个星期都不能锻炼。

exhibition [ˌeksi'biʃən] *n.* 展览，展览会；展品

【例】visit an art *exhibition* 参观艺术展//glass *exhibitions* 玻璃展品

exist [ig'zist] *vi.* 存在，生存

【例】Only about 1,000 pandas *exist* in China today. 中国现存大熊猫仅有1,000多只。

【衍】co-exist（*vi.* 共存）；existent（*adj.* 存在的，生存的）；non-existent（*adj.* 不复存在的）；existence（*n.* 存在，生存）

expand [ik'spænd] *vt.* 扩张 *vi.* 发展

【例】*expand* markets 拓展市场 // Metals *expand* when they are heated. 金属遇热膨胀。

expect [ik'spekt] *v.* 预料；期望，要求

【用】1. **expect sb. to do sth.** 期望或要求某人做某事：While you live in this house, I expect you to follow my rules. 你在这儿住时，希望你遵守我的规则。2. **be expected to do**（be）... 预料···；按要求：The movie is expected to be very popular. 这部电影预计会非常火爆。

【衍】unexpected（*adj.* 意外的，想不到的）；expectedly（*adv.* 预料之中地）；unexpectedly（*adv.* 出乎意料）；expectation（*n.* 预料；期望）

*expense [iks'pens] *n.* 费用，支出

【例】fees and *expenses* 费用

expensive [iks'pensiv] *adj.* 昂贵的，高消费的

【例】*expensive* region 高消费区 // The house rent is *expensive*. 房租很贵。

【衍】inexpensive（*adj.* 便宜的）

experience [iks'piəriəns] *vt.* 经历，体验 *n.* 经验；经历

【例】They are willing to *experience* different cultures. 他们愿意感受不同的文化。

【衍】inexperience（*n.* 缺乏经验）；experienced（*adj.* 经验丰富的）

experiment [iks'perimənt] *n.* 实验

【例】The result of the *experiment* was very good. 实验的效果非常理想。

【考】**do experiments** 做实验

expert ['ekspə:t] *n.* 专家，能手

【例】computer *experts* 计算机专家

explain [iks'plein] *vt.* 解释，说明

【记】ex（出）+plain（明白的）→讲解→解释

【例】Please *explain* why you're so late. 请解释一下你为什么这么晚才来。

【衍】explanation（*n.* 解释，说明）

*explicit [iks'plisit] *adj.* 清楚的；直率的

【例】I gave Bill *explicit* instructions. 我给了比尔明确的指示。

explode [iks'pləud] *v.*（使）爆炸；爆发

【记】联想记忆：探险（explore）遭遇爆炸（explode）

【例】A bomb *exploded* in the street on Sunday. 星期日那天，一枚炸弹在街上爆炸。

*explore [iks'plɔ:] *v.* 探险；探索

【例】It allows us to *explore* the cities of the next century. 它可以让我们去下个世纪的城市探险。//I was out *exploring* and saw a new kind of flower. 我出外勘查，发现了新品种的花。

【衍】explorer (*n.* 探险者，探险家)

export [iks'pɔːt] *vt.* 输出 *vi.* 出口

['ekspɔːt] *n.* 出口（物）

【记】词根记忆：ex（出）+port（运）→运出去（的东西）→出口（物）

【例】This country *exports* automobiles to the United States. 该国向美国出口汽车。// Wool is one of the chief *export* of Australia. 羊毛是澳大利亚的主要出品物资之一。

*expose [iks'pəuz] *vt.* 暴露；揭露

【记】词根记忆：ex（出）+pos（放）+e→放出来→（使）暴露

【例】*expose* a plot 揭露阴谋 // Some chemicals cannot be *exposed* to the sun. 一些化学物质不能暴露在阳光下。

It's him!!
expose

【考】1. **expose sth.** 揭露… 2. **be exposed to** 被暴露在…

express [iks'pres] *vt.* 表达；表示 *n.* 快车

【记】联想记忆：ex（出）+press（挤，压）→挤出→表达

【例】I didn't know how to *express* myself properly. 我不知道怎样恰当地表达自己的意思。

expression [iks'preʃn] *n.* 表情；表达法，表达方式

【例】an *expression* of happiness/anger 高兴/生气的表情 // Knowing more words and *expressions*, you will find it easier to read and communicate. 认识更多的单词和短语后，你会发现阅读和交流变得更为简单。

【衍】expressionless (*adj.* 面无表情的)

*extension [iks'tenʃn] *n.* 伸展，延伸

【例】Tools are *extensions* of human hands. 工具是人类双手的延伸。

extra ['ekstrə] *adj.* 额外的，外加的

【例】I had to work *extra* hours to finish the report. 我得加班来完成这个报告。

extraordinary [iks'trɔːdnri; iks'trɔːdənəri] *adj.* 非常的；非凡的

【记】extra（额外的）+ordinary（平常的）→平常之外的→非常的

【例】 *extraordinary* situations 特殊情况 // *extraordinary* achievements 非凡的成就

extreme ［iks'triːm］*adj.* 极端的，偏激的

【例】 *extreme* opinions 极端的看法

【衍】 extremely（*adv.* 极端地，非常地）

eyesight ［'aisait］*n.* 视力，视觉

【记】 组合词：eye（眼睛）+sight（视力）→视力

【例】 Tom's *eyesight* is poor. 汤姆的视力很差。

facial ［'feiʃl］*adj.* 面部用的

【例】 a *facial* cream 面霜

fact ［fækt］*n.* 事实，现实

factory
n. 工厂

【考】 1. **in fact** 事实上，实际上 2. **as a matter of fact** 事实上，实际上：I'm going there tomorrow, as a matter of fact. 实际上我明天就要去那儿。

*fade ［feid］*v.* 褪色，使消退，枯萎

【例】 The color of this silk material will not *fade*. 这种绸布料子不会褪色。

fail ［feil］*v.* 失败，不及格，衰退

【用】 **fail to do sth.** 未能做成某事：They failed to finish the work on time. 他们没能按时完成工作。

【例】 I *failed* my French test. 我的法语考试没有及格。//His eyesight is *failing*. 他的视力正在衰退。

【衍】 failure（*n.* 失败）

fair ［fɛə］*adj.* 公平的，晴朗的，白皙的 *n.* 集市，展览会

【例】 It's not *fair*. 这不公平。// If the weather is *fair* tomorrow, we'll go shopping. 明天天气晴朗的话，我们就去购物。// a world *fair* 世界博览会

【衍】 unfair（*adj.* 不公平的）

fair

fairly ［'fɛəli］*adv.* 相当；还算；公正地

【记】 来自fair（*adj.* 公平的）

【例】 He is a *fairly* good boy. 他是个很好的孩子。//He speaks English *fairly* well. 他英语讲得相当好。

【辨】**fairly, quite, rather, pretty**

这四个单词都有"相当"的意思，用法也比较相似，但是：1. 从程度上说**fairly**是最轻的一个，**quite**比**fairly**语气稍强，**rather**在程度上比**quite**更重一些，**pretty** 和**rather** 差不多，但大多数情况下用于非正式文体，语气从弱到强的排序为fairly < quite < rather ≈ pretty，具体为：They were getting along fairly well with each other. 他们相处还不错。//He was quite polite, but he wasn't ready to help me. 他很有礼貌，但并不愿意帮助我。//There's something rather strange about the way he talks to you. 他跟你说话的样子真有点怪。//Twenty-five is pretty old to take up ballet dancing. 二十五岁才学跳芭蕾，年纪就太大了。2. **rather**和**quite**可放在不定冠词前，也可放在不定冠词之后,还可以和动词连用,而**fairly**和**pretty**没有这些用法。如：That is quite/rather a surprising result. = That is a quite/rather surprising result. 那个结果令人非常吃惊。//I rather/quite like to go for a walk after supper. 我非常喜欢在晚饭后出去散步。3. 只有**rather** 可以修饰比较级，还可和**too**连用。如：This computer is rather more expensive than that one. 这台电脑比那台更昂贵。//This book is rather too difficult for the beginners. 这部书对初学者来说太难了。

*faith [feiθ] *n.* 信仰，信念；信任

【考】1. **in faith** 确实，的确 2. **have faith in** 相信，信任 3. **lose faith in** 失去对…的信念；不再信任

【衍】faithful（*adj.* 忠实的）

fall [fɔːl] *v.* (fell, fallen, falling) 落（下），降落；跌倒 *n.* (英autumn) 秋季

【考】1. **fall apart** 倒塌 2. **fall behind** 落后 3. **fall in love with sb.** 爱上… 4. **fall off** 跌落，从…上掉下 5. **fall asleep** 入睡 6. **fall ill** 生病

false [fɔːls] *adj.* 假的，不正确的

【记】反义词：true（*adj.* 正确的，真的）

【例】*False* friends are more dangerous than open enemies. 假情假意的朋友比公开的敌人更危险。// *false teeth* 假牙

false teeth

familiar [fəˈmiliə] *adj.* 熟悉的

【考】1. **be familiar with** 对某事物熟悉，通晓 2. **be familiar to** 为…所熟悉：These stories are familiar to us. 我们都熟知这些故事。

【辨】familiar, similar

familiar, similar 在词形上相似，用法上接近，容易混淆。familiar 意为"熟悉的"，惯用搭配有 be familiar with, be familiar to; similar 意为"相似的"，惯用搭配为 be similar to，表示"与…相像"。

*fancy [ˈfænsi] *adj.* 奇特的；空想的 *n.* 空想，假想 *vt.* (fancied, fancied, fancying) 想像，空想

【例】a *fancy* dress ball 化妆舞会

fantasy [ˈfæntəsi] *n.* 幻想，白日梦

【记】发音记忆："范特西"→听着周杰伦的《范特西》，陷入无限的想像→想像，幻想

【例】The young man lives in a world of *fantasy*. 这个年轻人生活在幻想之中。

【衍】fantastic (*adj.* 极好的，美妙的；奇异的)

far [fɑː] *adj./adv.* (farther/further, farthest/furthest) 远的(地)

【考】1. **as/so far as I know** 就我所知 2. **as/so far as I am concerned** 就我而言，我认为 3. **so far** 迄今为止 4. **by far** 最，…得多 5. **far from** 远非，完全不

fare [feə] *n.* (乘车或船等的)费用，票(价)

【记】联想记忆：far (远)+e→路程比较远，需要乘车买票→费用，票

【例】a taxi *fare* 出租汽车费

*fasten [ˈfɑːsn; ˈfæsn] *v.* 扎牢，扣住

【记】词根记忆：fast (牢的，紧的)+en (使)→使紧，使牢固→扎牢

【例】Please *fasten* your seat belt well. 请系紧您的安全带。

fasten

fault [fɔːlt] *n.* 过错，缺点，毛病

【考】1. **at fault** 有责任，有错: My memory is at fault. 我记错了。2. **it is sb.'s fault** 是某人的失误 3. **find fault with...** 批评…，挑…的错

【衍】faulty (*adj.* 有过失的，有缺点的)

favour [ˈfeivə] (美favor) *n.* 恩惠，好感，帮助

【记】发音记忆："飞吻"→姑娘对那个小伙子很有好感，于是给了他一个飞吻

【考】1. **in favour of sb./sth.** 支持… 2. **in sb.'s favour** 对某人有利

3. **do sb. a favour** 帮某人的忙，答应某人的请求

【衍】favourable（*adj.* 赞成的；有利的）

favourite [ˈfeivərit]（美 favorite）*adj.* 特别喜爱的 *n.* 特别喜爱的人（或物）

【例】Oranges are my *favorite* fruit. 橘子是我最喜爱的水果。

fax [fæks] *n.* 传真

【例】send a *fax* 发送传真

fear [fiə] *n./v.* 害怕，恐惧，担忧

【记】联想记忆：f+ear（耳朵）→危言耸听→害怕，恐惧

【考】1. **for fear of sth./doing sth.** 惟恐…，忧虑… 2. **with fear** 吓得，怕得：He was shaking with fear. 他害怕得直发抖。

单元自测

1. He got to the station early, _____ missing his train. （2004江苏）

    A. in case of   B. instead of

    C. for fear of   D. in search of

2. Would you _____ to put on this blouse?

    A. do me a favour   B. do a favor for me

    C. do me the favor   D. do the favor to me

3. "I don't think it's my _____ that the TV blew up. I just turned it on, that's all." said the boy. （2003上海）

    A. error   B. mistake   C. fault   D. duty

4. You're standing too near the camera. Can you move _____?

    A. a bit far   B. a little farther   C. a bit of farther   D. a little far

5. As she _____ the newspaper, Granny _____ asleep.

    A. read; was falling   B. was reading; fell

    C. was reading; was falling   D. read; fell

6. His father looks young, but _____ fact he is _____.

    A. in; in the forties   B. in; in his forties

    C. in the; in the forties   D. in; in his forty

7. She intended _____ but the look on your face suggested "No".

    A. explain   B. to explain   C. explanation   D. to be explained

8. Want to type faster? Just come to our school to have more _____.

    A. chance   B. experience   C. success   D. practice

9. The computer is _____. That is to say, the price of the computer is _____.
   A. expensive; high   B. high; expensive
   C. high; high   D. expensive; expensive

10. You are _____ to finish the work before six.
   A. suggested   B. hoped   C. expected   D. agreed

11. Good food, not _____, that's how one gets fat.
   A. enough exercises   B. exercises enough
   C. enough exercise   D. exercise enough

12. —I'm sorry I stepped outside for a smoke. I was very tired.
   —There is no _____ for this while you are on duty.   （2003北京）
   A. reason   B. excuse
   C. cause   D. explanation

13. It was a _____ difficult exam and many students failed in it.
   A. fairly   B. too   C. rather   D. enough

14. _____ to sunlight for too much time will do harm to one's skin.   （2002上海卷）
   A. Exposed   B. Having exposed
   C. Being exposed   D. After being exposed

15. There was an _____ look on his face when the actress appeared.
   A. excited   B. excite   C. exciting   D. excitedly

答案：CACBB BBDAC CBCCA

Man cannot discover new oceans unless he has courage to lose sight of the shore.   *—Gide*
人只有鼓起勇气，告别海岸，才能发现新的海洋。
————吉德

Word List 18

*feast [fiːst] *n.* 盛宴；节日；令人愉悦的事情
【例】to give a *feast* 举行宴会//a *feast* for the eyes 赏心悦目的事

*federal ['fedərəl] *adj.* 中央的（政府等），联邦的
【例】Switzerland is a *federal* republic. 瑞士是联邦制共和国。

fee [fiː] *n.* 费，费用
【记】发音记忆："费"
【例】a school tuition / *fee* 学费

feed [fiːd] *v.* (fed, fed, feeding) 喂（养），饲（养），吃（饲料）
【记】播种就是给土地喂（feed）种子（seed）
【考】1. feed on 以…为食 2. be fed up (with...)（对…）厌倦，受够了

feed

feel [fiːl] *vt.* (felt, felt, feeling) 感觉；触摸；认为 *vi.* 摸索，寻找 *link. v.* 觉得；摸起来
【用】1. feel用作动词，表示人的感觉或感情时，可用进行时态：I feel lonely. 我觉得孤独。//I am feeling better now. 我现在感觉好多了。注意：feel表示某物给人的感觉时不能用进行时态：This cloth feels smooth. 这块布摸起来很光滑。2. feel用作及物动词，后可接名词、代词、复合宾语或从句：We can't see air but we can feel it. 我们看不到空气，但能感觉到它。//I felt that he liked me very much. 我觉得他很喜欢我。
【考】1. feel like doing sth. 想做… 2. feel as if/though 仿佛…：Her chest felt as if it was about to burst. 她的胸膛仿佛快要爆炸了。
【衍】feeling (*n.* 感情；感觉)

fellow ['feləu] *n.* 同伴，伙伴

134

【例】We were school *fellows*. 我们曾经是同学。

female [ˈfiːmeil] *adj.* 女性的，雌性的 *n.* 女性，女人

【例】*female* animals 雌性动物

fence [fens] *n.* 栅栏，篱笆

【例】A *fence* is built for the safety of the area. 修建栅栏是为了确保该地区的安全。

ferry [ˈferi] *n.* 渡船

【例】A *ferry* crosses the river every hour. 每小时有一条渡船过河。

festival [ˈfestəvl] *n.* 节日

【例】the Spring *Festival* 春节

fetch [fetʃ] *v.* 去取来，去请来

【记】和 catch (*v.* 抓) 一起记

fever
n. 发烧

【例】The dog *fetched* the stick back. 小狗衔回了那根木棒。// to *fetch* a doctor 去请医生

few [fjuː] *adj.* 不多的，少数的 *pron.* 不多，少数

【考】1. **a few** 少数几个，一些 2. **only a few** 只有几个；没有多少 3. **quite a few** 相当多 4. **not a few** 相当多

*fiction
n. 虚构；编造

【辨】**few, little, a few, a little**
这几个词都有"少数"的意思。**few** 和 **little** 有否定含义，所在句被看作否定句：He has few friends. 他几乎没有朋友。而 **a few** 和 **a little** 是肯定含义：He has a few friends. 他只有几个朋友。**few** 和 **a few** 用于修饰可数名词，**little** 和 **a little** 用于修饰不可数名词。

*fibre [ˈfaibə] (美 fiber) *n.* 纤维

【例】a cotton *fibre* 棉花纤维

fierce [fiəs] *adj.* 猛烈的，激烈的

*field
n.

【例】a *fierce* wind 劲风 // a *fierce* competition 一场激烈的竞争
【衍】fierceness (*n.* 强烈)

fight [fait] *n./v.* (fought, fought, fighting) 打仗(架)，争论

【考】1. **fight against** 与…战斗，对抗…
2. **fight with** 和…作战 3. **fight for** 为…而战

fight

*figure [ˈfigə] *n.* 数字；人物 *v.* (美口语) 认为；(在心里) 描绘

【记】发音记忆："菲戈"→菲戈是绿茵场上的著名人物（figure）

【考】**figure out** 计算出，弄明白：I cannot figure out why he quitted his job. 我弄不明白他为什么辞职。

file [fail] *n.* 文件，档案

【例】We will keep your resume on *file*. 我们将把你的简历存入档案。

fill [fil] *v.* 填空，装满，充满

【考】1. **fill in sth.** 填充，填写 2. **fill up sth. with sth.** 用…将…填满 3. **be filled with...** 充满了…

final ['fainl] *adj.* 最后的 *n.* 决赛；期末考试

【例】the *final* round 决赛

***finance** ['fainæns] *n.* 财政，金融

【例】People who work in banks know about *finance*. 在银行工作的人懂金融。

find [faind] *vt.* (found, found, finding) 找到，发现；感到 *n.* 发现

【用】find可以接复合宾语，即find+宾语+宾补，注意：宾语和宾补之间为被动关系时，宾补用过去分词：I find my mobile phone stolen. 我发现手机被偷了。接宾语+宾补的动词：ask, advise, call, consider（认为），choose, elect, find, force, feel（认为，觉得），hear, help, like, let, make, order, persuade, see, tell, watch等。

【考】**find out** 找出，认识到，获知：Could you find out what time the train leaves? 你能找出火车什么时间发车吗？

【辨】**find, look for**

find, look for 都有"找"的意思。但**find**意为"找到"，侧重于结果：I didn't find my shoes. 我没找到我的鞋。**look for**意为"找寻"，侧重于过程：I'm looking for my shoes, but I haven't found it yet. 我在找我的鞋，但还没找到。

***fingernail** ['fiŋgəneil] *n.* (手)指甲

【记】组合词：finger（指头）+nail（指甲）→ 手指甲

【例】My *fingernails* need cutting. 我的指甲该剪了。

finger
n. 手指

finish ['finiʃ] *v.* 结束，做完

【用】**finish doing...** 做完某事：I finished cleaning the room. 我打扫完房间了。

fire [ˈfaiə] *n.* 火，火灾 *vt.* 点火；射击；解雇
【考】1. **catch fire** 着火 2. **make a fire** 生火 3. **set fire to** 放火 4.（**be**）**on fire** 着火，起火 5. **fire at sb./sth.** 朝…射击

***firework** [ˈfaiəwə:k] *n.*（*pl.*）烟花，焰火
【例】set off a few *fireworks* 燃放焰火

firm [fə:m] *n.* 公司，企业 *adj./adv.* 坚固的(地)，坚定的(地)
【例】Tom works in a big *firm*. 汤姆在一家大公司工作。// a *firm* belief 坚定的信念

fit [fit] *v.*（fit/fitted, fit/fitted, fitting）(使)适合 *adj.* 适合的，健康的
【考】1. **be fit for** 适合于 2. **keep fit** 保持健康

> 【辨】**fit, suit, match**
> **fit** 表"适合"之意时，多用来指"大小、形状等适合"及"服装合身"，而不表示服装的款式、颜色是否合适，如：The pair of shoes doesn't fit me. 这双鞋我穿不合脚。而 **suit** 侧重于"符合需要、口味、条件等"，尤其用来指"衣着的式样、颜色或发式与人相配"：This coat suits you well. 这件衣服的式样很合适你。**match** 指"相配，配得上"时，多指人或物在"品质、颜色"等方面相当或相配，如：It's difficult to match the color of the old paint. 很难找到与旧画颜色相配的色彩。

fix [fiks] *v.* 修理，安装；确定，决定
【考】1. **fix up** 修理；使固定 2. **fix one's eyes on...** 注视… 3. **fix one's**（**thoughts, attention**）**on...** 专注于…

flag [flæg] *n.* 旗；标志
【例】the national *flag* 国旗

flame

flame [fleim] *n.* 火焰，光辉
【例】The sticks burst into *flames*. 木柴烧起来了。

flash [flæʃ] *n.* 闪，闪光，转瞬间 *v.*(使)闪光，(使)闪现
【记】联想记忆：fl+ash（灰）→一下子变成了灰→转瞬间
【考】1. **in a flash** 很快地，立即：I'll be back in a flash. 我马上就回来。2. **flash back** 回忆，回溯
【衍】flashlight（*n.* 手电）

flat [flæt] *adj.* 平的 *n.* 一套房间；公寓
【例】The earth is round, not *flat*. 地球是圆的，不是平的。

*flee [fliː] v. (fled, fled, fleeing) 逃走, 逃跑

【考】**flee from** 从⋯逃走: The customers fled from the bank when the alarm sounded. 警铃响起时, 顾客们纷纷从银行跑了出来。

flee

flesh [fleʃ] n. 肉, 肉体

【例】*flesh* and blood 血肉, 亲人

*flexible [ˈfleksəbl] adj. 柔软的, 灵活的

【记】词根记忆: flex (弯曲)+ible (⋯的)→弯曲的→柔软的

【例】a *flexible* schedule 灵活的时间表

flight [flait] n. 飞行, 航班; 楼梯的一段

【记】f+light (轻的)→身体轻飘飘的, 飞了起来→飞行

【例】*Flight* Number 152 to Beijing is ready to leave. 飞往北京的152次航班即将起飞。// a *flight* of stairs 一段楼梯

*float [fləut] v. 漂浮, 浮动

【记】联想记忆: 船 (boat) 在水里漂浮 (float)

【例】The boat *floated* down the river. 小船顺流而下。

flood [flʌd] n. 洪水 v. 淹没, 使泛滥

【记】血 (blood) 流成河 (flood)

【考】1. **flood in/into** 大量涌入: Letters flooded into the office. 信件潮水般涌入办公室。2. **a flood/floods of** 大量的

flour [ˈflauə] n. 面粉, 粉

【例】Bread is made from *flour*. 面包是用面粉做的。

flow [fləu] v. 流动 n. 流, 流动

【记】联想记忆: f+low (低的)→水往低处流→流动

【例】Rivers *flow* into the sea. 河水流入大海。

flu [fluː] n. 流行性感冒

【例】bird *flu* 禽流感

*fluency [ˈfluːənsi] n. 流利, 流畅

【例】*fluency* of speech 口齿流利

focus [ˈfəukəs] v. 聚焦, 集中 n. 中心, 焦点

【考】**focus on...** 集中于⋯, 专注于⋯: The passage focuses on examination and equity. 这篇文章的主题是考试与公平。

fog [fɔg; fɔːg] n. 雾

【考】**in a fog** 困惑，迷惘：I'm in a complete fog about computer. 我对计算机一窍不通。

【衍】foggy（*adj.* 多雾的）

fold ［fəuld］*v.* 折叠，合拢

【记】和old（*adj.* 旧的，老的），hold（*v.* 拿，握）一起记

【考】**fold up** 折叠起来

【衍】unfold（*vt.* 打开，伸展）

folk ［fəuk］*adj.* 民间的

【例】*folk* music 民间音乐

follow ［ˈfɔləu］*v.* 跟随；遵循；仿效

【考】1. **as follows** 如下 2. **follow one's advice** 听从某人的劝告

【衍】following（*adj.* 以下的，接下来的）

follow

fond ［fɔnd］*adj.* 喜爱的，爱好的

【考】**be fond of...** 喜爱…：Tom is extremely fond of pointing out others' mistakes. 汤姆特别喜欢挑别人的毛病。

单元自测

1. The boy stood there with his eyes _____ on the picture.

   A. fixed   B. fixing   C. kept   D. keeping

2. My brother is very tall. The little bed won't _____ for him.

   A. prepare   B. care   C. fit   D. do

3. Our teacher wanted to _____ who broke the window.

   A. find   B. find out   C. look for   D. look

4. It is necessary that Mary _____ all the blanks on the application for admission to the university.

   A. fill in   B. fills in   C. will fill in D. must fill in

5. —Are the new rules working?

   —Yes. _____ books are stolen.

   A. Few   B. More   C. Some   D. None

6. —Do you like the material?

   —Yes, it _____ very soft.

   A. is feeling   B. felt   C. feels   D. is felt

7. He made a suggestion _____ she _____ the baby more frequently so that it will grow bigger.

A. when; fed   B. which; feeds   C. what; fed   D. that; feed

8. —Why is Jack always playing?

    —He has no _____ of time.

    A. sense   B. idea   C. effect   D. feeling

9. If（it is）convenient, please go to the post office and _____ me the parcel.

    A. bring   B. take   C. carry   D. fetch

10. Beijing plans to build more Olympic Games sites in university _____ resources after the Games _____.

    A. avoid wasting; will have finished   B. to avoid wasting; have finished

    C. avoid wasting; have finished   D. to avoid wasting; will have finished

11. It's not right for the dustmen to _____ the fallen leaves, for when the leaves are burning, they _____ poisonous gases.

    A. set fire to; give off   B. set fire on; give off

    C. set tire on; give out   D. set fire to; give out

12. When filled with a gas lighter than air, a balloon can _____ in the air.

    A. stop   B. float   C. wander   D. sail

13. I send you 100 dollars today, the rest _____ in a year. （2005湖南卷）

    A. follows   B. followed

    C. to follow   D. being followed

14. Tom's parents are too poor to pay his school _____.

    A. fee   B. fare   C. cost   D. tips

15. The British love to think of themselves as polite, and everyone knows how _____ they are of their "pleases" and "thank yous".

    A. keen   B. interested   C. fond   D. anxious

答案：ADBAA CDADB DBCAC

Not ignorance, but the ignorance of ignorance, is the death of knowledge. —Whitehead

不是无知本身，而是对无知的无知，才是知识的死亡。

——怀特海德

Word List 19

for [fɔː] *prep.* 为了；在⋯期间；对于 *conj.* 因为，由于

【例】I cooked dinner *for* Mary. 我给玛丽做了一顿饭。//I could not stay *for* the whole concert. 我不能整场音乐会都在场。

【考】1. **pay for** 为⋯付款 2. **be for** 支持，赞成 3. **look for** 寻找 4. **care for** 关心，喜欢，照顾 5. **stand for** 代表

*forbid [fə'bid] *v.* (forbade, forbidden, forbidding) 禁止，不许

【用】1. **forbid sb. to do sth.** 禁止某人做某事：I forbid you to go. 我不许你去。2. **forbid doing sth.** 禁止做某事：Smoking is forbidden in the concert hall. 演奏厅内禁止吸烟。

> 【辨】**forbid, ban**
>
> **forbid** 与 **ban** 都有"禁止"的意思。**forbid** 为常用词，多指"命令、要求某人不做某事"；**ban** 语气比较重，多指权威机关"正式禁止"，含有"严厉谴责"之意，只能用事物作其宾语。

force [fɔːs] *vt.* 强迫，迫使 *n.* 力量，武力

【用】**force sb. to do...**（=force sb. into doing sth.）强迫某人做某事

【考】1. **come into force** 生效,实行 2. **put in/into force** 施行,实施 3. **by force** 用暴力,强迫地

forecast ['fɔːkɑːst; 'fɔːkæst] *n.* 预知 *vt.* (forecast / forecasted, forecast / forecasted, forecasting) 预告,预测

【记】组合词：fore（前面的）+cast（抛；一瞥）→向前看→先见

【例】the weather *forecast* 天气预报 // Hurricane has been *forecast* for tomorrow afternoon. 天气预报说明天下午有飓风。

forecast

forehead [ˈfɔrid; ˈfɔːhed] *n.* 前额
【记】组合词：fore（前面的）+head（头）→前额
【例】There is a pain in my *forehead*. 我额头疼。

foreign [ˈfɔrən; ˈfɔːrən] *adj.* 外国的   *foreigner*
【例】a *foreign* language 一门外语

*foresee [fɔːˈsiː] *vt.* (foresaw, foreseen, foreseeing) 预见，预知
【记】组合词：fore（前面的）+see（看）→提前看到→预见
【例】The difficulties couldn't have been *foreseen*. 这些困难无法预见。

F *forest* n. 森林

forever [fəˈrevə] *adv.* 永远，永恒地
【例】No one can live *forever*. 没有人能够永生。

forget [fəˈget] *v.* (forgot, forgotten, forgetting) 忘记，忘掉
【用】1. **forget doing sth.** 忘记曾做过…：I'll never forget meeting my school headmaster for the first time. 我永远无法忘记和小学校长初次见面时的情景。2. **forget to do** 忘记去做…：She forgot to post the letter. 她忘记寄信了。注意：后接doing和to do时含义不同的动词还有：regret, remember, stop, try等，doing表示动作已发生，to do表示动作还未发生。stop doing sth. 停下来正在做的事，stop to do 停下来去做另外一件事；try to do sth. 努力做某事；try doing sth. 试着做某事。
【衍】forgetful* (*adj.* 健忘的，不留心的)

forgive [fəˈgiv] *vt.* (forgave, forgiven, forgiving) 原谅，宽恕
【考】1. **forgive sb. for sth.** 为某事原谅某人 2. **forgive sb. for doing sth.** 原谅某人做了某事：Tom cannot forgive himself for not seeing her mother before she died. 汤姆永远不能原谅自己，因为他未能在母亲去世前见她一面。

fork [fɔːk] *n.* 叉，餐叉
【记】for+k（发音：客）→给客人用的餐具→餐叉
【例】a *fork* and knife 一副刀叉

form [fɔːm] *n.* 表格；形式；结构 *v.* 形成，组建
【例】fill out the *form* 填好这个表格 // *form* good habits 形成良好习惯
【考】**in the form of** 以…的形式

*format [ˈfɔːmæt] *n.* 版式，格式
【记】联想记忆：form（形式）+at→形式→版式
【例】It's the same book, but a new *format*. 这是同一本书，不过是新版式。

*former ['fɔ:mə] *adj.* 以前的，从前的；（两者之中的）前者

【考】**the former...the latter...** 前者…后者…

*fortnight ['fɔ:tnait] *n.* 两星期

【例】In a *fortnight's* time I will be home. 两星期后我会回家的。

fortunate ['fɔ:tʃənit] *adj.* 幸运的，侥幸的

【记】来自fortune（*n.* 运气）

【例】He is *fortunate* enough to find a good job. 他找到了份好工作，真是太幸运了。

*fortune ['fɔ:tʃə:n] *n.* 财产；运气

【考】1. **make a fortune** 赚大钱，发财 2. **seek/try one's fortune** 碰运气

【衍】misfortune（*n.* 不幸）

forward(s) ['fɔ:wəd(z)] *adj.* 早的；前进的 *adv.* 向前，前进

【例】They moved the meeting *forward* from the 20th to the 18th. 他们把会议日期从20号提前到18号。

【考】1. **look forward to**（**+n. / doing**）盼望，期待：We are all looking forward to our holiday. 我们都盼着假期（的到来）。2. **put forward** 提出

*foster
v.

found [faund] *vt.* 成立，建立

【例】You should *found* your claim on facts. 你的主张应该以事实为基础。

fox
n. 狐狸

*fountain ['fauntin; 'fauntn] *n.* 喷泉；源泉

【例】The library is a *fountain* of information. 图书馆是信息的源泉。

*fragile ['frædʒail; 'frædʒl] *adj.* 易碎的，脆的

【例】The thin glass is *fragile*. 薄玻璃容易碎。

*fragrant ['freigrənt] *adj.* 香的，芬芳的

【例】The air in the garden was *fragrant*. 花香满园。

*framework ['freimwə:k] *n.* 框架，结构

【记】组合词：frame（框架，结构）+work（机件）→框架，结构

【例】This bridge over the river has a steel *framework*. 这座跨江大桥是钢骨构架。

franc [fræŋk] *n.* 法郎

【记】法国（France）的法郎（franc）

free [fri:] *adj.* 自由的，空闲的；免费的

【考】1. **for free** 免费 2. **free of charge** 免费 3. **set...free** 释放… 4. **be**

free from/of 免受…

【衍】freedom（*n.* 自由）

freeway [ˈfriːwei] *n.* 高速公路

【记】组合词：free（自由）+way（道路）→车辆通行无阻→高速公路

【例】A *freeway* runs through the village. 一条高速公路穿过那个村庄。

freeway

freeze [friːz] *v.* (froze, frozen, freezing)（使）结冰

【记】联想记忆：free（自由）+ze→让水失去自由→结冰

【例】We will *freeze* those fruit in the refrigerator. 我们将把那些水果冻在冰箱里。

【衍】freezing*（*adj.* 极冷的）；frozen（*adj.* 冻结的；冷酷的）

frequent [ˈfriːkwənt] *adj.* 经常的，频繁的

【例】Rains are *frequent* here in early summer. 初夏时节这里经常下雨。

fresh [freʃ] *adj.* 新鲜的；不熟练的

【例】*fresh* fruits 新鲜的水果// She's quite *fresh* to office work. 她没有办公室工作的经验。

*friction [ˈfrikʃən] *n.* 摩擦，摩擦力

【记】联想记忆：润滑油的功能（function）是减小摩擦力（friction）

【例】There is some *friction* among the family members. 家庭成员间有些摩擦。

fridge [fridʒ]（=refrigerator）*n.* 冰箱

【例】a solar energy *fridge* 太阳能冰箱

friendly [ˈfrendli] *adj.* 友好的

【考】**be friendly to** 对…友好：He's not quite friendly to us. 他对我们不是特别友好。

【衍】friendship（*n.* 友谊，友情）

frighten [ˈfraitən] *vt.* 使惊恐，吓唬

【记】联想记忆：fright（看作 fight 打架）+en→看打架，很害怕→使惊恐

【考】**frighten... off/away** 吓跑，吓走…

【衍】frightened（*adj.* 受惊的，受恐吓的）

frighten

frog
n. 青蛙

from [frɔm] *prep.* 从；从…起；距；来自

【考】1. be/come from... 来自 2. from time to time 不时
3. from now on 从现在起 4. from...to/till... 从…到…

*frontier [ˈfrʌntiə;frʌnˈtiər] n. 国境，边界；前线

【例】a *frontier* town 边疆城市

frost [frɔst;frɔːst] n. 霜

【例】The grass was covered with *frost*. 草被霜覆盖。

fruit [fruːt] n. 水果；结果

【例】His failure is the *fruit* of laziness. 他的懒惰导致了他的失败。

fry [frai] v. 油炸，油煎

【例】She *fried* the eggs in a pan. 她在平底锅里煎鸡蛋。

fuel [ˈfjuːəl] n. 燃料

【例】Gas and coal are *fuels*. 煤气和煤都是燃料。

full [ful] adj. 满的，充满的，完全的 adv. 完整地，十分地

【考】1. be full of... 充满…：The bus timetables are full of mistakes. 公车时间表到处是错误。2. at full speed 全速地

【衍】fully（adv. 充分地，完全地）

fun [fʌn] n. 乐趣，娱乐

【考】1. make fun of... 取笑…，和…开玩笑 2. for fun 为了消遣

【衍】funny（adj. 有趣的，好笑的）

function [ˈfʌŋkʃən] n. 功能，作用，职责 vi. 起作用；行使职责

【例】The *function* of a chairman is to lead and control meetings. 主席的职责是领导全体并主持会议。

*fundamental [ˌfʌndəˈmentəl] adj. 基础的，基本的

【例】a *fundamental* law 根本法则，基本定律

*funeral [ˈfjuːnərəl] n. 葬礼

【例】attend a *funeral* 参加丧礼

✱furnished [ˈfəːniʃt] adj. 配备了家具的

【记】来自furnish（v. 装配，配备）

【例】She rents a *furnished* flat. 她租了一套备有家具的公寓。

furniture [ˈfəːnitʃə] n.（总称）家具

【例】a piece of *furniture* 一件家具

单元自测

1. It's _____ to swim in summer.
   A. a fun   B. a great funny   C. fun   D. very fun

2. _____ story it is!
   A. What a funny   B. What funny   C. How a funny   D. How funny

3. Their cheerful voice showed that they were having a _____ discussion.
   A. noisy   B. serious   C. complete   D. friendly

4. Get the car thoroughly checked; I want to be _____ worry on the trip.
   A. clear of   B. free of   C. clear from   D. free from

5. He was looking forward _____ what the matter was.
   A. to see   B. to seeing   C. to be seeing D. to have seen

6. They have _____ the habit of _____ that shop which deals _____ silk.
   A. developed; doing in; with   B. got into; doing with; in
   C. had; dealing in; with   D. formed; dealing with; in

7. —I'd like to take a week's holiday.
   — _____, we're too busy.   （2004全国卷3）
   A. Don't worry   B. Don't mention it
   C. Forget it   D. Pardon me

8. —What's the weather forecast _____ tomorrow?
   —Sorry, I don't know.
   A. for   B. to   C. with   D. of

9. The murderer refused to come out, so the police had no choice but _____.
   A. forced open the door   B. to force the door open
   C. force the door open   D. breaking into the house

10. —At lunch time, I'd like to have a chat（闲谈）with you.
    — _____ Have what with me?
    A. I apologize.   B. Pardon?
    C. I see.   D. Forgive me.

11. Many graduates in China do their best to go abroad to seek their _____.
    A. luck   B. chance   C. fortune   D. fate

12. —Do you remember the traffic accident?
    —Yes, actually, I have experienced nothing _____.
    A. more frightened   B. more frightening
    C. very frightening   D. the most frightening

13. —Could you tell me _____ whom you have bought the present?

—Oh, yes. It is Dr. White, _____ whom we had learned a lot.

    A. to; from   B. for; from   C. by; with   D. with; out of

14. —Help yourself to some fish.

    — _____. I'm full.

    A. Of course   B. That's all right   C. Not at all   D. No, thank you

15. —Sorry. I _____ to post the letter for you.

    —Not at all. I _____ post it myself.

    A. forgot; will   B. forget; will

    C. forgot; am going to   D. will forget; am to

答案：CADDB DCABB CBBDA

Our destiny offers not the cup of despair, but the chalice of opportunity.   —*Nixon*

命运给予我们的不是失望之酒，而是机会之杯。

——尼克松

Word List 20

future [ˈfjuːtʃə] *n.* 将来

【衍】futureless（*adj.* 无前途的，无希望的）

【辨】**in future, in the future**

in future 强调 "今后"，相当于 from now on：You should be more honest in job application in future. 你今后找工作时，可得诚实一些。而 **in the future** 强调 "将来"，相当于 in time yet to come：Will humans live on the moon in the future? 人类将来会在月球上居住吗？

gain [gein] *v.* 获得，挣得 *n.* 收获

【记】联想记忆：及时雨（rain）带给农家好收成（gain）

【例】*gain* some experience 获得经验//No pains, no *gains*. 不劳无获。

*gallery [ˈgæləri] *n.* 画廊，美术品陈列室

【例】The man has been running the *gallery* for 15 years. 这个人经营这家画廊已经15年了。

*gallon [ˈgælən] *n.* 加仑（液体容量单位）

【记】发音记忆

【例】This barrel can hold 50 *gallons* of water. 这个桶可以装50加仑的水。

garage [ˈgærɑːʒ; gəˈrɑːʒ] *n.* 汽车间（库）

【例】There are three cars in the *garage*. 车库里有3辆车。

garbage [ˈgɑːbidʒ] *n.* 垃圾

【例】*garbage* truck 垃圾车

garlic [ˈgɑːlik] *n.* 大蒜

*garment [ˈgɑːmənt] *n.* 衣服，外衣

【例】Wash dark-colored *garments* separately. 把深色衣服分开洗。

*gather [ˈɡæðə] v. 聚集，采集

【考】1. **gather together** 聚在一起 2. **gather around...** 聚集在…周围：Everyone gathered around the table. 大家都围在桌子旁。

【衍】gathering (n. 收集，聚集)

*gay [ɡei] adj. 快活的，愉快的 n. (男) 同性恋

【例】The children were all gay at the thought of the coming holidays. 孩子们一想到即将来临的假日，都很高兴。

general [ˈdʒenrəl] adj. 大体的，总的；一般的

【例】general idea 大意 // general manager 总经理

【考】**in general 一般而言，大体上**

【衍】generally (adv. 一般地，通常)

G

generation [ˌdʒenəˈreiʃn] n. 代，一代

【记】词根记忆：gener (出生，产生) +ation→代，一代

【例】generation gap 代沟

generous [ˈdʒenərəs] adj. 慷慨的，大方的

【例】He is a generous man. 他为人大方。

【衍】generously (adv. 慷慨地)

gentle [ˈdʒentl] adj. 温柔的，轻轻的

【例】gentle comedy 轻喜剧

【衍】gentleman (n. 先生；绅士)；gentlemanly (adj. 绅士派头的)

geography [dʒiˈɔɡrəfi] n. 地理学

【例】a geography textbook 地理课本

*geometry [dʒiˈɔmətri] n. 几何学

【例】I don't like geometry in school. 我不喜欢上几何课。

gesture [ˈdʒestʃə] n. 姿势；手势

【例】Do you know the meaning of the gesture? 你知道这个手势代表什么意思吗？

get [ɡet] vt. (got, got, getting) 得到，到达 link.v. 变得

【用】1. **get+adj.** 变得…：Is your headache getting better? 你头疼好点儿了吗？2. get可以接复合宾语，宾补常是不定式、介词短语、过去分词或形容词：I will get my brother to help you. 我叫我弟弟来帮你。//You can't get eight people into that car. 你没法让八个人坐进那辆车里去。

【例】It's getting dark outside. 天黑了。

【考】1. **get along/on（well）with...** 与…相处得（好）2. **get down to** 开始认真做… 3. **get rid of** 摆脱，除去 4. **get through** 通过，打通（电话）5. **get out of** 从…出来 6. **get away** 逃脱，离开 7. **get across** 通过；理解 8. **get over** 克服；恢复 9. **get ready to do...** 准备好做… 10. **get in/into** 进入，到达 11. **get out** 出去 12. **get up** 起床 13. **get off** 下来；出发 14. **get around** 四处走动；传播开来 15. **get used to do...** 习惯做…

gifted ['giftid] *adj.* 有天赋的，有才华的

【记】来自gift（*n.* 天赋，才华）

【例】Newton was a *gifted* scientist. 牛顿是一名有天赋的科学家。

giraffe [dʒi'rɑːf] *n.* 长颈鹿

give [giv] *v.* （gave, given, giving）给，付出

【用】1. give多接双宾语，即**give sb. sth.**（=**give sth. to sb.**）把某物给某人：He gave me some advice. 他给了我一些建议。2. **given...** 考虑到，鉴于，假使：Given time, he'll make a first-class tennis player. 假以时日，他会成为一个一流的网球运动员。//Given the rain, we'll stay home. 如果下雨，我们就呆在家里。

【例】Collecting coins *gives* him great pleasure. 收集硬币给他带来了很多乐趣。

【考】1. **give up** 放弃 2. **give in** 屈服，让步 3. **give off** 放出，发出（光、热等）4. **give out** 分发；发出（气味等）；用尽

glad [glæd] *adj.* 高兴的，乐意的

【考】**be glad to do...** 乐意或高兴做某事：I am so glad to get your call. 接到你的电话我非常高兴。

【衍】gladly（*adv.* 高兴地；乐意地）

glance [glɑːns;glæns] *v./n.* 扫视，匆匆一看

【记】大街上瞥（glance）美女，脚下失衡（balance）

【考】1. **glance at...** 瞥眼看…，扫视… 2. **glance through / over...** 浏览…

【例】I liked the girl at first *glance*. 第一眼看见这个女孩我就喜欢上了她。

glare [glɛə] *v.* 瞪眼，怒目而视；闪耀 *n.* 强光

【例】Light from headlights of the car was *glaring* in the darkness. 汽车前灯的灯光在黑暗中闪耀着。

150

【考】**glare at...** 瞪…：The teacher glared at the student who was late. 老师生气的盯着那名迟到的学生。

*globe [gləub] *n.* 地球仪；地球

【记】发音记忆："哥伦布"→由此不难联想到地球吧→地球

【例】She turned the *globe* to point out New York. 她转动地球仪指出纽约的位置。

【衍】global（*adj.* 全球的）

globe

G

glory ['glɔːri] *n.* 光荣，荣誉

【例】a crown of *glory* 华丽的皇冠

go [gəu] *v.* (went, gone, going) 去，走；进行，进展 *link. v.* 变得，变成

【例】On Monday, I *go* shopping. 星期一我去购物。//Some diseases can make you *go* blind. 某些病会导致失明。

【考】1. **go over** 复习；查看，查阅 2. **go through** 通过；经历；全面检查 3. **go along with** 陪伴；赞同 4. **go about** 着手做某事；四处走动 5. **go on (doing)...** 继续做… 6. **go off** 离开；爆炸 7. **go into** 进入；从事某一行业 8. **go in for** 喜欢 9. **go after** 追逐，追求 10. **go around** 来回走动 11. **go by** 走过，顺便拜访

*goal [gəul] *n.* 目标；进球得分；(足球) 球门

【例】He kicked the ball straight into the *goal*. 他直接把球踢入了球门里。

【考】**achieve one's goal** 实现某人的目标：She wants to achieve her goal at all costs. 为了达到目的她不惜一切代价。

golf [gɔlf] *n.* 高尔夫球

【记】发音记忆

【例】He won the *golf* match by two shots. 他以两杆成绩赢得了这场高尔夫球比赛。

*goods [gudz] *n.* 商品，货物

【例】name-brand *goods* 名牌商品

*goose [guːs] *n.* (*pl.* geese) 鹅

govern ['gʌvn] *v.* 统治；管理

【例】The Liberal Democratic Party *governed* Japan for more than 40 years. 自由民主党统治日本40多年。

【衍】government (*n.* 政府)

gradual ['grædʒuəl] *adj.* 逐渐的，渐进的

【记】词根记忆：grad（级，阶段）+ual→分阶段的→逐渐的

【例】a *gradual* change 逐渐的变化

【衍】gradually（*adv.* 逐渐地）

graduate ['grædʒueit] *v.* 毕业 *n.*（大学）毕业生；研究生

【用】注意：graduate 是瞬间动词，不能跟段时间连用，表示毕业了多长时间。表示这种延续性概念时可用 be away from school 来替换。

【例】He *graduated* from Beijing Language and Culture University. 他毕业于北京语言文化大学。// middle school *graduates* 中学毕业生

【考】**graduate from...** 从…（学校）毕业

【衍】graduation（*n.* 毕业，毕业典礼）

grain [grein] *n.* 谷物，谷类

【例】We use only the best *grain* in our bread. 我们只用最好的谷物做面包。

gram [græm] *n.* 克（重量单位）

【例】The necklace weights 350 *grams*. 这条项链重350克。

grand [grænd] *adj.* 宏伟的，盛大的

【例】*grand* opening 隆重开业//*grand* master 高段棋手；在任何方面有特殊成就者

graph [grɑːf；græf] *n.* 图表，曲线图

【例】What does the *graph* show? 这张图表显示了什么？

grasp [grɑːsp；græsp] *vt.* 抓住，紧握；领会

【记】联想记忆：他见到她宛如抓住（grasp）一根救命稻草（grass）

【例】The boy climbed onto the wall and *grasped* the pole. 男孩儿爬上墙头抓住竿子。//Do you *grasp* what I mean? 你明白我的意思了吗？

grateful ['greitful] *adj.* 感激的，感谢的

【考】**be grateful to sb. for sth.** 因某事感激某人：We are grateful to you for your advice. 我们非常感激你的建议。

gravity ['græviti] *n.* 地心引力，重力

【例】The surface *gravity* on Mars is only about 38% of the surface *gravity* on Earth. 火星的地面重力只有地球地面重力的38%。

greedy ['griːdi] *adj.* 贪婪的

【记】联想记忆：绿色的（green）吸血鬼很贪婪（greedy）

【例】He is a *greedy* man. 他是一个贪婪的人。

greengrocer ['gri:ngrəusə] *n.* 蔬菜水果商

【记】组合词：green（绿色）+grocer（零售商）→蔬菜水果商

greet [gri:t] *vt.* 问候，向…致敬

【记】见面（meet）的时候互致问候（greet）

【例】She *greeted* me with a nod. 她点头向我问好。

【衍】greeting（*n.* 问候）

grocer ['grəusə] *n.* 零售商人；食品店

【例】His father was a *grocer*. 他父亲是一名杂货商。

【衍】grocery（*n.* 杂货；杂货店）

group [gru:p] *n.* 组，群　　　*ground　n. 地面*

【例】age *group* 年龄段/组

grow [grəu] *v.* (grew, grown, growing) 种植；生长，发育 *link. v.* 渐渐变得，变成

【用】**grow to do...** 渐渐形成某种态度：I think you will grow to like him when you know him better. 我想，当你对他有更多了解之后就会喜欢他了。

【例】Do you *grow* many plants yourself? 你自己也种许多植物吗？// The weather is *growing* cold. 天气渐渐变冷了。

【考】**grow up** 长大，成年

【衍】growth（*n.* 生长，增长）；growing（*adj.* 成长的，增加的）

guarantee [gærən'ti:] *vt./n.* 保证，担保

【记】联想记忆：guar（看作guard保卫）+antee→保证

【例】He can't *guarantee* that he will come on time. 他不能保证准时来。

单词自测

1. They know her very well. They had seen her _____ up from childhood.
   A. grow　　　B. grew　　　C. was growing　　D. to grow

2. He had hoped _____ this term, but he couldn't finish his thesis in time.
   A. him to graduate　　　　B. that he graduate
   C. he would graduate　　　D. his graduation

3. I'm glad _____ you that you can have the job.

A. that tell B. of telling C. of to tell D. to tell

4. How can they _____ there in such a short time?

A. get to B. arrive C. arrive at D. get

5. My watch _____ 20 seconds. Would you be so kind as to set it backwards?

A. wins B. gets C. gains D. loses

6. If you want to become a scientist _____, you should study harder _____.

A. future; future B. in future; in future

C. in the future; in future D. in future; in the future

7. She was always _____ with her children, never hitting nor scolding them.

A. calm B. gentle C. strict D. careful

8. The simple joy of reading a book is something we take for granted. But many people have had to _____ this pleasure because of poor eyesight.

A. give in B. give off C. give out D. give up

9. I don't doubt _____ Mary will devoted all her spare time _____ her lessons.

A. that; to go over B. that; to going over

C. if; to go over D. whether; to going over

10. I would be very _____ if you could give me an early reply.

A. pleasant B. grateful C. satisfied D. helpful

11. _____ him and then try to copy what he does.

A. Mind B. Glance at C. Stare at D. Watch

12. Charley Oakley, _____ NBA star, hasn't lost _____ game in the past three years.

A. an; a B. a; a C. the; a D. an; the

13. _____ general, his composition is not bad, but some examples he chose are terrible.

A. In B. On C. For D. Of

14. The Liberal Democratic Party _____ Japan for more than 40 years.

A. controlled B. powered C. governed D. charged

15. Tim loves to play _____ golf, while his brother Mark doesn't like it at all. He prefers to play _____ piano.

A. the; the B. the; / C. /; / D. /; the

答案：ACDDC CBDBB DAACD

Word List 21

guard [gɑːd] v. 保卫，看守 n. 防护装置，警戒

【例】They used poisonous snakes to *guard* the exhibition objects. 他们用毒蛇看守展品。

【衍】guardian（n. 护卫，保护人）; unguarded（adj. 没有设防的）

guidance ['gaidəns] n. 引导，指导

【记】联想记忆：guid（看作guide指引，指导）+ance（名词后缀）→指引，指导

【例】marriage *guidance* service 婚姻咨询服务

guilty ['gilti] adj. 有罪的，犯法的，做错事的

【例】I felt *guilty* about lying to you. 对你撒了谎，我感到很内疚。

guitar [gi'tɑː] n. 吉他，六弦琴

【记】发音记忆

【衍】guitarist（n. 吉他手）

gym [dʒim]（=gymnasium）n. 体操；体育馆，健身房

【例】at the *gym* 在体育馆

【衍】gymnastics（n. 体操）

habit ['hæbit] n. 习惯，习性

【考】1. **develop/form/get into a habit**（of）养成一个（…）习惯：He developed a habit of smoking. 他养成了抽烟的习惯。2. **have a habit of...** 有一个…的习惯

【衍】habitual（adj. 习惯的）; habitually（adv. 习惯地）

【辨】habit, custom

habit通常指个人的习惯，往往不需有意识地去想就能完成

custom指的是某个群体在经过长时间的实践后形成的习

155

*haircut [ˈhɛəkʌt] *n.* (男子) 理发

【记】组合词: hair (头发) +cut (剪) →理发

【例】I think I need a *haircut*. 我想我该理发了。

hall [hɔːl] *n.* 大厅, 礼堂; 门厅, 过道

【记】在大厅 (hall) 里办舞会 (ball)

【例】the Town *Hall*=the City *Hall* 市政厅//dining *hall* 食堂

hamburger [ˈhæmbɜːgə] *n.* 汉堡包

【记】发音记忆

【例】I ordered a *hamburger* and a milkshake. 我点了一个汉堡和一份奶昔。

★hammer [ˈhæmə] *n.* 锤子, 锣锤 *v.* 敲, 锤击

【例】It is easy to do the repair. All you need is a *hammer* and some nails. 只需要一把锤子和一些钉子就能把它修好。//She *hammered* on the door with her hands. 她用手锤打着门。

hand [hænd] *n.* 手; 指针 *vt.* 交付

【例】*hand* luggage 手提行李

【考】1. **shake hands with...** 与…握手 2. **take/hold one's hand** 拉着某人的手 3. **put up one's hand=raise one's hand** 举手 4. **hand in** 交上 5. **hand out** 分发 6. **be at hand** 在手边; 即将到来 7. **hand over** 移交 8. **hand in hand** 手拉手; 联合 9. **in hand** 在手头上; 在掌握中 10. **give sb. a hand** 帮助某人 11. **hand down** 把…传下去 12. **Hands up!** 举起手来!

【衍】handful* (*n.* 一把; 少数, 少量); handy* (*adj.* 便利的, 顺手的)

handle [ˈhændl] *vt.* 处理 *n.* 柄, 把

【记】hand (手) +le→方便手操作的东西→柄, 把手

【例】I was impressed by her *handling* of the affair. 我觉得她对此事的处理很了不起。

hang [hæŋ] *vt.* (hung/hanged, hung/hanged, hanging) 悬挂, 装饰

【用】hung和hanged都是hang的过去式或过去分词, 但hang指悬挂时其过去式和过去分词只能用hung, 指绞死时只能用hanged。可记为: 这世界真是不公平: 规则的被绞死, 不规则的反被挂起来了事。

【例】There was a big mirror *hanging* on the wall. 墙上挂着一面大镜子。

【考】1. **hang out/around** 闲荡 2. **hang on** (打电话时) 不挂断

(handwritten notes in margin:)
handbag
n. 小手提包
handkerchief
n. 手帕
handsome
a. 英俊的
handwriting
n. 书法
*handy
a. 便利的

3. **hang up** 挂断电话

happen ['hæpən] *v.* (偶然)发生，碰巧

【用】1. **happen to do**（**be**）**...** 碰巧做了（是）…：They happened to meet the writer of the novel. 他们碰巧遇上了那部小说的作者。2. **sth. happen to sb.** 某事发生在某人身上：What would happen to me if I fall from the window? 如果我从窗户掉下去会发生什么事呢？3. **It happens**（**happened**）**that...** 碰巧…：It happened that I knew the answer. 我碰巧知道答案。

【衍】happenings（*n.* 事件，意外发生的事件）

【辨】**happen, take place, occur**
三者都可表示"发生"，但**happen**强调的是意外或偶然发生的事件；**take place**通常指经过安排才发生的事件；**occur**既可指自然发生，也可指有意安排，用法较为正规。

happiness
n.幸福

harbour ['hɑːbə] *n.* (美harbor) 港口

【例】We can overlook the *harbour* from the window of our room. 从屋子的窗户我们可以俯瞰那个港口。

hardly ['hɑːdli] *adv.* 几乎不

【用】1. hardly是否定副词，不与其他表示否定的词语像no, nothing等连用，如：He hardly did anything. 他几乎什么也没有做。2. **hardly...when...** 表示"刚…就…"，当hardly放在句首时句子需要倒装，如：The game had hardly begun when it started raining.=Hardly had the game begun when it started raining. 比赛刚开始就下起雨来了。

【例】I can *hardly* hear the radio. Would you please turn it up? 我几乎听不见广播，请你把声音开大一些好吗？

*hardship ['hɑːdˌʃip] *n.* 困难，艰辛

【记】联想记忆：hard（艰苦的）+ship（船）→同舟共济度难关→困难

【例】The novel shows the *hardship* of her childhood. 小说讲述了她童年时期的艰苦生活。

harm [hɑːm] *n./vt.* 伤害，损伤

【考】**do harm to...** 给…带来伤害：Being exposed to sunlight for too much time will do harm to one's skin. 长时间的阳光照射会对皮肤造成伤害。

【衍】harmful（*adj.* 有害的）；harmless（*adj.* 无害的）

*harmony [ˈhɑ:məni] *n.* 协调，融洽

【例】We live together in *harmony*. 我们和睦地住在一起。

【衍】harmonious (*adj.* 和谐的，和睦的)

harvest [ˈhɑ:vist] *n./v.* 收割，收获 (物)

【例】A skilled worker can *harvest* 9~14 kilograms of tea leaves a day. 娴熟的工人每天可以采9~14公斤的茶叶。

*hatch [hætʃ] *v.* (鸟、鸡) 孵蛋

【例】Nearly all eggs have *hatched*. 几乎所有的蛋都孵出了小鸡。

have [hæv] *vt.* (had, had, having) 有，使，令 *aux.v.* 帮助构成完成时态

【用】have接复合宾语，主要句型有：1. **have sb. do sth.** 让某人做某事：If anyone happens to drop in while I am out, have him or her leave a message. 如果我出去时有人来访，让来人留个口信儿。注意：have的宾补是不定式要省略to，相同用法的动词还有：notice, help (to), feel, hear, listen to, make, let, watch, see, look at, observe 等。2. **have sb./sth. doing...** 让⋯⋯一直做⋯⋯：He had us laughing all through the meal. 他让我们一顿饭都笑个不停。3. **have sth. done** 让某事被(别人)做；遭遇：You have had your hair cut. 你剪头发了。//We had our money stolen. 我们的钱被偷了。

【考】1. **have trouble/difficulty** (**in**) **doing...** 做⋯⋯有困难 2. **have nothing to do with...** 和⋯⋯无关

*headline [ˈhedlain] *n.* (报刊的) 标题；(*pl.*) 头条新闻

【记】head (头) +line (行) → 文章开头的一行字 → 标题

【例】Have you read the *headlines* of today's paper? 你读今天报纸的头条新闻了吗？

headline

headmaster [ˌhedˈmɑ:stə] *n.* 中小学校长

【记】组合词：head (头) +master (主人) → 学校最大的主人 → 校长

【例】He is a *headmaster* of a middle school. 他是一所中学的校长。

【衍】headmistress (*n.* 女校长)

health [helθ] *n.* 健康，卫生

【记】健康 (health) 是最大的财富 (wealth)

【例】He is in poor *health*. 他的健康状况很差。

【衍】healthy (*adj.* 健康的，健壮的)；healthful (*adj.* 有益健康的)；

unhealthy（*adj.* 不健康的，对健康有害的）

heap ［hi:p］*n.* 堆 *vt.* 堆起来

【例】There is a *heap* of sand. 那儿有一堆沙子。// He *heaped* all the plates on the table. 他把所有的盘子都堆在桌子上。

hear ［hiə］*v.*（heard, heard, hearing）听见，听说，得知

【考】1. **hear of/about** 听说 2. **hear from** 收到…的来信 3. **hear... doing/do...** 听见…做…

【辨】**hear, hear of/about, listen to**

hear, hear of/about, listen to 都有"听"的意义。**hear** 侧重与"听到"，强调"听"的结果；**listen to** 侧重于"听"的动作，不一定能听到；**hear of/about** 侧重于"听说"，指间接听别人说到，不是亲自听到。

*hearing ［ˈhiəriŋ］*n.* 听力

【记】hear（听）+ing→听力

【例】You had a problem with your *hearing*. 你的听力有问题。

heat ［hi:t］*n.* 热 *v.* 加热

【例】body *heat* 体温//The fireplace *heated* the house. 壁炉让屋子暖和起来。

【衍】heated（*adj.* 热烈的，激昂的）

heaven
n.天堂，天空

heel ［hi:l］*n.* 脚后跟

【例】Her shoes rubbed her *heels*. 她的鞋磨脚后跟。

height ［hait］*n.* 高，高度

【记】high（*adj.* 高的）的名词形式

【例】What is your *height*? 你多高？

helicopter ［ˈhelikɔptə］*n.* 直升飞机

【例】There is no place to land the *helicopter* here. 直升机无法在这里降落。

*helmet ［ˈhelmit］*n.* 头盔

【例】You'd better wear a *helmet* when you ride your motorcycle. 骑摩托车时最好戴上头盔。

helmet

help ［help］*n./v.* 帮助，帮忙；有帮助，有用

【用】1. **help sb.（to）do sth.** 帮助某人做某

hero
n. 英雄

H

事：I helped him load the car. 我帮他装车。 2. **help(to) do sth.** 帮忙，有助于：The kids helped clean up the kitchen. 孩子们帮忙打扫厨房。3. **help sb. with sth.** 帮助某人做某事：My mom helps me with my homework. 妈妈辅导我做功课。

【考】1. **with the help of** 在…的帮助下 2. **help sb. out** 帮助某人解决困难 3. **help out** 帮忙 4. **help oneself to sth.** 自用某物 5. **can't help doing...** 忍不住做某事：Anne is such a good cook that I can't help eating everything she makes. 安妮是个很棒的厨师，我忍不住吃了她做的所有东西。

*herb [həːb; (h)əːrb] *n.* 草药

【记】发音颠倒过来似中文"薄荷"→薄荷也是一种草药

hesitate [ˈheziteit] *v.* 犹豫，踌躇

【记】联想记忆：he（他）+sit（坐）+ate→他坐在那，犹豫不决→犹豫

【用】**hesitate to do...** 做…犹犹豫豫：Don't hesitate to tell me what you want. 想要什么尽管说。

hesitate

嫁给我!! 嫁给我!!

hide [haid] *v.* (hid, hidden, hiding) 掩饰，隐藏

【例】The man *hid* in a car. 那个男的藏在车里。

hire [ˈhaiə] *vt.* 租用

【例】They *hired* a bathing machine. 他们租用了一辆游泳更衣车。

hit [hit] *n./v.* (hit, hit, hitting) 打，撞；击中

【考】**hit on...** 偶然发现…：I hope that someone will hit on a solution to our problem. 我希望有人能想出办法以解决我们的问题。

hold [həuld] *v.* (held, held, holding) 拿，握住；举行

【考】1. **hold on** 稍等，别挂电话 2. **hold on to...** 紧紧抓住…；坚持… 3. **hold to...** 坚持…；握紧 4. **hold up** 举起 5. **hold back...** 隐瞒；抑制…

【例】*hold* a party 举办晚会

【衍】holder (*n.* 持有者，占有者)

*holy [ˈhəuli] *adj.* 神圣的

【例】*holy* war 圣战

homeland [ˈhəumlænd] *n.* 祖国

【例】They were forced to leave their *homeland*. 他们被迫离开了祖国。

honour [ˈɔnə] (美honor) *vt.* 尊敬，给予荣誉 *n.* 荣誉，光荣

【例】They *honoured* him with a special dinner. 他们专门设宴招待他以示尊敬。

【考】**It is one's honour to do...** 做…是某人的荣幸：It is my honour to help you. 帮助你是我的荣幸。

*hook [huk] *n.* 钩子 *vt.* 钩住，用钩子挂

coat hook

【记】就看（look）了一眼，魂儿就被"钩"（hook）住了

【例】He hung his coat on the *hook*. 他把大衣挂在了钩子上。// *Hook* the rope on the nail. 把绳子挂在那根钉子上。

a coat rack 衣架

hope [həup] *n./v.* 希望

【用】1. **hope to do...** 希望做…：We should not hope to get rewards without hard work. 不努力工作我们就别想得到奖赏。2. **hope (that)** 希望…：I hope (that) I can receive your photo as soon as possible. 希望能尽快收到你的照片。3. **hope for...** 希望，期待…注意：hope后不能接复合宾语，如果要表达希望某人做某事，需要用宾语从句或其他形式，如：I hope that you will succeed. (=I hope for your success.) 我希望你能成功。

【衍】hopeful (*adj.* 有希望的；有前途的)；hopeless (*adj.* 没有希望的；不可救药的)

【辨】**hope, wish**

对于有可能实现的事情时用**hope**，如：I hope you will help me. 我希望你能帮助我（我这样想也相信你会这样做）。对于不可能实现或实现的可能性很小时用**wish**，如：I wish I were 20 years younger. 但愿我能年轻20岁（这是不可能的事情）。而且**wish**后接**that**从句时要用虚拟语气。另外，**hope**后不能接双宾语或复合宾语，**wish**则可以。

单元自测

1. In the singing class the group leader _____ out a collection of new songs to each member.

   A. found   B. handed   C. put   D. called

2. —Is this raincoat yours?

   —No, mine _____ there behind the door.

A. is hanging   B. has hung   C. hangs   D. hung

3. Look, many people are gathering there. What is _____?

    A. going on   B. happened   C. matter   D. taken place

4. It is _____ any wonder that his friend doesn't like watching television much.

    A. no   B. such   C. nearly   D. hardly

5. Don't _____ to correct me if I made a mistake.

    A. pause   B. stop   C. mind   D. hesitate

6. We thought of selling this old furniture, but we've decided to _____ it. It might be valuable.

    A. hold on to   B. keep up with   C. turn to   D. look after

7. I _____ an answer to my letter within a few days.

    A. hope   B. wait   C. look through   D. expect

8. Mr. Johnson was _____ in the leg while fighting Japanese during the war.

    A. hurt   B. harmed   C. injured   D. wounded

9. As a result of destroying the forests, a large _____ of desert _____ covered the land.

    A. number; has   B. quantity; has   C. number; have   D. quantity; have

10. I _____ her voice at once on the phone, though we hadn't seen each other for ten years.

    A. heard   B. knew   C. realized   D. recognized

11. Students sometimes support themselves by _____ of taking evening jobs.

    A. ways   B. offers   C. means   D. helps

12. The area was badly _____ by a great storm.

    A. hurt   B. knocked   C. beaten   D. hit

13. We desire _____ a _____ person.

    A. hiring; studied   B. to hire; studied

    C. hiring; learned   D. to hire; learned

14. —You haven't lost the ticket, have you?

    — _____. I know it's not easy to get another one at the moment.

    A. I hope not   B. Yes, I have   C. I hope so   D. Yes, I'm afraid so

15. Tom suggested that we _____ such a meeting, but Jenny insisted that it _____ of great importance.

    A. not hold; should be   B. didn't hold; be

    C. hold; was   D. not hold; was

答案：BCADD ADDBD CDDAD

Word List 22

horse n. 马   hospital n. 医院

horrible ['hɔrəbl; 'hɔːrəbl] *adj.* 令人恐惧的，恐怖的

【例】What's that *horrible* smell? 什么东西这么难闻？

host [həust] *n.* 主人，节目主持人 *vt.* 招待，主持

【例】I'm glad to *host* the forum. 很高兴主持这次的论坛。

【衍】host**ess** (*n.* 女主人)

housework ['hauswəːk] *n.* 家务劳动

housewife
n. 家庭主妇

【记】组合词：house（房子）+work（工作）→家里的工作→家务劳动

【例】You have only 12 minutes to do the *housework*. 你仅有12分钟来做家务。

however [hau'evə] *adv.* 可是，然而，尽管如此 *conj.* 无论

【用】1. however表转折时，可以放在句首、句中或句末，注意要用逗号隔开：The book is expensive; however, it's worth it. 这本书很贵，但它物有所值。2. however作连词时相当于no matter how，意为"无论如何"，引导让步状语从句：You should try to get a good night's sleep however much work you have to do. 无论有多少工作要做，你都应该好好睡上一觉。

【辨】**however, but, although**（**though**）

表示转折时，**however**是连接副词，放在句首、句中、句末都可以，需要用逗号隔开，如：I'd like to go with you. However, my hands are full.（=I'd like to go with you. My hands are full, however.）虽然我很想和你一块去，但是我太忙了。**but**是并列连词，只能放在~成转折关系的两个分句或句子之间，如：I'd like to go~but my hands are full. 虽然我很想和你一块去，但~**although**和**though**是从属连词，引导让步状语~/ Though I'd like to go with you, my hand~

husband
n. 丈夫

一块去，但是我太忙了。注意：汉语常常使用"虽然…但是…"这个连词词组，但在英语中 **although**（**though**）和 **but** 绝对不能同时使用。

*howl [haul] *v.* 嚎叫，嚎哭

【记】发音记忆：how（音似：嚎）+l→嚎叫

【例】The dog was *howling* in the yard. 狗在院子里嚎叫。

howl

hug [hʌg] *v.*（hugged, hugged, hugging）紧抱，拥抱 *n.* 拥抱

【例】The child was *hugging* her doll. 那孩子紧抱着她的洋娃娃。// He gave his daughter a big *hug*. 他紧紧抱着自己的女儿。

hug

human [ˈhjuːmən] *adj.* 人的，人类的 *n.* 人，人类

【例】*human* history 人类史

【衍】human being（*n.* 人类）; humanitarian（*n.* 人道主义）

humour [ˈhjuːmə]（美humor）*n.* 幽默，幽默感

【例】He has a good sense of *humour*. 他很幽默。

【衍】humorous（*adj.* 富于幽默的）

hunt [hʌnt] *v./n.* 寻找；狩猎，猎取

【例】The police are *hunting* down the escaped convict. 警察正在追捕逃犯。// treasure *hunt* 寻宝

【考】**hunt down** 搜寻直到找到：Wherever you go, I can *hunt* you down. 不论你走到哪儿，我都能抓到你。

【衍】hunter（*n.* 猎人）; hunting（*n.* 打猎；搜寻）

*hurricane [ˈhʌrikən] *n.* 飓风，狂风

【记】联想记忆：hurri（看作hurry匆忙）+cane→来得很匆忙的风→飓风

【例】The *hurricane* destroyed our homes. 飓风毁掉了我们的家园。

hurry [ˈhʌri] *v.* 赶快；急忙 *n.* 匆忙，仓促

【考】1. **hurry up** 快点；催促：Could you hurry them up? 你能不能催他们一下？2. **in a hurry** 匆忙；赶忙：Why are you in such a hurry? 你干嘛这么着急？3. **in no hurry** 不用着急，慢点

hurt [həːt] *v.*（hurt, hurt, hurting）伤害

【例】You *hurt* my feelings. 你伤了我的心。

【辨】hurt, injure, wound

hurt 既可指心灵上的伤害，也可指肉体上的伤害，强调疼痛的感觉；injure 多用于意外事故带来的肉体上的伤害；wound 一般指在战争或打斗中的伤害（如枪伤等）。

hurt

*hydrogen [ˈhaidrədʒən] *n.* 氢

【例】Water contains *hydrogen* and oxygen. 水中含有氢和氧。

*identification [aiˌdentifiˈkeiʃən] *n.* 辨认，鉴定；身份证明

【例】Let me see your *identification* card. 让我看看你的身份证。

【考】**identification with** 认同：I have no identification with what you said. 我不认同你说的话。

identity [aiˈdentəti] *n.* 身份；一致

【例】Only when your *identity* has been checked, will you be allowed in. 核实身份后你才可以进入。

idiom [ˈidiəm] *n.* 习语，成语

【例】How many *idioms* have you learned today? 你今天学了多少条习语？

*ignore [igˈnɔ:] *vt.* 不理睬；忽视

【例】Why are you *ignoring* me? 你为什么不理我？

ignore

illegal [iˈli:gəl] *adj.* 违法的，不合规定的

【记】il（不）+legal（合法的）→不合法的

【例】Cigarette advertising on TV is *illegal* in many countries. 在许多国家，在电视上给香烟做广告是违法的。

【衍】illegally（*adv.* 非法地）

illness n. 疾病

imagine [iˈmædʒin] *v.* 想像，设想

immediately ad. 立即

【用】1. **imagine+doing...** 想像做…：I can't imagine being rich. 我从没有想过变得富有。注意：imagine后需要跟动作时只能用doing而不能用to do。2. **imagine+从句**，如：I can imagine what you told me about the forest. 我可以想像出你告诉我的关于那片森林的情况。

*immigration [ˌimiˈgreiʃən] *n.* 移民

【例】There are strict controls on *immigration* into this country. 移民到这个国家有严格的限制。

*imply
v. 暗示 意味着

*import [im'pɔːt] *vt./n.* 进口，输入

【记】词根记忆：im（进入）+port（运送）→往里运送→进口

【例】We have to *import* crude oil to meet growing demand. 我们不得不进口原油以满足日益增长的需求。

importance [im'pɔːtəns] *n.* 重要性

【例】They place great *importance* on children getting good study results. 他们十分重视让孩子取得优异的成绩。

*impress [im'pres] *vt.* 留下印象

【记】词根记忆：im（进入）+press（压）→压进去→留下印象

【例】Your pretty face really *impressed* me. 你美丽的容颜给我留下了非常深刻的印象。

【衍】impression（*n.* 印象，感觉）；impressive（*adj.* 印象深刻的）

improve [im'pruːv] *v.* 改进，更新

【例】My advisor encouraged me to take a summer course to *improve* my writing skills. 指导老师鼓励我参加暑期课程来提高写作技巧。

【衍】improvement（*n.* 改进；进步）

inch [intʃ] *n.* 英寸

【例】Luckily, the bullet narrowly missed the captain by an *inch*. 幸运的是，子弹从距离上尉一英寸的地方飞过，没有击中他。

incident ['insidənt] *n.* 事件

【例】Not too long ago, an *incident* that happened at Walt Disney touched me greatly. 不久前，发生在迪斯尼的一件事深深地触动了我。

include [in'kluːd] *vt.* 包含，包括

【用】**including sb./sth. = sb./sth. included** 如：Many people like the book, including me/me included. 许多人喜欢这本书，我也不例外。

【例】The activities *include* singing pop songs and playing classical and folk music. 活动内容包括演唱流行歌曲、演奏古典和民族音乐。

income ['inkʌm; 'inˌkʌm] *n.* 收入，所得

【记】联想记忆：in（进入）+come（来）→进来的东西→收入，所得

【例】He needs a high *income* to support such a large family. 他需要有高收入才能供养得起这样一个大家庭。

increase [in'kriːs] *v.* 增加，繁殖 *n.* 增加，加大

【例】You may have to *increase* your budget. 也许你不得不增加预算。

【考】**increase by...** 增加了…; **increase to...** 增长到…

indeed [inˈdiːd] *adv.* 确实，实在

【例】He speaks English well *indeed*, but of course not so fluently as a native speaker. 他英语确实说得不错，但还是不如本土人士说得流利。

independent [ˌindiˈpendənt] *adj.* 独立的，有主见的

【例】Symbols and the things they stand for are all *independent* of each other. 符号与它们代表的事物之间是相互独立的。

【衍】independently (*adv.* 独立地); independence (*n.* 独立)

indicate [ˈindikeit] *vt.* 指出，显示

【记】词根记忆：in+dic（说）+ate（做）→说出→指示，指出

【例】These figures *indicate* that our sales are increasing. 这些数字表明我们的销售额在增加。

Industry n.部门,行业,企业

influence [ˈinfluəns] *n./vt.* 影响

【例】What *influenced* your career choice? 什么影响了你对职业的选择？

【考】**influence upon/on...** 对…有影响：Listening to the music has a calming influence on her. 听音乐对她起了一种镇静的作用。

＊infer v.推论,意味着

inform [inˈfɔːm] *v.* 通知，告诉

【例】The police *informed* him that his car had been stolen. 警察通知他说他的车被盗了。

【考】**inform sb. of sth.** 通知某人某事：I informed my boss of the change of schedule. 我通知了老板计划有所改动。

【衍】information (*n.* 信息)

initial [iˈniʃəl] *adj.* 开始的，最初的

【例】After he'd overcome his *initial* shyness, he became very friendly. 他克服了开始的羞涩之后，变得非常友好。

injure [ˈindʒə] *vt.* 损害，伤害

【例】He *injured* an arm in a car accident. 他在一次车祸中伤了一只手臂。

【衍】injury (*n.* 受伤处)

inn [in] *n.* 小旅店，小饭店

【记】联想记忆：in（进入）+ n（想像成一扇小门）→进入一扇小门→小旅店

ink n.墨水

【例】the Holiday *Inn* 假日旅馆

innocent [ˈinəsnt] *adj.* 清白的，无罪的

【例】I'm an *innocent* man. 我是无辜的。

insect [ˈinsekt] *n.* 昆虫

【例】Cockroach is a disgusting type of *insect.* 蟑螂是一种非常恶心的昆虫。

insert [inˈsəːt] *vt.* 插入

【例】*Insert* a quarter in the coin slot, and then dial the number. 往投币孔里投进一枚25美分的硬币，然后拨号。

insert

inside prep.& ad 内部又在 内部

insist [inˈsist] *v.* 坚持，坚决认为

【用】1. insist表示"坚持"时，后接that从句常用虚拟语气，即should do 的形式，should 可以省略，如：The mother insisted that her daughter go to the graduation dance. 妈妈坚持让自己的女儿参加毕业舞会。2. insist表示"坚持认为、坚持说"的时候，that从句不用虚拟语气，如：He insists that there is an important difference between the two. 他坚持认为这两者间有着重大的区别。

【考】**insist on sth./doing sth.** 坚持（做）某事：Father insisted on taking her to the hospital. 父亲坚持要带她去医院。

inspect [inˈspekt] *vt.* 检查；审视

【例】He *inspected* the car for signs of rust. 他检查了汽车，看看有没有生锈的迹象。

【衍】inspection（*n.* 检查，视察）

inspire [inˈspaiə] *v.* 鼓舞，激励；启示

【例】I was *inspired* to work harder by her example. 我以她为榜样激励自己更加努力地工作。

【衍】inspired（*adj.* 得到灵感的）

instant [ˈinstənt] *adj.* 立即的；速食的 *n.* 瞬间

【例】*instant* noodle 方便面

【衍】instantly（*adv.* 立即地）；instance（*n.* 例子；事实）

instead [inˈsted] *adv.* 代替，顶替

【记】in（在…内）+stead（看作steal偷）→从中做手脚，偷天换日→代替

【例】It is too wet to go for a walk; let's go swimming *instead.* 天气太

潮湿了不适合散步，我们不如去游泳吧。

【考】**instead of** 代替；而不是：We students should be honest and try to get good results by studying hard instead of cheating in examinations. 作为学生，我们应该诚实并通过努力学习在考试中取得好成绩，而不是利用作弊来取得高分。

institute [ˈinstitjuːt; ˈinstituːt] *n.* 协会，学院

【例】research *institute* 研究所

*institution [ˌinstiˈtjuːʃən; ˌinstiˈtuːʃən] *n.* 公共机构，协会

【例】a financial *institution* 一家金融机构

单元自测

1. Mother will wait for him to have dinner together, _____.
   A. however late is he　　　　B. however he is late
   C. however is he late　　　　D. however late he is

2. —I'm afraid I can't finish the book within this week.
   — _____.
   A. Pleased go ahead　　　　B. Hurry up
   C. Not at all　　　　D. Take your time

3. My chest _____ when I make a deep breath, doctor.
   A. harms　　B. wounds　　C. hurts　　D. injures

4. _____ my finishing reading the magazine, you can have it _____.
   A. On; immediately　　　　B. At; quickly
   C. For; fortunately　　　　D. With; likely

5. The problem is _____ to us. We must discuss it at once.
   A. great importance　　　　B. of important
   C. of great importance　　　　D. of very importance

6. There is a new problem involved in the popularity of private cars _____ road conditions need _____.
   A. that; to be improved　　　　B. which; to be improved
   C. where; improving　　　　D. when; improving

7. The National Day and the International Labour Day are great _____ in our country.
   A. things　　B. accidents　　C. incident　　D. events

8. There are 50 students in our class _____ Zhou Lan.
   A. includes　　B. beside　　C. including　　D. that

9. It is rather cold today, but tomorrow we expect the temperature to _____.

   A. develop   B. grow   C. increase   D. rise

10. The bell _____ the end of the period rang, _____ our heated discussion.

   A. indicating; interrupting   B. indicated; interrupting

   C. indicating; interrupted   D. indicated; interrupted

11. The old man was unfortunately knocked down by a car and badly _____.

   A. damaged   B. harmed   C. injured   D. wounded

12. The couple _____ staying in the countryside for their summer holidays.

   A. wanted to   B. insisted on   C. stuck to   D. intended

13. We'll have tea in the garden _____ the house.

   A. in the place of   B. instead of in   C. instead in   D. in place of

14. —How do you _____ we go to Beijing for our holidays?

   —I think we'd better fly there. It's much more comfortable.   （2004福建）

   A. insist   B. want   C. suppose   D. suggest

15. You see the lightning _____ it happens, but you hear the thunder later.

   A. the moment   B. while   C. the time   D. an instant

答案：DDCAC ADCDA CBBDA

Our greatest glory consists not in never falling but in rising every time we fall.   —Goldsmith

我们最值得自豪的不在于从不跌倒，而在于每次跌倒之后都爬起来。   ——戈德史密斯

Word List 23

instruct [in'strʌkt] v. 指示，教导；通知

【记】联想记忆：in+struct（看作strict严厉的）→教不严，师之惰→教导

【例】A computer can only do what you have *instructed* it to do. 电脑只能按照你的指示运作。

【衍】instruction (*n.* 说明，须知；教导)；instructor (*n.* 教师；讲师)

instrument ['instrumənt] *n.* 乐器；工具，器械

【例】musical *instrument* 乐器

*insure [in'ʃuə;in'ʃuər] v. 确保，给…保险

【记】联想记忆：in+sure（确定的）→确保

【考】**insure...against...** 给…上保险：My house is insured against fire. 我的房子上了火险。

【衍】insurance (*n.* 保险)

intelligence [in'telidʒəns] *n.* 智力，聪明

【例】*intelligence* test 智力测验

*intend [in'tend] v. 想要，打算

【用】**intend (sb.) to do sth.** 打算（让某人）做某事：I didn't intend to stay outside for long. 我不打算在外面待很久。

【衍】intended (*adj.* 有意的，故意的)；intention (*n.* 意图，目的)

interest ['intrist] *n.* 兴趣，趣味；利息 *vt.* 使产生兴趣

【考】1. **be interested in=have an interest in** 对…感兴趣：He has an interest in word games. 他对字谜游戏感兴趣。2. **a place of interest** 名胜

【衍】interesting (*adj.* 有趣的)；uninterested (*adj.* 不感兴趣的)；disinterested (*adj.* 客观的；漠不关心的)

interpreter [in'tə:pritə] *n.* 翻译员，口译人员

【例】He wants to work as an *interpreter*. 他想做一名

171

interrupt [ˌintəˈrʌpt] *v.* 打扰，打断

【记】词根记忆：inter（在…之间）+rupt（断裂）→在中间断裂→中断，中止

【例】I didn't mean to *interrupt* you. 我不是有意打断你。

interval [ˈintəvəl] *n.* 间歇，间隔；幕间休息

【记】词根记忆：inter（在…之间）+val（表名词）→间距

【考】**at intervals** 每隔一段（时间或距离）：You should visit the dentist at regular intervals. 你应该定期去看牙医。

interview [ˈintəvjuː] *n./v.* 采访，会见，面试

【记】词根记忆：inter（相互）+view（看）→相互观察→面试，交谈

【例】She has an *interview* this weekend. 她周末有个面试。

【衍】interviewer（*n.* 会见者；面试官）；interviewee（*n.* 被访问者；面试者）

introduce [ˌintrəˈdjuːs; ˌintrəˈduːs] *vt.* 介绍；引进

【例】This is the new technology we *introduced* last month. 这就是我们上个月引进的新技术。

【考】**introduce...to...** 把…介绍给…

【衍】introduction（*n.* 引进，介绍）

introduce

invent [inˈvent] *vt.* 发明，创造

【例】Do you know who *invented* the roller skates? 你知道是谁发明了旱冰鞋吗？

【衍】invention（*n.* 发明，创造）；inventor（*n.* 发明家）；inventive（*adj.* 善于创造的，发明的）

invite [inˈvait] *vt.* 邀请，招待

【用】**invite sb. to do sth.** 邀请某人做某事：I am often invited to give talks to biology students in colleges. 大学经常邀请我去给生物学专业的学生做演讲。

【例】He wanted to *invite* them to dinner. 他想邀请他们吃饭。

【衍】invitation（*n.* 邀请，请帖）；uninvited（*adj.* 未被邀请的）

iron [ˈaiən] *n.* 铁；熨斗 *v.* 熨烫

【例】A new *iron* has been discovered on that planet. 在那个行星上发现了一种新的铁元素。// She washed and *ironed* her dress. 她把衣服洗干净，然后熨平。

*irrigation [ˌɪriˈgeɪʃən] n. 灌溉

【记】来自irrigate（v. 灌溉）

【例】*Irrigation* needs lots of water. 灌溉需要大量的水。

island
n. 岛

jam [dʒæm] v. (jammed, jammed, jamming)

（使）阻塞 n. 果酱；阻塞

【例】The fax machine has *jammed* again. 传真机又卡住了。

【考】**traffic jam** 塞车

jacket
n. 夹克

jar
n. 罐

jaw
n. 口部

traffic jam

*jet [dʒet] v. 喷射 n. 喷气式飞机；喷射

【例】The spring *jetted* out. 泉水喷涌而出。

jeans
n. 牛仔裤

jeep
n. 吉普

*jewelry [ˈdʒuːəlri] n. （总称）珠宝，首饰

【例】Helen wore lots of *jewelry*. 海伦戴着许多首饰。

*jog [dʒɔg] v. (jogged, jogged, jogging) 慢跑

【记】联想记忆：一边慢跑（jog）一边遛狗（dog）

【例】She likes doing *jogging* in the morning. 她喜欢早上慢跑。

join [dʒɔɪn] v. 参加，加入；连接；会合

【考】**join in** 参加，加入：We all joined in the singing. 我们一起歌唱。

joke
n. & v.
（开）玩笑

【辨】**join, join in, take part in**

join 常用来指加入一个团体或组织并成为其中的一员，如参军、入团、入会等；**join in** 多用来指参与到竞赛、娱乐、谈话等活动中去；**take part in** 指参加比赛或大型的活动，并在其中发挥积极作用。

journalist [ˈdʒɜːnəlist] n. 记者，新闻工作者

【例】Tom was a *journalist* of a local TV station. 汤姆是当地一家电视台的记者。

journey [ˈdʒɜːni] n. 旅行，路程

【例】The *journey* around the world took the old sailor nine months. 老水手用9个月的时间完成了环球旅行。

judge [dʒʌdʒ] v. 判断，评价 n. 裁判，法官

【例】Cars are *judged* on fuel efficiency（耗油量）rather than speed. 汽车是按耗油量而不是按速度来判断它们的性能的。

【考】**judging by/from** 根据…判断

judge

【衍】judgment（n. 裁判，判断）

*jungle [ˈdʒʌŋgl] n. 丛林，密林

【记】发音记忆："长高"→树木参天→丛林

【例】There are many poisonous snakes in the *jungle*. 丛林里有许多毒蛇。

junior [ˈdʒuːnjə] adj. 初级的；年少的

【记】联想记忆：jun（看作June六月）+ ior → 小孩子过六一儿童节→年少的

【例】*junior* high school 初中

just [dʒʌst] adv. 刚才，恰好；只是，仅 adj. 公正的

【考】1. **just now** 刚刚，不久之前；现在 2. **just then** 就在那时

justice [ˈdʒʌstis] n. 正义，公正；司法

【记】just（正义）+ice→正义，公平

【例】Judges should base their judgments on *justice*. 法官的判决应该建立在公正的基础上。

kangaroo [ˌkæŋgəˈruː] n. 大袋鼠

keep [kiːp] v.（kept, kept, keeping）保留；保存；使…保持某种状态 link. v. 保持，继续

kangaroo

【用】1. **keep (on) doing...** 继续做某事，一直做某事：Did he give up or keep on trying? 他是放弃了还是在继续努力？

2. **keep sb. from doing sth.** 阻止某人做某事：What can you do to keep it from happening again? 你能做什么来阻止它再次发生？ 3. keep可以接复合宾语，宾补常用分词、形容词、副词和介词短语等，表示使保持某种状态：Doctors will keep her in hospital for at least another week. 医生至少还会让她再住院一星期。//The noise kept him awake. 噪音使他睡不着。

【例】You can *keep* that book—I have another copy. 你可以留着那本书，我还有一本。// *Keep* that cat away from me! 别让那只猫靠近我！//Will the fish *keep* until tomorrow? 鱼能放到明天吗？// keep silent 保持沉默

【考】1. **keep in touch with sb.** 和某人保持联系 2. **keep off** 禁止接近；防止 3. **keep in mind** 记住，谨记 4. **keep up** 保持；继续；不低

落 5. **keep up with** 跟上，不落后

kettle [ˈketl] *n.* (烧水用的) 水壶

Keyboard
n. 键盘

【例】The water in the *kettle* had all boiled away. 壶里的水完全烧干了。

kick [kik] *v./n.* 踢

kid
n. 联系；小孩

【例】The baby was lying on its back, *kicking* its legs in the air. 婴儿平躺着，两腿向空中踢。

kilo [ˈkiːləu; ˈkiləu] *n.* 千克；千米

kill
v. 杀死

【例】The shopkeeper gave us short weight: we got 9 *kilos* instead of 10 *kilos*. 店主给我们的分量少了：只有9千克而不是10千克。

kilogram [ˈkiləugræm] *n.* 千克

Kilometre
n. 千米

【记】组合词：kilo（千）+gram（克）→千克

【例】He bought 10 *kilograms* of apples. 他买了10公斤苹果。

* kindergarten [ˈkindəˌɡɑːtən] *n.* 幼儿园

kindness
n. 仁慈；放纵

【记】联想记忆：kind（看作kid孩子）+er+garten（看作garden乐园）→孩子的乐园→幼儿园

Kingdom
n.

【例】My part-time job is to look after children at a *kindergarten*. 我在一所幼儿园做兼职，照看小孩子。

knee [niː] *n.* 膝盖

【例】I got down on my *knees* and pleaded for help. 我跪下来寻求帮助。

knock [nɔk] *n./v.* 敲；打；击

Knife
n. 小刀

【考】1. **knock at/on** 敲打 2. **knock down** 把…撞倒；拆卸 3. **knock into sb.** 撞到某人

labour [ˈleibə]（美 labor）*n.* 劳动，劳力

lab
=laboratory
n. 实验室

【记】旧时的港口（harbour）有很多劳力（labour）

【例】Building a house requires a lot of *labour*. 盖一栋房子需要大量的劳力。

lack [læk] *n./v.* 缺乏，缺少

*lamb
n. 小羊

【例】There is a *lack* of trust between us. 我们之间缺乏信任。

*lame [leim] *adj.* 跛的，残废的

【记】发音记忆："累母"→孩子瘸了，当母亲的当然累了

lame
"累母"

【例】the *lame* person 跛子

lamp [læmp] *n.* 灯，油灯；光源

【例】the electric *lamp* 电灯

land [lænd] *n.* 陆地 *v.* 登陆；降落

【例】dry *land* 旱地 // The pilot *landed* the plane safely. 驾驶员使飞机安全降落。

【考】**land on...** （飞机等）降落于…

*lantern [ˈlæntən] *n.* 灯笼

【记】Lantern Festival 元宵节，即灯笼节

单元自测

1. He _____ smoking in order to keep fit.
   A. got down to   B. intended not to
   C. managed to break away   D. tried to give up

2. It is believed that if a book is _____, it will surely _____ the reader.
   A. interested; interest   B. interesting; be interested
   C. interested; be interesting   D. interesting; interest

3. When first _____ to the market, these products enjoyed great success.
   A. introducing   B. introduced   C. introduce   D. being introduced

4. It is well known that Thomas Edison _____ the electric lamp.
   A. invented   B. discovered   C. found   D. developed

5. We _____ her to join us, but she refused.
   A. persuaded   B. made   C. insisted   D. invited

6. China, the world's most populous nation, _____ the WTO on November 10, 2001, _____ China a new place at the table of nations.
   A. attended; given   B. joined; offering
   C. joined; offered   D. took part in; giving

7. When I got home, I found the door open. A terrible thought suddenly _____ me— had anyone broken into the house?
   A. struck   B. beat   C. knocked   D. attacked

8. There was a second knock at the door. It was the second time I _____ that evening.
   A. was interrupted   B. was interrupting
   C. had interrupted   D. had been interrupted

9. —How does it happen that your business goes wrong?
   —But I have done all that is _____ by law.

A. requested B. judged   C. desired   D. required

10. —What did you say to me?

  —Nothing, I _____ to myself.

  A. just talked   B. was just talked

  C. have just talked   D. was just talking

11. It's very important for a student to _____ a good state of mind while taking the college entrance examination.

  A. keep up   B. keep on   C. keep off   D. keep out

12. It is not my _____ to argue with you.

  A. aim   B. goal   C. intention   D. object

13. You should go and visit your old parents at _____.

  A. sometimes B. interval   C. intervals   D. frequency

14. The little boy asked his friends not to make _____ of him.

  A. laugh   B. fun   C. joy   D. joke

15. Jack's younger sister is three years _____ to him.

  A. junior   B. prior   C. senior   D. later

答案：DDBAD BADDA ACCBA

All that you do, do with your might; things done by halves are never done right.

               —Stoddard

做一切事情都应尽力而为，不可半途而废。

            ——斯托达德

Word List 24

★ **lap** ［læp］ *n.* 大腿；（跑道的）一圈

last ［lɑːst；læst］ *adj./adv.* 最近，最后 *v.* 持续，维持

【例】The *last* person to arrive was Tom. 最后到的是汤姆。//When did you *last* go on vacation? 你最近一次度假是在什么时候？//This table should *last* a lifetime. 这张桌子够用一辈子。

【考】1. **at last** 最后，最终 2. **the last but one** 倒数第二

【衍】lasting（*adj.* 耐久的，持久的）；last name（*n.* 姓）

latter ［ˈlætə］ *n.*（两者之中的）后者

【例】I offered Robert peas and carrots, and he chose the *latter*. 我拿出了豌豆和胡萝卜，罗伯特选择了后者。

laughter ［ˈlɑːftə；ˈlæftə］ *n.* 笑，笑声

【例】I heard my friends' *laughter*, so I asked them what was so funny. 我听见了朋友的笑声，便问他们什么这么好笑。

*****laundry** ［ˈlɔːndri］ *n.* 洗衣店；要洗的衣服

lay ［lei］ *v.*（laid, laid, laying）放，搁；产（卵）

*****league** ［liːg］ *n.* 联盟，社团

【记】联想记忆：联盟（league）成员都是同事（colleague）

【例】National Football *League* 国际足球联盟

leak ［liːk］ *v.* 漏，泄漏

【例】Water *leaked* from the cracked glass. 水从破玻璃杯中渗出。

least ［liːst］ *n.* 最少，最少量

【例】He was the one who did the *least* of the work and got the most of the money. 他就是那个干活最少、拿钱最多的人。

【考】**at least** 至少

leather [ˈleðə] *n.* 皮革

【记】联想记忆：天气（weather）对皮（leather）毛（feather）制品的保存有影响

leave [liːv] *v.* (left, left, leaving) 离开；留下；遗忘

【用】1. leave 表示让…处于某种状态时，接复合宾语，宾补是现在分词、过去分词、形容词、介词短语等：Don't leave the water running while you brush your teeth. 你刷牙时不要让水一直流着。2. 表示把某物"忘在某地方"时，用leave，不可用forget：I left my bag at home. 我把包忘在家里了。

【考】1. leave for... 前往…，去… 2. leave out 遗漏；不考虑 3. leave alone 不管，不理会

(手写) lecture n. 讲课演讲

(手写) leg n. 腿

legal [ˈliːgəl] *adj.* 法律的，法定的

【例】He is the only *legal* heir of the rich man. 他是这位富翁的惟一法定继承人。

length [leŋθ] *n.* 长，长度

【考】at length 最后；详细地：At length we arrived at our destination. 我们终于到达了目的地。

let [let] *vt.* (let, let, letting) 让

【用】let sb. do sth. 让某人做某事：Let them do it themselves. 让他们自己去干吧。

【考】1. let alone 更不用说 2. let out 放走；泄漏 3. let off 排放 4. let in 让…进来；使陷入

(手写) ＊lemon n. &a 柠檬

(手写) ＊lemonade n. 柠檬汁

(手写) lend (lent, lent) n. 把…借给

【辨】let's, let us

let's, let us 都有"让我们做…"之意。let's包含说话者，反义疑问句中用"shall we"；let us 一般不包括说话者，反义疑问句和其他祈使句一样，用"will you"。

level [ˈlevl] *n.* 水平线，水平 *adj.* 平坦的

【例】the *level* of water in the bottle 瓶中的水位 // high *level* 高水平

＊**liberation** [ˌlibəˈreiʃən] *n.* 解放

【例】the African *liberation* movements 非洲解放运动

＊**liberty** [ˈlibəti] *n.* 自由

【记】图书馆（library）内享受阅览自由（liberty）

＊**librarian** [laiˈbreəriən] *n.* 图书管理员，图书馆馆长

179

【记】librar（y）（图书馆）+ian（人）→图书馆馆长

license ['laisəns] n. 执照，许可证

librarian

【记】发音记忆：“来审视”→审视合格才能发执照→执照

【例】driving *license* 驾驶执照

lie [lai] n. 谎言 vi.（lay, lain, lying）躺，卧，平放；位于 vt.（lied, lied, lying）说谎

【例】*lie* detector 测谎仪//The newspaper is *lying* next to the couch. 报纸在床旁边。//*Lie* still and don't make any noise. 躺着别动，也不要制造任何噪音。

【考】1. **a white lie** 善意的谎言 2. **lie down** 躺下 3. **lie in** 存在于

lift [lift] n.（美 *elevator*）电梯 vt. 举起，抬起 vi. 升起，（云、烟等）消散

【例】wait for the *lift* 等电梯 // Please *lift* the box and put it on the table. 请把盒子抬起来放到桌子上。

light [lait] n. 光，灯，灯光 vi.（lit / lighted, lit / lighted, lighting）点（火），变亮 adj. 明亮的；轻的；浅色的

【考】**light up** 点燃，亮起来：The good news lit Jane's face up. 那个好消息让简的脸熠熠生辉。

lightning ['laitniŋ] n. 闪电

【记】联想记忆：light（光）+ning→极强的光→闪电

lightning

like [laik] n. 爱好 prep. 像，跟…一样 v. 喜欢，喜爱

【辨】**like, as**

两词都有“像…”之意，但用法却不同，不可以互换。**like**一般用作介词，其后接名词或代词，不接从句。如：He cried like a baby. 他哭得像个小孩子。而**as**用作连词，其后往往接从句，如：Do exactly as I say. 照我说的办。另外**as**也可用作介词，但意思是“作为，以…身份”，如：He used his umbrella as a walking-stick. 他把雨伞当作手杖用。

likely ['laikli] adj. 很可能的

【用】**be likely to** 可能：Jim is likely to have a higher salary. 吉姆很有可能得到更高的薪水。

limit [ˈlimit] *vt.* 限制，限定；减少

【例】My mother *limits* the amount of food that I eat. 我母亲限制我的饭量。

line [lain] *n.* 直线，排 *v.* 画线于，(使)成行

【例】We waited in *line* for an hour to buy tickets. 我们排了一个小时的队去买票。

【考】**be in line** 排成一行，成直线

link [liŋk] *v.* 连接，联合 *n.* 链环，链接

【例】Many people *link* the number 13 with bad luck. 许多人把13和霉运联系在一起。

lion n. 狮子

lip n.

liquid n.&a.

literature [ˈlitəritʃə] *n.* 文学

【衍】literary (*adj.* 文学的)

litre [ˈliːtə] (美liter) *n.* 升；公升(容量单位)

【记】联想记忆：metre(米)是长度单位，litre(公升)是体积单位

litter [ˈlitə] *v.* 乱丢杂物

【记】把little的"l"乱丢，错拿放成"r"→乱扔

【例】The park was *littered* with beer cans. 公园里，啤酒罐丢得到处都是。

little [ˈlitl] *adj.* (less, least) 小的；少的

【考】1. **a little** 一些，一点 2. **not a little** 很多；非常 3. **little by little** 逐渐地

live [liv] *vi.* 生活，居住 *vt.* 过着，经历 *adj.* 活的；直播的

【例】Although Lucy is 26 now, she still *lives* with her parents. 尽管露西已经26岁了，但她还和父母住在一起。

【考】1. **lead/live a...life** 过着…的生活 2. **live on...** 以…为生 3. **live off** 靠…生活

lively [ˈlaivli] *adj.* 活泼的；充满生气的

【例】Everyone had fun at the *lively* party. 在那个生动有趣的舞会上，大家玩得都很开心。

【辨】**alive, living, lively**

alive和**living**用来指活着并继续生存的生物体，**alive**为表语形容词，常用来作表语，如：Is the tiger still alive? 那只老虎还活着吗？**alive**也可作后置定语，此时等同于**living**，如：There isn't a dinosaur living (=alive) today. 如今没有活着的恐龙了。**living**一般

置于名词前(也可置于名词后)。**lively**意为"活泼的",常用来作表语或宾语补足语,如: The teacher tried to make his class lively and interesting. 老师试着把课讲得生动有趣。

load [ləud] *n.* 担子,货物

【例】I set down my heavy *load* when I reached the bus station. 到达公交车站时,我把重担卸了下来。

*loaf [ləuf] *n.* 一个面包

local [ˈləukl] *adj.* 当地的,地方的

【例】the *local* government 当地政府

lonely [ˈləunli] *adj.* 孤独的,寂寞的

【例】She feels rather *lonely* in the strange town. 在这座陌生的城市里,她感到很寂寞。

【辨】**alone, lonely**

alone强调不和他人在一起但并不意味不快乐,**lonely**常指痛苦地意识到自己独自一人,如: Tom is alone in the room, but he doesn't feel lonely. 汤姆独自在房间里,但他不感到孤单。**alone**为表语形容词,**lonely**既可作表语也可作定语。

loose [lu:s] *adj.* 松散的,宽松的

【例】I had to wear a belt because my pants were so *loose*. 因为裤子太松了,我得系皮带。

loose

lose [lu:z] *vt.* (lost, lost, losing) 失去,丢失

【例】*lose* weight 减肥//*Lost* & Found 失物招领处//*lose* the game 输了比赛

【衍】loss* (*n.* 丧失;损耗)

*lounge [laundʒ] *n.* 休息厅,休息室

【记】loung(看作long长的)+e→躺在长椅上休息→休息厅

luggage [ˈlʌgidʒ] *n.* (总称)行李

【例】My *luggage* was stolen at the bus station. 我的行李在公交车站被偷了。

mad [mæd] *adj.* 发疯的,生气的

【例】If your parents get *mad*, you could try to have a conversation with them about it. 如果惹父母生气了，你可以试着通过交谈来解决。

magic ['mædʒik] *n.* 魔法，魔术 *adj.* 有魔力的

maid n.女佣

【例】Do you believe in *magic*? 你相信魔法吗？

【衍】magical （*adj.* 魔术的；不可思议的）; magician （*n.* 魔术师）

magic

main [mein] *adj.* 主要的

mail n.及v.邮政

【例】*main* idea 大意//*main* building 主楼

【衍】mainly （*adv.* 主要地）

mainland ['meinlænd] *n.* 大陆

【记】组合词：main（主要的）+land（陆地）→大陆

【例】the Antarctic *mainland* 南极洲大陆

单元自测

1. —Is it your favourite place?
   —On the contrary, it's the _____ place that I want to visit.
   A. worst   B. last   C. best   D. latest

2. If only he _____ quietly as the doctor instructed, he would not suffer so much now.
   A. lies   B. lay   C. had lain   D. should lie

3. Hundreds of jobs _____ if the factory closes.
   A. lose   B. will be lost   C. are lost   D. will lose

4. There seems to be nothing _____ to do but _____ for the doctor.
   A. leave; send   B. left; to send   C. left; send   D. leaving; send

5. Bill, often regarded as one of the best students in his class, _____ to be a student who cheated in the exam.
   A. came out   B. turned out   C. sent out   D. let out

6. He is ill and has _____ in bed for two days already.
   A. lied   B. lain   C. laid   D. layed

7. The speaker _____ his voice so as to be heard.
   A. increased   B. lifted   C. rose   D. raised

8. Jack doesn't look _____ his father, but he walks _____ his father does.
   A. as, as   B. like, like   C. as, like   D. like as

9. My parents are _____ to come to the school tomorrow.

A. possibly   B. likely   C. probable   D. possible

10. The expenses should _____ what you can really afford.

    A. limit to   B. be limited to   C. not beyond   D. not over

11. The street has changed a lot and it _____ many high buildings.

    A. has been put up   B. is lined with

    C. has appeared   D. has been added to

12. —Shall I tell Ann how to improve her English speaking?

    —Yes, but _____ of suggestions may discourage her.

    A. a list too long   B. a too long list

    C. too long a list   D. a list of too long

13. The accident is _____ fresh in my memory than when it happened.

    A. little   B. more   C. no less   D. without

14. The lessons given by Mr. Smith are always _____ and interesting.

    A. lovingly   B. lovely   C. lively   D. vividly

15. Although the old man lives in a small house _____, he never feels _____.

    A. lonely; lonely   B. alone; alone   C. alone; lonely   D. lonely; alone

答案：BCBCB BDDBB BCCCC

The tragedy of life is not so much what men suffer, but what they miss.
                —*Carlyle*

生活的悲剧不在于人们受到多少苦，而在于人们错过了什么。
                ——卡莱尔

Word List 25

major [ˈmeidʒə] *adj.* 主要的，成年的 *n.* 主修专业
【例】The waste produced by *major* industries is harmful to both nature and human life. 主要工业产生的废物对自然界和人类的生活都有危害。//What is your *major*? 你的专业是什么？

majority [məˈdʒɔriti; məˈdʒɔːriti] *n.* 多数
【例】The *majority* was/were in favour of banning smoking. 大多数人支持禁烟。
【衍】minority（*n.* 少数，少数民族）

make [meik] *vt.* (made, made, making) 制造，做；使成为
【用】make后接复合宾语时，可以充当宾补的有名词、形容词、非谓语动词等。主要句型有：1. **make+宾语+do sth.** 使宾语做…：The announcement made the whole world cheer. 这个宣告使全世界的人都欢呼起来。//Mama made him clean up the plate. 妈妈让他洗盘子。注意：如改为被动句，宾补必须是to do形式：He was made to clean up the plate by mama. 妈妈让他洗盘子。可用于该句型的动词还有feel, hear, let, watch, see等。2. **make+宾语+adj.** 使宾语…：Having fun with friends makes us happy. 和朋友一起玩儿使我们快乐。可用于该句型的动词还有feel, find, think, drive等。3. **make+宾语+n.** 使宾语成为…：The contest made her a star. 这次比赛使她成了明星。可用于该句型的动词还有elect, choose, consider, name, call等。4. **make+宾语+done**，使宾语被…：When we talk with others we make ourselves understood not just by words. 当我们与他人交谈时，并不仅仅靠语言来让别人理解。5. 如果补是不定式或从句，常常使用形式宾语的句型，即**make+n. +宾语**：People in the west make it a rule to buy Christ for their relatives and friends. 西方人把给亲朋好友一种惯例。可用于该句型的动词还有feel, find

【考】1. **make money** 挣钱 2. **make bed** 整理床铺 3. **make a living** 谋生 4. **make use of** 利用 5. **make up of** 构成 6. **make up one's mind** 下决心 7. **make sure** 保证，确保 8. **make out** 做，理解 9. **make sense** 有意义 10. **make it** 做成某事，成功

【辨】**be made from, be made of**
两个词组都是"由…制成"的意思，**be made from** 已经无法看出原料的性质、特征等，而 **be made of** 可以看出。如：This kind of paper is made from agricultural waste. 这种纸是由农业废料制成的。//The desk is made of wood. 这张桌子是木头做的。注意：当某物是由多种材料组成时，无论能否看出原料的性质、特征等，均用 be made from。

manage [ˈmænidʒ] *vt.* 管理，达成 *vi.* 应付过去
【记】联想记忆：man（人）+age→人来管理→管理
【用】**manage to do…** 设法做到（manage 后不可接 doing）：We managed to bring the price down. 我们设法把价格降下来。
【例】She *managed* the school very well. 她把学校管理得井井有条。//Can you *manage* another piece of cake? 你还能再吃一块点心吗？//Although they can *manage* without each other, they do better together. 虽然没有对方他们也能应付，但在一起他们能做得更好。
【衍】management（*n.* 管理）；managerial（*adj.* 管理的）；manager（*n.* 经理）

【辨】**manage to do… , try to do…**
manage to do… 表示"设法做某事"，并已经成功；**try to do…** 则表示"尽力，设法去做某事"，未必成功，如：We managed to solve the problem without your help. 我们在没有你帮助的情况下解决了这个问题。（问题已解决）//We tried to solve the problem without your help. 我们打算在没有你帮助的情况下解决这个问题。（尽力去解决，但未必能解决）

manner [ˈmænə] *n.* 方式；举止；(*pl.*) 礼貌，规矩
【记】联想记忆：man（男人）+ner→做男人就得有风度→风度，礼貌
【例】He has his own *manner* of acting. 他有自己的表演风格。// table *manners* 饭桌礼仪，用餐的规矩
【衍】mannerly（*adj./adv.* 有礼貌的/地）

mankind
M n. 人类

*marathon [ˈmærəθən; ˈmærəθɑn] n. 马拉松

【记】发音记忆

*march n. & v. 行进，行进

【例】Radcliffe won her first *marathon* title in the New York City *Marathon*. 拉德克利夫在纽约市马拉松比赛上赢得了自己的第一个马拉松冠军。

mark [mɑːk] n. 标记；分数 v. 做记号，标记

*market n. 市场

【用】**mark...with...** 做记号：We marked where we were now with X on the map. 我们在地图上自己所处的位置标了一个X的记号。

【例】For some Amercians, automobile is a *mark* of social position. 对于一些美国人来说，汽车是社会地位的标志。//foot *marks* 脚印// Each stone is *marked* with a number. 每块石头都标有号码。

marry [ˈmæri] v. (married, married, marrying) 和…结婚

【记】结婚 (marry) 是令人幸福快乐的 (merry) 事

【用】1. **marry sb.** 和某人结婚 (注意：不用任何介词)：Bill married a famous actress. 比尔娶了一位著名的演员。2. marry和get married 都是非延续性动词，因此不能与表示一段时间的状语连用；表示结婚已有一段时间应用be married：They married fifty years ago. (= They have been married for fifty years.) 他们结婚已有50年了。

【衍】marriage (n. 结婚，婚姻)

*mask [mɑːsk; mæsk] n. 口罩，面罩 (具)，遮盖物 v. 戴面具，掩饰

【例】A man wearing a *mask* robbed the store. 一个头戴面具的男子抢劫了这家商店。

*mass [mæs] n. 众多，大量；(pl.) 群众

【例】*mass*-produced 批量生产的 // The *masses* are the makers of history. 人民群众是历史的创造者。//mass media 大众传媒

mask

【衍】massive (adj. 大量的)

master [ˈmɑːstə; ˈmæstə] vt. 精通，掌握 n. 主人；硕士

*mat n. 垫子

【例】People should work harder to *master* computer use. 人们应该努力掌握计算机的使用。//the *master's* degree 硕士学位

match [mætʃ] v. 相配，相称 n. 比赛；火柴

【例】No warship our enemy had could *match* ours in speed or in fire-power. 敌方的战舰，不论是在速度还是在火力上，都无法和我们的相媲美。// a well-*matched* couple 非常般配的一对儿 //

the final *match* 总决赛

material [mə'tiəriəl] *n.* 材料，原料；物质

【例】building *materials* 建筑材料

*matter ['mætə] *n.* 事情，物质；原因 *vi.* 要紧，有重大关系

【用】**no matter** 无论（与疑问词连用，引导让步状语从句）: No matter where you go, I will follow you. 无论你去哪儿，我都会跟随你。

【例】What's the *matter*? 什么事？ // It doesn't *matter* to me what you do. 你做什么对我并不重要。

【考】1. **as a matter of fact** 实际上 2. **It doesn't matter.** 不要紧，没关系。（用于回答别人的道歉）

*mature [mə'tjuə] *adj.* 成熟的，成年的

【记】联想记忆：自然（nature）中的一切慢慢变得成熟（mature）

【例】She's very *mature* for her age. 相对于她的年龄而言，她已经很成熟了。//A *mature* crocodile can grow up to 20 feet long. 成年鳄鱼可以长到20英尺长。

*maximum ['mæksiməm] *n./adj.* 最大量（的），最大限度（的）

【例】The fine for disobeying the rule of road closures is a *maximum* of $5,000. 违反道路禁行令的最高罚金可达5,000美元。

may [mei] *modal v.* 可以；也许，可能

【例】You *may* leave if you want to. 你想走就可以走了。//Something *may* have happened to her. 她可能出了点什么事。

【辨】**may, might, could**

might 可以作为 **may** 的过去式表示可以做的事情或可能发生的事情；**might** 也可以代替 **may**，这时表示口气委婉或是实现的可能性更小一些。表示可能性时 **may** 和 **might** 常用于肯定句或否定句，不用于疑问句，语气比 **could** 弱。**might** 表示的可能性比 **may** 更小。

mean [mi:n] *v.* (meant, meant, meaning) 意味着，意思是

【用】1. **mean...** 意思是…: What do you mean by saying that? 你说这话是什么意思？ 2. **mean+*n.*/doing/从句** 意味着: I decide to work out the problem even if it means sitting up all night. 我决心要做出这道题，即使这意味着要熬个通宵。3. **mean to do...** 打算做…: I didn't mean to hurt you. 我本意不是要伤害你。

【例】She *meant* more to me than anyone. 对我来说，她比任何人都

重要。

【考】**mean a lot /nothing**（**to...**）（对…）很重要/根本不重要

*means ［miːnz］*n.* 方法，手段

【用】means为单复数同形的名词：What do you think is the fastest means to become a millionaire? 你认为成为百万富翁最快的方法是什么呢？

【例】Plants can defend themselves by using both physical and chemical *means.* 植物可以用物理以及化学的方法保护自己。

【考】1. **by means of** 依靠，凭借：The workers lift the load by means of a crane. 工人们借助起重机把重物吊起。2. **by no means** 绝不：It is by no means easy to finish this paper. 要完成这篇论文一点都不容易。3. **by all means** 尽一切办法，一定

*meanwhile ［'miːnwail; 'miːnhwail］*adv.* 同时

【记】mean（意味）+while（当…的时候）→意味着当…的时候发生…→同时

【例】Your teacher will be back soon. *Meanwhile*, get on with your work. 你们的老师不久就要回来了。现在赶紧做你们的作业。

measure ［'meʒə］*v.* 测量，权衡 *n.* 方法，措施

【用】**take measures**（**to do sth.**）采取措施（做某事）：Governments will take measures to reduce levels of harmful waste. 政府将采取措施减少有害废物。

【例】This building *measures* roughly 200 square meters. 这座建筑大约占地200平方米。//an emergency *measure* 紧急措施

【衍】measurement（*n.* 测量）

medical ［'medikl］*adj.* 医学的，医疗的

【例】*medical* services 医疗服务

*medium ［'miːdiəm］*adj.* 中间的，中等的 *n.*（*pl. media*）媒介

【例】The man is blond and of *medium* height. 那个男人一头金发，中等身材。

【考】**mass media** 大众传媒

meet ［miːt］*v.*（met, met, meeting）遇见，会面；满足 *n.* 集会

【例】It is nice to *meet* you. 很高兴见到你。//*meet* the demands/needs 满足要求//sports *meet* 运动会

*memorial ［mə'mɔːriəl］*n.* 纪念碑，纪念物 *adj.* 纪念的

【例】There is a war *memorial* in the center of town. 市中心有一座战

Meat n.肉

medal n.奖牌,纪念章

Medicine n.药,医学

Meeting n.会,集会

melon n.瓜

189

member
n. 成员

争纪念碑 √
【衍】memory (n. 记忆，回忆)

mend [mend] v. 修理，修补

【例】The hem of my skirt needs *mending*. 我裙子的边儿需要补一下。

mental ['mentl] adj. 精神的，脑力的

【记】发音记忆："满头"→满头大汗，脑力不支→脑力的

【例】Forgiveness can be helpful to your *mental* and physical health. 宽容有助于你的身心健康。//*mental* disorders 精神错乱

mention ['menʃn] vt. 提到，说起 n. 提及

menu
n. 菜单

【例】She doesn't *mention* her daughter in her will. 她在遗嘱中没有提到她的女儿。

【考】1. **mention sth. to sb.** 向某人提起某事 2. **not to mention** 更不用说 3. **Don't mention it.** 不用谢。

*merchant ['mə:tʃənt] n. 商人，生意人 adj. 商业的，商人的

【例】Our city will have an open-air market for *merchants*. 我市将为做生意的人建立一个露天市场。

mercy ['mə:si] n. 怜悯

【例】They will show no *mercy* to you if you are caught. 如果你被抓了，他们绝不会手下留情的。

【考】1. **at the mercy of** 任凭…的摆布 2. **without mercy** 毫不留情地 3. **show mercy to sb.** 同情某人

【衍】merciful* (adj. 仁慈的；宽大的)

*merely ['miəli] adv. 仅仅，只不过

merry
a. 欢乐的

【例】The store *merely* broke even in its first year. 这家商店仅仅开张一年就倒闭了。

*mess [mes] n. 凌乱 v. 弄乱

【考】1. **What a mess!** 太乱了！ 2. **mess (sth.) up=mess up (sth.)** 把东西弄乱；把某事搞砸

【衍】messy* (adj. 乱七八糟的)

message ['mesidʒ] n. 消息，留言；要旨

metal
n. 金属

method
n. 方法

metre
n. 米

【例】If anyone happens to drop in while I am out, have him or her leave a *message*. 如果我不在的时候有人来拜访，让他（她）留个信儿。//What is the *message* of this story? 这篇故事的主旨是什么？

【衍】messenger (n. 报信者，使者)

*microscope ['maikrəskəup] *n.* 显微镜

【记】词根记忆：micro（微）+scope（看）→用来看微小的东西→显微镜

*microwave ['maikrəweiv] *n.* 微波

【记】词根记忆：micro（微）+wave（波）→微波

middle ['midl] *n.* 中间，当中 *adj.* 中部的，中间的，中级的

【例】in the *middle* 在中间// *middle* school 中学// *middle* children 排行中间的孩子// *middle*-aged people 中年人

【辨】**middle, centre**

二者都有"中间"的意思，但 **centre** 常用来指一个准确的点，如：the centre of the city 市中心，而 **middle** 用于不太准确的位置；当考虑事物的长度而不是面积时常用 **middle**，如：I am walking in the middle of the road. 我正在马路中间。**middle** 可以用于时间但 **centre** 不行，如：in the middle of the night 午夜。

midnight
n. 午夜

mild.
a. 温和的

millionaire
n. 百万富翁

mind [maind] *n.* 思想 *v.* 介意

【用】1. **mind + doing**：介意…：He doesn't mind lending you his dictionary. 他不介意把字典借给你。//I hope you don't mind my asking, but where did you buy those shoes? 希望你不介意我问一下，你的鞋子从哪里买的？2. **Do/Would you mind + doing.../+if...?** 用于请求对方同意或帮忙：I'll be away on a business trip. Would you mind looking after my cat? 我要出差，你介意照顾我的小猫吗？// Do you mind if I sit here? 我坐这儿你介意吗？注意：在回答 Do/Would you mind...? 的问句时，如表示不介意常用：Of course not./Not at all./No, please. 等；如果表示介意常用：I'm sorry but I do.

【考】1. **absent-minded** 心不在焉的，**open-minded** 思想开放的，**single-minded** 坚决的 2. **Never mind.** 没关系 3. **keep...in mind** 牢记在心 4. **make up one's mind** 下定决心 5. **change one's mind** 改变主意

mine [main] *n.* 矿藏 *v.* 开采，挖掘 *pron.* 我的（名词性物主代词）

【例】coal *mine* 煤矿

【衍】miner（*n.* 矿工）

*mineral ['minərəl] *n.* 矿物质，矿物

【记】mine（矿）+ral→矿物质

【例】*mineral* water 矿泉水

191

*minimum [ˈminiməm] *n.* 最小量，最小值 *adj.* 最小的

【记】mini（小的）+mum→最小的

【例】The *minimum* you would pay for a double room in a central area is $50 a person in our city. 我市中心地区的旅店双人间的最低价位是每位50美元。

【衍】minimize（*v.* 最小化）

*minister [ˈministə] *n.* 部长；牧师

【例】the Prime *Minister* 首相//the Foreign *Minister* 外交部长

*ministry [ˈministri] *n.* （政府的）部门

【例】the *Ministry* of National Defense 国防部

minority [maiˈnɔrəti] *n.* 少数；少数民族

【记】minor（较小的）+ity（名词后缀）→少数

【例】Some people want change, but they're in the *minority*. 有些人想要变革，但他们只是少数人。

minus [ˈmainəs] *adj.* 负的 *prep.* 减去

mirror
M n.镜子

【记】联想记忆：min（看作mini小的）+us→把东西变小→减去

【例】The right answer is *minus* 6. 正确答案是负6。// 200 *minus* 100 makes 100. 200减去100等于100。

miss [mis] *v.* 错过；想念

*missile
n.导弹 发射

【用】**miss+n./+doing**（不能接to do作宾语）：He missed the bus. 他没赶上车。//He barely missed being killed by a car. 他差点被汽车撞死。

【衍】missing（*adj.* 丢失的，迷路的，不见了的）；unmissable（*adj.* 不应失误的）

mistake [miˈsteik] *v.* (mistook, mistaken, mistaking) 弄错 *n.* 错误

【记】mis（错）+take（拿）→拿错→弄错

【考】1. **make a mistake=make mistakes** 犯错误 2. **by mistake** 错误地：His luggage was removed by mistake. 他的行李被误拿了。 3. **mistake...for...** 错把…当作…

【衍】mistaken（*adj.* 错误的）；mistakenly（*adv.* 错误地）

misunderstand [ˌmisˌʌndəˈstænd] *vt.* (misunderstood, misunderstood, misunderstanding) 误会，不理解

【记】mis（错）+understand（理解）→理解错误→误会

【例】You *misunderstood* my words. 你误解了我的话。

【衍】misunderstanding（*n.* 误会，误解）

mix ［miks］*v.* 混合，搅拌

mixture n. 混合物

【例】No matter what society it is, men and women *mix* socially on a day-to-day basis. 不论在什么社会，男女每天少不了要打交道。

【考】**mix up** 弄乱；混淆：Don't mix up all my important papers. 不要把我的重要文件弄乱了。

【衍】mixture（*n.* 混合物）

✱ mobile ［'məubail; 'məubl］*adj.* 活动的，可移动的

✱modem n. 调制解调器

【记】英里（mile）是活动的（mobile）距离

【考】**mobile phone=cell phone** 移动电话，手机

modest ［'mɔdist］*adj.* 谦虚的，谦逊的

model n 模型式样

【例】He's too *modest* to tell you he's the champion. 他很谦虚，不会告诉你他就是冠军。

moral ［'mɔrəl; 'mɔːrəl］*adj.* 道德的，精神的 *n.* 道德，寓意

modern a.现代化的

【例】I can't help your plan with money, but I'll give you *moral* support. 我拿不出钱来支持你们的计划，但是我会给你们精神上的支持。

mommy n.妈妈

【衍】morally（*adv.* 道德上地）；morality（*n.* 道德）

monitor n.班长　*month n.月*　*✱monument n.纪念.*　*✱mop n&v.拖把*

M

单元自测

1. She talked a lot, but we couldn't _____ what she meant.

   A. make up　　　B. make out of　　C. make up of　　D. make out

2. —How can you _____ with so few people and so little money?

   —It's really a hard job.

   A. deal　　　B. manage　　　C. do　　　D. come

3. —Excuse me. Is this the right way to the Summer Palace?

   —Sorry, I am not sure. But it _____ be.

   A. might　　　B. will　　　C. must　　　D. can

4. _____ words and expressions have come into the language from American English.

   A. A great many　　　　　B. A great deal of

   C. A large amount of　　　D. The number of

5. The lion is considered the king of the forest as it is a(n) _____ of courage and power.

   A. example　　　B. sign　　　C. mark　　　D. symbol

6. My uncle _____ until he was forty-five.

    A. married   B. didn't marry   C. was not marrying D. would marry

7. The life of London is made up of many different _____.   （2001上海）

    A. elements   B. sections   C. materials   D. realities

8. I've visited a lot of different places and stayed in a lot of different hotels, and nothing else _____ this one.

    A. takes   B. matches   C. makes   D. compares

9. Mr. Brown did not believe that such things _____ much.

    A. minded   B. happened   C. troubled   D. mattered

10. Johnny, you _____ play with the knife, you _____ hurt yourself.

    A. won't; can't   B. mustn't; may   C. shouldn't; must D. can't; shouldn't

11. —Why haven't you bought any butter?

    —I _____ to but I forgot about it.

    A. liked   B. wished   C. meant   D. expected

12. Though _____ rich, he was better off than at any other period in his life.

    A. by any means   B. by some means

    C. by all means   D. by no means

13. —How about eight o'clock outside the cinema?

    —That _____ me fine.

    A. fits   B. meets   C. satisfies   D. suits

14. —James, I am sorry I used your computer when you were away this morning.

    — _____.

    A. That's all right   B. It's a pleasure

    C. You are welcome   D. Don't mention it

15. No matter what you do, you should put your _____ into it.

    A. mind   B. heart   C. brain   D. thought

答案：BADDC BDBAB DAAAB

Word List 26

more [mɔ:] (much/many的比较级) *adj.* 更多的 *adv.* 更 *pron.* 更多的…；另外的…

【用】1. more作副词，除了与至少有两个音节的形容词或副词构成比较级，还可以修饰动词：I couldn't agree with you more. 我非常赞同你的意见。2. more作代词，可以和many, much, some, any, no, a few, a little等以及数词连用：I couldn't eat any more. 我再也吃不下了。//I'll take three more. 我再要三个。

【例】I need one *more* stamp before my collection is completed. 我还需要一枚邮票才能完成我的收集。

【考】1. **more or less** 或多或少，大体上 2. **more than** 多于，超过 3. **no more than** 不过，仅仅，和…一样都不 4. **not more than** 至多；不比…更… 5. **what's more** 而且，此外，更有甚者 6. **more and more** 越来越 7. **the more..., the more...** 越…，越… 8. **once more** 再一次 9. **no more = not... any more** 不再

【辨】no more than, not more than

二者在数量上进行比较的时候**no more than**=only是"仅仅、只有"的意思，如：There are no more than 8 chairs in the room. 屋子里只有8把椅子。而**not more than** = the most是"最多、不超过"的意思，如：There are not more than 8 chairs in the room. 屋子里最多有8把椅子。二者在程度上进行比较的时候**no more than**是"两者都不"的意思，如：A is no more important than B. A和B都不重要。而**not more than**是"比不上、不及"的意思，如：A is not more important than B. A没有B重要。

motivation [ˌməutiˈveiʃən] *n.* 动机

【例】What is your *motivation* to quit your job? 你辞

motto [ˈmɔtəu] *n.* 箴言，格言

【例】Our team's *motto* is "Be the Best." 我们队的座右铭是"永争第一"。

*mountainous ['mauntinəs] *adj.* 多山的

【记】mountain（山）+ous→多山的

【例】Mountain lions live in *mountainous* areas of the western United States. 美洲狮生长在美国西部的多山地区。

*mourn [mɔːn] *v.* 哀痛；哀悼

【例】She is still *mourning* the death of her father. 她仍然在为父亲的逝世哀悼。

move [muːv] *v.* 移动，搬动，搬家

【例】Don't *move*! 不许动！

【考】1. move up 上升 2. move on 继续前进 3. move about 来回走动 4. move out 搬出 5. move around 走来走去

【衍】movement（*n.* 运动，活动）；remove（*v.* 移动；搬家）

multiply ['mʌltiplai] *v.* (multiplied, multiplied, multiplying)（使）相乘；增加

【记】词根记忆：multi（多）+ply→变多→增加

【例】Eight *multiplied* by one equals eight. 8乘以1等于8。

murder ['məːdə] *n./v.* 谋杀

【例】A man is being questioned in relation to the *murder*. 一名男子因涉嫌谋杀正在接受审问。

murder

*musical ['mjuːzikəl] *adj.* 音乐的，爱好音乐的 *n.* 音乐喜剧

【记】music（音乐）+al→音乐的

【例】*musical* instrument 乐器

must [mʌst] *modal v.* 必须，应当；肯定（表示推测）

【用】1. must 用来表推测时只可用于肯定句，推测现在用must+do/be，推测过去用 must +have +done/been：He looks strange today. Something must have happened to him. 他今天看起来有点奇怪，肯定出了什么事儿。2. 在回答由must引起的问题时，否定的答复常用needn't或don't have to，而不用must not。

【辨】must, have to

have to比较强调客观需要，而must着重说明主观看法，如：I must

mushroom
n. 蘑菇

musical
a&n 音乐的

musician
n. 音乐家

mouse
n. 鼠标

moustache
n. 小胡子

mouth
n. 嘴

move
M v. 移动

movement
n. 运动，活动

mud
n. 泥

muddy
a. 多泥的

*multiply
v. 乘

murder
谋杀

tidy up the room. 我必须把屋子打扫干净。（主观想法）; I have to
tidy up the room. 我不得不把屋子打扫干净。（客观需要）

name [neim] *n.* 名字, 名称 *vt.* 命名, 名叫
【考】**name after** 以…来命名: This island was named after the man
who discovered it. 这个岛是以发现者的名字命名的。
【衍】namely (*adv.* 即, 也就是)

narrow ['nærəu] *adj.* 狭窄的
【例】The street is too *narrow* to run so many cars. 这条街太窄了, 容
不了这么多车。
【衍】narrowly (*adv.* 狭窄地)

nation ['neiʃn] *n.* 民族, 国家
【例】industrialized *nations* 工业国 // the United *Nations* 联合国
【衍】national (*adj.* 国家的, 全国性的); nationality (*n.* 国籍)

*nationwide ['neiʃənwaid] *adj.* 全国性的
【记】组合词: nation (国家) + wide (广阔的) → 遍及全国 → 全国性的
【例】Police carried out an *nationwide* manhunt to catch that murder.
警察展开了全国搜捕以抓获凶手。

native ['neitiv] *adj.* 本土的, 本国的
【例】*native* language 母语

nature ['neitʃə] *n.* 自然; 性质
【例】I love getting close to *nature*. 我十分喜欢亲近大自然。
【考】**by nature** 生来
【衍】natural (*adj.* 自然的); naturally (*adv.* 自然地); unnatural (*adj.*
不自然的)

near [niə] *prep.* 在…附近, 靠近 *adj.* 近的 *adv.* 附近, 邻近
【例】The missing boys were last seen playing *near* the river. 人们最
后一次看见那些走失的男孩们时, 他们在河边玩耍。// in the *near*
future 在不久的将来

nearby ['niə'bai] *adj.* 附近的 *adv.* 在附近
【例】There was an old man sitting quietly on a bench *nearby*. 有位老
人静静地坐在附近的长凳上。

【辨】**near, close**
二者意思几乎相同, 但是在某些短语的搭配中不可互换, 如: the

near future 不久的将来//the near distance 近处，它们中的 **near** 不可用 **close** 替换；同样 a close friend 密友//close behind 紧随中的 **close** 亦不可用 **near** 替换。

nearly ［'niəli］*adv.* 将近；几乎

【例】This blue star sapphire is worth *nearly* six hundred thousand dollars. 这颗蓝宝石的价值将近60万美元。

【辨】**nearly, almost**

这两个单词都有"几乎"的意思，在肯定句中和动词否定形式前可以互换，如：I almost/nearly didn't wake up on time. 我几乎睡过了头。主要不同在于：**almost** 可以和 any, no, none, never, nobody, nothing 连用，但是 **nearly** 不可。如：Almost no one knows it. 几乎没人知道这件事。

necessary ［'nesisəri］*adj.* 必需的，必要的

【例】It's *necessary* to be prepared for a job interview. 在面试前做好准备是很有必要的。

【衍】unnecessary（*adj.* 不必要的）

need ［ni:d］*vt.* 需要 *modal v.* 必须 *n.* 需要，需求

【用】1. need 用作情态动词，通常用于否定句和疑问句：—Need you go now? —No, I needn't. / Yes, I must. —你现在必须走吗？—不，不必。/是的，必须走。2. **needn't have done ...** 本不必做…（实际已做）：Catherine, you needn't have cleaned my room; I could manage it myself. 凯瑟琳，你不必打扫我的房间的，我自己能行。3. 主语是物时，need 后面常用 doing 形式来表示被动（也可以用不定式的被动式）：Your hair needs cutting.（=Your hair needs to be cut.）你的头发需要剪了。类似用法的动词还有 want, require, demand 等。

【例】You don't *need* to describe her, because I have met her several times. 你不用给我形容她长什么样子，我已经见过她几次了。

*negotiate ［ni'gəuʃieit］*v.* 谈判，协商

【例】They are *negotiating* a new contract. 他们就一份新的合同进行谈判。

neighbourhood ［'neibəhud］（美 neighborhood）*n.* 四邻，邻近地区

【记】neighbour（邻居）+hood→四邻

N

neck
n. 颈，脖子

necklace
n. 项链

【例】Tim and Jane live in the same *neighbourhood*. 提姆和简住得很近。

neither ['naiðə] *adj./pron.*（两者）都不 *conj.* 也不

【用】1. **neither A nor B** 作主语时主谓一致采用就近原则，即根据B的单复数来决定谓语动词和代词的形式：Neither the children nor he has ever had his supper. 他和孩子们都没吃晚餐。如果A、B部分是句子则句子要倒装，如：Neither has he been to Beijing, nor will he do so. 他没有去过北京，也不想去。2. **neither of** 短语作主语时，谓语动词用单数：Neither of her sons goes to college. 她的两个儿子都没上大学。3. **neither/nor+be/have/do+**主语，此结构表示前面的内容也适用于另一个人或物：I have never had a girlfriend. Neither has he. 我从来没有女朋友，他也一样。

【辨】**neither, none**

neither用于否定两者：Neither of my two sisters is here. 我两个姐姐都不在这儿。而 **none** 否定三者或三者以上：None of the pupils knew the answer. 学生中谁都不知道答案。**neither**作主语时，谓语动词为单数，**none**作主语时，谓语动词单复数皆可。

never ['nevə] *adv.* 决不，从来没有

【用】never用于句首时句子要倒装：Never will I forget the day on which I got married. 我永远也忘记不了结婚的那一天。

next [nekst] *adj.* 最近的；紧挨着的，隔壁的；下一次 *adv.* 随后，然后，下一步 *n.* 下一个人（东西）

【例】the *next* day 第二天

【考】**next to** 和…挨着

*****noble** ['nəubl] *adj.* 高贵的，贵族的

【例】Jane was born in a *noble* family. 简出身于一个贵族家庭。

noble

nobody ['nəubədi] *pron.* 没有人，谁也不 *n.* 小人物

【用】1. nobody后面不接of短语，如果要表示某范围中没有一个人，用neither of... 或none of...：To my disappointment, neither of my parents agreed with me. 令我失望的是，父母都不赞同我。2. nobody是否定代词，因此所在句的反意疑问部分要用肯定形式：Nobody was absent from the meeting, were

199

nephew
n. 侄子,外甥

nervous
a. 紧张的

nest
n. 巢,隐蔽处

net
n. 网

network
n. 网络

niece
n. 侄女,外甥女

they? 这次会议没人缺席，是吗？类似的否定代词还有nothing, none, few, little等。

nod [nɔd] *v./n.* (nodded, nodded, nodding) 点头，点

【考】**nod at sb.** 朝某人点头

none [nʌn] *pron.* 无任何东西或人

【用】none作主语时句子谓语动词用单、复数均可：Trees were cut but none were/was planted. 树木只砍不栽。//None of the telephones is/are working. 这些电话中没有一部是可以用的。

【考】**second to none** 最佳的，首届一指的

【辨】**nobody, no one, none**

1. **nobody** 和 **no one** 只能指代人，**none** 既可指代人又可指代物。

2. **no one** 和 **none** 能后接of，**nobody** 无此用法，如能说no one of us或none of us而不能说nobody of us。3. **nobody** 和 **no one** 作主语时，谓语动词用单数，**none** 作主语时谓语动词既可用单数也可用复数。

non-stop [ˌnɔn'stɔp] *adj./adv.* 不停的(地)，不断的(地)

【例】It is a ridiculous idea that someone wants to build a *non-stop* machine. 有人想制造永动机，这想法真是太荒谬了。

nor [nɔː] *conj.* 也不

【例】In this village of 1, 000 persons, half can not read *nor* write. 在这个1,000人的村子里，有一半人不会读和写。

note [nəut] *n.* 便条，笔记，注释 *vt.* 记录，注意

【例】He *noted* that the room was very clean. 他注意到屋子很干净。

【考】**take notes** 做笔记

notice [ˈnəutis] *n.* 通告，注意 *v.* 注意到

【用】notice后可接复合宾语，宾补有do, doing和done三种形式，此时意义和用法类似于see。notice sb. do sth.表示注意到某人做某事的全过程：I noticed you cross the street. 我看到你过了马路。notice sb. doing sth. 强调注意到某人正在做某事，如：I noticed you crossing the street. 我看到你正在过马路。而notice sth. done 表示注意到某物被…，如：No one noticed the flowers on the table changed. 没人注意到桌子上的花被换过。注意类似用法的动词还有hear, watch等。

【考】**take notice of...** 注意…

【衍】noticeable (*adj.* 显而易见的；值得注意的); unnoticed (*adj.* 不引人注意的；被忽视的)

*numb [nʌm] *adj.* 麻木的

【记】数字（number）化的年代让人麻木（numb）

【例】It was so cold that my hands were *numb*. 天这么冷，我的手都冻僵了。

number [ˈnʌmbə] *n.* 数字，号码；数量

【用】the number of + 可数名词复数 + 谓语动词用单数，意为"…的数量"; a number of + 可数名词复数 + 谓语动词用复数，意为"大量的…"。

【例】What is your phone *number*? 你的电话号码是多少？

*nutrition [njuːˈtriʃn;nuːˈtriʃn] *n.* 营养

【记】安利纽崔莱（Nutrilite）提倡有营养的（nutrition）健康生活

【例】Good *nutrition* is important. 营养好很重要。

obey [əˈbei] *v.* 服从，顺从

【例】A soldier's duty is to *obey* orders. 服从命令是士兵的职责。

【衍】disobey (*v.* 违反，不服从)

object [ˈɔbdʒikt] *n.* 物体；目标；宾语

[əbˈdʒekt] *v.* 反对

【记】确定目标（object）和主题（subject）

【例】He can draw without looking at the *object* he draws. 他不看实物凭想像就能把它画出来。

【考】**object to (doing) ...** 反对（做）…: I strongly object to your suggestion. 我强烈反对你的提议。

【衍】objection (*n.* 反对，抗议)

observe [əbˈzəːv] *v.* 观察；遵守

【记】联想记忆: ob（反）+serve（服务）→服务要通过观察才能反映→观察

【用】observe作观察讲时，宾语形式有名词/代词、复合宾语和从句三种，即:

1. **observe+*n./pron.*:** He has observed stars all his life. 他一生都在观察星星。 2. **observe+*n./pron.* +do/doing...**（被动语态为be

observe

observed+to do/doing）: I observed the film star walking in the street. 我见到那个电影明星在街上走。3. **observe+从句**: I observed what was going between my parents. 我注意到我父母之间所发生的事。

【例】*observe* the orbit of the moon 观测月球轨道// Please *observe* the speed limit while driving. 开车时请遵守速度限制。

【衍】observer（*n.* 观察者，观察员）; observation（*n.* 观察）

*obtain [əb'tein] *vt.* 获得，得到

【例】Where did you *obtain* such a thing? 你从哪儿得到的这个东西？

*obvious ['ɔbviəs] *adj.* 明显的，显而易见的

【例】The truth may not always be *obvious*. 真理并不总是显而易见。

【衍】obviously（*adv.* 明显地）

occupy ['ɔkjupai] *vt.* 占领，占据

【例】Caring for the baby *occupies* most of her time. 她的大部分时间都用来照顾宝宝了。

【衍】occupation*（*n.* 占据；职业）

*occur [ə'kə:] *vi.* 发生，出现

【记】词根记忆：oc+cur（跑，发生）→发生，出现，同根词还有：current（*adj.* 当前的）

【例】What you said will never *occur*. 你说的永远也不会发生。

【考】**occur to sb.** 某人想到：A new idea occurred to him. 他想到了一个新主意。

【衍】occurrence（*n.* 发生，出现）

Oceania [ˌəuʃi'einiə] *n.* 大洋洲

【记】ocean（海洋）+ia→被大海环绕的洲→大洋洲

of [ɔv] *prep.* …的

【用】1. 表示范围：Of all choices, this is the best. 所有选择中，这是最好的。2. "of + 抽象名词"相当于这个名词的同根形容词，如：of importance=important，这类抽象名词还有value, use, help等。

【例】The result *of* the experiment was very good. 实验的结果非常理想。//the city *of* Beijing 北京市//an old friend *of* mine 我的一个老朋友

off [ɔf;ɔ:f] *prep./adv.* 离（走）开

【例】have/take a day *off* 休息一天

【考】1. **put off** 推迟，脱下 2. **turn off** 关掉，使转变方向 3. **take off** 起飞 4. **get off** 下车 5. **let off** 投放（炸弹），排放 6. **give off** 发出，

放出(蒸汽、气味等) 7. **set off** 出发，使爆炸 8. **shut off** 关掉，切断
9. **show off** 炫耀 10. **live off** 靠…生活 11. **cut off** 切断，隔绝
12. **run off** 逃跑，流掉 13. **go off** 离开，消失 14. **send off** 寄出，派
遣 15. **be off one's head** 神经错乱

*offence [ə'fens] (美offense) *n.* 犯罪，过错；冒犯，攻击

【记】联想记忆：of+fence（篱笆）→越过了别人家的篱笆→冒犯

【例】Drunk driving is a serious *offence*. 酒后驾车属严重违例。

offer ['ɔfə; 'ɔːfə] *v./n.* 提供，提出，出价

【用】1. **offer sb. sth. (=offer sth. to sb.)** 主动拿给或提供某人某物：
The school offered their students free room and board. 这所学校为学
生提供免费食宿。2. **offer to do...** 主动提出做…：He offered to take
me back home. 他主动提出送我回家。

office ['ɔfis; 'ɔːfis] *n.* 办公室

【例】post *office* 邮局

【衍】officer (*n.* 军官)；official (*n.* 官员；*adj.* 官方的，正式的)

*offshore [ˌɔf'ʃɔː; ˌɔːf'ʃɔː] *adj./adv.* 近海的(地)，向海的(地)

【记】off（离开）+shore（海岸）→稍离开海岸的→近海的

【例】an *offshore* wind 吹向海面的风

单元自测

1. —Have you finished your report yet?

   —No, I'll finish in _____ ten minutes.

   A. another   B. other   C. more   D. less

2. —Tom is never late for work. Why is he absent today?

   —Something _____ to him.

   A. must happen   B. should have happened

   C. could have happened   D. must have happened

3. —I think you might have got drunk at the party.

   —Well, I _____.

   A. mostly did   B. nearly had   C. almost did   D. almost had

4. —Shall I tell John about it?

   —No, you _____. I've told him already.

   A. needn't   B. wouldn't   C. mustn't   D. shouldn't

5. —Can you come on Monday or Tuesday?

   —I'm afraid _____ day is possible.

A. either   B. neither   C. some   D. any

6. I made a call to my parents yesterday. To my disappointment, _____ of them answered it.

    A. either   B. none   C. neither   D. nobody

7. —Do you mind if I open the window?

    — _____ I feel a bit cold.

    A. Of course not.   B. I'd rather you didn't.

    C. Go ahead.   D. Why not?

8. Mary never does any reading in the evening, _____.

    A. so does John   B. John does too   C. John doesn't too   D. nor does John

9. He glanced over at her, _____ that though she was tiny, she seemed very well put together.   （2005广东）

    A. having noted   B. noted   C. to note   D. noting

10. We don't know whether _____ of the students who will pass the college entrance exam is big or small.

    A. a number   B. the number   C. a lot   D. plenty

11. There had been noisy scenes at the end of the match, the losers _____ the final decisions.

    A. objected to   B. objecting to   C. opposing to   D. opposed

12. So far, several ships have been reported missing _____ the coast of Bermuda Island.

    A. off   B. along   C. on   D. around

13. Although the working mother is very busy, she still _____ a lot of time to her children.   （2000上海）

    A. devotes   B. spends

    C. offers   D. provides

14. _____ a boy, the man was taken away by the police.

    A. Supposing to murder   B. Supposed to murder

    C. Supposing to have murdered   D. Supposed to have murdered

15. Mother told Jim to _____ the milk until it boiled and then turn off the gas.

    A. glance   B. watch   C. observe   D. notice

答案：A D C A B   C B D D B   B A D C B

Word List 27

often ['ɔfn; 'ɔːfn] *adv.* 经常地

【例】How *often* do you go to the library? 你多久去一次图书馆?

【考】more often than not 经常, 多半

oil [ɔil] *n.* 油, 石油 *vt.* 给…上油

【记】发音记忆: "哦! 油"→油, 石油

【例】This motor burns less *oil* but works better. 这种发动机耗油更少, 效率更高。//The machine needs to be *oiled*. 这台机器需要上油了。

【衍】oily (*adj.* 油的); oilfield* (*n.* 油田)

old [əuld] *adj.* 老的, 旧的

【例】the *old* people 老年人//the *Old* English 古英语

【辨】older, elder

older和elder都有"年长"的意思。older可用来指人或物, 而elder只能用来指人并且不可用在比较级中, 如: Jane is Mary's elder sister. 简是玛丽的姐姐。Jane is older than Mary. 简比玛丽年纪大。(此时就不能用elder)。elder本身就可以作名词而older不可以。

on [ɔn] *prep.* 在…上, 在…时候, 在…地方, 关于 *adv.* 继续

【用】1. 涉及具体某天的时间用on: on Friday 在星期五//on that afternoon 在那天下午//on Christmas Eve 在圣诞夜 2. **on + n./doing...** 一…就…: On his arrival, I told him what had happened. 他一到, 我就告诉他发生了什么事情。

【考】1. **on the moment** 立刻 2. **on time** 按时, 准时 3. **on holiday/vacation** 度假 4. **on the other hand** 另一方面 5. **on the contrary** 正相反 6. **on the /one's way**(to)在…的路上 7. **on the whole** 基本上, 大体上 8. **on show** 在展出 9. **on and on** 继续不停的 10. **on dut-** 班; 上班 11. **on one's own** 独立地, 自主地 12. **on foot** 步行

once [wʌns] *n./adv.* 一次；曾经 *conj.* 一旦

【例】I go to school *once* a week. 我每周上一次课。// *Once* you meet her you'll never forget her. 你一旦见到她就永远也忘不了她。

【考】1. **at once** 立刻，马上；同时 2. **once again=once more** 再一次 3. **once in a while** 偶尔 4. **all at once** 突然

one [wʌn] *num.* 一 — *pron.* 一个（人或物）；任何人（泛指）

【用】one作代词，代替前文出现过的可数名词，表示单数用one，表示复数用ones：We've been looking for houses but haven't found one we like yet. 我们一直在看房子，但是还没有找到一个喜欢的。//Cars do cause us some health problems—in fact far more serious ones than mobile phones do. 汽车的确导致一些健康问题——实际上比手机导致的健康问题严重得多。

【考】1. **one at a time** 一次一个 2. **at one time** 曾经；同时 3. **one by one** 一个接一个 4. **one-way** 单行的 5. **one more+**n. 再来一个… 6. **one day** 有一天；总有一天 7. **one another**（三人或三人以上）互相 8. **at one time or another** 曾经

【衍】oneself（*pron.* 亲自，自己）

【辨】**one, ones, that, those, it**
这五个代词都可以指代前面出现过的名词，以避免重复。**one**和**ones**只能代替可数名词，具有泛指性质，往往带有修饰语，如：This question is one of great importance. 这个问题很重要。**that**和**those**具有特指性质，**that**常用于代替不可数名词，**those**代替可数名词复数，如：Life in city is quite different from that in country. 城市生活和乡村生活非常不同。//The buildings in the capital are taller than those in other cities. 首都的建筑比其他城市的高大。**one**和**it**都可以代替上文提到的单数名词，但one用于泛指，相当于a+名词，**it**用于特指，相当于the+名词，如：I prefer a flat in the downtown to one（=a flat）in the suburb. 我更喜欢市中心而不是郊区的公寓。//The Parkers bought a new house but it（=the house）will need a lot of work before they can move in. 帕克夫妇买了一所新房子，但是那所房子需要好好收拾后才能入住。

onion [ˈʌnɪən] *n.* 洋葱

【记】联想记忆：on+i+on，记住它的结构就像洋葱的皮，一层一层

only [ˈəʊnlɪ] *adj.* 惟一的，仅有的 *adv.* 只，仅仅

【用】1. **only + to do** 想不到；结果只是（表示紧跟着上文动作的出人意料或不幸的结果）：The news reporters hurried to the airport, only to be told the film stars had left. 记者匆忙赶到机场，想不到被告知影星们已经离开了。2. only修饰的状语或状语从句放在句首，句子要用部分倒装的结构，如：Only then did I understand what she meant. 直到那时我才明白她的意思。//Only when the war was over was he able to go back home. 直到战争结束后，他才得以重返家乡。注意：如果only修饰的是主语，句子不要倒装，如：Only he has been friendly. 只有他是友好的。

【例】I am an *only* child. 我是独生子。// I'm *only* 15. 我年仅15岁。

【考】1. **not only...but**（**also**）**...** 不但，而且 2. **if only** 但愿，要是…就好了（需用虚拟语气）

open [ˈəupən] *adj.* 公开的，开着的 *v.* 打开，公开

【例】The door is *open*. 门开着。// They are aiming at *opening* up new markets. 他们打算打开新的市场。

【考】1. **open-air** 露天的 2. **open up** 展开；开张：She wanted to open up an Internet café. 她想开一家网吧。

【衍】openly（*adv.* 公开地）；opening*（*n.* 开放，口子）

*****opera** [ˈɔprə] *n.* 歌剧

【记】歌剧（opera）开始（open）了

【例】*opera* house 歌剧院

operate [ˈɔpəreit] *v.* 动手术；操作，运转

【例】The machine *operates* best at high speeds. 机器在高速运转时状态最佳。

【考】**operate on sb.** 给某人动手术

【衍】operation（*n.* 手术；操作）；operator（*n.* 操作者）

opinion [əˈpinjən] *n.* 看法，见解

【例】*Opinions* are divided on the question. 人们对这个问题看法不一。

【考】1. **in one's opinion** 在某人看来，某人认为 2. **opinion on/about...** 对…的看法或观点

*****oppose** [əˈpəuz] *v.* 反对

【记】词根记忆：op（反）+pose（摆姿势）→反的姿态→反对

【例】There are many people who *oppose* this view. 有很多人反对这种观点。

【衍】opposite（*adj.* 相反的，对立的）

optimistic [ˌɔptiˈmistik] *adj.* 乐观的

【例】We should be *optimistic* about our future. 我们应该对自己的未来持乐观态度。

*optional [ˈɔpʃənl] *adj.* 可选择的，随意的

【记】词根记忆：opt（选择）+ion+al→可选择的

【例】Evening classes are *optional*. 晚上的课是选修课。

【衍】option（*n.* 选择）

or [ɔː] *conj.* 或者；还是，否则

【例】I just don't care about whether you believe it *or* not. 我才不在乎你信不信呢。

【考】1. **either ... or ...** 或者…或者… 2. **or so** 大约，左右

oral [ˈɔːrəl] *adj.* 口头的，口述的

【例】*oral* English 英语口语

*orbit [ˈɔːbit] *n.*（天体等的）运行轨道

【例】The satellite is in *orbit* around the earth. 卫星在围绕地球的轨道上运行。

order [ˈɔːdə] *n.* 顺序；命令 *vt.* 命令；点菜；定货

【用】1. **in order to do.../in order that...** 目的是…，为了…：I got up early in order to catch the first bus. 我起床很早以便能赶上头班车。2. **order sb. to do sth.** 命令某人做某事：The doctor ordered me to stay in bed. 医生命令我卧床休息。3. **order+从句** 常用虚拟语气，即should do的形式，should可以省略：The manager ordered that we (should) deliver the parcel at once. 经理命令我们马上递送包裹。

【考】1. **out of order** 不整齐；出故障 2. **in order** 整齐；状态良好 3. **put/keep...in order** 使/保持…整齐 4. **postal order** 邮政汇票

【衍】orderly（*adj.* 整齐的，井然的 *adv.* 按顺序地，依次地）

【辨】**in order to, so as to**
in order to和**so as to**都可用来表示目的，用法相同，只不过**in order to**语气强，可以放在句中或句首，而**so as to**语气弱，不能放在句首。

ordinary [ˈɔːdinəri] *adj.* 普通的，平常的

【例】*ordinary* people 普通人

*organ [ˈɔːɡən] *n.* 器官

【例】Cancer can attack any of the body's *organs*. 癌症可以侵袭身体的任何器官。

【衍】organic (*adj.* 器官的；有机的；组织的)

organise [ˈɔːɡənaiz] (美organize) *v.* 组织

【例】I'm *organising* the evening party. 我正在筹备晚会。

【衍】organisation (*n.* 组织)；organiser (*n.* 组织者，创办者)

*origin [ˈɔridʒin] *n.* 起源；由来

【例】What is the *origin* of this saying? 这句俗语从何而来？

【衍】originate (*v.* 起源；发生)；original (*adj.* 原始的，最初的)；originally (*adv.* 最初，原先)

other [ˈʌðə] *pron./adj.* 其他的，另外的

【考】1. **each other** 彼此 2. **other than** 除了 3. **at any other time** 在其他任何时间 4. **the other day** 前几天 5. **every other day/year...** 每隔一天/年…

【辨】another, other, the other, others, the others

这几个单词或词组都可以翻译为"其他的"，但意义和用法有所区别。**another**指另外一个，后接单数名词(常省略或用one代替)：I saw one girl whispering to another. 我看到一个女孩在和另一个女孩耳语。**other**指另外的，后接复数名词：Disney soon drew other cartoon characters like Donald Duck. 迪斯尼很快又画出了像唐老鸭这样的其他卡通人物。**the other**指某范围中所有其余的，既可接单数名词(此时范围就是两个，**the other**指两者中的另外一个)，也可接复数名词，名词常可省略：The couple has two girls. One is 8, the other is 4. 这对夫妇有两个女孩，一个8岁，另一个4岁。//Jenny was not getting on very well with the other girls in her class. 詹妮和班上的其他女孩相处得不好。

others和**the others**是代词用法，后面不能再接名词，意义和**other, the other**相同，实际上是"other+复数名词"和"the other+复数名词"把名词省略后的简化形式：Some writers are greater than others. 一些作家比另一些作家更伟大。(此句中的others就相当于other writers) //Jack and the others paid no attention. 杰克和其他人都没留意。(此句中the others相当于the other people)

otherwise [ˈʌðəwaiz] *adv.* 否则，要不然

【例】You'd better finish your homework now, *otherwise* you'll get into trouble. 你最好现在就完成作业，不然会有麻烦的。

ought [ɔːt] *modal v.* 应当，应该

【考】**ought to do...** 应该做…：I wondered whether I ought to leave. 我想我是否应该离开。

> 【辨】**should, ought to**
>
> **should** 和 **ought to** 都表示"应该"的意思。二者用法基本相同，只是 **ought to** 常用来表示因责任、义务等该做的事情，口气稍重一些，而 **should** 则表示宜于做某事。

out [aut] *adv.* 在外，完结 *adj.* 外面的，出局的

【考】**out of** 从…里面；来自；在…外：He took the key out of his pocket. 他从兜里掏出钥匙。//Two out of three people voted no. 三人中有两个投了反对票。

*outcome [ˈautkʌm] *n.* 结果，成果

【记】来自词组 come out 结果

【例】No one knows what the *outcome* of the talk will be. 没有人知道谈判的结果会怎样。

outdoors [ˌautˈdɔːz] *adv.* 户外的，野外的 *n.* 户外

【例】stay *outdoors* 呆在户外 //Tom is a sports fan and a lover of the *outdoors*. 汤姆是个体育迷，也喜欢户外运动。

outer [ˈautə] *adj.* 外部的

【例】*outer* space 外太空

outgoing [ˈautgəuiŋ] *adj.* 好交际的，外向的；即将离职的

【记】组合词：out（出的）+going（去）→出去的→好交际的

【例】She is an *outgoing* girl. 她是个外向的女孩子。

outing [ˈautiŋ] *n.* 远足，郊游

【例】It's a pity the weather isn't better for our *outing* today. 我们今天出去游玩天气不见好，真遗憾。

*outline [ˈautlain] *n.* 大纲，轮廓；要点，概要 *vt.* 描绘轮廓；略述

【记】组合词：out（出来）+line（线条）→划出线条→轮廓

【例】The little boy drew an *outline* of his hand. 小男孩画了自己手的轮廓。

*output [ˈautput] *n.* 产量，输出量

【记】来自词组put out 产生

【例】an *output* of 100 tons a day 日产量100吨

outside [ˌaut'said] *n.* 外面，外表，外界 *adv.* 在外面，外表，外界 *adj.* 外面的，外表的 *prep.* 在…外

【例】On the *outside*, the house looked well cared for. 从外面来看，房屋保护得很好。// It is cold *outside*. 外面很冷。

【衍】outsider (*n.* 外人，局外人)

*outspoken [ˌaut'spəukən] *adj.* 坦率的

【记】组合词：out（出）+spoken（口头的，说的）→说出来的→坦率的

【例】He is an *outspoken* critic of the government. 他总是直言批评政府。

*outstanding [ˌaut'stændiŋ] *adj.* 突出的，显著的；杰出的

【记】out（超出）+stand（站）+ing→站出来的→鹤立鸡群的→突出的

outstanding

【例】He is an *outstanding* politician. 他是一名杰出的政治家。

★outward(s) ['autwəd(z)] *adv.* 向外，在外 *adj.* 向外的，外出的

【例】The door opens *outwards*. 这扇门向外开。

over ['əuvə] *prep.* 在…之上；超过 *adv.* 越过 *adj.* 完了，结束了

overcost
n. 校

【例】The lamp hung *over* the table. 那盏灯悬挂在桌子上方。//Do you think it's going to rain *over* the weekend? 你认为周末会一直下雨吗？

【考】1. **all over** 浑身；全部 2. **over and over again** 一而再再而三地 3. **over there** 在那边 4. **turn over** 打翻；翻身 5. **take over** 接管 6. **go over** 查看；复习 7. **look over** 从上面看过去；检查 8. **think over** 反复考虑

overcome [ˌəuvə'kʌm] *v.* 战胜，克服，胜过

【记】来自词组come over 战胜，支配

【例】If we work with a strong will, we can *overcome* any difficulty. 只要我们有毅力就能克服任何困难。

*overhead ['əuvəhed] *adj./adv.* 在高处，在空中

【记】over（在…之上）+head（头）→在头顶上的→在空中

【例】A plane flew *overhead*. 飞机从头顶飞过。

*overlook [ˌəuvə'luk] *vt.* 俯瞰，远眺

【记】来自词组look over 从…上面看过去

【例】It's a quiet and comfortable hotel *overlooking* a bay. 这是一个安静、舒适的酒店，俯瞰海湾。

*overweight [ˌəuvəˈweit] *adj.* 过重的，超重的

【记】组合词：over（超过）+weight（重量，体重）→超重的

【例】You are *overweight*. 你超重了。

*owe [əu] *v.* 欠；把…归于…

【用】1. owe sth. to... 把某事归因于…：She owes her success to good luck. 她把她的成功归结于运气好。2. **owe sth. to sb. = owe sb. sth.** 欠某人某物：We owe a lot to our parents. 我们欠父母的太多了。

own [əun] *adj.* 自己的 *vt.* 拥有

【例】I thought if I *owned* a restaurant I could eat there for free. 我想如果自己有家餐馆那就可以吃免费大餐了。

【考】1. **on one's own** 单独地，独自地 2. **of one's own** 某人自己的

【衍】owner（*n.* 所有者；主人）；ownership*（*n.* 所有权）

ownership
n. 所有制

oxygen [ˈɔksidʒən] *n.* 氧，氧气

【例】We depend on *oxygen* to live. 我们依靠氧气才能存活。

pace [peis] *n.* 步子，步速；节奏

【记】跳舞不是赛跑（race），要跟着节奏（pace）走

【例】The fence is only ten *paces* from the house. 围墙离屋子只有十步远。

【考】**keep pace with** 跟上…（的步伐）

Pacific [pəˈsifik] *adj.* 太平洋的

【例】the *Pacific* Ocean 太平洋

单元自测

1. Mary cares about clothes too much, and she _____ too much money _____ clothes.

   A. spends; in　　　B. cost; at　　　C. pays; to　　　D. spends; on

2. I don't drink wine as a rule, but I don't mind a glass _____.

   A. all the time　　B. more or less　　C. at any time　　D. once in a while

3. Is this the factory _____ you visited the other day?

   A. that　　　　　B. where　　　　　C. in which　　　　D. the one

4. The computer center, _____ last year, is very popular among the students in this

school.

A. open   B. opening   C. having opened   D. opened

5. My _____ of this weekend's activity is going out with some good friends.

A. idea   B. opinion   C. mind   D. thought

6. When the teacher took his place, the classroom became _____.

A. quiet and order   B. quietly and order

C. quiet and orderly   D. quite and orderly

7. Sarah has read lots of stories by American writers. Now she would like to read _____ stories by writers from _____ countries.

A. some; any   B. other; some

C. some; other   D. other; other

8. —You ought to have given some advice to them.

— _____, but who cared what I said?

A. So I ought   B. So ought I   C. So I did   D. So did I

9. The famous actors said, "Just do something nice for somebody. Pass it _____".

A. out   B. away   C. along   D. through

10. I prefer a flat in Inverness to _____ in Perth, because I want to live near my Mom's.

A. one   B. that   C. it   D. this

11. —Here you are! Two pounds of meat and a dozen eggs.

—Thank you. How much do I _____ you?

A. owe   B. offer   C. charge   D. cost

12. Martin is as strong as a horse. He is _____ ill.

A. often   B. sometimes   C. frequently   D. seldom

13. His father began to earn his living by writing music _____ he was twenty.

A. while   B. since   C. as old as   D. as early as

14. —Thank you very much.

—You are welcome. I was _____ glad to help.

A. too much   B. only too   C. not so   D. very much

15. The mother wanted her daughter _____ at once.

A. to operate   B. to be operated

C. to operate on   D. to be operated on

DACA CCCCA ADDBD

Word List 28

pack ［pæk］*n.* 包，背包；一群 *v.* 包装，整理

【例】Tom refused to *pack* his belongings. 汤姆拒绝把自己的东西打包。

【考】**pack up** 把…打包，整理

【衍】package（*n.* 包裹）

*packet ［'pækit］*n.* 小包裹；袋

【记】和pocket（*n.* 口袋）一起记

【例】He tore open the *packet* and found what he needed. 他撕开小包裹找到了自己需要的东西。

*paddle ［'pædl］*n.* 桨状物，蹼 *v.* 划桨，戏水

【例】She stepped into the canoe and picked up the *paddle*. 她跨进独木舟，拿起了桨。

pain ［pein］*n.* 疼痛；（*pl.*）努力

【记】一下雨（rain），关节就疼（pain）得厉害

【例】She was the only one with whom I could safely talk about all my fears and *pains*. 她是我惟一可以放心倾诉内心恐惧与痛苦的人。// *pain* killer 止痛片

【考】1. **in pain** 痛苦地 2. **take pains to do...** 不辞辛苦做… 3. **have a pain in...** …痛：I had a pain in my left hand. 我左手疼。

【衍】painful（*adj.* 疼痛的，使痛苦的）；painless（*adj.* 不痛的）

palace ［'pælis］*n.* 宫，宫殿

【记】颐和园：the Summer Palace

【例】Maybe you have been to many countries, but nowhere else can you find such a beautiful *palace*. 也许你去过很多国家，但只有在这里你才能见到如此富丽堂皇的宫殿。

pale ［peil］*adj.* 苍白的，灰白的

【例】On hearing the news of the accident in the coal mine, she went

214

pale. 一听到煤矿出事的消息，她脸色变得苍白。

*pan ［pæn］*n*. 平底锅，盘子

【记】发音记忆："盘"→盘子

*pancake ［'pæŋkeik］*n*. 薄煎饼

【记】组合词：pan（平底锅）+cake（饼）→平底锅上煎饼→薄煎饼

【例】Can we have *pancakes* for breakfast? 我们早餐可以吃煎饼吗？

*panic ［'pænik］*v*. (panicked, panicked, panicking)(使) 惊恐，恐慌 *n*. 惊慌，恐慌

【记】联想记忆：pan（盘子）+ic（发音似：一磕）→深夜里盘子一磕就噼里啪啦地碎了，造成恐慌

【例】No one *panicked*. 没有人惊惶失措。

panic

//The bad news caused *panic*. 这个坏消息引起了人们的恐慌。

*paperwork ［'peipəwəːk］*n*. 文书工作

【记】组合词：paper（文件）+work（工作）→日常文书工作

【例】His duty in our company is to do *paperwork*. 他在我们公司负责文书工作。

paragraph ［'pærəgrɑːf; 'pærəgræf］*n*. (文章的) 段落

【记】para+graph（写）→一部分一部分写→段落

【例】How many *paragraphs* are there in the passage? 这篇文章里有多少段？

*parallel ［'pærəlel］*n*. 平行线；类似 *adj*. 平行的

【考】**parallel to** 与…平行：Draw a line parallel to the base of the triangle. 划一条和三角形底边平行的线。

parcel ［'pɑːsl］*n*. 包裹

【例】When I opened the door, a *parcel* on the floor caught my eye. 当我打开门的时候看到地上有一个包裹。

pardon ［'pɑːdn］*vt./n*. 原谅，宽恕；对不起

Parent
n.父母

【用】**Pardon me. (=I beg your pardon.)** 的意思有以下几种：1. 表示请求对方的原谅。2. 用升调说表示请对方再说一遍，此时只说Pardon亦可。

【例】This book will teach you how to *pardon* others. 这本书将教你如何原谅别人。

parking ［'pɑːkiŋ］*n*. 停车

P

【例】All the *parking* spaces of this shopping mall were taken. 这个购物中心的停车位已满。

parrot [ˈpærət] *n.* 鹦鹉

【记】联想记忆：那只鹦鹉（parrot）爱吃胡萝卜（carrot）

【例】He had a *parrot* that he kept in a cage. 他在笼子里养了一只鹦鹉。

part [pɑːt] *n.* 部分；角色 *v.* 分离，分别

【例】If a small *part* of the plane were to fail, the plane would explode in the sky. 飞机上一个小零件出了问题都会使飞机在空中爆炸。// They *parted* enemies. 他们分手后成了死对头。

【考】1. **take part in** 参加 2. **play a part in...** 在…中起作用 3. **in part** 在某种程度上；部分地 4. **part with...** 与…分离

【衍】partly＊（*adv.* 部分地；在一定程度上）

*participate [pɑːˈtisipeit] *vi.* 参加，参与

【考】**participate in...** 参加…：She was invited to participate in a television debate. 她应邀参加一场电视辩论。

*particular [pəˈtikjulə] *adj.* 特殊的；个别的 *n.* (常 *pl.*)详情，细节

【例】An auction is usually advertised beforehand with full *particulars* of the articles to be sold. 拍卖会举办前会登出广告并会详细介绍拍卖品。

【考】**in particular** 特别，尤其

【衍】particularly (*adv.* 特别地；显著地)

partner [ˈpɑːtnə] *n.* 搭档，合作者

【记】联想记忆：part（部分）+ner→生活的一部分→搭档

【例】Sometimes an animal has a plant *partner*. 有时动物与植物之间存在着共生关系。

【衍】partnership (*n.* 合伙，合作关系)

pass [pɑːs; pæs] *v.* 传递；经过

【例】Time *passes* quickly. 时间过得很快。

【考】1. **pass on** 传递 2. **pass by** 经过 3. **pass away** 去世

passage [ˈpæsidʒ] *n.* (文章等的)一节；走廊

【记】pass（通过、经过）+age→通道

【例】This is the only *passage* to cross the river. 这是过河的惟一通道。

part-time
a ＆ ad. 兼职的/地

passenger [ˈpæsindʒə] *n.* 乘客，旅客

【例】The taxi driver often reminds *passengers* to take their belongings when they leave the car. 出租车司机在乘客下车时通常会提醒他们带好随身物品。

*****passer-by** [ˌpɑːsəˈbai] *n.* 过客，过路人

【例】Police are asking about *passers-by* who might have seen the accident. 警察正在询问有可能目睹这起事故的路人。

*****passive** [ˈpæsiv] *adj.* 被动的

【例】*passive* smoking 被动吸烟

passport [ˈpɑːspɔːt; ˈpæspɔːt] *n.* 护照

【记】pass（通过）+port（港口）→通过港口使用的证件→护照

【例】*Passport* Control 出境关卡

past [pɑːst; pæst] *adj.* 过去的，最近的 *n.* 过去，往事 *prep.* 经过；晚于

【例】in the *past* few days 在过去的几天//look back into the *past* 回顾过去//If someone wanted to reach the river at this point, he had to went *past* our camp. 如果有人想从这里过河就必须经过我们的营地。//Days went *past* without any news. 日子过去了，没有一点消息。

【考】**in the past** 在过去

*****patent** [ˈpætənt] *n.* 专利权

【例】The *patent* runs out in two years' time. 专利权两年后失效。

patient [ˈpeiʃnt] *n.* 病人 *adj.* 耐心的

【记】对待病人（patient）不耐心点（patient）可不行

【例】The *patient* kept coughing all night. 病人咳嗽了一整夜。

patient

【考】**be patient with...** 对…有耐心：Parents should be patient with their children. 父母对待孩子应该有耐心。

【衍】patiently（*adv.* 有耐心地）；impatient（*adj.* 没有耐心的）；impatiently（*adv.* 无耐性地）；patience（*n.* 容忍；耐心）

pattern [ˈpætn] *n.* 式样；模式

【记】伴侣（partner）相处的模式（pattern）都各不相同

【例】action *pattern* 行为模式

pavement [ˈpeivmənt] *n.* 人行道

217

【例】George was riding his small tricycle along the *pavement*. 乔治正在人行道上骑他的小三轮车呢。

pay ［pei］*v.* (paid, paid, paying) 付钱，给…报酬 *n.* 工资

【考】1. **pay for** 付款；偿还 2. **pay back** 偿还(借款)；报复 3. **pay up** 全部付清 4. **pay attention to** 注意 5. **pay a visit** 访问

【例】People in Sweden *pay* taxes on everything. 在瑞典，人们做任何事情都要上税。// I *paid* 10 yuan for the book. 我买这本书用了十元钱。// *pay* the bill 买单

【衍】payable (*adj.* 可付的，应付的)；payment (*n.* 付款；报答)；repay (*v.* 偿还)

peaceful ［'piːsful］*adj.* 和平的，安宁的

【记】来自peace (和平) +ful→和平的

【例】All human beings long for a *peaceful* world. 人类渴望一个和平的世界。

【衍】peacefully (*adv.* 和平地；安宁地)；peacefulness (*n.* 和平)

*pedestrian ［pi'destriən］*n.* 步行者，行人

【记】有坐火车 (train) 的人就有走路的人 (pedestrian)

【例】This area is for *pedestrians* only. 此处只许步行。

penny ［'peni］*n.* (*pl.* pence) 便士，美分

【例】If you buy more than ten, they knock 20 *pence* off the price. 如果你购买10个以上他们会给你便宜20便士。

pepper ［'pepə］*n.* 胡椒粉

【记】看成是 pe+p(e) +pe+r, 吃了胡椒粉，我喷，喷，喷，喷嚏打个不停

【例】Would you like salt and *pepper*? 要加盐和胡椒粉吗？

pepper

percent ［pə'sent］*n.* 百分之…

【记】词根记忆：per (每) +cent (百)→每个一百里有多少→百分之…, 也可写作per cent

【例】Only 58 *percent* of children in sub-Saharan Africa are drinking safe water. 在非洲撒哈拉以南的地区，只有百分之五十八的儿童能够喝到干净的水。

【衍】percentage (*n.* 百分率)

perfect ［'pəːfikt］*adj.* 完美的，极好的

【例】Practice makes *perfect*. 熟能生巧。

【衍】perfectly（adv. 完美地；很）；imperfect（adj. 有缺点的；未完成的）

*perform [pə'fɔːm] v. 表演，表现；履行

【记】联想记忆：per（每个）+form（形成）→每个人的一生都像是在表演一出戏

【例】In competitions, gymnasts have to *perform* on different pieces of equipment. 比赛时，体操运动员必须在不同的器械上表演。//Mike *performs* well at school. 麦克在学校表现很好。//*perform* a duty 履行职责//*perform* a research 进行研究

【衍】performance（n. 表演；性能）；performer（n. 表演者；执行者）

*perfume ['pəːfjuːm] n. 香味；香水

【记】喷上香水（perfume），粉墨登场表演（perform）

【例】They have several different *perfumes* on sale. 他们出售好几种香水。

perhaps [pə'hæps] adv. 可能，或

【例】*Perhaps* the weather will change this evening. 傍晚可能要变天。

period ['piəriəd] n. 时期，时代

*permanent ['pəːmənənt] adj. 永久的，持久的

【例】He wants a *permanent* job. 他想找个长久的工作。

*permit [pə'mit] v. (permitted, permitted, permitting) 许可，允许 n. 许可证，执照

【记】词根记忆：per+mit（放）→放进来→许可

【用】1. **permit doing...** 允许做某事：We do not permit smoking in the office. 我们不允许在办公室里抽烟。2. **permit sb. to do sth.** 允许某人做某事：They were not permitted to enter the building. 不允许他们进入这幢楼。

【例】You need a *permit* to park here. 在这里停车需要许可证。

【衍】permission（n. 允许，许可，同意）

personal ['pəːsənl] adj. 个人的，私人的

【记】来自person（人）+al→个人的

【例】I have something *personal* to discuss with you. 我有点私事和你商量。

【衍】personally（adv. 就自己而言）；impersonal（adj. 非个人的）；personality（n. 个性；人物）

personalization [ˌpəːsənəlaiˈzeiʃən] *n.* 个性化

【记】personalize（*v.* 个性化）

***personnel** [ˌpəːsəˈnel] *n.* 人员，职员

【记】来自person（人）+nel→人员

【用】personnel为集体名词，本身只有单数形式，但表达复数概念，作主语时，谓语动词用复数。

【例】All *personnel* are given a security badge. 所有职员都有安全证。

persuade [pəˈsweid] *v.* 说服，劝说；使相信

【用】persuade可接复合宾语，宾补常是动词不定式或介词短语，即：1. **persuade sb. (not) to do sth.** 说服某人（不）做某事：She persuaded me to phone the local college. 她说服我给当地的大学打电话。2. **persuade sb. into/out of doing sth.** 说服某人（不）做某事：I persuaded her into/out of going to the party. 我说服她（不）参加这次聚会。

【例】I *persuaded* her that what I had said was true. 我使她相信了我的话。

★ **pest** [pest] *n.* 害虫

【例】Gardeners use chemicals to kill garden *pest*. 园丁用化学药剂消灭害虫。

pesticide [ˈpestisaid] *n.* 杀虫剂

【记】词根记忆：pest（害虫）+i+cide（杀）→杀虫剂

【例】The food is free of *pesticides*. 这些食物没有杀虫剂污染。

单元自测

1. —Waiter!

—_____?

—I can't eat this. It's too salty. （2000全国）

A. Yes, sir   B. What   C. All right   D. Pardon

2. —Hi, Tracy, you look tired.

—I am tired. I _____ the living room all day.

A. painted   B. had painted

C. have been painting   D. have painted

3. My mother always gets a bit _____ if we don't arrive when we say we will.

A. anxious   B. ashamed   C. weak   D. patient

4. On entering another country, a tourist will have to _____ the customs.

   A. pass on   B. pass through   C. get over   D. get in

5. During the next ten years we both worked day and night to _____ the money we had borrowed.

   A. pay off   B. pay for   C. pay to   D. pay back

6. We went to Canada to travel and my cousin _____ as our guide.

   A. played   B. showed   C. acted   D. performed

7. —Do you think he'll succeed?

   —Well, he's helped by so many classmates, what's more, he works extremely hard. So he will _____ succeed.

   A. probably   B. perhaps   C. possibly   D. likely

8. The guard _____ the old man to pass after he showed him the pass.

   A. promised   B. agreed   C. let   D. permitted

9. Alice trusts you; only you can _____ her to give up the foolish idea.

   A. suggest   B. attract   C. tempt   D. persuade

10. Because the first pair of pants didn't fit properly, he asked for _____.

    A. another pants   B. other pants

    C. the others ones   D. another pair

11. —It's really an exciting game!

    —Why not _____ us?

    A. take part in   B. join in   C. join   D. attend

12. Those T-shirts are usually $35 each, but they have a _____ price of $19 in the Shopping Center.

    A. particular   B. especial   C. special   D. cheap

13. —Which city in China do you like best?

    —Oh, Beijing. I've only read about these places before, such as the Forbidden City! It is _____ exciting being there.

    A. finally   B. really   C. actually   D. personally

14. When we were told that we had to wait for a long time because of the weather, we said nothing but to wait _____.

    A. hurriedly   B. slowly   C. patiently   D. carefully

15. Three months _____, and Jack decided to return to his country.

    A. past   B. later   C. gone   D. passed

DDD CCBCD

Word List 29

pet [pet] *n.* 宠物，爱畜

【记】发音记忆："拍它"→轻拍宠物，让它舒服→宠物

【例】Do you mind if I keep *pets* in this house? 你介意我在屋子里养宠物吗?

Your pet ???!!

petrol ['petrəl] *n.* 汽油

【记】发音记忆："派车"→汽车有油才能派出

【例】We filled the car up with *petrol* before the long journey. 长途旅行前我们给车加满了汽油。

*****phenomenon** [fə'nɔminən] *n.* (*pl.* phenomena) 现象

【记】发音记忆："费脑迷呢"→他费脑筋琢磨这奇特的现象仍迷惑不解

【例】physical *phenomenon* 物理现象

phone [fəun] (= telephone) *v.* 打电话 *n.* 电话；电话机

【例】I've tried to *phone* my wife six times and I can't get through. 我试给妻子打了六个电话但都接不通。//mobile *phone* 手机

photographer [fə'tɔgrəfə] *n.* 摄影师

【记】词根记忆：photo (照片) +graph (写) +er (人) →摄影师

【例】There are a lot of *photographers*. 那里有很多摄影师。

phrase [freiz] *n.* 短语，习惯用语

【例】What does the underlined *phrase* mean? 划线的短语是什么意思?

physical ['fizikəl] *adj.* 身体的；物理的

【例】*physical* condition 身体状况 // *physical* means 物理方法

【衍】physically (*adv.* 身体上地)

physician [fi'ziʃən] *n.* (有行医执照的) 医生

【例】Dr. Black has been my *physician* for twenty years. 布莱克医生担任我的私人医师已经20年了。

physics ['fiziks] *n.* 物理 (学)

【例】The main subjects I studied at school included Chinese, maths, English, *physics*, chemistry and computer. 我在学校的主修课程包括语文、数学、英语、物理、化学和计算机。

【衍】physicist (*n.* 物理学家)

pick [pik] *v.* 拾起, 采集; 挑选

【记】捡起 (pick) 球大脚开 (kick) 出去

【考】1. **pick sth. up=pick up sth.** 捡起; 收拾; 获得 (尤指不经意间学到); 重新开始: Cathy picked up a lot of Spanish by playing with the native boys and girls. 和当地的孩子们一起玩耍让凯西学了一些西班牙语。2. **pick sb. up=pick up sb.** 用车接…: I can pick you up at the station and then we may have dinner together in town. 我可以去车站接你然后我们一起在城里吃饭。3. **pick out** 精心挑选: I picked this one out. 我挑了这一个。

【衍】picker (*n.* 采集者)

piece [piːs] *n.* 一块 (片, 张, 件…); 小的部分

【例】Down fell the mirror, breaking to *pieces*. 镜子掉下来摔碎了。

【考】**a piece of** 一块 (片, 张, 件…)

*pile [pail] *v.* 堆积, 积累 *n.* 堆

【考】1. **pile up** 堆积: My work is piling up. 我的工作越堆越多。2. **pile...on/onto...** 把…堆在…上: The boy piled the boxes on top of the other. 男孩儿把箱子一个个地堆在另一个的上面。

*pin [pin] *vt.* (pinned, pinned, pinning) 钉住, 别住 *n.* 别针; 胸针

pin

【例】He *pinned* the announcement up on the bulletin board. 他把告示钉在公告栏上。// She wore a diamond *pin*. 她佩戴了一枚钻石胸针。

pity ['piti] *n.* 怜悯, 同情; 憾事

【考】1. **feel pity for...** 可怜…: He felt no

pity

pity for that old man. 他对那个老人毫无怜悯之情。2. **What a pity!** 真遗憾!

place [pleis] *n.* 地方,处所 *vt.* 放置,安置

【例】I had been driving for at least an hour when I finally found his *place*. 我至少开了一小时的车才找到他的住所。//He *placed* the vase in the middle of the table. 他把花瓶放在桌子中间。

【考】1. **take place** 发生(不用于被动形式)2. **take the place of** 取代

plain [plein] *adj.* 平常的,普通的;明白的 *n.* 草原

【记】生活中,疼痛(pain)在所难免,再平常(plain)不过

【例】Bob likes *plain* home cooking. 鲍勃喜欢家常便饭。// *plain* language 平实的语言

【衍】plainly(*adv.* 平坦地;明白地)

plan [plæn] *n./vt.* (planned, planned, planning)计划,打算

【用】1. **plan to do...** 计划做…: He is planning to go to graduate school. 他打算念研究生。2. **plan on doing...** 打算或计划做某事,如: We plan on staying in Italy for a week. 我们打算在意大利待上一个礼拜。3. plan作名词可以与for搭配,如: have a plan for表示有一个做某事的计划//make a plan for为做某事制定计划

【衍】planning(*n.* 计划,规划); planner(*n.* 计划者)

plant [plɑːnt;plænt] *vt.* 种植;播种 *n.* 植物

【例】We will *plant* different kinds of trees, flowers and grass in and around our school. 我们将在学校及其周围种上各种花草树木。

play [plei] *v.* 玩;打(球);播放 *n.* 玩耍;戏剧

【考】1. **play with...** 玩耍,摆弄: John, you mustn't play with the knife; you may hurt yourself. 约翰,别摆弄刀子了,你会弄伤自己的。2. **put on a play** 上演话剧: The school usually puts on a play in the spring. 学校通常在春天上演一出话剧。3. **play a part/role in** 起作用;扮演角色: You played an important part in winning the game. 能赢得比赛你发挥了重要作用。

【衍】player(*n.* 选手;表演者); playful(*adj.* 好玩的,有趣的)

pleasant ['pleznt] *adj.* 令人愉快的,舒适的

【例】They had a *pleasant* chat over a cup of coffee. 他们一起喝了咖啡,谈得很开心。

【衍】unpleasant(*adj.* 令人不愉快的,讨厌的); pleasantness(*n.* 愉快,舒适)

please [pliːz] *v.* 请；使人高兴，令人满意
【衍】pleasing (*adj.* 令人高兴的)

pleased [pliːzd] *adj.* 高兴的
【用】1. **be pleased to do...** 乐意或高兴做…: He is pleased to see the woman. 他乐意见这位女士。2. **be pleased with...** 对…表示满意: I am very pleased with the quality of your work. 我对你的工作十分满意。3. **be pleased that** 对…表示满意或高兴: I am pleased that he gladly accepted our invitation. 他愉快地接受了我们的邀请让我很高兴。

pleasure [ˈpleʒə] *n.* 高兴，愉快
【考】1. **take/find pleasure in sth./doing sth.** 从（做）某事中得到乐趣: More and more people take pleasure in stamp collection. 越来越多的人从集邮中找到了乐趣。2. **It is a pleasure for sb. to do sth.= It is one's pleasure to do sth.** 某人很高兴做某事: It is a pleasure for me to write to you. 我很高兴给你写信。

【辨】**It is a pleasure / My pleasure, with pleasure, for pleasure**
It is a pleasure / My pleasure 用于回答 thank you; **with pleasure** 用于回答别人的求助，意思是欣然答应或乐意为之，如: —Could you do me a favor and take these books to my office? —你能帮我个忙把这些书拿到我办公室吗？ —With pleasure. —愿意效劳。**for pleasure** 是为了消遣的意思，如: She travels for business and for pleasure. 她旅行既是为了工作也是为了消遣。

*plot [plɔt] *vt.* (plotted, plotted, plotting) 密谋 *n.* 情节
【例】The *plot* is pretty boring. 故事情节枯燥无味。

*plug [plʌg] *vt.* (plugged, plugged, plugging) 把…塞住；接通电源 *n.* 塞子，插头
【例】Could you *plug* the TV set in, please? 你能插上电视机的电源吗？ //The *plug* doesn't fit the drain. 这个塞子和排水口不配套。

plug

plus [plʌs] *prep.* 加，加上
【例】I got a B *plus* (*B*⁺) on my history paper. 我的历史论文得了 B⁺。//Six *plus* two equals eight. 6加2等于8。

point [pɔint] *v.* 指，指向 *n.* 点；要点，观点；分数
【用】1. **point out sth./that** 指出: She pointed out that it was getting

dark. 她指出天快黑了。2. **There is no point in doing...** 做…无意义：There was no point in staying any longer. 再待下去毫无意义。

【例】Todd quickly turned round and *pointed* a gun at the man. 托德迅速转身用枪指着那个男人。//weak *points* 弱点//turning *point* 转折点

【考】1. **point of view** 观点 2. **point to/at** 指着，指向 3. **to the point of** 到…的程度 4. **at the point of** 就在…之前，快要…的时候

【衍】pointless（*adj.* 无意义的）

*poison [ˈpɔizn] *n.* 毒药

【记】联想记忆：毒害（poison）百姓，被送进监狱（prison）

【例】These snakes' *poison* could kill a person in ten minutes. 这些蛇的毒液能在十分钟内致人于死地。

【衍】poisonous*（*adj.* 有毒的；致命的）

polite [pəˈlait] *adj.* 有礼貌的，有教养的

【记】警察（police）很有礼貌（polite）

【例】It's not *polite* to ask a lady how old she is. 询问女士的年龄是不礼貌的。

【衍】politely（*adv.* 客气地，有礼貌地）；politeness（*n.* 有礼貌，优雅）；impolite（*adj.* 无礼的，粗鲁的）

political [pəˈlitikl] *adj.* 政治的

【记】和politics（*n.* 政治）一起记

【例】He is a *political* leader. 他是一名政治领袖。

【衍】politician*（*n.* 政治家，政客）；politics*（*n.* 政治）

pollute [pəˈluːt] *vt.* 污染

【例】Many cities around the world today are heavily *polluted*. 当今世界上的许多城市都受到了严重的污染。

【衍】pollution（*n.* 污染）

poor [pɔː] *adj.* 贫穷的，可怜的，差的

【用】the+形容词表示作为整体的"某一类人"，如：the poor指"穷人"，有类似用法的形容词还有dead, sick, blind, young, old, rich等。此类词作主语时，谓语动词应使用复数形式。

【例】Can you believe that in such a rich country there are so many *poor* people? 在如此富裕的国家里居然有这么多的穷人，你能相信吗？

【衍】poorly（*adv.* 贫穷地）

pop [pɔp] (=popular) *adj.* （口语）（音乐、艺术等）大众的，通俗的
【例】*pop* songs 流行歌曲

popular [ˈpɔpjulə] *adj.* 流行的，受欢迎的；大众的
【例】Chinese films are very *popular* in the U.S.. 中国电影在美国很受欢迎。// *popular* science 大众科学
【衍】popularity (*n.* 流行；普及); unpopular (*adj.* 不受欢迎的，不流行的); popularize (*vt.* 普及)

population [ˌpɔpjuˈleiʃn] *n.* 人口，人数
【例】The *population* of the United States is growing older and will continue to do so. 美国人口正在逐步老龄化，这种趋势还将继续下去。// *population* explosion 人口爆炸，人口激增

*porridge [ˈpɔridʒ; ˈpɔːridʒ] *n.* 稀饭，粥
【记】联想记忆：por (看作poor贫穷的) +ridge (山脊) →住在山脊上的穷人只能天天喝稀粥

*portable [ˈpɔːtəbl] *adj.* 轻便的，便携的
【记】联想记忆：port (港口) +able (易…的) →港口方便运输的→轻便的
【例】a *portable* computer 便携式电脑

position [pəˈziʃən] *n.* 位置，职位
【记】词根记忆：posit (放) +ion→放在那→位置
【例】I am applying for a *position* at IBM. 我正在申请IBM公司的职位。

*positive [ˈpɔzətiv] *adj.* 积极的；肯定的
【例】Try to be *positive* about your future. 试着对你的未来乐观一些。// Are you *positvie* that it was Maria you saw? 你确定看到的是玛丽亚吗？
【衍】positively (*adv.* 肯定地)

*possess [pəˈzes] *vt.* 占有，拥有
【例】He *possesses* many fine qualities. 他有很多优点。
【衍】possession* (*n.* 所有，拥有；财产，所有物)

possible [ˈpɔsəbl] *adj.* 可能的
【考】1. **as...as possible** 尽可能…的 2. **if possible** 如果可能的话：We'd like you to start work tomorrow if possible. 如果可能的话我们想让你明天就开始工作。

227

【衍】possibility（n. 可能，可能性）；impossible（adj. 不可能的）

*postpone [pəust'pəun] vt. 推迟，延期

【例】I'm afriad we'll have to *postpone* our meeting. 恐怕我们得推迟会议的时间。

*potential [pə'tenʃəl] adj. 潜在的，可能的 n. 潜力

【例】a *potential* danger 潜在的危险 // My coach said that I had lots of *potential*. 教练说我很有潜力。

pound [paund] n. 磅；英镑

【记】发音记忆

【例】Two *pounds* of carrots, please. 请给我两磅胡萝卜。//Millions of *pounds'* worth of damage has been caused by a storm last night. 昨晚的暴雨造成了上百万英镑的损失。

pour [pɔ:] v. 倾泻，不断流出

【记】发音记忆："破"→水罐破了，水流出→倾泻

【考】1. **pour...on...** 把…倒在…：If you pour water on flowers, they will flourish. 给花浇水它们就会盛开。2. **pour...into...** 把…倒进…：I opened a can of orange and poured it all into the bowl. 我打开一听橘汁，全部倒进了碗里。3. **pour in** 不断的涌入或涌出

power ['pauə] n. 力量；动力

【例】come to *power* 掌权//*power* station 发电站

【衍】powerful（adj. 效力大的；强有力的）；powerless（adj. 无能力的）

practice ['præktis]（美 practise）n./v. 练习，实践

【用】**practice sth./doing...** 练习做…：Boys are practicing playing basketball. 男孩子们正在练习打篮球。

【考】**put...into practice** 把…付诸实践

【衍】practical（adj. 实际的，实用的）；practically（adv. 实际上）

praise [preiz] n./vt. 赞扬，表扬

【记】联想记忆：p+raise（提高）→业绩提高，受到表扬

【考】**praise sb. for sth.** 因某事而表扬某人：The police officer was praised for his bravery. 这名警官因为英勇而受到表扬。

praise

*pray [prei] v. 祈祷，祈求

【例】Let us *pray*. 让我们祈祷吧。//I *prayed* that Tom would be all

right. 我祈祷汤姆一切平安。

【衍】prayer* (n. 祈祷)

*precious ['preʃəs] adj. 宝贵的，珍贵的

【考】**precious to...** 对…来说很珍贵：Her privacy is very precious to her. 隐私对她来说很宝贵。

pray

*precise [pri'sais] adj. 精确的，准确的

【例】The *precise* details of the deal are still a secret. 有关交易的确切细节还是个秘密。

*predict [pri'dikt] v. 预言；预报

【例】Eric in his book *predicts* a future world with sufficient material. 埃里克在自己的书中预言了一个物质充足的未来世界。

【衍】predictable (adj. 可预言的)；unpredictable (adj. 不可预知的)

单元自测

1. She _____ his number in the phone book to make sure that she had got it right.
   A. looked up　　B. looked for　　C. picked out　　D. picked up

2. If you don't take away all your things from the desk, there won't be enough _____ for my stationery.　　　(2000上海)
   A. area　　B. place　　C. room　　D. surface

3. It is necessary _____ me _____ my studies before a new term.
   A. for; to make a plan for　　B. of; making a plan for
   C. for; to make a plan of　　D. of; making a plan of

4. I _____ ping-pong quite well, but I haven't had time to play since the new year.
   A. will play　　B. have played　　C. played　　D. play

5. —Could you do me a favor and take these books to my office?
   —Yes, _____.
   A. for pleasure　　B. I could　　C. my pleasure　　D. with pleasure

6. The new machine is _____ people, because it saves money and energy as well.
   A. compared with　　B. used to　　C. popular with　　D. well-known to

7. According to the new research, gardening is a more _____ exercise for older women than jogging or swimming.　　　(2001上海)
   A. mental　　B. physical　　C. effective　　D. efficient

8. We have worked out the plan and now we must put it into _____.
   A. fact　　B. reality　　C. practice　　D. deed

229

9. Cathy, this is Mike. I _____ to tell you that I will be absent for lunch.

    A. have telephoned   B. was telephoning

    C. telephoned   D. am telephoning

10. Most buildings _____ in the 1976 earthquake in Tangshan. Now the city has _____ a new look.

    A. were falling to pieces; carried on   B. fell into ruins; turned up

    C. were fallen to pieces; appeared   D. fell into ruins; taken on

11. —Bruce, I really appreciate your handwriting.

    — _____ .

    A. I practice every day   B. Thank you very much

    C. No, I don't think so   D. Well, it's not good enough

12. This is the first time that I _____ for months.

    A. felt really pleased   B. have felt really pleased

    C. feel really pleased   D. have felt really pleasing

13. At the sight of the hunter, the deer was _____ away when its antlers(角) were _____ on the branches.

    A. at the point to run; got rid of   B. on the point of running; caught

    C. about to run; burst   D. on the moment of running; lost

14. All possible means _____ been taken to stop the river _____ .

    A. have; polluting   B. has; polluted

    C. have; from polluted   D. has; being polluted

15. Oh, John, _____ you gave us.

    A. how a pleasant surprise   B. how pleasant surprise

    C. what a pleasant surprise   D. what pleasant surprise

答案：ACCDD CCCDD BBBDC

Word List 30

prefer [pri'fə:] *vt.* (preferred, preferred, preferring) 宁愿 (选择)；更喜欢
【用】1. **prefer A to B** 二者之中更喜欢A：I prefer football to base-ball. 比起棒球，我更喜欢足球。//I prefer singing to acting. 我喜欢唱歌，不喜欢演戏。注意：本句型中的to是介词。2. **prefer to do...** 更喜欢做…：Some people prefer to drive without wearing a safety belt. 有些人开车宁可不系安全带。注意：本句型中的to是不定式符号。3. **prefer to do sth. rather than do sth.** 宁愿做某事而不愿做某事：I prefer to go to swim rather than stay at home. 我宁可去游泳也不愿呆在家里。4. **prefer sb. (not) to do sth.** 希望某人 (不) 做某事 5. **prefer that one (should) do sth.** 希望某人做某事
【衍】preferable (*adj.* 更可取的，更优越的)；preference* (*n.* 偏爱；优先选择)

*****pregnant** ['pregnənt] *adj.* 怀孕的
【例】She is *pregnant* with her third child. 她怀了第三个孩子。

*****prejudice** ['predʒudis] *n.* 偏见，成见
【考】**prejudice against** 对…的偏见：There is still a prejudice against foreigners. 对外国人仍然存有偏见。

prepare [pri'pɛə] *v.* 准备；配制
【例】John is *preparing* us a meal. 约翰正为我们做饭菜。
【考】1. **prepare for...** 为…做准备：He prepared well for the job interview. 对于面试，他做了充分的准备。2. **prepare to do...** 准备做…：He prepared to jump from the plane. 他做好了跳伞的准备。3. **prepare sb. to do sth./for sth.** 使某人做好做某事的准备，这的sb. 多是反身代词：I'll have to prepare myself for the n~ term in August. 我必须做好准备以迎接8月份开始的～
【衍】preparation* (*n.* 准备)

231

*prescription [pri'skripʃn] *n.* 处方, 药方

【例】The doctor gave me a *prescription* for some pills. 医生给我开了一些药丸。

present ['prezənt] *adj.* 当前的; 出席的 *n.* 礼物, 赠品

['pri'zent] *vt.* 赠送; 介绍

【考】1. **present at...** 出席…: All the people present at the party were his supporters. 出席晚会的人都是他的支持者。2. **at present** 目前, 现在 3. **present sth. to sb.=present sb. with sth.** 赠送, 给予: The mayor presented the prizes to the top students./ The mayor presented the top students with the prizes. 市长为最优秀的学生们颁发了奖品。

【衍】presentation* (*n.* 陈述; 介绍)

*preserve [pri'zə:v] *vt.* 保护, 保存

【记】联想记忆: pre (提前) +serve (服务) →提前做好服务工作→保护, 保存

【例】Store the coffee in a cool, dark place to *preserve* its flavor. 把咖啡置于阴凉、避光处以保持其味道。

*press [pres] *vt.* 压, 按 *n.* 压, 按; 新闻界, 出版社

【例】She *pressed* the wrong key on the computer. 她按错了计算机上的键。// freedom of the *press* 新闻自由

【衍】pressure (*n.* 压迫; 压力, 压强)

⇐press

pretend [pri'tend] *v.* 假装, 装作

【用】1. **pretend to do** (**be**) 假装…: She pretended to be interested in his story. 她假装对他的故事感兴趣。注意: pretend的宾语不能用doing形式。2. **pretend+that** 假装…: He pretended that he hadn't heard. 他假装没听见。

prevent [pri'vent] *v.* 防止, 阻止

【用】**prevent sb. (from) doing sth.** 阻止某人做某事: His injure will prevent him from playing in today's game. 他受了伤, 将不能参加今天的比赛。注意: 当prevent用于被动语态时, 介词from不能省略。和prevent意义和用法类似的单词有stop, prohibit, keep等。

【衍】prevention (*n.* 预防, 防止)

preview ['pri:'vju:] *vt.* 预演, 预习

【记】词根记忆：pre（提前）+view（看）→提前看→预习

【例】The audience that *previewed* the new movie didn't like it. 看了预演的观众都不喜欢这部电影。

*previous ['priːviəs] *adj.* 在前的，早先的

【例】I already studied this in my *previous* school. 我在先前的学校已经学过了。

pride [praid] *n.* 自豪，骄傲 *v.* （使）自豪，（使）自夸

【例】sense of *pride* 自豪感

【考】1. **take pride in** 为…感到骄傲 2. **pride oneself on...** 因…而得意：We pride ourselves on our high standards. 我们为我们的高标准而自豪。

primary ['praiməri; 'praiˌməri] *adj.* 初级的；首要的

【例】*primary* school 小学 // Her *primary* aim is to get into medical school. 她的首要目标是考上医科学校。

*primitive ['primitiv] *adj.* 原始的，远古的

【例】*Primitive* man made himself primitive tools from sharp stones and animal bones. 原始人用尖石块和兽骨为自己制作原始的工具。

*principle ['prinsəpl] *n.* 原则，原理

【例】We adhere to the *principle* that everyone should be treated fairly. 我们必须坚持人人都应该被平等对待这一原则。

【考】**on principle** 从原则上讲

print [print] *v.* 印刷

【例】The dictionary is being *printed* and it will soon come out. 字典正在印刷过程中，很快就可以出版。

【衍】printer（*n.* 印刷工人；打印机）

private ['praivit] *adj.* 私人的，私营的；秘密的

【例】It's illegal to read people's *private* letters without permission. 未经允许看别人的私人信件是违法的。

【考】**in private** 私下里，秘密地

【衍】privately（*adv.* 私下地）；privacy（*n.* 隐私）

*privilege ['privilidʒ] *n.* 特权，特别待遇

【例】Some of the prisoners are given special *privileges*. 有的囚犯享有特权。

probably ['prɔbəbli] *adv.* 很可能，大概

【例】I invited her to the party but she *probably* won't come. 我邀请她参加晚会，但是她可能不会来。

*procedure [prə'si:dʒə] *n.* 程序，手续

【例】Writing a cheque is quite a simple *procedure*. 签支票的手续很简单。

process ['prəuses; 'prɔses] *vt.* 加工，处理 *n.* 程序；方法

【例】They are still *processing* the research data. 他们还在处理研究数据。// Unlike watching TV, reading is a highly active *process*. 与看电视不同，阅读是一个非常积极主动的过程。

【衍】processer (*n.* 处理器)

produce [prə'dju:s; prə'du:s] *v.* 生产，制造

【例】That factory *produces* cars. 那家工厂生产小汽车。// *mass-produced* 大量生产的

【衍】production (*n.* 生产，制造); producer (*n.* 生产商); reproduce (*vt.* 再生产；繁殖)

*profession [prə'feʃn] *n.* 职业，专业

【例】Law is a very difficult *profession*. 法律是一门很难的专业。

【衍】professional (*n.* 专业人员; *adj.* 专业的，职业的); preprofessional (*adj.* 职业前的，为从事职业做准备的)

professor [prə'fesə] *n.* 教授

【例】university *professors* 大学教授

profit ['prɔfit] *n.* 利润，益处 *v.* 盈利，获益于

【例】Your company can *profit* in several years by using our plan. 采用我们的计划可以让你们公司在几年内盈利。

【衍】profitable (*adj.* 有利可图的); nonprofit (*adj.* 非赢利的，无利可图的)

programme ['prəugræm] (=program) *n.* 节目，项目 *v.* 为…编制程序

【例】TV *programme* 电视节目 //They can now *programme* computers to recognize your voice. 现在他们能设置程序，让电脑识别你的声音。

【衍】programmer (*n.* 程序员)

progress ['prəugres; 'prɔgres] *n.* 进步，上进 *vi.* 进展；进行

【例】No *progress* was made in the trade talk. 贸易谈判没有取得任何进展。//As the disease *progresses*, patients might lose the ability to move. 随着病情的恶化，患者可能会丧失行动能力。

【考】1. **in progress** 在行进中 2. **make progress (in)**（在某方面）取得进展

【衍】progressive（*adj.* 前进的；进步的）

*prohibit [prə'hibit] *vt.* 禁止，阻止

prohibit

【考】**prohibit sb. from doing sth.** 阻止某人做某事

project ['prɔdʒekt] *n.* 项目，工程

【例】*project* manager 项目经理 // water *projects* 水利工程

【衍】projector（*n.* 投影机）

promise ['prɔmis] *v.* 答应，允诺；预示 *n.* 答应，允诺；希望，前景

【用】1. **promise to do sth.** 允诺做某事：I have promised to meet him at the airport at 3:30 tomorrow afternoon. 我答应他明天下午3:30机场见。 2. **promise sth. to sb.** 允诺给某人某物：I can't give you the CD; I've promised it to James. 我不能把这张CD给你，我已经答应给詹姆士了。3. **promise+that** 从句 答应，许诺：I promised my father that I would come back home before 5:00 p.m.. 我答应父亲下午5:00前回家。

【例】This year *promises* to be another good one for harvests. 今年看来又是个丰收年。//a young player of great *promise* 一个很有前途的年轻演员

【衍】promising（*adj.* 有希望的，有前途的）

*promote [prə'məut] *vt.* 促进，提升；推销

【例】The organization *promotes* cancer research. 该机构推动了癌症研究的发展。// The company has used pretty little girls to *promote* their goods. 公司雇用年轻漂亮的女孩推销商品。

pronounce [prə'nauns] *v.* 发音

【记】联想记忆：pron（代词）+（n）oun（名词）+ce→又是代词又是名词，怎么发音？

【例】How do you *pronounce* your name? 你的名字怎么念？

【衍】pronunciation（*n.* 发音）

proper ['prɔpə] *adj.* 恰当的，合适的

【例】Please put the books back on the *proper* shelves. 请把书放回适当的位置。

【衍】properly（*adv.* 适当地；完全地）

protect [prə'tekt] *vt.* 保护

【考】**protect...from (doing) sth.** 保护…免受…: Wear sunglasses to protect your eyes from sunlight. 戴上太阳镜, 保护眼睛免受阳光的损害。

【衍】protection (*n.* 保护)

proud [praud] *adj.* 自豪的, 骄傲的

【考】**be/feel proud of** 对…感到骄傲: I am really proud of the independence I've achieved. 我为自己的独立而骄傲。

【衍】proudly (*adv.* 骄傲地)

prove [pru:v] *vt.* 证明, 证实 *vi.* 证明是, 结果是, 原来是

【例】He has *proved* his courage in the battle. 他已在作战中证明了他的勇气。

【用】1. **prove+(to be) +*n./adj.*** 证明是…: She may prove to be the most suitable person for the job. 结果她可能是最适合干这项工作的人。//Your plan proved to be workable. 你的计划证明是可行的。注意: 此句不能说成: Your plan is proved to be workable. 即prove一词用主动形式表被动含义, 不使用被动语态。2. **prove+that从句**: But Einstein was able to prove that light coming from the stars was bent as it passed the sun. 然而爱因斯坦却能证明从恒星来的光线经过太阳时变弯曲了。

provide [prə'vaid] *v.* 提供

【用】**provide sb. with sth. (=provide sth. for sth.)** 为…提供…: We'll provide you with a room of your own. 我们将为你提供一间属于你自己的房间。

province ['prɔvins] *n.* 省

【例】Canada has 10 *provinces* and 3 territories. 加拿大有10个省和3个行政区。

*****psychology** [sai'kɔlədʒi] *n.* 心理学

【记】psycho (心理学) +logy→心理学

public ['pʌblik] *adj.* 公共的, 公众的, 国家的 *n.* 公众

【例】*public* transport 公共交通; 公交车辆// The gardens are open to the *public*. 公园对公众开放。// *public* policy 国家政策

【衍】publicity (*n.* 公开); publicly (*adv.* 公然地; 舆论上地)

publish ['pʌbliʃ] *v.* 出版, 发行

【例】This magazine is *published* monthly. 这本杂志是月刊。

【衍】publisher (*n.* 出版商)

pull [pul] *v.* 拉，拖 *n.* 拉力，引力

【考】1. **pull down** 拆毁；使降低 2. **pull up** 追上；停止 3. **pull in** 进站，靠岸 4. **pull on** 穿，戴；继续拉 5. **pull out** 撤离，离站 6. **pull over** (使) 开到路边 7. **pull away** 脱身，离开

pump [pʌmp] *vt.* 用泵抽水；抽 *n.* 抽水机，泵

【例】Air must be *pumped* into the plane so that the passengers can breathe. 必须将空气抽入飞机供乘客们呼吸。

*punctual ['pʌŋktʃuəl] *adj.* 准时的

【记】发音记忆："碰个巧"→碰巧刚好→准时的

【例】Please try to be more *punctual* in the future. 以后请尽量准时。

punish ['pʌniʃ] *vt.* 惩罚，处罚

【记】没有完成 (finish) 任务受到惩罚 (punish)

【用】**punish sb. for sth.** 因某事惩罚某人：His parents punished him for coming home late. 因为回家晚了父母处罚了他。

【衍】punishment (*n.* 惩罚)

*purchase ['pɜːtʃəs] *n./vt.* 购买

【例】Milk of this brand can be *purchased* in many shops. 这种牌子的牛奶在很多商店都可以买到。// He gave his son some money for the *purchase* of his school books. 他给他儿子一些钱买课本。

*pure [pjuə] *adj.* 纯的，不掺杂的

【例】*pure* science 纯科学 (有别于应用科学)

【衍】purely (*adv.* 纯粹地；完全地)

purpose ['pɜːpəs] *n.* 目的，意图

【考】**on purpose** 故意：I am sorry but I didn't do it on purpose. 对不起，我不是故意那么做的。

【衍】purposefully (*adv.* 有目的地)；purposely (*adv.* 故意地)

put [put] *vt.* (put, put, putting) 放，摆

【例】Where did the man *put* his cellphone? 那个男人把手机放在哪里了？

【考】1. **put away** 把…放好 2. **put on** 穿上；把…放在 3. **put out** 扑灭 4. **put up** 抬起；建造；张贴 5. **put off** 推迟 6. **put up with** 忍受，容忍 7. **put forth** 提出 8. **put down** 放下；拒绝 9. **put back** 放回原

处 10. **put an end to** 结束，中止 11. **put...into practice** 实行 12. **put on weight** 长胖

| **puzzle** | ['pʌzl] *n.* 难题；(字、画)谜 *v.* (使)迷惑，困扰 |

【例】I like doing crossword *puzzles.* 我喜欢玩填字游戏。

【考】**puzzle over/about...** 为…冥思苦想或伤脑筋：Doctors puzzled about her illness. 医生们冥思苦想也不明白她到底得了什么病。

puzzle

【衍】puzzled (*adj.* 迷惑不解的)

*pyramid ['pirəmid] *n.* 角锥形，金字塔

【例】The *Pyramids* of Egypt were built as tombs. 埃及的金字塔是建来作坟墓的。

*quake [kweik] *n./vi.* 震动

【例】Suddenly, the earth began to *quake.* 突然，大地猛烈地震动起来。

*qualification [ˌkwɔlifiˈkeiʃn] *n.* 资格，条件；资格证书

【例】medical *qualification* 医学证书

【考】**qualification for** (做某事的)资格，条件：Previous experience is not an essential qualification for this job. 以前的经验并不是获得这份工作的必要条件。

【衍】qualify (*v.* 使有资格，限制)

单元自测

1. The college entrance examination is coming, and the students are _____ it.
   A. preparing
   B. prepared for
   C. prepared
   D. preparing for
2. All the people _____ at the party were his supporters.
   A. present
   B. thankful
   C. interested
   D. important
3. His poor health _____ him joining in almost any public activity.
   A. stop
   B. prevented
   C. forbade
   D. kept
4. She is always ready to help people in trouble because she thinks it's a _____.
   A. decision
   B. chance
   C. pride
   D. pleasure
5. Our bodies are strengthened by taking exercise. _____, our minds are developed by learning.

A. Probably   B. Likely   C. Similarly   D. Generally

6. —Nancy is not coming tonight.

    —But she _____!

    A. promises   B. promised   C. will promise   D. had promised

7. Dogs are kept to _____ the houses from thieves at night.

    A. guard   B. defend   C. protect   D. prevent

8. Which country helps to _____ food _____ England?

    A. provide; for   B. provide; in

    C. provide; to   D. provide; on

9. The stone under her feet rolled down; she was _____ into the river, and she called out for help.

    A. being pushed   B. pushed   C. pulled   D. being pulled

10. He went to town _____ buying a new television.

    A. with a purpose of   B. with the purpose of

    C. in the purpose of   D. on purpose of

11. In Disneyland every year, some 800,000 plants are replaced because Disney refuses to _____ signs asking his guests not to step on them.

    A. put down   B. put out   C. put up   D. put off

12. On Sundays I prefer _____ some friends to _____ home alone.

    A. to visit; stay   B. visiting; stay   C. visiting; staying   D. to visit; staying

13. We had thought the examination would be difficult, but it _____ easy.

    A. turned   B. came   C. appeared   D. proved

14. If the law and order _____, neither the citizen nor his property is safe.

    A. are not preserved   B. is not preserved

    C. were not preserved   D. have not been preserved

15. —I'm trying to use this machine, but it won't start.

    —Let me show you how to start it. See, all you have to do is _____ the button.

    A. to press   B. press   C. to turn   D. turn

答案：D A B D C B A A C B C C D A A

Word List 31

quality [ˈkwɔliti] *n.* 质量；品质

【例】Generally speaking, the more expensive the camera is, the better its *quality* is. 一般来说，相机的价格越高质量越好。//He has all the *qualities* of a good teacher. 他具有一位优秀教师应该具备的所有品质。

quantity [ˈkwɔntiti] *n.* 数量

【例】We aim at quality rather than *quantity*. 我们的目标是质量而非数量。

【考】1. **a（large）quantity of=quantities of** 大量的（既可修饰可数名词，也可修饰不可数名词）：As a result of destroying the forests, a large quantity of desert has covered the land. 由于人类破坏森林，造成大片沙漠覆盖了陆地。2. **in quantity** 大量地：Tom sells drugs wholesale and in quantity. 汤姆大量批发销售药品。

quarrel [ˈkwɔrəl; ˈkwɔːrəl] *n./vi.* 争吵，吵架

【例】We had a *quarrel* about money. 我们就钱的问题争吵起来。

【考】1. **quarrel about/over...** 因…而争吵 2. **quarrel with sb.** 与某人吵架：Why are you always quarrelling with your friends? 你为什么总是和你的朋友吵架？

quarrel

【衍】quarrelsome（*adj.* 喜欢吵架的）

*questionnaire [ˌkwestʃəˈnɛə] *n.* 调查表，问卷

【记】question（询问）+naire→问卷

【例】I had to fill out a health *questionnaire* at the doctor's office. 我需要在医生的办公室里填写一张健康调查问卷。

*queue [kjuː] *vi.* 排队 *n.* 行列，长队

【例】I hope people will not jam but *queue* whenever and wherever needed. 我希望需要时人们能够排队而不要拥挤。

【考】1. **join the queue** 排队 2. **jump the queue** 插队 3. **stand/wait in a queue** 排队等待

*quit [kwit] *v.* (quitted, quitted, quitting)离开；停止

【记】联想记忆：我是不是该安静（quiet）地走开（quit），还是勇敢留下来

【例】If I don't get a pay raise, I'll *quit*. 如果不给我加薪，我就不干了。

quite [kwait] *adv.* 完全，十分

【例】We wanted to get home before dark, but it didn't *quite* turn out as planned. 我们想在天黑前到家，但是没能按计划做到。

【考】1. **quite a few** 很多的，大量的 2. **quite a number of** 相当多的

race [reis] *n.* 种族；比赛 *v.* 赛跑，比赛

【例】human *race* 人类 //a bike tour and *race* 自行车旅行竞赛// Thirteen vehicles lined up last March to *race* across the Mojave Desert. 十三辆汽车于去年三月整队，角逐莫哈韦沙漠越野赛。

range [reindʒ] *n.* 范围；射程

【例】That subject is outside my *range*. 这个课题超出了我的研究范围。//The gun has a *range* of five miles. 这把枪的射程是5英里。

【考】**a wide range of** 大范围的…

rare [rɛə] *adj.* 罕见的，稀有的

【记】联想记忆：稀有的（rare）东西要小心（care）对待

【例】Skilled and responsible retail managers are *rare*. 熟练而又有责任心的零售经理比较少见。

*rate [reit] *n.* 比率；价格；速度 *v.* 估价；认为

【例】the death *rate* 死亡率//What is the *rate* for printed matter? 邮寄印刷品的邮资是多少？ //He *rated* the movie excellent. 他认为这部电影很好看。

【考】**at this rate** 照这种样子

rather [ˈrɑːðə; ˈræðə] *adv.* 相当，宁可

【用】1. **rather than** 与其…，不如…；是…而不是…（连接两个平行句子成分）：It is what you do rather than what you say that matters. 重要的是你做了什么而不是说了什么。注意：连接两个不定式时，rather than后面的那个不定式可以带to，也可以不带to。

2. would rather do... (than do...) 宁可做…（而不做…）: I'd rather walk than take a bus. 我宁愿走路也不愿坐公共汽车。

reach [riːtʃ] *v.* 到达；（伸手）够到

【例】*reach* an agreement 达成一项协议

【考】1. **reach out** 伸出 2. **reach for** 伸手去拿

react [riˈækt] *vi.* 起反应，起作用；反抗

【记】词根记忆：re（相反）+act（行动）→产生相反的行动→反抗

【考】**react to...** 对…做出反应：TV could react to the sudden event quickly. 电视能迅速对突发事件做出反应。

【衍】reaction（*n.* 反应；反作用）

ready [ˈredi] *adj.* 准备就绪的

【考】**be ready to do.../for...** 做好准备做…：We are ready to go. 准备就绪只待出发。

real [riəl] *adj.* 真实的,确实的

【例】*real* life 现实生活

【衍】really（*adv.* 真正地）；reality（*n.* 真实,现实）

realize [ˈriəlaiz] *vt.* 认识到；实现

【记】联想记忆：real（真实的）+ize（使…）→使变得真实→实现

【例】I failed in the final examination last term and only then did I *realize* the importance of study. 上学期期末考试我没有通过,直到那时我才意识到学习的重要性。

reason [ˈriːzn] *n.* 理由,原因 *v.* 说服,劝说

【记】和season（*n.* 季节）一起记

【例】The *reason* why she was ill was that she had drunk cold water. 她是因为喝了凉水才生病的。

【衍】reasonable（*adj.* 合乎情理的）；reasoning（*n.* 推理）

> 【辨】**reason, cause, excuse**
> **reason** 与 **conclusion**（结论）相对,指的是用来解释某种看法或行为的"理由",常与for搭配使用：the reason for changing the plan 变更计划的理由; **cause** 与 **effect**（结果）相对,指的是某个客观存在事件的直接原因,"起因",常与of搭配使用：the cause of the fire 起火的原因; **excuse** 意为"借口,托辞",往往指为推卸责任或逃避惩罚而找的借口：Stop making excuses! 别再找借口了！

receive [ri'si:v] v. 收到，得到

【例】I hope I can *receive* your photos as soon as possible. 我希望能尽快收到你寄来的照片。

【衍】accept（v. 接受）

recognize ['rekəgnaiz] vt. 认出；承认

【例】I *recognized* Tom the moment I saw him. 我一见到汤姆就认出他来了。

*__recommend__ [ˌrekə'mend] v. 推荐

【记】re（再）+commend（看作command需要）→一而再再而三的被需要→推荐

【例】Who *recommended* you to our company? 谁把你推荐到我们公司的？

【衍】recommendation（n. 推荐）

recover [ri'kʌvə] vi. 痊愈 vt. 恢复；重新获得

【考】**recover from** 恢复：It may take him a month to recover from the operation. 他手术后需要一个月的康复时间。

【衍】recovery（n. 恢复，痊愈）

*__recreation__ [ˌrekri'eiʃn] n. 消遣，娱乐

【例】Basketball is the usual *recreation* of them after school. 篮球是他们放学后通常的娱乐。

【衍】recreational（adj. 休养的；娱乐的）

recycle [ˌri:'saikl] v. 再循环，回收

【记】re（重新）+cycle（圈，循环）→再循环

【例】*recycled* paper 再生环保纸

reduce [ri'dju:s;ri'du:s] vt. 减少，缩减

【例】*reduce* pressure 减小压力

*__refer__ [ri'fə:] v. (referred, referred, referring) 谈到，提到

【考】**refer to** 提到，涉及：Is that the small town you often refer to? 这就是你常提到的那个小镇吗？

*__referee__ [ˌrefə'ri:] n. 仲裁人，调解人，【体】裁判员

【例】chief *referee* 裁判长

*__reference__ ['refərəns] n. 涉及；参考；证明书

【记】refer（提及）+ence（名词后缀）→提及，涉及

【例】a *reference* book 参考书

*reflect [ri'flekt] *vt.* 反射，反映

【例】Her work *reflects* intelligence. 她的工作反映出了她的聪明才智。

【衍】reflection（*n.* 反射；反映）

*refresh [ri'freʃ] *v.* （使）精神振作；更新

【记】词根记忆：re（重新）+fresh（新鲜）→更新

【例】A cool drink *refreshed* me after my long walk. 走了很长的一段路后，一杯冷饮让我恢复了精神。

【衍】refreshing（*adj.* 提神的，令人耳目一新的）

refuse [ri'fju:z] *v.* 拒绝，不愿

【用】**refuse to do sth.** 拒绝做某事：He refused to listen to her suggestions. 他不愿意接受她的建议。注意：refuse后只能接to do，不能接doing，类似用法的动词还有：want, hope, expect, intend, demand, plan, ask, decide, promise, agree, offer, prepare, manage, fail, learn, afford等。

regard [ri'gɑ:d] *v.* 当作，看待*n.* 关心，注意；致意

【考】1. **regard...as...** 把…当作…：He regarded reading as a headache. 他把读书当成件令人头疼的事。2. **in/with regard to** 关于：I've nothing to say with regard to your complaints. 对于你的投诉，我无话可说。

【衍】regardless*（*adj.* 不管，不顾，不注意）

*register ['redʒistə] *n.* 记录，登记簿*v.* 登记，注册

【例】a *register* of births and deaths 出生和死亡记录 // He *registered* the birth of his child. 他给孩子做了出生登记。

regret [ri'gret] *n.* 遗憾，懊悔；令人遗憾的事*vt.* （regretted, regretted, regretting）遗憾；后悔

【用】1. regret作名词时，如果表示遗憾、懊悔的情绪，为不可数名词；如果意为感到遗憾的事、歉意，则为可数名词。I can't come—please give them my regrets. 我不能来了，请代我向他们表示歉意。2. **regret doing sth. (=regret to have done sth.)** 为做过某事而遗憾：Have you ever regretted doing something you shouldn't have done? 你是否曾经为做了不该做的事情而遗憾？ 3. **regret to do sth.** 为要做某事而遗憾（动词常为say, inform, tell等表示"通知、告诉"含义的词）：I regret to say that you have failed your exam. 我很遗憾地告诉你，你考试不及格。 4. 后接doing和to do时含义不同的动词

还有：forget, remember, stop, try等：后接doing表示动作已发生，接to do表示动作还未发生。

【例】My only *regret* is that I could not devote more time to the just cause. 我惟一的憾事是不能花更多的时间于这一正义事业上。// Have a care of what you say or you may *regret* it. 注意自己说的话，不然你会后悔的。

【考】1. **have no regrets** 毫无遗憾：He said he had no regrets about leaving the university. 他说他对离开大学毫不遗憾。2. **much to one's regret** 令某人非常遗憾或抱歉的是：Much to my regret, I must leave now. 很抱歉我现在得走了。

regular ['reɡjulə] *adj.* 规则的，经常的
【例】the train's *regular* schedule 火车正常时刻表
【衍】regularly (*adv.* 有规律地；经常地)

*relate [ri'leit] *v.* 有关；涉及
【考】**relate to sth.** 涉及，和…相关：The symbols relate to an earlier system. 这些标志和早期的制度有关。
【衍】related (*adj.* 有关的，相关的)

relation [ri'leiʃn] *n.* 关系；亲属
【例】*Relation* between the two countries has reached a crisis point. 两国关系已达到出现危机的地步。
【考】**in/with relation to** 与…相关；涉及…：in relation to the murder 涉嫌谋杀

relax [ri'læks] *v.* (使)放松，轻松
【例】Don't worry about it; just try to *relax*. 不要为这事担心，放松些。
【衍】relaxing (*adj.* 令人放松的)；
relaxed (*adj.* 放松的，舒畅的)；
relaxation (*n.* 放松，消遣)

relax

relay ['ri:lei] *n.* 接力，接替 *v.* 接替，转运
【记】联想记忆：re (重新) +lay (放置)→重新放置→转运
【例】new *relays* of troops 新补充的部队

remain [ri'mein] *vi.* 余下，留下 *link.v.* 保持，仍是
【用】remain作系动词：The price has gone down, but I doubt whether it will remain so. 价格有所下降，但我怀疑它是否会持续下去。
【考】**It remains to be seen...** …有待观望：Having a trip abroad is

certainly good for the old couple, but it remains to be seen whether they will enjoy it. 到国外旅行对老年夫妇当然很好，但是他们是否喜欢还有待观望。

remember [ri'membə] v. 记得；纪念

【辨】**remember to do, remember doing**
remember to do... 记得去做…：Remember to close the door. 记得把门关上。**remember doing...** 记得曾做过…：I don't remember ever smiling so wide. 我不记得我曾笑得这么开心过。

remind [ri'maind] vt. 提醒，使记起
【记】词根记忆：re(重新)+mind(头脑，思想)→重新浮现在脑海→提醒，使记起

【辨】**remind sb. of sth. , remind sb. to do sth.**
remind sb. of sth. 提醒某人某事：Uniforms remind the wearers of their purpose and duties. 制服提醒穿着者他们的目的和责任。
remind sb. to do sth. 提醒某人去做某事：The taxi driver often reminds passengers to take their belongings when they leave the car. 出租车司机经常提醒乘客离开时拿好他们的东西。

remove [ri'mu:v] vt. 移动，拿走；去除
【记】re+move(移动)→移动
【例】*remove* your hat 摘掉你的帽子 // *remove* the dishes from the table 将盘子从桌子上拿走 // The boss *removed* his name from consideration. 老板将他的名字排除在考虑的范围之外。

reply [ri'plai] n./vi. (replied, replied, replying) 回答，答复
【考】**reply to** 回答，做出反应：Many people replied to our advertisement. 许多人都对我们的广告做出了反应。

***representative** [ˌrepri'zentətiv] n. 代表
【记】represent (v. 代表)+ative→代表
【例】a *representative* of a company 公司的代表

***request** [ri'kwest] n./vt. 要求，请求
【记】联想记忆：re (一再)+quest (看作question提问)→一再提问→请求
【例】These materials are in great *request*. 这些材料有很大的需求量。// Visitors are *requested* not to touch the exhibits. 游客们被要求不要触摸展品。

require [riˈkwaiə] *vt.* 需求；要求

【用】1. **require** + 从句，从句谓语用虚拟语气结构 **(should) +do**：It is required that all passengers (should) show their tickets. 旅客都要检验车票。2. **require sb. to do sth.** 要求某人做某事，常用被动形式：Students are required to bring their own pens and pencils. 规定学生们要自带钢笔和铅笔。3. **require+doing (= + to be done)**：The floor requires cleaning/to be cleaned. 地板需要清洁了。类似require（后接现在分词表示被动含义）的动词还有want, need等，如：The floor wants/needs cleaning. 地板需要清洁了。

【例】To solve the problem *requires* the efforts of the whole society. 解决这个问题需要全社会的努力。

【衍】requirement（*n.* 需要，必要的条件）

【辨】request, require
除作动词外，**request** 还可作名词使用；而**require**只能作动词。当它们都作动词时，**require** 的前两个用法都适用于**request**，但**request**没有后接doing的用法。另外request一词是指很有礼貌的请求，多含担心因种种原因对方不能答应的意味。而**require**强调根据事业、需要或纪律、法律等而提出的要求。

rescue [ˈreskju:] *vt./n.* 营救，援救

【记】联想记忆：res（看作rest休息）+cue（线索）→救援人员放弃休息寻找线索

【考】**come to sb.'s rescue** 救援某人：We came to his rescue and pulled him out of the river. 我们来救他，把他从河里拉了出来。

rescue

research [riˈsə:tʃ] *n./v.* 研究，调查

【记】联想记忆：re+search（搜寻）→不断搜寻资料进行研究

【例】a *research* on space 关于太空的研究

【衍】researcher（*n.* 研究者）

*__resemble__ [riˈzembl] *vt.* 像，类似

【例】He strongly *resembles* his mother. 他酷似他的母亲。

*__reserve__ [riˈzə:v] *n./vt.* 保留，储备；预订

【记】联想记忆：re（一再）+serve（服务）→一再为之服务，是为了储备客户→储备

【例】I *reserve* the right to disagree. 我保留持不同意见的权利。

【衍】reservation（*n.* 预订，保留）；reserved（*adj.* 预订的，缄默的）

单元自测

1. Living in a town can't compare with living in the country _____ as shopping, entertainment, and traffic.

   A. in many cases   B. in some ways   C. in such respects   D. at any rate

2. —You don't look well. What's wrong with you?

   —Why? I'm _____ myself.

   A. coming to   B. quite   C. of   D. by

3. —Can you shoot that bird at the top of the tree?

   —No, it's out of _____.

   A. range   B. reach   C. control   D. distance

4. —What about the weather here in winter?

   —It's _____ warmer than in the north of this country.

   A. fairly   B. rather   C. quite   D. very

5. Their ladders could _____ the top of the building.

   A. got   B. arrive in   C. come up   D. reach

6. When you write to him, please _____ him.

   A. give my loves to   B. give my regard to

   C. remember me to   D. give my wishes for

7. Not until all the fish died in the river _____ how serious the pollution was.

   A. did the villagers realize   B. the villagers realized

   C. the villagers did realize   D. didn't the villagers realize

8. —You were brave enough to raise objections at the meeting.

   —Well, now I regret _____ that.

   A. to do   B. to be doing   C. to have done   D. having done

9. The meeting will start at 3:00, so I will _____ you at 2:40.

   A. call for   B. accept   C. call at   D. receive

10. Can you _____ our headmaster at the first sight?

   A. know   B. recognize   C. tell   D. think

11. —The cars give off a great deal of waste gas into streets.

   —Yes. But I'm sure something will be done to _____ air pollution.

   A. reduce   B. remove   C. collect   D. warn

12. The dictionary he _____ was not on the bookshelf.

A. spoke to   B. looked up   C. point out   D. referred to

13. They seldom _____ in bed after 5:00 a.m. even though they are on holiday.

A. remained   B. slept   C. was   D. continued

14. In our childhood, we were often _____ by Grandma to pay attention to our table manners.

A. demanded   B. reminded   C. allowed   D. hoped

15. I wonder if you have forgotten _____ the novel from me last week. Will you please remember _____ it here tomorrow?

A. to borrow; to bring

B. borrowing; bring

C. borrowed; bring

D. borrowing; to bring

答案：CBABD CADAB ADABD

We cannot always build the future for our youth, but we can build our youth for the future.   —*Roosevelt*

我们不能总是为我们的青年造就美好未来,但我们能够为未来造就我们的青年一代。   ——罗斯福

Word List 32

*resign [ri'zain] *v.* 辞去，辞职

【记】词根记忆：re（不）+sign（加上记号）→不加记号→辞职

【例】He *resigned* from a board of directors because of his age. 因为年龄问题，他从董事会中辞职了。

*resist [ri'zist] *vt.* 抵抗；挡开

【记】词根记忆：re（反）+sist（站）→反过来站→抵抗

【用】**resist+doing...** 忍住不…：She could hardly resist laughing. 她忍不住要笑。

【衍】resistance（*n.* 抵抗）

respond [ri'spɔnd] *v.* 回答；做出反应

【考】**respond to...** 对…做出反应：They usually respond to it in one of these three ways. 他们经常以这三种方式中的一种回应它。

responsibility [riˌspɔnsə'biliti] *n.* 责任

【记】responsib(le)（责任）+ility→责任心

【例】A father has many *responsibilities*. 父亲要尽许多责任。

【衍】irresponsibility（*n.* 无责任）

rest [rest] *n.* 休息；剩余的部分，其余的人（物）*vi.* 休息，歇息

【考】1. **the rest of...** 剩余的…：The rest of the students will take part in the competition. 剩下的学生将参加那个竞赛。2. **rest on/upon...** 依据；停留在：Your argument rests on a statement that can't be proved. 你的论点是以一项无法证明的陈述为依据的。

*restriction [ri'strikʃn] *n.* 限制

【记】restrict（限制，约束）+ion→限制

【例】supply on *restriction* 限制供应

【衍】restrict（*vt.* 限制，约束）

return [ri'tə:n] *v.* 归还，返回 *n.* 返回，来回

【例】*return* ticket 往返票

【考】**return to** 重新回到（地方、话题等）：I am always dreaming of returning to the small village where I was born. 我一直梦想着回到我出生的那个村庄。

review ［ri'vju:］ *vt.* 复习；重新调查 *n.* 复习；复查；评论

【记】re（重新）+view（看）→重新看→复习

【例】to *review* the situation 回顾形势//book *review* 书评//to *review* last week's lessons 复习上周的功课

*revolution ［ˌrevə'lu:ʃn］ *n.* 革命，变革

【例】Industrial *Revolution* 工业革命

*rhyme ［raim］ *n.* 韵，押韵 *v.* （使）押韵，作诗

【例】nursery *rhyme* 儿歌

*rid ［rid］ *vt.* （rid/ridded, rid/ridded, ridding）使…摆脱

【考】**get rid of** 摆脱；除去：Mary is trying to get rid of the mice in her house. 玛丽试图除掉她家里的老鼠。

*ridiculous ［ri'dikjuləs］ *adj.* 荒谬的，可爱的

【例】a *ridiculous* suggestion 荒谬的意见

*rigid ［'ridʒid］ *adj.* 刚硬的，刚性的；严格的

【例】*rigid* ideas 固执的看法

ring ［riŋ］ *v.* （rang, rung, ringing）（钟、铃等）响；打电话 *n.* 电话铃声；环形物（如环、圈、戒指等）

【例】He *rang* me at noon. 他中午打电话给我了。//growth *rings* of trees 树的年轮

*ripe ［raip］ *adj.* 成熟的，熟的

【记】联想记忆：稻熟（ripe）米（rice）香

【例】*ripe* old age 高龄 // *ripe* sweet tomatoes 成熟的甜西红柿

*ripen ［'raipən］ *v.* （使）成熟

【记】rip(e)（成熟的）+en（使…）→使…成熟

【例】These peaches are *ripened* by the sun. 这些桃子是被太阳晒熟的。

rise ［raiz］ *vi.* （rose, risen, rising）*n.* 上升，上涨

【例】Only with hard work can you expect to get a pay *rise*. 只有努力工作你才有望得到加薪。

【辨】**rise, raise**

rise 为不及物动词,表示某物自己往上升: The sun rises in the east. 太阳从东方升起。而 **raise** 为及物动词,可接宾语,可用于被动语态: Raise your hands. 举起手来。

risk [risk] *n.* 冒险,风险 *vt.* 冒…的危险

【用】**risk doing** 冒险做…: He got well-prepared for the job interview, for he couldn't risk losing the good opportunity. 他为面试做了充分准备,因为他不能冒险丢失这个好机会。

【考】**take a risk** 冒险: The best leaders know that taking a risk is not a thoughtless exercise. 最好的领导知道冒险并不是盲目的行动。

rob [rɔb] *v.* (robbed, robbed, robbing) 抢夺,抢劫

【考】**rob sb. of sth.** 抢某人的某物: I was robbed of my bag. 我的包被抢走了。

【衍】**robber** (*n.* 抢劫者)

roll [rəul] *v.* 滚动,打滚 *n.* 面包圈,卷状物

【例】The dog *rolled* in the mud. 狗在泥地里打滚。

【考】**roll up** 到达,出现: Bill finally rolled up two hours late. 迟到了两小时后,比尔终于来了。

roll

rot [rɔt] *v.* (rotted, rotted, rotting) 腐烂,腐败

【例】The beams had *rotted* away. 横梁已经腐烂了。

rough [rʌf] *adj.* 粗糙的,粗略的

【例】Elephants have their own way to tell the shape of an object and whether it is *rough* or smooth. 大象有自己的方法来识别物体的形状以及它是粗糙还是光滑。//*rough* conditions 艰苦的条件//a *rough* person 粗人

round [raund] *adv.* 转过来 *prep.* 环绕一周,围着 *adj.* 圆的,球形的

【例】We were sitting *round* the fire, eating and talking. 我们围坐在炉火边,边吃边谈。

【考】1. **look round** 环顾;观察 2. **get round** 避免;说服;走动;传开来 3. **go round** 流行,传播 4. **all year round** 终年,一年到头 5. **a round trip** 往返旅途

*roundabout ['raundəbaut] *adj.* 绕道的；不直接的 *n.* 转盘路

【记】组合词：round（圆圈）+about（附近）→在附近绕圈→迂回的，拐弯抹角的；绕道的

【例】a *roundabout* way of traveling 迂回的旅行路线

*routine [ru:'ti:n] *n.* 常规，日常事务

【记】联想记忆：例行公事（routine）就是按常规路线（route）走

【例】a *routine* medical examination 常规体检

*royal ['rɔiəl] *adj.* 王室的，皇家的；第一流的

【记】联想记忆：皇室的（royal）的忠诚（loyal）臣民

【例】the *royal* family 王室，皇族

*ruin ['ru:in] *v.* (使) 毁坏；(使) 毁灭 *n.* (*pl.*) 废墟；遗迹

【例】Crops are *ruined* by the war. 因为战争，庄稼被毁。

*sacred ['seikrid] *adj.* 宗教的；庄严的，神圣的

【例】Cats were *sacred* to the Egyptians in ancient time. 猫对于古埃及人来说是圣物。

*sacrifice ['sækrifais] *n./v.* 牺牲，奉献

【例】Parents *sacrifice* themselves to their children. 家长为孩子奉献了自己的一切。

sail [seil] *v.* 航行，开航 *n.* 帆；航行

【例】Months ago we *sailed* ten thousand miles across the Pacific. 几个月前我们跨越太平洋航行了一万英里。

same [seim] *n.* 同样的事 *adj.* 同样的，同一的

【例】Your watch is the *same* as mine. 你的表和我的一样。

【考】1. **at the same time** 同时 2. **on the same day** 同一天 3. **in the same way** 相同的方式 4. **the same as...** 和…一样

satisfaction [ˌsætis'fækʃn] *n.* 满意

【例】What he has done is far from *satisfaction*. 他所做的远不能令人满意。

【考】**satisfaction with...** 对…满意

satisfy ['sætisfai] *v.* 满足，使满意

【例】People buy to *satisfy* both body and soul. 人们买东西是为了满足身心两方面的需求。

【衍】satisfying (*adj.* 令人满意的); satisfied (*adj.* 感到满意的)

say [sei] *v.* (said, said, saying) 说，讲

【用】1. **say... to sb.** 向某人说…：say hello to sb. 向某人问候 2. **It is said that** 据说…：It is said that the site of an ancient city has been discovered at the bottom of the lake. 据说在湖底发现了一座古城的遗址。

【考】1. **that is to say** 也就是说 2. **say to oneself** 心中暗想

【辨】**say, speak, talk, tell**

say 是普通用语，一般接说话的具体内容，如：He said hello to every person. 他向每个人问好。**speak** 一般用作不及物动词，强调讲话这一动作本身；用作及物动词只接某种语言。如：—What did you think of her speech? —She spoke for one hour but didn't say much. —你认为她的演讲怎么样？—她说了一个小时但是没有说出多少内容。**talk** 与 **speak** 一样侧重于动作，不过 **talk** 更侧重"与人交谈时的连贯说话"如：We talked about music all night. 我们整夜都在谈论音乐。**tell** 表示把某件事情告诉某人、讲述故事等，如：I told him my address. 我告诉他我的地址。

*scan [skæn] v. (scanned, scanned, scanning) 细看；浏览；扫描

【记】发音记忆："四看"→四下看→细看

【例】He *scanned* the newspaper while having his breakfast. 他在吃早饭的时候浏览了一下报纸。

*scare ['skɛə] v. 惊吓，威吓；受惊

【记】联想记忆：s+care（在意）→太过在意，担惊受怕→受惊

【例】The dog *scared* the stranger away. 狗把那个陌生人吓跑了。

scare

*sceptical ['skeptikl] adj. 怀疑的，怀疑论的

【例】The *skeptical* student refused to accept the theory of evolution. 这个喜欢怀疑的学生拒绝接受进化论。

schedule ['skedʒul] n. 时刻表 vt. 安排，排定

【例】bus *schedule* 公共汽车时刻表//The tests are *scheduled* for six months' time. 这些测试预计用六个月完成。

scissors ['sizəz] n. (pl.) 剪刀，剪子

【用】**glasses, jeans, scissors** 等由两部分组成的东西，只用复数的形式，谓语动

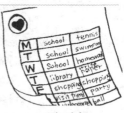

schedule

词也使用复数。如：The scissors are sharp. 这把剪刀很锋利。若想表示单数含义，可使用a pair of来修饰这类名词，谓语动词亦使用单数，如：This pair of scissors is made in HangZhou. 这把剪刀是杭州制造的。

【例】John cut the paper with *scissors*. 约翰用剪刀剪开那张纸。

*scold [skəuld] *vt.* 责骂，谴责

【记】联想记忆：s+cold（冷）→冷酷无情→责骂

scold

【考】**scold sb. for sth.** 为某事责骂某人：The teacher scolded Jimmy for running in the classroom. 老师因为吉米在教室中跑而批评他。

*scratch [skrætʃ] *v.* 抓，划破；乱涂 *n.* 乱写；抓痕

【记】联想记忆：s+cratch（看作catch抓住）→抓

【例】Because the puppy was *scratching*, I gave it a bath. 小狗不停地抓搔，所以我给它洗了个澡。

scream [skri:m] *v.* 尖叫，尖声喊叫 *n.* 尖叫（声）

【记】女孩子们看到冰激凌（ice-cream）就会尖叫（scream）

【例】The woman *screamed* as she saw the dog attacked her child. 那女人看到狗攻击她的孩子时尖叫起来。

screen [skri:n] *n.* 幕，荧光屏

【例】TV *screen* 电视荧光屏

*sculpture ['skʌlptʃə] *n.* 雕塑（术），雕像

【例】Don't touch any of the *sculptures* at the museum. 不要触摸博物馆里的任何雕像。

search [sə:tʃ] *n./v.* 搜寻，搜查

【记】网页上的搜索就是这个单词search

【考】1. **search out...** 找出… 2. **in search of...** 搜寻…

【辨】**1. search, search for**
search指"搜身/搜查某物"，宾语是搜查的对象，如：The police searched the thief but found no weapon on him. 警察搜查了小偷，但没找到武器。**search for**指"搜寻某人/某物"，宾语是搜查的目的：He searched for his keys. 他找他的钥匙。

2. look for, search for, be after

以上三个词组都指"找"的动作或过程，与 find（找到）强调"找"的结果相对。**look for** 是普通用语，语气较弱；**search for** 是"搜寻"，语气较强。**be after** 表示"尾追"，如：The police are after him. 警方正在追捕他。

second [ˈsekənd] *n.* 秒 *num.* 第二 *adj.* 二等的

【例】We learn English as our *second* language. 英语是我们的第二语言。

【考】**second to none** 最棒的：Fred is second to none in math in our class. 佛瑞德是我们班数学学得最好的。

【衍】secondly（*adv.* 第二，其次）；millisecond（*n.* 毫秒）

section [ˈsekʃn] *n.* 段，部分，部门

【例】There is heavy traffic on some *sections* of the freeway. 高速公路的某些路段发生了严重的交通堵塞。

security [siˈkjuəriti] *n.* 安全

【例】*security* rules 安全法规

【衍】secure（*adj.* 安全的，可靠的）

see [siː] *v.*（saw, seen, seeing）看见，看到；领会

【用】see 可以接复合宾语，宾补是不定式（省略 to）、现在分词和过去分词：I saw him drive off. 我看见他开车走了。//I hope to see the plan carried out. 我希望看到计划得到实施。

【例】go to *see* a doctor 去看医生//Do you *see* what I mean? 明白我的意思了吗？

【考】1. **see to** 处理，照料 2. **see sb. off** 给某人送行

seek [siːk] *v.*（sought, sought, seeking）试图；寻找，寻求

【记】联想记忆：see（看）+k→更深入地看→寻找

【例】He *sought* to make peace. 他企图讲和。//Most men *seek* wealth; all men seek happiness. 大多数人寻求财富，所有的人追求幸福。

seem [siːm] *link.v.* 似乎，好像

【用】seem 用作系动词，主要句型有：1. **seem+*adj./n.*** 看上去好像：It seems cruel not to give some money to beggars. 不给乞丐点钱似乎很残忍。2. **seem to do（be）...** 似乎，好像：I seem to hear a voice in the distance. 我好像听到远处有说话声。3. **It seems... /seemed**

that... 似乎：It seems that she's gone away. 好像她已经走了。4. **It seems... /seemed as if...** 看起来好像（常用虚拟语气）：It seemed as if no one cared. 看来好像没人在意。5. **seem like...** 好像...：He seems like a nice guy. 他看上去是个不错的家伙。

*seize [siːz] *v.* 抓住（时机等）

【例】He *seized* the boy's arm. 他抓住了那个男孩的手臂。

seldom ['seldəm] *adv.* 很少，不常

【用】1. seldom是否定副词，因此后接反意疑问句时，用肯定形式：He seldom cries, does he? 他很少哭，是吗？2. seldom位于句首，句子的谓语要用倒装形式：Seldom did I ask him for help. 我很少向他请求帮助。类似的副词或短语还有never, hardly, neither/nor, only by, no sooner...than..., not until, so等。3. 表示动作发生频率的副词有：never（从不），seldom（很少），sometimes（有时），often（经常），always（总是）。

【辨】**hardly, seldom**

两个副词都具有否定意义。**hardly**否定动词的动作，如：We could hardly move. 我们几乎不能动。**seldom**指动词的动作很少发生，如：He seldom bathed. 他很少洗澡。

单元自测

1. The old man can't hope to _____ the pain in his knee in a few days.
   A. get rid of　　　B. be off　　　C. get off　　　D. get over

2. As we all know, the sun _____ in the east and sets in the west.
   A. raises　　　B. raising　　　C. rising　　　D. rises

3. He _____ his life when he saved the child from the fire.
   A. spent　　　B. cost　　　C. risked　　　D. lived

4. I have heard about the shop _____.
   A. to be stolen　　B. robbed　　C. robbed of　　D. being robbed of

5. Does any one know how the news _____?
   A. get over　　　B. get up　　　C. get round　　　D. turn round

6. It rained for two weeks on end, completely _____ our holiday.
   A. ruined　　　B. to ruin　　　C. ruining　　　D. was ruined

7. The company's employment policy makes it clear that men and women have _____ opportunities.

A. balanced   B. equal   C. same   D. natural

8. What he has done is far from _____.

    A. satisfactory   B. satisfied   C. satisfaction   D. satisfy

9. —What did you think of her speech?

    —She _____ for one hour but didn't _____ much.

    A. spoke; speak   B. spoke; say

    C. said; speak   D. said; say

10. The guards caught the spy and _____ him very carefully.

    A. asked for   B. searched for   C. looked for   D. searched

11. Having a trip abroad is certainly good for the old couple, but it remains _____ whether they will enjoy it.   （2002全国）

    A. to see   B. to be seen   C. seeing   D. seen

12. It was no use _____ persuade him to give up smoking. What he _____ was happiness _____ health.

    A. seeking to; ask; rather than   B. seeking to; sought; rather than

    C. to seek; sought; more than   D. to seek; ask; more than

13. I must be getting fat—I can _____ do my trousers up.   （2004全国二）

    A. fairly   B. hardly

    C. nearly   D. seldom

14. —What do you think of the book?

    —Oh, excellent. It is worth _____ second time.

    A. to read a   B. to read the   C. reading a   D. being read the

15. Ten minutes _____ an hour when you are waiting for a phone call.

    A. liked   B. likes   C. seemed   D. seems

答案：ADCBC CBCBD BBBCD

Word List 33

select [si'lekt] *vt.* 选择，挑选，选拔 *a.* 精选的

【例】Our shops *select* only the very best quality product. 我们商店都是精选的质量最好的产品。

【衍】selection (*n.* 选择)

*seminar ['seminɑ:] *n.* 研究会，讨论发表会

【例】The teacher made some of his lessons *seminars*, which were welcomed by the students. 这位教师把他的部分课程变成了讨论会，很受学生欢迎。

send [send] *vt.* (sent, sent, sending) 打发，派遣；送，邮寄

【用】1. send常接双宾语，即 **send sb. sth. (=send sth. to sb.)** 送/寄某物给某人：Foreign countries can send their programmes to China. 外国可将他们的电视节目传送到中国。常接双宾语的动词还有：give, lend, buy, show等。2. send可以接复合宾语，即 **send sb. to do sth.** 使某人做某事：Photographers are sent to take the pictures. 摄影记者被派去拍照片。当send的宾补为doing形式时，即 **send sb. doing**，表示"使某人突然做…"：The fire sent everyone running out of the building. 大火让所有人从房子里跑了出来。

【考】1. **send out** 发出，放出 2. **send off** 邮寄；送行 3. **send up** 发射 4. **send for sb.** 让人去请某人

senior ['si:niə] *adj.* 年长的，资深的；高年级的 *n.* 上级，长辈；高年级学生

【记】词根记忆：sen (老) +ior→年长的

【例】*senior* adults 长者//*senior* lecturers 高级讲师

sense [sens] *n.* 感觉，意识

【例】*sense* of sight 视觉//*sense* of humor 幽默感

【考】**make sense** 有意义

【衍】sensitive (*adj.* 敏感的；灵敏的)

separate ['sepəreit] v. (使)分开，(使)分离

['seprət] adj. 单独的，分开的

【例】Doctors completed a 20-hour operation to have *separated* one-year-old twins at the head. 医生们用20小时完成了一岁连体双胞胎的头部分离手术。//The system enables glass, plastic, paper, and other rubbish to go into *separate* boxes. 该系统可使玻璃、塑料、纸和其他垃圾进入不同的垃圾箱。

【衍】separation* (n. 分离，隔离)

serve [sə:v] vt. 服务，招待；服役

【例】The dining-room *serves* three meals a day from 7:00 am to 7:00 pm. 这个餐厅从早七点到晚七点提供三餐。//No matter what he is wearing, you must *serve* him. 不管人家穿着如何，你都要为他服务。

【考】1. serve as 作为：The stone served as a road sign. 这块石头被用作一块路标。2. serve for 充当，用作：The box serves for a table. 这个箱子作为餐桌使用。

*session ['seʃn] n. 会议；开庭

【考】in session 在开会，在开庭

set [set] vt. (set, set, setting)设置，调整；树立 n. 一套；设备

【例】I forgot to *set* my alarm and I overslept. 我忘记设闹铃，睡过头了。//He took the case out of her hand and *set* it on the floor. 他从她手里拿过箱子放在地板上。//Competition helps to *set* self-respect. 竞争有利于树立自尊心。//The sun hardly *set*. 太阳几乎不落山。

【考】1. set up 建立，建造 2. set out to do 着手做… 3. set out/off 出发 4. set sb./sth. free 解放… 5. set aside 留出 6. set records 创造记录 7. set apart 分开 8. set about... 开始… 9. set a pace 定步调 10. set fire to... (=set...on fire) 纵火焚烧… 11. set an example 树立榜样 12. (be) set in... 以…为背景 13. a set of 一组，一套

settle ['setl] vi. 安家，定居 vt. 解决 (问题)

【例】They helped the rare bird *settle* in Kent. 他们帮助这种稀有的鸟在肯特郡安家落户。//All the problems were *settled*. 所有的问题都解决了。

【考】settle for sth. 满足于某物

【衍】settled (adj. 固定的); settler (n. 移民者，殖民者); settlement (n. 殖民；新拓居地)

shake [ʃeik] *vt.* (shook, shaken, shaking) 使摇动；震动

【例】*shake* the head 摇头

【考】**shake hands with sb.** 和…握手

shall [ʃæl] *modal. v.* 将要，会；应该；…好吗？

【用】1. shall可用于构成一般将来时，但仅限于陈述句第一人称：We shall have a new manager. 我们将有一个新经理。2. shall表示说话人的允诺或警告，限于陈述句第二人称和第三人称：You shall follow the doctor's advice. 你得遵照医嘱。3. 表示征求意见或者提出建议，限于疑问句第一人称和第三人称：Shall I tell him you're here? 我应该告诉他你来了吗？

shape [ʃeip] *n.* 形状，外形 *vt.* 使成形；制造，塑造

【例】pear-*shaped* 梨形的

【考】1. **in shape** 在外形上处于良好状态；健康 2. **out of shape** 变形；不健康

share [ʃɛə] *v.* 分享，共同使用 *n.* 一份；股份

【例】The manufacturer and the dealer *shared* in the expense of advertising. 制造商与经销商共同承担广告费用。// They sell *shares* in companies at the stock exchange. 他们在证券交易所出售公司股票。

【考】**share sth. with sb.** 与某人分享某物：She shared all her knowledge with the whole scientific world. 她将自己的全部知识与整个科学界共享。

sharp [ʃɑːp] *adj.* 尖锐的；敏锐的；整点的

【例】*sharp*-eyed people 目光敏锐的人 // 6:00 *sharp* 六点整

【衍】sharpen* (*vt.* 使锐利，削尖)

*****shelter** [ˈʃeltə] *n.* 掩蔽，隐蔽处

【例】a *shelter* for the homeless 无家可归者的收容所

shelter

SHELL SWEET SHELTER

S

shock [ʃɔk] *vt.* 使震惊 *n.* 震动，冲击

【例】*shock* wave 冲击波

【衍】shocking (*adj.* 令人震惊的，令人厌恶的)；shocked (*adj.* 感到震惊的)

shoot [ʃuːt] *vt.* (shot, shot, shooting) 射击，射中；摄影 *n.* 嫩枝，苗，芽

【记】联想记忆：sh+oot (看作root根) →从根部长出新芽

【例】Can you *shoot* that bird at the top of the tree? 你能射中树梢上

的那只鸟吗? //She had *shot* many pictures when she was in China. 她在中国拍摄了很多照片。//Processing tea *shoots* into the familiar dry tea leaves requires great care and skill. 把茶树嫩叶加工成我们熟悉的干茶叶需要十分仔细也需要精湛的技巧。

【考】**shoot up** 射击;迅速生长

【衍】shot (*n*. 射击,开枪,开炮)

*shortly [ˈʃɔːtli] *adv.* 不久

【例】*Shortly* afterwards, the police stopped the car and both thieves were arrested. 过了没有多久,警察截住了那辆汽车,两个贼都被抓获了。

should [ʃud] *modal. v.* 应当,应该

【用】1. should表示应该,与ought to同义: Parents should talk with their children frequently. 父母应经常和孩子交谈。2. 表示可能: It's nearly seven o'clock. Jack should be here at any moment. 快七点了,杰克可能随时会到。3. 构成虚拟语气,表示要求或建议: I suggest you (should) ask Mr. Wu. 我建议你去问问吴老师。4. should have done... / should not have done...本应该做却没做…/本不该做却做了…: I was really anxious about you. You shouldn't have left home without a word. 你让我很担心,你不应该一句话也不说就离开了家。

show [ʃəu] *v.* (showed, shown/showed, showing) 给…看,出示,显示 *n.* 展示,展览(会);演出

【例】talk *show* 脱口秀 //He *showed* great interest in music. 他对音乐很感兴趣。

【考】1. **show sb. around** 领某人到处参观 2. **on show** 正在被展出 3. **show off** 炫耀 4. **show up** 露出,露面

*shrink [ʃriŋk] *v.* (shrank, shrunk 或 shrunk, shrunken) 收缩;缩短

【例】The pupils of the eyes will automatically *shrink* in strong light. 瞳孔在强光下会自动收缩。

What?
shrink

shut [ʃʌt] *n./vt.* (shut, shut, shutting) 关闭 *adj.* 关闭的

【例】John *shut* everybody out of the kitchen. 约翰把所有的人都关在厨房外面。

【考】1. **shut down** 关闭,倒闭 2. **shut off** 关掉,切断 3. **shut up** 住口

*shuttle [ˈʃʌtl] *n.* (往返于两个定点之间的)车辆、飞机等

【例】She caught a *shuttle* to Washington D.C.. 她搭上一辆开往华盛顿的往返公车。//the space *shuttle* 航天飞机

*significance [sig'nifikəns] *n.* 意义，重要性

【例】Few people realized the *significance* of the discovery. 很少有人意识到这一发现的重要性。

【衍】significant (*adj.* 有意义的，重要的)

similar ['similə] *adj.* 相似的，像

【考】be similar to... 与…相似的：Your ring is similar to mine. 你的戒指和我的那个很像。

【衍】similarly (*adv.* 类似地); similarity (*n.* 类似，类似处)

since [sins] *conj.* 从…以来；由于 *prep./adv.* 从…以来

【用】1. 引导时间状语从句，主句多用完成时：She has wanted to be a dancer since she was a child. 从儿时起，她就想当一名舞蹈演员。2. 引导原因状语从句：Since it was raining, we didn't go out. 由于下雨了，我们就没出去。3. It is+一段时间+since从句 (注意从句中用短暂性动词和持续性动词的区别)：It's two years since he joined the League. 他入团已经两年了。//It's two years since he was a League member. 他退团已经两年了。

【辨】since, as, because, for

这四个词都可以引导原因状语，**because**语气最强，表示直接而明确的原因，常用于回答why引起的问句，如：He had to stay at home yesterday because he was ill. 因为病了，他昨天只得呆在家里。**as**语气较弱，只是附带说明较明显的原因，如：She was well paid, as she had done the work well. 她的薪水很高，因为她干得出色。**since**语气也比**because**弱，陈述的理由往往是对方所知道的，常译作"既然"，如：Since you can't answer the question, perhaps we'd better ask someone else. 既然你无法回答这个问题，我们最好再问问别人。**for**语气最弱，只是就前一句做逻辑推理或解释一下理由，引导一个表示原因的并列句，for一般不用于句首，如：Maybe he is ill, for he is absent today. 他今天没有来，可能是病了。

single ['siŋgl] *adj.* 单一的，单个的

【例】*single* parent 单亲//*single*-minded pursuit 专注的追求

sink [siŋk] *v.* (sank, sunk, sinking) (使) 下沉；消沉；陷入 *n.* 洗涤槽，污水槽

【例】The British had to *sink* this warship. 英国人必须击沉这艘军舰。

【考】**sink in** 陷入：I sank in my thoughts. 我陷入沉思。

【衍】unsinkable (*adj.* 不会下沉的)；sinking (*n.* 沉没)

situation [ˌsitjuˈeiʃn] *n.* 形势，情况

【例】a dangerous *situation* 危险的境地

skill [skil] *n.* 技能，技巧

【例】writing *skills* 写作技巧

【衍】skillful (*adj.* 熟练的，精湛的；灵巧的)

skip [skip] *vi.* (skipped, skipped, skipping) 跳过；跳读

【例】A newspaper reader can select what he is interested in and *skip* what he thinks is boring. 读报人可以选择他感兴趣的部分来阅读而略过他认为无聊的部分。

*slide [slaid] *v.* (slid, slid, sliding) 滑行，滑动 *n.* 幻灯片；滑道

【例】Some boys are *sliding* on the ice. 一些男孩子在溜冰。

slight [slait] *adj.* 轻微的，细小的

【记】联想记忆：s+light (轻的)→轻微的

【例】*slight* mistake 微小的错误//*slight* movement 轻微的运动

【衍】slightly (*adv.* 轻微地)

*slim [slim] *adj.* 苗条的，纤细的

【例】In order to become *slim*, she eats like a bird. 为了变苗条，她吃得很少。

*slip [slip] *v.* (slipped, slipped, slipping) 溜 (进/走)，滑动 *n.* 片，纸片；滑倒

【例】She *slipped* away without being seen. 她悄悄溜走，未被人看见。//He took a *slip* of paper out of his pocket. 他从衣袋里拿出一张纸条。

smell [smel] *vt.* (smelled/smelt, smelled/smelt, smelling) 嗅，闻 *vi.* 有臭气 *link.v.* 闻起来 *n.* 气味

【用】1. **smell+***adj.* 闻起来怎么样：The flower smells sweet. 这种花闻起来又香又甜。2. **smell as if+**从句 闻起来好像…：The house smells as if it hasn't been lived in for years. 房子里的味道闻起来让人感觉这里很多年没人住了。3. 不带表语和状语，常指有难闻气味：This meat is beginning to smell. 这肉有味儿了。

*sniff [snif] *v.* 用力吸；嗅，闻

【例】She *sniffed* the drink suspiciously. 她怀疑地闻了闻饮料。

so [səu] *conj.* 因此，所以 *pron./adv.* 如此，这么

【用】1. 作并列连词，表示"所以"，注意不能和because连用：This question is simple, so I can answer it. 这个问题很简单，我能回答。 2. 作代词，代替前面提到的事物或情况以避免重复：I think so. 我认为是这样的。//I told you so. 我告诉过你。 3. 作副词，表程度：We got so wet and dirty. 我们浑身又湿又脏。//so short a time 这么短的时间

【考】1. **so as to** 为了 2. **or so** 大约 3. **so far** 到目前为止 4. **so that** 目的是，以便 5. **so...that...** 如此…以至于…

> 【辨】**so, such**
> 这两个单词作副词时都可用来加强语气，表示"如此…，这样…"，但在用法上有所不同：1. 用于有形容词修饰的单数可数名词时，位置不同，即such+a/an +*adj.* +*n.* 和so+*adj.* +a/an +*n.* 两种结构：such a good teacher=so good a teacher 这么好的一位老师 2. **so** 可以修饰many, much, little, few, 而**such**不可以：so much work 这么多的工作；但当little表示"小"而非"少"之意时，用**such**修饰，如：Such little animals eat so much grass. 那么小的动物吃了那么多的草。3. 复数名词和不可数名词，以及没有形容词修饰的单数可数名词之前用**such**修饰，不能用**so**，如：We had such fun. 我们玩得真开心。//You are such a fool. 你真是个大傻瓜。

social ['səuʃl] *adj.* 社会的；社交的；群居的

【例】Correct ideas come from *social* practice. 正确的思想来自社会实践。//The bee, like the ant, is a *social* insect. 蜜蜂同蚂蚁一样是群居性昆虫。

society [sə'saiəti] *n.* 社会

【例】During those years many young students were angry at *society*. 在那些岁月里，许多年轻学生对社会愤愤不平。

software ['sɔftwɛə] *n.* 软件

【记】组合词：soft（软的）+ware（器件）→软件

【例】common *software* 通用软件

*solar ['səulə] *adj.* 太阳的

【例】*solar* system 太阳系//*solar* power 太阳能

some [sʌm] *adj.* 一些，若干；有些；某一 *pron.* 若干，一些

【用】1. 作形容词，修饰可数名词复数或不可数名词，表示"一些，一点"：I have some trouble. 我碰上了一点麻烦。2. 修饰数词，表示"大约"：It happened some twenty years ago. 这大约是20年前的事了。3. 修饰单数可数名词，表示"某一"：He went to some place in Africa. 他到非洲某地去了。4. 作代词，单独用或与of连用：Many of them become fat. And some have bad teeth. 他们之中有很多人发胖了，并且有些人的牙齿也坏了。

【辨】**some, any**

这两个词作形容词时都有"一些"之意。**some**用在肯定句中，如：Please give me some water. 请给我点水。而**any**用在否定句以及含有怀疑或否定的句子中，如：They don't have any children. 他们没有孩子。在疑问句中一般用**any**，但在表示问话者期待得到肯定答复或表示提议、邀请时用**some**，如：Would you like some more cakes? 你再吃点蛋糕好吗？

soon [su:n] *adv.* 不久，很快，一会儿

【用】**no sooner... than** 一…就…：I had no sooner left than she called. 我刚走她就打来了电话。注意：当no sooner位于句首时，其后的部分应使用倒装语序：No sooner was the frost off the ground than the work began. 地上的霜一消散，人们就开始工作了。

【考】1. **as soon as possible** 尽快 2. **sooner or later** 迟早 3. **soon after** 不久之后

*sorrow [ˈsɔrəu] *n.* 悲伤，悲痛

【例】To her great *sorrow*, her dog died in a traffic accident. 她的爱犬死于车祸，为此她悲伤不已。

sort [sɔːt] *v.* 分类，拣选 *n.* 种类，类别

【考】**sort of** 副词词组，表示"有几分，多少"：When you give someone a tip, you're sort of being polite. 当你给小费时，在某种程度上你是在礼貌待人。

*soul [səul] *n.* 灵魂，心灵

sound [saund] *vi.* 发出声音 *vt.* 宣告 *link.v.* 听起来 *n.* 声音

【用】sound作系动词，主要用法有：1. **sound like** 听起来像…：I

don't want to sound like I'm speaking ill of anybody, but the manager's plan is unfair. 我不想让自己听起来像是在说别人的坏话，但是经理的计划确实不公平。2. **sound**+*adj.* 听起来…：The disc sounded fantastic at the party that night. 那晚聚会上放的唱片听起来棒极了。

sour ［ˈsauə］*adj.* 酸的

【例】If you leave milk on the table, it goes *sour* quickly. 如果把牛奶放在餐桌上，它会很快变酸的。

sour

***sow** ［səu］*v.* （sowed, sowed/sown, sowing）播种

【记】一排排（row）播种（sow）

【例】It is important to remove weeds before *sowing* seed in the soil. 播种前清除杂草是很重要的。

***spade** ［speid］*n.* 铲子；纸牌中的黑桃

【例】The soldiers dug in the stony soil with *spade*. 士兵用铲子在满是石头的地上挖坑。

【考】**call a spade a spade** 有话直说，实事求是

SPADE

spare ［speə］*adj.* 空闲的；多余的，剩余的 *vt.* 提供；匀出，分出

【用】1. **spare time** 空闲时间 2. **spare (sb.) some time** （为某人）抽出时间 3. **spare no effort (to do sth.)** 不遗余力（做某事）：I'll spare no effort to help you. 我将不遗余力地帮助你。

speak ［spiːk］*v.* （spoke, spoken, speaking）说，讲；谈话；发言

【用】1. **speak to/with sb. (of/about sth.)** 与某人谈（某事）2. **speak+** 语言：Do you speak English? 你讲英语吗？

【考】1. **speak out** 大声地说 2. **generally speaking** 一般而言

S

单元自测

1. When anybody in our village is ill, Dr. Green will _____.

   A. send for   B. send off   C. be sent   D. be sent for

2. You'd better _____ some money for special use.

   A. pick up   B. set aside   C. put off   D. give away

3. Mineral oil is of no use to man until it _____ into different products, such as oil for trains, petrol for cars, etc.

A. separates   B. is separating
C. has been separated   D. will be separated

4. —When shall we start?

   —Let's _____ it at 8:30. Is that all right?   (2002北京)

   A. set   B. meet   C. make   D. take

5. It was so noisy outside that he couldn't _____ down to read.

   A. settle   B. put   C. sit   D. lie

6. —We want someone to design the new art museum for us.

   — _____ the young fellow have a try?

   A. May   B. Shall   C. Will   D. Need

7. Let Harry play with your toys as well; Clare you must learn to _____.

   A. support   B. care   C. spare   D. share

8. _____ by his death, his wife was determined _____ on working.

   A. Deeply shocked; to go   B. Deeply shocked; on going
   C. Shocked deeply; to go   D. Shocked deeply; on going

9. —Excuse me, may I ask you some questions?

   —Sorry, I'm too busy and haven't even a minute to _____.

   A. spend   B. spare   C. share   D. stop

10. It has been announced that candidates _____ remain in their seats until all the
    papers have been collected.

    A. can   B. will   C. may   D. shall

11. It's nearly seven o'clock. Jack _____ be here at any moment.

    A. must   B. need   C. should   D. can

12. I think it will rain this afternoon, but my brother thinks _____.

    A. seriously   B. similarly   C. logically   D. otherwise

13. —How long has this bookshop been in business?

    — _____ 1982.

    A. After   B. In   C. From   D. Since

14. Can you believe that in _____ a rich country there should be _____ many poor
    people?

    A. such; such   B. such; so   C. so; so   D. so; such

15. —I'd like _____ information about the management of your hotel, please.

    —Well, you could have _____ word with the manager. He might be helpful.

    A. some; a   B. an; some   C. some; some   D. an; a

答案：DBCCA ADABD CDDBA

Word List 34

*spear [spiə] *n.* 矛

【例】Washington Monument is a very tall building that looks like a *spear* shooting into the sky. 华盛顿纪念碑是一座极高的建筑, 外形像直刺苍穹的长矛。

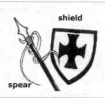

shield

spear

special ['speʃəl] *adj.* 特别的, 专门的

【例】Take *special* care tonight because the road is icy. 路面结冰了, 今晚要格外小心。//His *special* satisfaction comes from volunteer work. 他从义务服务中得到最大满足。

【衍】specialist* (*n.* 专家, 专科医生); especial (*adj.* 特别的, 特殊的)

*specific [spə'sifik] *adj.* 特殊的; 明确的

【例】Don't use words, expressions, or phrases known only to people with *specific* knowledge. 不要使用只有具备特殊知识的人才懂的词语或表达方式。

speech [spi:tʃ] *n.* 演讲

【例】Martin Luther King's *speech* "I have a dream" is still famous. 马丁·路德·金《我有一个梦想》的演讲仍然富有盛名。

speed [spi:d] *v.* (speeded/sped, speeded/sped, speeding) (使) 加速 *n.* 速度

【考】1. **high speed** 高速 2. **speed up** 加速

spend [spend] *vt.* (spent, spent, spending) 度过; 花费 (钱、时间等)

【用】1. **spend** + 时间 + (**in**) **doing sth.** 在某事上花费多少时间: People spent much more time watching TV than reading books. 人们花在看电视上的时间比花在读书上的时间多得多。2. **spend** + 金钱 + **on sth.** 为某事物花费多少时间/金钱: In my opi necessary to spend all this money on a new compute 新电脑花这么多钱没有必要。

269

【辨】spend, cost, pay, take

这四个单词都有"用,花费"之意,区别在于:1.主语不同:**spend,
pay**的主语是人,**cost**的主语是物,**take**的主语多为形式主语it。
如:He will pay the bill. 他会买单。//The book cost me 20 yuan. 这
本书花了我20元钱。// It takes a lot of money to buy a house. 买一
所房子要花一大笔钱。2.宾语不同:**pay**的宾语是钱,**take, spend**
和**cost**的宾语既可以是钱,也可以是时间,cost还可以跟双宾语。如:
It took me a lot of time to prepare for the speech. 准备演讲花了我很
多时间。//His carelessness cost him his life. 粗心大意让他付出了生
命的代价。

*spin ［spin］*vt.*（spun, spun, spinning）纺纱;旋转 *n.* 旋转

【例】I *spun* a coin on the table. 我在桌子上旋转一枚硬币。

*spirit ［'spirit］*n.* 精神,灵魂

【例】Maori believe that the *spirit* stays with the body for three days
after death. 毛利人相信,灵魂在人死后会在尸体内存留三天。

【衍】spiritual（*adj.* 精神的;心灵的）

spit ［spit］*v.*（spat, spat, spitting）吐唾沫;吐痰

【例】Don't *spit*. 不要随地吐痰。

splendid ［'splendid］*adj.* 灿烂的,辉煌的;（口语）
极好的

【记】词根记忆:splend（明亮）+id（…的）
→让人眼前一亮的→灿烂的

【例】Peacocks are dressed in feathers of *splendid* colors. 孔雀披着一
身灿烂夺目的羽毛。

*split ［split］*vt.*（split, split, splitting）撕开,切开

【例】My trousers *split*. 我的裤子撕破了。

*sponsor ［'spɔnsə］*n.* 赞助者;主办者 *vt.* 赞助;主办

【记】联想记忆:spons（音似:四帮四）+or→四帮四,一对一→赞助

【例】He would *sponsor* the young man to the Olympics. 他将资助那
个年轻人参加奥运会。

spot ［spɔt］*n.* 斑点,污点;场所,地点 *vt.*（spotted, spotted, spotting）沾
上污渍,弄脏;认出,发现

【例】*spot* mistakes 发现错误

spray ［sprei］*n.* 水雾,喷雾（器）*v.* 喷洒

【例】When he opened the can, the soda *sprayed* out all over him. 他一打开罐子，就喷了一身汽水。

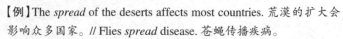

spray

spread [spred] *n./v.* (spread, spread, spreading) 延伸，展开；传播

【记】联想记忆：sp+read（阅读）→通过阅读来扩展我们的视野→延伸

【例】The *spread* of the deserts affects most countries. 荒漠的扩大会影响众多国家。// Flies *spread* disease. 苍蝇传播疾病。

【考】spread out 展开

*squeeze [skwi:z] *n.* 紧握，捏 *v.* 压榨，挤

【例】She gave my hand a *squeeze*. 她捏了捏我的手。// *Squeeze* hard to get all the water out of the sponge. 使劲把海绵里的水都挤出来。

*stable ['steibl] *adj.* 稳定的

【记】联想记忆：s+table（桌子）→像桌子一样四平八稳→稳定的

【例】Markets are flourishing and prices are *stable*. 当前市场繁荣，物价稳定。

*stadium ['steidiəm] *n.* (露天) 体育场

【例】A new *stadium* has been built for the Olympic Games. 一座为奥运会建造的新体育场已经完工。

staff [stɑːf; stæf] *n.* 全体职员

【例】the *staff* of a school 教职员工

*stain [stein] *n.* 污点，瑕疵

【例】a coffee *stain* 咖啡渍

【衍】stainless* (*adj.* 无瑕疵的，不锈的)

stand [stænd] *vi.* (stood, stood, standing) 站立 *vt.* 承担，忍受 *n.* 站；台

【例】Modern plastics can *stand* very high and very low temperatures. 现代塑胶可以经受极度高温或低温。// a self-checkout *stand* 自动收银台

【考】1. **stand up** 起立 2. **stand for** 代表

standard ['stændəd] *n.* 标准，规格 *adj.* 标准的，一流的

【记】联想记忆：stand（站）+ard→站有站相→标准

【例】*standard* room（旅馆的）标准间

stare [stɛə] *v.* 盯着看，凝视

【记】联想记忆：凝视（stare）星（star）空

【考】**stare at...** 凝视…

start ［stɑːt］ *n./v.* 开始，着手；出发

【用】1. **start+*n.*/doing** 开办/创办…：When he left university he had earned enough money to start his own business. 毕业时，他赚的钱已经足够开办自己的企业了。2. **start+to do** 开始做…：They started to use English, but they also brought in some words from their own languages. 他们开始使用英语，但也把自己语言中的一些词汇带到了英语里。

【考】1. **start out** 出发，动身 2. **start off** 出发，开始 3. **start with...** 以…作为开头

*starve ［stɑːv］ *v.* 饿死，挨饿

【例】Many live in luxury while others are *starving*. 许多人生活奢侈，而其他人却饿得要死。

【衍】starvation*（*n.* 饥饿；饿死）

star　　starve

state ［steit］ *n.* 状态；国家，州 *vt.* 宣称

【例】*state* of health 健康状况//*state*-run companies 国有企业//A recent report *stated* that the number of Spanish speakers in the U.S. would be higher than the number of English speakers by the year 2090. 最近一份报告称，到2090年，美国说西班牙语的人将多于说英语的人。

【衍】statement（*n.* 声明；陈述）

*statesman ［ˈsteitsmən］ *n.*（*pl.* statesmen）政治家

【例】In his last years the *statesman* wrote his autobiography. 这位政治家在晚年撰写了自传。

【衍】statewoman（*n.* 女政治家）

*statistics ［stəˈtistiks］ *n.* 统计表，数字，数据

【例】*Statistics* prove that you are safer in a plane than in a car. 数据证明，乘飞机要比乘汽车安全。

*statue ［ˈstætʃuː］ *n.* 雕像

【例】the *Statue* of Liberty 自由女神像

status ［ˈsteitəs; ˈstetəs］ *n.* 身份，地位

【例】Greek and Roman hairstyles were determined according to class,

S

age and marital（婚姻的）*status*. 古希腊人和古罗马人的发型取决于他们的阶级、年龄和婚姻状况。

stay ［stei］*v.* 保持，停止，阻止 *n.* 逗留（时间）

【用】**stay+*adj.*** 保持…：How does sea water *stay* clean? 海水是怎样保持清洁的呢? //stay alive 维持生存

【例】Mike is eager to *stay* away from the busy city life for a while. 麦克渴望离开繁忙的都市生活一段时间。//How long are you *staying* in Xi'an? 你准备在西安待多久?

【考】**stay up** 熬夜

*steady ［ˈstedi］*adj.* 稳固的；平稳的

【记】什么事情都做好准备（ready）做起来就很平稳（steady）

【例】The birth rate in Europe has been in a *steady* decrease since the 1960s. 20世纪60年代以来，欧洲的出生率一直稳步下降。

steep ［sti:p］*adj.* 险峻的，陡峭的

【记】每一级台阶(step) 只能放一(e)只脚，真够陡峭的（steep）

【例】It was the *steepest* mountain I had ever climbed. 这是我爬过的最陡的山。

step ［step］*v.* (stepped, stepped, stepping) 走；跨步 *n.* 脚步；台阶

【例】I took a few *steps* back. 我往后退了几步。//The teacher *steps* back and becomes an adviser. 那位教师退而变成了一位顾问。

stick ［stik］*v.* (stuck, stuck, sticking) 粘住；坚持 *n.* 木棒（棍）

【例】Once a decision has been made, all of us should *stick* to it. 一旦做出决定，我们都应该坚持它。// We made the fire out of dry *sticks*. 我们用干柴枝来生火。

still ［stil］*adj.* 静止的，平静的 *adv.* 仍然，还

【例】Time has stood *still* for me from that moment. 从那一刻起对我来说时间就静止了。//Please tell me how the accident came about. I am *still* in the dark. 请告诉我事故是怎么发生的，我还被蒙在鼓里呢。

stop ［stɔp］*vt.* (stopped, stopped, stopping) 停止；阻止 *n.* 停；（停车）站

【用】1. stop后可接动名词和不定式作宾语，但二者的意思不同。

stop doing... 表示停止做某事：Stop talking, OK? 别说了行不行？而 **stop to do...** 表示停下手中正在做的事情去做另一件事：He stopped to look outside the car. 他停下来看了看车外。2. **stop sb.（from）doing sth.** 阻止某人做某事：The mother tried to stop her young daughter going out on dates. 母亲试图阻止小女儿外出约会。

*stout [staut] *adj.* 结实的，矮胖的

【例】He has a *stout* makeup. 他体格健壮。

stout

straight [streit] *adj. /adv.* 直的（地）

【例】He looked at me *straight* in the eye. 他直视着我的眼睛。//Come *straight* home after school. 放学后直接回家。

*straightforward [ˌstreit'fɔːwəd] *adj./adv.* 正直的（地），坦率（地）

【记】组合词：straight（直的）+forward（向前的）→直截了当的→坦率的

【例】I have always been honest and *straightforward*. 我一直都正直、坦率。

*strength ['streŋθ] *n.* 力量，力气

【例】Bill was doing a lot of physical exercise to build up his *strength*. 比尔进行大量的运动以增长力气。

【辨】**strength, force, power**

这三个词都有"力，力量"之意。**strength**指内在力量，能用以从事、忍受或抵抗许多事物，如：By strength of will and optimism he overcame his illness. 他凭着坚定的意志和乐观的心态战胜了病魔。**power**主要指人事物潜在的力量、职权或政权，如：Only man of all animals has the power to reason. 所有动物中只有人类具有思考能力。**force**主要指自然界的力量、暴力、压制力等，如：If you drop something, the force of gravity will pull it to the floor. 如果你扔下一样东西，地心引力就把它吸到地面上。

*strengthen ['streŋθən] *v.* 加强，增强

【例】Our bodies are *strengthened* by taking exercise. Similarly, our minds are developed by learning. 锻炼使我们的身体强壮，同样，学习使我们的头脑发达。

*stress [stres] *n.* 压力 *vt.* 强调

【例】Many managers suffer from *stress*. 许多经理都承受着压力。// An army spokesman *stressed* that all the soldiers had been ordered to issue clear warnings before firing any shot. 军方发言人强调，所有士兵已被命令在开枪前必须发出明确警告。

strict [strikt] *adj.* 严格的，严密的

【考】**be strict with...** 对…很严格/严厉：My mother is very strict with me. 母亲对我非常严厉。

strict

*strike [straik] *vt.* （struck, struck/stricken, striking）罢工；侵袭；敲；划燃 *n.* 罢工

【例】The clock *struck* as we left. 就在我们离开时，钟响了。//Train services are now back to normal after last week's *strike* in New York. 上周纽约的罢工结束后，火车恢复了运行。

struggle [ˈstrʌgl] *n./v.* 努力，斗争，挣扎

【例】I *struggled* to get free. 我争取获得自由。

Help!!! Help!!!

struggle

*style [stail] *n.* 风格，时尚

【例】*style* of dress 着装风格

subject [ˈsʌbdʒikt] *n.* 题目，主题，学科，主语，主体

【例】What is the *subject* of the book? 这本书的主题是什么？//My favorite *subject* is chemistry. 我最喜欢的学科是化学。

【衍】subjective* (*adj.* 主观的)

*submit [səbˈmit] *vt.* (submitted, submitted, submitting) 提交，递交

【例】I *submitted* my papers to the examiner. 我把试卷交给监考人。

*subscribe [səbˈskraib] *v.* 捐赠，订阅

【例】*Subscribe* now and you will get 10% discount off. 现在订阅的话你会得到九折优惠。

*substitute [ˈsʌbstitjuːt; ˈsʌbstituːt] *vt.* 替换

【考】**substitute sth. for sth.** 用某物替换某物：The researcher substituted a ball for the toy train. 研究者用一只球替换了玩具火车。

succeed [səkˈsiːd] *vi.* 成功 *vt.* 继承，接替

【考】**succeed in** (**doing**) **something** 成功做成某事：He succeeded in the examination. 他考试通过了。

【衍】success (*n.* 成功); successful (*adj.* 成功的); successfully (*adv.* 成功地)

单元自测

1. —What do you think of this matter?

   —This is a matter of _____ importance I think.

   A. especial   B. fairly   C. rather   D. special

2. Some passengers complain that it usually _____ so long to fill in travel insurance documents.

   A. costs   B. takes   C. spends   D. spares

3. The soldier's wet clothes needed _____ on the grass to dry in the sun.

   A. unfolding   B. unfold   C. spreading   D. spread

4. I'm your friend; I'll always _____ you about any question.

   A. stand by   B. stand up   C. stand on   D. make up to

5. Hearing the news, Miss Gao _____ at me in surprise for a while.

   A. glanced   B. stared   C. regarded   D. noticed

6. At first I had some trouble with my car, but finally I managed _____.

   A. to get starting it   B. it to get started

   C. to get it started   D. getting it started

7. In the dark forests _____, some large enough to hold several English towns.

   A. stand many lakes   B. lie many lakes

   C. many lakes lie   D. many lakes stand

8. He has left out the most important reason why he _____ last night.

   A. stayed up   B. put up   C. picked up   D. kept up

9. —Tom, I can't find your mobile phone.

   —Why? It was there just now. _____ somewhere on my way home?

   A. Steal   B. Stealing   C. Stolen   D. Being stolen

10. Once a decision has been made, all of us should _____ it.

    A. direct to   B. stick to   C. lead to   D. refer to

11. —Is the paint on the door dry?

    —It _____ has to dry for another day or two.

    A. still   B. already   C. yet   D. even

12. We must do something to _____ factories _____ waste water into the river before it is cleaned.

    A. stop; pouring   B. prevent; to pour

    C. keep; pouring   D. stop; to pour

13. He is always full of _____ as though he never know tiredness.

    A. strength   B. energy   C. force   D. spirit

14. Quite a few people used to believe that disaster _____ if a mirror was broken.

    A. was sure of striking   B. was sure of having struck

    C. was sure to be struck   D. was sure to strike   （2002全国）

15. Walt was not sure if people would like the film. If it had not been _____, he would have lost everything.

    A. succeeded   B. success   C. a success   D. successes

答案：DBCAB CBACB AABDC

We must accept finite disappointment, but we must never lose infinite hope.   *—Martin Luther King, Jr.*

我们必须接受失望，因为它是有限的，但千万不可失去希望，因为它是无穷的。   ——马丁·路德·金

S

Word List 35

such [sʌtʃ] *adv.* 那么，如此 *adj.* 这样的，那样的 *pron.* (泛指) 人，事物

【用】1. **such+a/an+**(*adj.*) **+n.** : **such a loss** 这样的损失 2. **such+**复数名词/不可数名词：The ladies took only tea and coffee and such drinks. 女士们只喝茶、咖啡以及诸如此类的饮料。//such unselfish love 如此无私的爱 3. **no/any/all/many +such+** 可数名词：As I know, there is no such car in this neighborhood. 据我所知，这附近没有这样的车。4. **such...that...** 如此…以至于：They were such fun that I spent the whole day with them. 他们有趣极了，所以我和他们待了一整天。//We were in such an anxious rush that we forgot the airline tickets. 我们如此匆忙以至于忘拿飞机票了。

【考】**such as** 诸如，例如

【衍】so (*conj./pron./adv.* 如此，这么)

***suck** [sʌk] *v.* 吸，吮

【例】She was *sucking* lemonade through a straw. 她正在用吸管吸柠檬汁。

sudden [ˈsʌdn] *adj.* 突然的

【例】He was caught in a *sudden* storm. 他遇到一场突如其来的风暴。

【考】**all of a sudden** 突然

【衍】suddenly (*adv.* 突然地)

suffer [ˈsʌfə] *v.* 受苦，遭受

【例】The town *suffered* a lot of damage from the storm. 风暴给城镇带来了巨大的损失。

【考】**suffer from...** 忍受，遭受：She is suffering from a knee injury. 她在遭受膝伤的煎熬。

【衍】suffering* (*n.* 痛苦，苦难)

suggest [səˈdʒest] *vt.* 建议；提出；暗示

278

【用】1. **suggest** +*n.*/**doing** 建议；使想起：Could you suggest some low-priced hotels? 你能介绍几个便宜些的旅馆吗？ 2. **suggest+宾语从句**，表示建议时从句使用虚拟语气，即谓语用 (should)+do：I suggest they repeat the experiments and see for themselves. 我建议他们重复实验亲自看看。注意：suggest作"提出，暗示"讲时不用 (should)+动词原形，而使用直陈语气，如：The opponents of the examination system suggest that examinations are an evil force. 考试制度的反对者认为考试是一种罪恶的力量。

【衍】suggestion（*n.* 建议）

suit ［sjuːt］*vt.* 适合 *n.* 一套（衣服）

【例】—How about eight o'clock outside the cinema? —That *suits* me fine. —八点在电影院外怎么样？—那对我挺合适。

【衍】suitable（*adj.* 合适的，适宜的）

super ［ˈsjuːpə］*adj.* 超级的，极好的

【记】S.H.E的歌曲*superstar*

【例】the *super* aged 高龄老人

【衍】superman（*n.* 超人）

*****superb** ［sjuːˈpəːb］*adj.* 庄重的，华丽的，极好的

【例】You get a *superb* view of the lake from here. 从这里观赏到的湖景最美丽。

*****superior** ［sjuːˈpiəriə］*n.* 长者；上级 *adj.* 较高的，上好的

【例】Standard, *superior* and luxurious rooms are all available. 标准间、高级间和豪华间都有。

supply ［səˈplai］*n.* 供给；供应品 *v.* 供给，提供

【考】**supply sth. to sb.(=supply sb. with sth.)** 为某人提供某物：We supply raw materials to many factories. 我们为很多工厂提供原材料。

S

【辨】**supply, provide, offer**
三个单词都有提供的意思，但**supply**常侧重于大量、持续以及补充的意味，如：Our task is to supply vegetable all the year round. 我们的任务是全年供应蔬菜。而**provide**侧重于提前做好准备以提供给需要者的意味，如：The big market provides live fish from all parts of the country. 这个大市场供应来自全国各地的活鱼。**offer**虽然常翻译成"提供"，但实际是询问别人是否想要什么东西，如：He offered me a cigarette. I shook my head. 他敬我一支烟，我摇头拒绝了。

support [sə'pɔːt] *vt./n.* 支持，赞助；赡养

【例】The blacks' revolution won a nationwide *support*. 黑人的革命运动赢得了全国范围内的支持。// *support* a family 赡养一个家庭

suppose [sə'pəuz] *vt.* 猜想，假定 *vi.* 料想

【用】**be supposed to do**（**be**）1. 被猜测…: The Snowman is supposed to live in the highest mountain in the world—Mount Everest. 人们猜想雪人居住在世界最高的山峰——珠穆朗玛峰。2. 应该…: We were supposed to have a chemistry class, but the teacher was out of town for a meeting. 我们本应该上化学课，但老师出城开会去了。

*****supreme** [suːˈpriːm] *adj.* 极度的；极大的，最高的

【例】*supreme* importance 最重要//a *supreme* ruler 最高统治者

sure [ʃuə;ʃuər] *adj.* 确信，肯定 *adv.*（口语）的确，一定，当然

【考】1. **be sure about** 有把握，确信 2. **be sure to do**... 一定会 Quite a few people used to believe that disaster was sure to strike if a mirror was broken. 很多人曾经相信如果镜子被打碎那么灾难肯定就会降临。3. **be sure that**... 确信 I'm sure we will win. 我确信我们会赢。4. **make sure that**... 使确定: She looked up his number in the phone book to make sure that she had got it right. 她从电话本查了他的号码以确保号码没错。5. **for sure** 确实

*****surgeon** ['sɜːdʒən] *n.* 外科医生

*****surplus** ['sɜːpləs] *n.* 剩余，过剩

【记】词根记忆: sur（超过）+plus（加，多余的）→剩余

【例】*surplus* population 过剩人口

*****surround** [səˈraund] *vt.* 围绕，包围

【记】联想记忆: sur+round（圆）→形成一个圆→围绕

【例】A high wall *surrounds* the garden. 一堵高墙环绕着花园。

surrounding [səˈraundiŋ] *adj.* 周围的 *n.* 围绕；（*pl.*）环境

【记】来自surround（包围，围绕）+ing→周围的

【例】The house is set in beautiful *surrounding*s. 这房子周围环境优美。

survive [səˈvaiv] *vi.* 幸存，生还 *vt.* 比…活得长

【例】In such dry weather, the flowers will have to be watered if they are to *survive*. 在这样干燥的天气下，这些花必须浇水才能存活。

【衍】survival*（*n.* 生存，幸存）

suspect [sə'spekt] v. 怀疑 n. 犯罪嫌疑人

【记】词根记忆：sus+pect(=spect看)→ 在下面看一看→怀疑

【例】I *suspect* she is lying. 我怀疑她在 说谎。

【衍】suspected (*adj.* 可疑的)

suspect

swallow ['swɔləu] vt. 吞下；咽下 n. 燕子

【记】联想记忆：s+wall（墙）+ (l) ow → 燕子在墙角垒窝

【例】Chew your food properly before *swallowing* it. 食物仔细嚼碎后再咽下。

swallow

*swap [swɔp] v. (swapped, swapped, swapping) 交换

【考】**swap sth. for sth.** 用某物换某物：I'll swap my orange for your apple. 我用橙子换你的苹果。

*swear [sweə] v. (swore, sworn, swearing) 发誓，诅咒

【例】I *swear* I won't lie to you. 我发誓不会对你撒谎。

sweep [swiːp] vt. (swept, swept, sweeping) 扫除，打扫

【例】I just *swept* the floor. Don't drop crumbs! 我刚扫完地，不要 把面包屑掉到地上！

sweet [swiːt] *adj.* 甜的；新鲜的；可爱的 n. 甜食；芳香

【例】*sweet* memories 甜蜜的回忆 // *sweet* winds 清新的风

swell [swel] v. 肿胀，增大

【例】His feet *swelled* so large that he could hardly put his boots on. 他 的脚肿得连靴子都穿不上了。

*swift [swift] *adj.* 快的，迅速的

【衍】swiftly (*adv.* 很快地，即刻)

*swing [swiŋ] v. (swung, swung, swinging) 挥舞，摆动 n. 秋千

【记】容祖儿有一首歌叫《挥着（swing）翅膀（wing）的女孩》

【例】He *swung* at me. 他朝我挥手。

*switch [switʃ] v./n. 更换，转换

【例】They *switched* seats. 他们交换了座位。

*sword [sɔːd] n. 剑，刀

symbol ['simbl] n. 符号，象征

sword

【记】联想记忆：符号（symbol）是为了简单的（simple）表达意思才创造的

【例】The lion is a *symbol* of courage and power. 狮子是勇气和力量的象征。

*sympathy [ˈsimpəθi] *n.* 同情

【例】I have a lot of *sympathy* for children who cannot afford to go to school. 我十分同情上不起学的孩子。

*symphony [ˈsimfəni] *n.* 交响乐

*symptom [ˈsimptəm] *n.* 症状

【例】She showed all the *symptoms* of an allergy. 她表现出过敏的所有症状。

system [ˈsistəm] *n.* 体系，系统

【例】Language is a highly developed *system* of symbols. 语言是一种高度发达的符号系统。

take [teik] *v.* (took, taken, taking) 拿走；接受，接纳

【用】1. take表示做或进行，可以和许多名词搭配：**take a photo** 拍照片//**take a test** 参加考试//**take a shower** 洗个澡//**take a rest** 休息一下//**take a look at...** 看一看… 2. take表示花费、需要，其主语可以是人，也可以是物，并常用形式主语句型：**It takes/took (sb.) some time/money to do sth.** 做某事花费（某人）多少时间/金钱：It will take me hours to do all this work. 我得花好几个小时才能做完这项工作。

【例】Don't forget to *take* your umbrella. 别忘了带上你的雨伞。// *take* action 采取行动 // *take* medicine 吃药 // *take* the bus 乘公共汽车 // You should *take* her advice. 你应当接受她的建议。

【考】1. **take advantage of...** 利用… 2. **take away** 拿走，夺走 3. **take care of...** 照顾… 4. **take charge of...** 负责… 5. **take one's time** 不用着急，慢慢来 6. **take it easy** 放松；不要着急 7. **take part in...** 参加… 8. **take up...** 从事… 9. **take off** 起飞；脱下 10. **take place** 发生 11. **take over...** 接管… 12. **take trouble to do sth.** 不辞辛苦做某事

*talent [ˈtælənt] *n.* 天才，才能

【例】There must be a use for my *talent*. 天生我材必有用。// *talent* show 才艺大赛

talk [tɔːk] *v.* 谈话，议论 *n.* 谈话，会谈；演讲

【例】*talk* show 脱口秀//peace *talks* between two countries 两国间的和平对话

【考】1. **talk to/with sb.** 和…交谈 2. **talk about sb./sth.** 谈论… 3. **give a talk** 做讲座，演讲：I'm writing to ask you to come and give a talk on American films. 我写信是想邀请你来做一个有关美国电影的讲座。

*target [ˈtɑːɡit] *n.* 目标，对象；靶子

【例】She became the *target* of most of our jokes. 我们总是拿她开玩笑。

6 7 8 9 ● 9 8 7 6

target

taste [teist] *n.* 味道，品味，爱好 *vt.* 品尝；觉察…味道 *vi.* 品尝，有味道 *link.v.* 吃起来，滋味是

【用】taste可以用作系动词，后常接形容词或like介词短语：The chicken tasted good. 这鸡味道很好。//The coffee doesn't taste like anything I have ever had before. 这咖啡跟我以前喝过的咖啡味道完全不一样。

【例】I don't go in for rock and roll. It's much too noisy for my *taste*. 我不喜欢摇滚乐，它对于我来说太吵了。//I took the medicine mixed in orange juice, but I can still *taste* it. 我把药和橘子汁掺和起来喝，但还是能尝出药的味道。

tear [tɛə] *v.* (tore, torn, tearing) 扯破，撕开 *n.* 眼泪

【例】burst into *tears* 突然大哭起来//fight back *tears* 强忍泪水//She picked up the envelope and *tore* it open. 她拿起信封，撕开了。

【考】1. **tear up** 撕毁，撕碎 2. **tear down** 拆毁

*tease [tiːz] *v.* 取笑，嘲弄

【记】联想记忆：tea（茶）+se→大家一起喝茶，取笑对方→取笑

【例】Stop *teasing* your brother. 别再逗弄你弟弟了。

*technique [tekˈniːk] *n.* 技术，技巧

【记】词根记忆：tech（技术，工艺）+nique→技术

【例】Scientists are developing new *techniques* for treating cancer. 科学家们正在研究治疗癌症的新方法。

【衍】technical*（*adj.* 技术的，工艺的）

technology [tekˈnɔlədʒi] *n.* 技术，科技

【记】词根记忆：tech（技术，工艺）+nology→技术，科技

【例】high *technology* 高科技//information *technology*（IT）信息技术

technology

tell [tel] *v.*（told, told, telling）告诉，吩咐；辨别，知道

【用】1. tell词义为"告诉"时，一般需接双宾语，句型有：**tell sb. sth./从句** 告诉某人某事：Tell me your name. 告诉我你的名字。//Calm down and tell me what happened. 冷静下来，告诉我发生了什么事？**tell sb. about sth.** 告诉某人有关某事的情况：Did you tell him about the party? 你告诉他晚会的事了吗？2. **tell sb. to do** 吩咐某人做某事：The woman tells her son to keep his room in order. 妈妈告诉儿子要保持屋子的整洁。3. **tell the difference between** 分辨，识别：I can't tell the difference between the twins. 我分辨不出这对双胞胎谁是谁。做"分辨"讲时，tell前一般为can。

【例】*tell* the truth 说实话，讲真话 // *tell* white lies 说善意的谎话// *tell* jokes/stories 讲笑话/故事

*temporary [ˈtemprəri; ˈtempəreri] *adj.* 暂时的，临时（性）的

【例】*temporary* workers 临时工

【衍】permanent（*adj.* 永久的）

*tend [tend] *vt.* 照管，护理 *vi.* 趋向，往往是

【记】联想记忆：ten（十）+d→没有十全十美，只能趋向完美→趋向

【例】A team of gardeners *tends* the grounds. 一组园艺工人照看这块场地。

【考】**tend to do sth.**：倾向于做…，往往会…：Students from well-respected schools tend to have good jobs. 名校毕业的学生往往会找到好工作。

【衍】tendency*（*n.* 趋向，倾向）

*tense [tens] *adj.* 紧张的 *n.* 时态

【记】发音记忆："弹死"→没有弹性了→因为是拉紧的→紧张的

【例】What's the matter? You seem *tense*. 怎么了？你看上去很紧张。

【衍】tension*（*n.* 紧张；拉紧）

*tentative [ˈtentətiv] *n.* 试验；假设 *adj.* 试验性的，试探的

【例】We've made *tentative* plans for a holiday but haven't decided anything certain yet. 我们考虑了几个度假的初步计划，但是还没

284

有做出任何决定。

---

*terminal ['tə:minl] *n.* (火车，汽车，飞机的) 终点站；终端

【例】All international flights leave from *Terminal* C. 所有国际航班都由C站起飞。//Each desk had its own computer *terminal*. 每张桌子都有自己的计算机终端设备。

单元自测

1. They are _____ little children that they can't do _____ many things in _____ short a time.
   A. such; so; such   B. such; so; so   C. so; so; so   D. so; such; such

2. —Where does your English teacher come from?
   —I am not sure, but his Chinese _____ Shanghai.
   A. hears   B. shows   C. suggests   D. sounds

3. The tailor made him a new _____.
   A. clothes   B. dress   C. wear   D. suit

4. He was _____ to be a musician, but he became a lawyer.
   A. considered   B. thought   C. said   D. supposed

5. Not _____ the word, he looked it up in the dictionary.
   A. sure of   B. being sure of   C. be sure about   D. sure

6. It is _____ to hear that he has decided to go abroad.
   A. surprise   B. surprised   C. surprising   D. to surprise

7. Some people lose heart at the first _____ of unusual difficulties.
   A. signals   B. emblems   C. signs   D. symbols

8. Whatever rank you may be in, it would be wrong to _____ the law into your own hands.
   A. bring   B. hold   C. take   D. seize

9. My teacher often said in class "Let's _____ in English."
   A. say   B. talk   C. speak   D. tell

10. Popular music is liked by many people, but it is not to everyone's _____.
    A. manners   B. share   C. smell   D. taste

11. At the moment, we can't _____ who will be chosen our monitor.
    A. know   B. speak   C. tell   D. read

12. The storm came up all of a(n) _____ and damaged lots of wooden houses.
    A. time   B. abrupt   C. sudden   D. haste

13. _____ such heavy pollution already, it may now be too late to clean up the river.

A. Having suffered B. Suffering　　　C. To suffer　　　D. Suffered

14. The basic needs of the world's population should be _____ first.

A. provided　　　B. supplied　　　C. met　　　　　D. satisfied

15. Nick is looking for another job because he feels that nothing he does _____ his boss.　　　　　　　　　　　　　　　　　（2000春季 北京安徽）

A. serves　　　B. satisfies　　　C. promises　　　D. supports

答案：BCDDA CCCBD CCACB

You are not in charge of the universe; you are in charge of yourself.

—Bennett

你并不掌管整个宇宙，但你得掌管你自己。

——贝内特

Word List 36

*terror ['terə] *n.* 恐怖；可怕的人

【例】She screamed in *terror*. 她惊恐地叫了起来。

【衍】terrorist（*n.* 恐怖分子）；terrorism（*n.* 恐怖主义）

than [ðæn] *conj.* 比

【例】He could run much faster *than* I could. 他跑得比我快多了。

【考】1. **more than** 多于，不仅仅 2. **no more than** 只是，仅仅 3. **not more than** 不超过，不如…多 4. **rather than** 胜于 5. **other than** 除了，不同于

that [ðæt] *adj./pron.* 那，那个 *conj.*（引导从句，无词义）*adv.* 那么，那样

【用】1. that用于引导名词性从句（主语从句、宾语从句、表语从句、同位语从句）和定语从句。引导名词性从句时没有词义，引导定语从句时指代先行词的意义。另外，that在引导宾语从句时可以省略，在定语从句中作宾语时也可以省略，其他情况则不可省略。2. that用于指代上文提到的不可数名词，以避免重复：I'm moving to the countryside because the air there is much fresher than that in the city. 我要搬到乡下去，因为那的空气比城市的要清新得多。that也可指代上文提到的一种情况：—I have never been to Paris. —That's a pity. —我从来没去过巴黎。—那很遗憾。

【考】1. **That's all right.** 没关系。2. **so/such...that...** 如此…以至于…

【辨】**that, which**

that和which在引导定语从句时，以下情况只能用**that**：1. 先行词中既有人又有物时；2. 先行词被all, anything, everything等不定代词以及first, only, any等修饰时；3. 先行词被形容词最高级修饰时。以下情况只能用**which**：1. 定语从句由介词加关系代词引导时；2. 在非限定性定语从句中。

that, what

that和**what**都可以引导主语从句、宾语从句和表语从句。区别在于，**that**只起引导作用，不充当任何句子成分，也没有实际意义；而**what**除了起引导作用，同时还在其引导的从句中作某个句子成分，本身的含义也根据句子内容而有所不同。如：I can prove that she did it. 我能证明是她干的。//I can prove what she said. 我能证明她所说的话。

*theft [θeft] *n.* 盗窃案

【记】和thief (*n.* 小偷) 一起记

【例】the anti-*theft* security alarm 防盗警报装置

*theme [θi:m] *n.* 主题

【记】联想记忆：the+me→就是我→我就是主题

【例】*theme* park 主题公园

then [ðen] *adv.* 当时，那时；然后；那么（通常用于句首或句尾）

【例】I was 25 *then* and had just gotten married. 那时我25岁，刚刚结婚。//She took a shower, and *then* went to bed. 她洗了个淋浴，然后就睡觉了。

【考】1. **now and then** 偶尔，时不时 2. **from then on** 从那时起 3. **even then** 尽管那样，即使那时 4. **just then** 就在这时候，那时候 5. **since then** 从那以后

*theory ['θiəri] *n.* 理论

【记】联想记忆：the+ (st) ory→故事就是故事，不能从理论上去分析→理论

【考】**in theory** 在理论上：In theory, the plan should work. 从理论上讲，这个计划应该可行。

【衍】theoretical* (*adj.* 理论的)

there [ðεə] *int.* 那！你瞧！（表示引起注意）*n.* 那里 *adv.* 在那里

【用】1. there和be, seem, appear, remain, stand, exist等动词连用，表示"有，存在"的意思：There is nothing new under the sun. 太阳底下无新事。2. there常放于句首以加强语气，如谓语动词是go, come, leave, start, stand, lie等，主谓要倒装：There comes my boyfriend. 我男朋友过来了。但必须注意的是，若主语是代词，则不用倒装：There he comes. 他过来了。具有类似用法的副词还有：here, now, then等。

【例】Martha had been working for Miller Laboratories for two years, but she was not happy *there.* 玛撒在米勒实验室工作两年了，但她在那儿一点也不开心。

therefore [ˈðɛəfɔː] *adv.* 因此，所以

【例】The equipment is complicated and *therefore* expensive. 这种仪器结构复杂，因此价格昂贵。

think [θiŋk] *v.* (thought, thought, thinking) 想，思索；认为

【用】1. think如果接否定意义的宾语从句，否定形式转移到think上：I don't think it is necessary to call him. 我认为没有必要给他打电话。类似否定转移用法的动词还有：suppose, believe, hope, expect等。2. I think so. 我认为是这样。I think not.=I don't think so. 我认为不是这样。如：—She is the best singer! —I don't think so. —她是最好的歌手! —我不这样认为。可用于这种表达方式的动词还有expect, believe, suppose, guess等。

【考】1. **think of** 看待；想到，想起 2. **think about** 考虑，思考 3. **think over** 仔细考虑，琢磨 4. **think out** 彻底思考，解决：I don't think you have thought out all the consequences of your action. 我想你并没有考虑清楚自己行为所带来的后果。

【衍】thinking* (*n.* 思索；见解，想法)

*thirst [θɜːst] *n.* 渴，口渴

【例】He woke up with a terrible *thirst.* 他醒来时饥渴难耐。

【衍】thirsty (*adj.* 口渴的)// a thirst for knowledge 对知识的渴望

*thorough [ˈθʌrə; ˈθʌrəu] *adj.* 彻底的

【例】She did a *thorough* job of researching her paper. 她对自己的论文做了详尽彻底的研究。

【衍】thoroughly (*adv.* 彻底地)

though [ðəu] *conj./adv.* 虽然，可是，尽管

【用】1. though作连词，与although在大多数情况下可以互换使用，但though比较口语化。though可以用even修饰，although无此用法。She wore a fur coat, even though it was a very hot day. 她穿了件皮衣，尽管那天非常热。2. though用作副词，可以放在句中或句末：—How is everything going on with you in Europe? —Quite well. Not so smoothly as I hoped, though. —你在欧洲一切还好吗? —很好，尽管不如我希望的那样顺利。注意：although永远没有作副词的用法。

【考】1. even though 尽管，虽然 2. as though（=as if）好像，仿佛

thought [θɔːt] *n.* 思考，思想；念头

【例】I was sank in my *thoughts*. 我陷入了沉思。

【衍】thoughtful（*adj.* 思考的；体贴的）；thoughtless（*adj.* 欠考虑的）

*thrill [θril] *n.* 激动，兴奋；刺激 *vt.* 使激动；使胆战心惊

【记】联想记忆：thr+ill（病）→病人不宜太激动→激动

【例】I'll never forget the *thrill* of my son's birth. 我永远也忘不了儿子出生时自己的那种兴奋。

【衍】thriller*（*n.* [口] 富有刺激性的东西）；thrilled（*adj.* 激动的，兴奋的）

through [θruː] *prep./adv.* 穿过；从始至终

【考】1. glance through 浏览 2. get through 打通（电话）；通过

3. go through 经受

*throughout [θruːˈaut] *prep.* 遍及，贯穿

【例】There is no rainfall *throughout* the year. 全年都没有下雨。

throw [θrəu] *v.*（threw, thrown, throwing）投，掷，扔

【考】1. throw away 扔掉，丢弃 2. throw up 呕吐

> 【辨】throw... at... , throw... to...
> throw... at... 把…扔向…，目的是打中，常带有攻击性：The kids were throwing stones at a row of bottles. 孩子们向一排瓶子扔石子儿。throw... to... 把…扔给…，目的是让对方接住：She threw the ball to him. 她把球扔给他。

thus [ðʌs] *adv.* 这样；因而

【例】The new machine will work twice as fast, *thus* greatly reducing costs. 新机器的运转速度将提升一倍，因而大大降低了成本。

【衍】hence（*adv.* 因此，从此）；therefore（*adv.* 因此，所以）

tick [tik] *n.* 钟表的滴答声；记号 *v.* 发出滴答声

【记】联想记忆：验票员在票（ticket）上做记号（tick）

【例】The only sound was the *tick* of the clock. 听到的只有钟的滴答声。

tie [tai] *v.*（用绳、线）系，拴，扎 *n.* 关系；领带；绳子，结

【例】The aim of these activities is to strengthen the *ties* between the Chinese and American students. 这些活动的目地是加强中美学生之间的联系。

【考】1. **tie up** 捆绑；束缚，阻碍：The prisoners were tied up and taken away. 犯人被绑起来带走了。2. **tie ... to ...** 把…绑在…上：He tied his horse to a tree. 他把马绑在了树上。

*tight [tait] *adj./adv.* 紧的（地）

【记】联想记忆：合缝太紧了（tight），连光（light）都透不进

【例】She had her eyes *tight* shut. 她把眼睛闭得紧紧的。

【衍】tightly（*adv.* 紧紧地，牢固地）；tighten（*v.* 绷紧，拉紧）

till [til] *conj./prep.* 直到，直到…为止

【用】till作连词时，常用来引导时间状语从句，但不能位于句首。1. 用于肯定句，主句动词常为延续性动词，表示这个动作一直延续到till所表示的时间为止。如：The crazy fans would wait till the movie star arrived. 这些疯狂的影迷会一直等到影星来为止。2. 用于否定句，主句的动词一般是非延续性的，它所表示的动作直到till所表示的时间才发生：Mary didn't sleep till her mother came back. 直到妈妈回来，玛丽才睡。

*tire ['taiə] *vt.* 使疲劳 *n.* 轮胎

【例】Doing so much housework *tired* me. 做这么多家务活把我给累坏了。

【考】1. **be tired of** 对…感到厌倦 2. **be tired with/from** 因…感到疲劳

【衍】tired（*adj.* 疲劳的，疲倦的）

*tissue ['tiʃuː] *n.* 薄的纱织品；薄纸；（动、植物的）组织

【例】facial *tissue* 面巾纸

tissue

together [tə'geðə] *adv.* 一起，共同

【例】Our school is quite close to our home, so we could go to school *together* by bike. 学校离家很近，所以我们可以一起骑车去上学。

【考】**gather together** 集合在一起

*tolerate ['tɔləreit] *vt.* 忍受，容忍

【例】I won't *tolerate* your rude behavior any more. 我再也无法忍受你的粗鲁行为了。

too [tuː] *adv.* 也；又；太；很

【用】1. 表示"也"，常放在句末，不能用于否定句：We're going to

the movies. Can you come too? 我们要去看电影。你能一块儿去吗？
注意：否定句中表示"也"的含义用either：I can't play tennis and I can't play golf either. 我不会打网球也不会打高尔夫球。 2. **too...to do...** 太…以至于不能做…：Hoffman was too nervous to speak. 霍夫曼太紧张了，以至于话都说不出来了。3. **cannot...too...** 怎样…也不过分；越…越好：You cannot be too careful. 你越小心越好。

【辨】**too much... , much too...**

too much 修饰不可数名词，意为"太多的…"：There is too much salt in the soup. 汤里放的盐太多了。**much too** 修饰形容词或副词，意为"太…"：Allen had to call a taxi because the box was much too heavy to carry all the way home. 艾伦不得不打的，因为那箱子太沉了，无法搬回家。

total ［'təutl］*adj.* 总数的；总括的；完全的 *n.* 合计 *vt.* 合计为
【例】a *total* yearly budget 年度总预算//He has a *total* of four hours of sleep each day. 他每天总共才睡四个小时。
【衍】totally (*adv.* 总合地，完全地)

touch ［tʌtʃ］*v.* 触摸，接触 *n.* 接触；联系 *vt.* 感动
【例】I *touched* his shoulder, but no reaction. 我碰了碰他的肩膀，但他没反应。//Not too long ago, an incident that happened at Walt Disney *touched* me greatly. 前不久发生在迪斯尼乐园的一件事令我非常感动。
【考】1. **get in touch (with...)** (和…) 取得联系 2. **be/keep/stay in touch (with...)** (和…) 保持联系
【衍】touched (*adj.* 感动的)；untouched (*adj.* 未触及的，不受感动的)

*tough ［tʌf］*adj.* 结实的；棘手的
【例】a *tough* cop 身强体壮的警察//Life is *tough* in the city. 都市生活并不好过。

*tournament ［'tuənəmənt; 'tɜ:rnmənt］*n.* 比赛，锦标赛
【记】联想记忆：tour (旅行) +ament→到世界各地去打锦标赛还可以顺便旅行

toward(s) ［tə'wɔ:d(z); tɔ:rd(z)］*prep.* 向，朝，对于
【例】The little boy came out running *towards* his mother with tears in his eyes. 小男孩出来后哭着朝妈妈跑去。
【衍】forward(s) (*adv.* 向前地，向将来地)；backward(s) (*adv.* 向后

地，相反地）；upward(s)（*adv.* 以上，向上）

trade [treid] *n.* 贸易 *vt.* 买卖

【例】the World *Trade* Center 世贸中心

【衍】trader（*n.* 商人）

tradition [trə'diʃn] *n.* 传统，惯例

【例】diet *tradition* 饮食习惯

【衍】traditional（*adj.* 传统的，惯例的）

train [trein] *v.* 培训，训练 *n.* 火车

【例】If you want to take up this job, you should first be *trained* for three months. 如果你想从事这份工作必须先接受三个月的培训。

【衍】training（*n.* 培训，练习）；trainee（*n.* 受训者，练习生）

*tram [træm] *n.* 有轨电车

*transform [træns'fɔ:m] *v.* 转变，转换

【记】词根记忆：trans（转）+form（形式）→形式的转换→转变

【例】Ballet classes *transformed* her from a common girl to a graceful dancer. 芭蕾舞学习让她从一个平凡的少女变成了优雅的舞者。

translate [træns'leit] *v.* 翻译

【记】词根记忆：trans（转）+late→将一种语言转为另外一种语言→翻译

【例】The article was written in German and *translated* into Chinese. 这篇文章是用德文写的，并被译成中文。

【衍】translation（*n.* 翻译；译文）；translator（*n.* 翻译家，译者）

*transparent [træns'pærənt] *adj.* 显然的；透明的

【例】*transparent* lies 明显的谎言 // Anna was wearing a nearly *transparent* shirt. 安娜穿着一件几乎透明的衬衣。

【衍】obvious（*adj.* 明显的）；evident（*adj.* 明显的，显然的）；apparent（*adj.* 显然的，外观的）

transport [træns'pɔ:t] *n.* 运输，传送器 *vt.* 运输，传送

【记】词根记忆：trans（转）+port（运，送）→传送

【例】public *transport* 公共交通工具//Cars help farm families to *transport* their children to faraway schools. 汽车为农村家庭把孩子送到很远的学校上学提供了便利。

【衍】transportation（*n.* 交通，运输）

*trap [træp] *v.* 使陷入困境 *n.* 陷阱，圈套

【例】He got *trapped* in a cave. 他中了陷阱，掉进了洞穴里。

*treat [tri:t] *vt.* 对待，看待；治疗

【例】We *treated* each other as brothers and sisters. 我们亲如兄弟姐妹。// One of the patients he *treated* was Laura. 劳拉是他治疗过的病人之一。

【衍】treatment（*n.* 治疗，疗法）

*tremble ['trembl] *v.* 颤抖，挥动

【例】The poor girl *trembled* in the cold. 可怜的女孩儿冻得直发抖。

*trend [trend] *n.* 倾向，趋势；时尚

【记】《时尚》杂志就叫TREND

【例】The "do-it-yourself"（DIY）*trend* continues to grow in the U.S. DIY继续风靡美国。

*trial ['traiəl] *n.* 审判；试验

【例】This murder *trial* will last six weeks. 这宗谋杀案的审理将持续6周。

triangle ['traiæŋgl] *n.* 三角形 *adj.* 三角形的

【记】词根记忆：tri（三）+angle（角）→三角形

trouble ['trʌbl] *n.* 问题；疾病；麻烦 *vt.* 使苦恼，使忧虑，使麻烦

【用】1. **have trouble (in) doing...** 在⋯上有困难 2. **take trouble to do...** 费心或费力去做⋯ 3. trouble表示抽象意义上的"烦恼"时是不可数名词；指"烦心事，令人烦恼的事"时是可数名词。

【例】heart *trouble* 心脏病 //I wanted to tell my friend about my *trouble*. 我打算把烦恼告诉朋友。

【考】1. **get into trouble** 招致不幸，陷入困境 2.（**be**）**in trouble** 处于困难中 3. **have trouble with...** 和⋯有纠纷；有⋯病痛：He has trouble with his memory. 他记忆力不好。

【衍】troubled（*adj.* 麻烦的；杂乱无章的）；troublemaker（*n.* 惹麻烦的人，捣乱者）；troublesome*（*adj.* 令人烦恼的；讨厌的）

单元自测

1. —The magician said he would change a stone into a piece of gold.

　—No, it's a trick. He's _____ a common man.

　A. no more than　　B. not more than　　C. more than　　D. no less than

2. It was not until 1920 _____ regular radio broadcasts began.

　A. while　　　　B. which　　　　C. that　　　　D. since

3. We waited and waited. _____ we had been looking forward to.
   A. The hour then came
   B. Then did the hour come
   C. The hour came
   D. Then came the hour

4. He injured his leg and _____ could not play in the game.
   A. for   B. therefore   C. but   D. so

5. He gave us another piece of advice, _____ of great help to the research work.
   A. which I think it is
   B. I think which is
   C. which I think is
   D. I think it is

6. —How is everything going on with you in Europe?
   —Quite well. Not so smoothly as I hoped, _____.
   A. though   B. instead   C. either   D. too

7. _____, she jumped into the river to save the drowning girl.
   A. With no a moment's thinking
   B. Without a moment's thought
   C. Without a moment's thinking
   D. With no thought of herself

8. —Can't you stay a little longer?
   — _____.
   A. I don't think so
   B. I believe not
   C. I am afraid not
   D. I don't believe it

9. Follow your doctor's advice, _____ your cough will get worse.
   A. or   B. and   C. then   D. so

10. We are only _____ glad to do anything we can _____ her.
    A. very; help   B. too; to help   C. too; help   D. very; helping

11. Here's my card. Let's keep in _____.
    A. touch   B. relation   C. connection   D. friendship

12. In _____ Chinese culture, marriage decisions were often made by parents for their children.
    A. remote   B. historic   C. traditional   D. initial

13. Which doctor is _____ her for her sickness?
    A. dealing with   B. treating   C. curing   D. operating

14. No _____ that you failed in the exam. You have always been so careless.
    A. matter   B. trouble   C. wonder   D. way

15. The book is said _____ into many languages.
    A. to be translating
    B. to be translated
    C. to have translated
    D. to have been translated

ABCAB ACBCD

295

Word List 37

true [truː] *adj.* 真正的，确实的，正确的
【例】*true* love/friendship 真正的爱情/友谊
【考】**come true** 成为现实
【衍】untrue（*adj.* 不真实的，不正确的）; truly（*adv.* 真正地，真实地）

trust [trʌst] *vt./n.* 相信，信任，信赖
【例】a lack of *trust* 缺乏信任
【衍】trustworthy（*adj.* 可信赖的）; trustful（*adj.* 相信的，信任的）

truth [truːθ] *n.* 事实；真理
【例】tell the *truth* 说实话//hide the *truth* 隐瞒真相
【衍】untruth（*n.* 假话）; truthful（*adj.* 诚实的，说实话的）

try [trai] *v.* (tried, tried, trying) 尝试，试图；努力
【用】1. **try to do** 尽力去做某事，结果不定：I'm trying to put everything in order in my new flat. 我想把新公寓里的所有东西都归置好。2. **try doing...** 尝试做某事：I try holding my breath to stop sneezing. 我试着屏住呼吸以止住打喷嚏。
【考】1. **try one's best** 尽某人最大的努力 2. **try on** 试穿

*tube [ˈtjuːb; ˈtuːb] *n.* 管子
【例】a *tube* of toothpaste 一管牙膏

*tune [tjuːn; tuːn] *n.* 曲调，调子
【例】The naughty boy played some amusing *tunes* in class. 那个淘气的男孩儿在班上演奏了一些令人发笑的曲子。

turn [təːn] *v.* 旋转；转变；转弯 *n.* 轮流
【用】1. **turn out to be** 结果是，原来是：The weather turned out to be very good, which was more than we could expect. 结果天气非常好，这大大超出了我们的预料。2. **turn+n./adj.** 变成/变得…：Lu Xun was a medical student before he turned writer. 鲁迅成为作家之前是

296

学医的。注意：turn后接名词时不需要冠词。

【例】Her face *turns* red. 她脸红了。// at the *turn* of the century 世纪之交

【考】1. **turn away** 走开，转过脸 2. **turn down** 调低（声音）；拒绝
3. **turn in** 上交 4. **turn into**（使）变成 5. **turn on/off** 打开/关闭
6. **turn out** 生产；证实，发觉是 7. **turn over** 翻转；移交 8. **turn to**
转向；变成；求助于 9. **turn up** 调大（声音）；出现，到来 10. **in turn**
轮流，按次序

twice [twais] *adv.* 两次；两倍

【例】When I got ill, I took medicine *twice* a day. 我生病时每天吃两次药。

*twist [twist] *v.* 拧，扭曲 *n.* 扭曲，歪曲

【例】John stepped into a hole and *twisted* his ankle. 约翰踩到一个洞里扭伤了脚踝。

twist

*typhoon [tai'fuːn] *n.* 台风

【记】发音记忆："台风"

【例】violent *typhoon* 强台风

*typical ['tipikl] *adj.* 典型的；象征性的

【记】联想记忆：typ（看作type典型）+ical→典型的

【例】It was *typical* of her to forget. 她这人就是爱忘事。// He was from a *typical* French family. 他来自一个典型的法国家庭。

【衍】typically（*adv.* 典型地；代表性地）

ugly ['ʌɡli] *adj.* 丑陋的，难看的

【例】the *ugly* duckling 丑小鸭

*unable [ʌn'eibl] *adj.* 不能的，不能胜任的

【记】un（不）+able（能够的）→不能的

【例】The boy is *unable* to reach the cup. 男孩够不着杯子。

*unbearable [ʌn'bɛərəbl] *adj.* 无法忍受的

【记】un（不）+bear（忍受）+able（可…的）→无法忍受的

【例】The heat outside is *unbearable*. 外面的高温真让人难以忍受。

*unbelievable [ˌʌnbi'liːvəbl] *adj.* 难以置信的

【记】un（不）+believ(e)（相信）+able（可…的）→难以置信的

【例】What happened to me that day is just *unbelievable*. 那天发生在我身上的事情简直令我无法相信。

*uncertain [ʌn'səːtn] *adj.* 不确定的

【记】un（不）+certain（确定的）→不确定的

【例】Whether he will come or not is *uncertain* yet. 他是否会来还不确定。

【衍】uncertainty（*n.* 不确定）

*uncomfortable [ʌnˈkʌmftəbl；ʌnˈkʌmfərtəbl] *adj.* 不舒服的，不安的

【记】un（不）+comfort（舒服）+able（可…的）→不舒服的

【例】Her father looked nervous and *uncomfortable* in front of the camera. 她父亲在相机前显得紧张不安。

* unconditional [ˌʌnkənˈdiʃənl] *adj.* 无条件的，绝对的

【记】un（不）+conditional（有条件的）→无条件的，绝对的

【例】an *unconditional* surrender 无条件投降

*unconscious [ʌnˈkɔnʃəs] *adj.* 不省人事的，无意识的

【记】un（不）+conscious（有意识的）→无意识的→不省人事的

【例】After Tom hit his head, he was *unconscious* for several minutes. 被汤姆击中头部后他昏迷了几分钟。

under [ˈʌndə] *adv.* 在下 *prep.* 在…下面，向…下面

【例】*under* the pressure 在压力之下 //Several new railways are *under* construction in China. 中国有几条新铁路正在建设中。

【考】1. **under control** 在控制之中 2. **under...condition** 在…情况下

【辨】**under, below, beneath**

三者都有"在…下方"的意思。**under**在正下方，反义词为**over**，如：The book is under the desk. 书在桌子底下。**below**指位于比某物低的位置，但不一定在其正下方，反义词为**above**，如：The temperature in the house is below zero. 房间里的温度在零度以下。**beneath**为正式用语，除文学用语外已较少使用。

*underline [ˌʌndəˈlain] *vt.* 在…下面划线；强调

【记】组合词：under（在…下）+line（划线）→在…下面划线

【例】the *underlined* words 划线单词

understand [ˌʌndəˈstænd] *v.* (understood, understood, understanding) 懂得，理解

【例】Do you *understand* Spain? 你懂西班牙语吗？

【衍】understanding（*n.* 谅解，理解）

*undertake [ˌʌndəˈteik] *vt.* (undertook, undertaken, undertaking) 承担；保证

【例】*undertake* a post 担任一个职位

【衍】undertaking（*n.* 事业，企业）

*underwear [ˈʌndəwɛə] *n.* 内衣

【记】组合词：under（在…内）+wear（穿）→穿在里面的衣服→内衣

【例】We should change our *underwear* every day. 内衣应该天天换。

*unemployment [ˌʌnimˈplɔimənt] *n.* 失业（状态）

【例】*unemployment* insurance 失业保险

unfair [ˌʌnˈfɛə] *adj.* 不公平的，不公正的

【记】记忆方法：un（不）+fair（公平的，公正的）→不公平的，不公正的

【例】This is *unfair*. 这不公平。

【衍】unfairly（*adv.* 不公正地）

*unfit [ˌʌnˈfit] *adj.* 不适宜的，不相宜的

【记】un（不）+fit（合适）→不适宜的

【例】This house is *unfit* to live in. 这栋房屋不宜居住。

*unfortunate [ʌnˈfɔːtʃənit] *adj.* 不幸的，倒霉的

【记】un（不）+fortunate（幸运的）→不幸的

【例】I was *unfortunate* enough to loss my keys. 我把钥匙丢了，真是够倒霉的。

【衍】unfortunately（*adv.* 不幸地）

uniform [ˈjuːnifɔːm] *n.* 制服

【记】词根记忆：uni（单一）+form（形式）→单一形式→制服

【例】School *uniforms* are becoming more and more popular across the USA. 校服在美国变得越来越流行。

*union [ˈjuːniən] *n.* 联合，联盟

【记】词根记忆：uni（单一）+on（人，物）→使人都朝着同一个方向走→联合

【例】the Student *Union* 学生会//the European *Union* 欧盟

*unique [juːˈniːk] *adj.* 惟一的，独特的

【记】词根记忆：uni（单一）+que（…的）→惟一的，独特的

【例】The picture of Mona Lisa is a *unique* work of art. 名画蒙娜·丽莎是件独一无二的艺术品。

unit [ˈjuːnit] *n.* 单元，单位

【例】an army *unit* 一支部队

*unite [juːˈnait] *v.* 联合，团结

【例】She *unites* common sense with vision. 她把想像力与常识联系在一起。

【衍】reunite（*v*. 再联合，重聚）

*universal [ˌjuːniˈvəːsl] *adj.* 普遍的，全体的

【例】War causes *universal* misery. 战争给世人带来苦难。

universe [ˈjuːnivəːs] *n.* 宇宙

【记】词根记忆：uni（单一）+vers（转）+e→一个旋转着的整体空间→宇宙

【例】There are many galaxies in the *universe*. 宇宙中有许多星系。

university [ˌjuːniˈvəːsiti] *n.* 大学

【例】a top *university* 一所顶级大学//open *university* 开放大学，函授大学，电大

unless [ənˈles] *conj.* 如果不，除非

【例】It is known to all that *unless* you exercise regularly, you won't keep good health. 众所周知，经常锻炼才会有健康的体质。

*unlike [ʌnˈlaik] *prep.* 不像，和…不同

【例】His latest novel is quite *unlike* his earlier ones. 他最近一部小说的风格与其早期作品的迥然不同。

*unrest [ˌʌnˈrest] *n.* 不安；骚动

【记】词根记忆：un（不）+rest（休息，安静）→不安

【例】social *unrest* 社会动荡不安

until [ənˈtil] *prep./conj.* 直到…为止，在…以前

【用】1. 主句谓语动词是延续性的，表示动作一直进行，到until表示的时间才停止：I watched until she was out of sight. 我一直看着，直到她从视野中消失。2. 主句谓语动词常为非延续性的，表示动作一直不发生，直到until表示的时间才发生：My uncle didn't marry until he was forty-five. 我叔叔直到45岁才结婚。3. **Not until+时间状语（从句）+ 助动词（did，will）+主语…**，即否定词用于句子开头，句子部分倒装：Not until he was forty-five did my uncle marry. 我叔叔直到45岁才结婚。4. **It+be+ not until +时间状语（从句）+that…**：It was not until he was forty-five that my uncle married. 我叔叔直到45岁才结婚。

【辨】until, till

till和until可以用在口语和书面语中。until较till更为正式；until可

以放在句首而**till**则不可, 如: Until you finish your homework don't think about watching television. 除非你完成家庭作业, 否则别想看电视。

unusual [ʌnˈjuːʒl] *adj.* 不平常的, 异常的

【记】un (不) +usual (平常的) →不平常的

【例】Snow is an *unusual* sight in this warm place. 下雪在这个温暖的地方是一种罕见的现象。

【衍】unusually (*adv.* 不寻常地)

***unwilling** [ʌnˈwiliŋ] *adj.* 不愿意, 勉强的

【例】They were *unwilling* to help him. 他们不愿意帮他。

【衍】unwillingly (*adv.* 不情愿地); unwillingness (*n.* 不情愿)

up [ʌp] *adv.* 向上; 在上方 *adj.* 上面的 *n.* 上升 *v.* (upped, upped, upping) 举起; 提高 *prep.* 向高处

【例】She *upped* and left. 她起身走了。

【考】1. **up to** 多达 2. **be up to sb.** 是某人的义务或职责 3. **ups and downs** 沉浮; 兴衰

***update** [ˌʌpˈdeit] *vt./n.* (使) 现代化; 更新

【记】up (向上) +date (日期) →日期不断向前推→更新

【例】Please *update* your database quickly. 请尽快更新你的数据库。

upon [əˈpɔn] *prep.* 在…上面

【用】upon与on意义相同, 但语气较为正式: The village stands upon a hill. 村庄坐落在一座小山上。

***upper** [ˈʌpə] *adj.* 较高的, 较上的

【例】What is the *upper* limit to the human life span? 人类最长能活多久?

***upset** [ˌʌpˈset] *adj.* 心烦的, 苦恼的 *vt.* (upset, upset, upsetting) 使苦恼

【记】联想记忆: up (上) +set (放置) →心七上八下的→使…心烦意乱

【例】My parents were in a huge argument, and I was really *upset* about it. 我父母吵得很凶, 让我非常苦恼。

upstairs [ˌʌpˈstɛəz] *adv.* 在楼上, 到楼上

【记】up (上面) +stairs (楼梯) →在楼上

【例】go *upstairs* 上楼

***upward(s)** [ˈʌpwəd(z)] *adv.* 向上, 往上

【记】词根记忆：up（向上）+ward（方向）→向上

【例】The plane is flying *upward*. 飞机正往高处飞去。

*urban [ˈəːbən] *adj.* 城市的，市内的

【例】the *urban* population 城市人口

*urge [əːdʒ] *vt.* 催促，力劝

【用】urge sb. to do sth. 催促某人做某事：He urged her to go to bed early. 他催促她早点睡觉。

*urgent [ˈəːdʒənt] *adj.* 急迫的，紧急的

【例】I must post this letter now; it's *urgent*. 这封信很急，我必须现在就把它寄出去。

use [juːz] *n./vt.* 利用，应用

【考】1. make (better/the best) use of（较好地/充分地）利用 2. come into use 开始投入使用 3. use up 用光

【衍】useful (*adj.* 有用的，有益的); useless (*adj.* 无用的); user (*n.* 使用者，用户)

used [juːzd] *adj.* 用过的；旧的，二手的

【用】used car 二手汽车

used to *aux. v.* 过去常常

【例】My mother *used to* dance a lot. 我母亲过去经常跳舞。

> 【辨】used to do, be used to do, be used to+ *n.* /doing
>
> **used to do** 意为过去常做某事，如 I used to get up early. 我以前常常早起。**be used to do** 意为被用来做某事，如：Water is used to produce electricity. 水被用来发电。**be used to+*n.* /doing...** 意为习惯于做某事，如 He is used to sleeping late and getting up early. 他习惯了晚睡早起。

单元自测

1. The lawyer listened with full attention, _____ to miss any point.

   A. not trying   B. trying not   C. to try not   D. not to try

2. I can hardly hear the radio. Would you please _____? （1995全国）

   A. turn it on   B. turn it down   C. turn it up   D. turn it off

3. Americans eat _____ vegetables per person today as they did in 1910.

A. more than twice   B. as twice as many

C. twice as many   D. more than twice many

4. Buying such a streamline car has always been _____ his dreams.

   A. on   B. over   C. above   D. beyond

5. Little _____ what you said. I wish you had repeated it!

   A. did I understand   B. I understood

   C. I did understand   D. have I understood

6. The men will have to wait all day _____ the doctor works faster.

   A. if   B. unless   C. where   D. that

7. It was only when I reread his poems recently _____ I began to appreciate their beauty. （1998全国）

   A. until   B. that   C. then   D. so

8. They do not seem to _____ with knives and forks.

   A. use for eating   B. be used to eating

   C. use to eat   D. used to eat

9. Mother _____ us stories when we were young.

   A. was used to tell   B. is used to telling

   C. used to tell   D. used to telling

10. This medicine, taken on time 3 times a day, can be very _____ for a cold.

   A. healthy   B. useful   C. strong   D. effective

11. Without fact, we cannot form a worthwhile opinion, for we need to have factual knowledge _____ our thinking.

   A. which to be based on   B. upon which to base

   C. which to base upon   D. to which to be based

12. Simon thought his computer was broken _____ his little brother pointed out that he had forgotten to turn it on.

   A. until   B. unless   C. after   D. because

13. The vast majority of nations have agreed to _____ their efforts to bring peace.

   A. connect   B. joins   C. unite with   D. unite

14. _____, I don't like her idea.

   A. Telling the truth   B. Being told the truth

   C. Tell the truth   D. To tell the truth

15. When climbing the hill John was knocked unconscious by an _____ rolling stone.

   A. untouched   B. unexpected

   C. unfamiliar   D. unbelievable

ꓭ ꓷ ꓷ Ɐ ꓭ   ꓷ Ɔ Ɐ 8

Word List 38

useless ['juːslis] *adj.* 无用的
【例】This is a *useless* knife, because the handle is broken! 这把小刀没用了，因为刀把坏了。

user ['juːzə] *n.* 使用者，用户
【例】a *user* of public transportation 公共交通的使用者

usual ['juːʒl] *adj.* 通常的，平常的
【考】**as usual** 照常，照例：As usual, I slept late that Saturday morning. 和平时一样，那个星期六早晨我起得很晚。

*vacant ['veikənt] *adj.* 空的，空白的
【例】a *vacant* position 空缺职位

*vague [veig] *adj.* 含糊的，不清楚的
【例】Through the fog we saw the *vague* outline of a ship. 透过雾，我们看到了船模糊的轮廓。

*vain [vein] *adj.* 自负的；徒劳的
【例】She is very *vain* about her voice. 她对自己的声音很自负。//a *vain* attempt 无用的尝试
【考】**in vain** 徒劳

*valid ['vælid] *adj.* 有效的
【例】This card is *valid* for three months. 这张卡三个月内有效。

*valley ['væli] *n.* 山谷，溪谷
【例】a spacious *valley* 宽阔的山谷

valuable ['væljuəbl] *adj.* 值钱的，贵重的
【例】Real friendship is more *valuable* than money. 真正的友谊比金钱更宝贵。

value ['væljuː] *n.* 价值，益处 *vt.* 估价，评价
【例】What is the *value* of your house? 你的房子值多少钱? // You'll find this map of great *value* in helping you to get round London. 当你

游览伦敦时，你会发现这张地图用处很大。

*variety [vəˈraɪəti] *n.* 种种，种类

【考】**a great/wide variety of** 各式各样的：Tom didn't come for a variety of reasons. 汤姆因为种种原因而没有来。

various [ˈveərɪəs] *adj.* 各种各样的，不同的

【例】The products we sell are many and *various*. 我们出售的产品是多种多样的。

【辨】**various, different**

二者都有"不同的"之意。**various**强调种类的不同，意为"各种不同的"，"各式各样的"，如：The boy invented various reasons for being late. 男孩为自己的迟到编造了各种理由。**different**强调事物之间的区别或本质的不同，有时侧重对比但并不注重差别，如：The colors of the two boxes are different. 那两个盒子的颜色不同。

vehicle [ˈviːikəl; ˈviːhikəl] *n.* 车辆

【例】The military has some amphibious *vehicles*. 部队有一些水陆两用车。

*version [ˈvəːʃən; ˈvəːʒn] *n.* 译文，版本

【例】These books are the Chinese *versions* of Shakespeare. 这些书是莎士比亚作品的中文译本。// the film *version* of a famous novel 根据名著改编的电影版本

very [ˈveri] *adv.* 很，非常 *adj.* 恰好的，正好的

【用】very作形容词时，用来加强语气：That's the very thing I've been looking for. 那正是我要找的东西。

vest [vest] *n.* 背心，内衣

【例】a bullet-proof *vest* 防弹背心

*via [ˈvaiə] *prep.* 经，经过，经由

【例】I sent the letter *via* airmail yesterday. 我昨天把信用航空邮件寄了出去。

*vice [vais] *n.* 恶习，缺陷 *prep.* 副，次；代替

【记】联想记忆：罪恶（vice）和美好（nice）只差一个字母

【例】virtue and *vice* 善与恶// *vice* president 副总统；大学副校长

*victim [ˈviktim] *n.* 受害人，牺牲品

【记】联想记忆：有胜利者（victor），就会有受害者（victim）

【例】He was the *victim* of a road accident. 他是一场交通事故的受害者。

video [ˈvidiəu] *n.* 录像，视频

【例】Do we have any blank *videos*? 我们有空白录像带吗？

*videophone [ˈvidiəufəun] *n.* 可视电话

【记】组合词：video（视频）+phone（电话）→可视电话

【例】*Videophone* is very helpful in our daily life. 在我们的日常生活中，可视电话非常有用。

view [vju:] *n.* 看法；景色

【考】1. in one's view 按…的观点 2. in view of 鉴于，由于 3. **in full view of / in the view of** 在被…完全看得见的地方 4. **a point of view** 一个观点

vinegar [ˈvinigə] *n.* 醋

【例】apple *vinegar* 苹果醋

*violate [ˈvaiəleit] *vt.* 违反，干扰

【例】*violate* a law 犯法

*violence [ˈvaiələns] *n.* 暴力；强烈

【例】an act of *violence* 暴力行为

violent [ˈvaiələnt] *adj.* 暴力的；猛烈的

【例】a *violent* attack 猛烈的进攻

*violin [ˌvaiəˈlin] *n.* 小提琴

【记】朱自清的《荷塘月色》中有一个经典的比喻："如梵阿玲上奏着的名曲"，其中的"梵阿玲"即为violin一词的音译。

*virtue [ˈvɔ:tʃu:] *n.* 美德，正直的品行

【例】Being honest is always thought of as a *virtue*. 诚实一直被认为是种美德。

*virus [ˈvaiərəs] *n.* 病毒

【例】We should be watchful of computer *viruses*. 我们应当警惕计算机病毒。

*visa [ˈvi:zə] *n.* 签证

【例】entry *visa* 入境签证

visit [ˈvizit] *n./v.* 参观，访问，拜访

【例】*Visiting* time in this hospital is from 3 pm to 5 pm. 这家医院的探望时间为下午3点至5点。

【考】**pay a visit to** 去参观；拜访

【衍】visitor（*n.* 访问者，参观者）

visual [ˈvɪʒuəl] *adj.* 看的，视觉的

【记】词根记忆：vis（看）+ual（…的）→视觉的

【例】the *visual* arts 视觉艺术

*vital [ˈvaɪtl] *adj.* 重大的，生死攸关的

【例】a *vital* injury 致命伤

*vivid [ˈvɪvɪd] *adj.* 生动的，鲜明的

【例】a *vivid* description 栩栩如生的描绘

【衍】vividly（*adv.* 生动地，鲜明地）

vocabulary [vəˈkæbjuləri] *n.* 词汇，词汇表

【例】He has a very large *vocabulary*. 他词汇量很大。

*voluntary [ˈvɔləntri; ˈvɔləntəri] *adj.* 自愿的

【例】She is a *voluntary* worker at the hospital. 她在这家医院做义工。

*volunteer [ˌvɔlənˈtiə] *v.* 自愿 *n.* 志愿者

【例】We all *volunteered* to paint the house. 我们都是自愿来粉刷房子的。

*vote [vəut] *v.* 选举，投票

【用】**vote for/against** 投票赞成/反对：Vote for Johnson—the people's friend! 请投约翰逊一票——他是人民的朋友！

voyage [ˈvɔiidʒ] *n.* 航行，旅行

【例】They made a *voyage* to the distant island. 他们航行去远方的小岛。

*wag [wæg] *v.*（wagged, wagged, wagging）摇动，摆动

【例】The dog was *wagging* its tail and barking. 那只狗摇着尾巴大叫。

wage [weidʒ] *n.* 工资，报酬

【例】How can I keep a family on such a low *wage*? 这么点工资，我怎么养家？

waist [weist] *n.* 腰部，腰围

【例】She has a very small *waist*. 她腰很细。

wait [weit] *v.* 等待 *n.* 等待，等待时间

【例】They are *waiting* in line to get their tickets. 他们正在排队等候买票。

【考】1. **wait for** 等待 2. **wait on** 服侍，招待 3. **wait a minute** 等一下 4. **can't wait to do...** 迫不及待要做…

【衍】waiter（*n.* 男招待）；waitress（*n.* 女招待）；waiting-room（*n.* 侯

诊室；候车室）

wake [weik] v. （waked/woke, waked/woken, waking）醒来，叫醒

【考】1. **wake up** 醒来 2. **wake sb. up** 把某人叫醒：I want you to wake me up at 7:00 a.m.. 我想让你7点叫醒我。

walk [wɔːk] n. 散步 v. 走路，步行

【例】She *walks* to school every day. 她每天走着去上学。

【考】1. **go for a walk** 散步 2. **walk out** 走出 3. **walk around**（sth.）四处走走；绕着某物走

*walnut ['wɔːlnʌt] n. 胡桃，胡桃木

【记】联想记忆：wal（看作wall墙）+nut（坚果）→坚果皮跟墙一样硬→胡桃

wander ['wɔndə] v. 游荡；漫步；流浪

【记】联想记忆：去流浪（wander）吧，途中充满了奇迹（wonder）

【例】As I moved up the hill, my attention *wandered* for a few minutes. 上山的时候我走神了几分钟。

【考】**wander about/around** 徘徊，游荡

want [wɔnt;wɔːnt] v. 想要，需要

【用】1. **want to do...** 想做…：We wanted to get back home before dark. 我们想在天黑前回到家。2. **want sb. to do sth.** 想让某人做某事：Parents want their children to be attentive to their studies. 父母想让孩子们专心学习。3. **sth.+want+doing**（to be done）某事物需要被做：This work wants doing at once. =This work wants to be done at once. 这工作需要马上就做。need, require等动词也有类似用法。

【衍】unwanted（*adj.* 不必要的；多余的）

war [wɔː] n. 战争

【考】1. **go to war** 发动战争 2. **be at war with** 与…交战 3. **declare war on...** 向…宣战 4. **World War II** 第二次世界大战

*ward [wɔːd] vt. 保卫，看护 n. 病房，收容所

【例】The cancer *ward* is on the fifth floor of the hospital. 癌症病房在医院的第五层。

*warehouse ['weəhaus] n. 仓库；大商店

【记】组合词：ware（器皿）+house（房子）→放器皿的房子→仓库

warm [wɔːm] *adj.* 暖和的；热情的 v.（使）暖和

【例】The children jumped up and down to keep *warm*. 孩子们上下跳

动保持身体暖和。

【考】**warm up** 热身；变暖：Runners are warming up for the next race. 运动员正在为下一场比赛做热身。

【衍】warmth（*n.* 温暖；热情）；warming（*n.* 升温）

单元自测

1. — How often do you eat out?

    — _____, but usually once a week.

    A. Have no idea   B. It depends   C. As usual   D. Generally speaking

2. If women were _____ in this country, they would be given better jobs.

    A. cared   B. valued   C. fed   D. treated

3. Sometimes it was a bit boring to work there because there wasn't always _____ much to do.

    A. such   B. that   C. more   D. very

4. We volunteered to collect money to help the _____ of the earthquake.

    A. victims   B. folks   C. fellows   D. villagers

5. One of the advantages of living on the top floor of a high rise is that you can get a good _____.

    A. sight   B. scene   C. view   D. look

6. This is the first time for him to _____ your beautiful country.

    A. call on   B. pay a visit to   C. drop in   D. come

7. —Hank Stream didn't turn up last night, did he?

    —No. We _____ for him. A whole night was wasted.

    A. needn't have waited   B. couldn't have waited

    C. needn't have to wait   D. didn't need to wait

8. He lay in bed, _____, listening to the songs on the radio.

    A. awake   B. awoke   C. wake   D. woke

9. She was afraid _____ because she was afraid _____.

    A. to swim; to drown   B. to swim; of drowning

    C. of swimming; to drown   D. of swimming; of drowning

10. —Has the cyclist been seen _____ down by a car?

    —Yes, and he _____ a timely medical treatment.

    A. be knocked; hopes   B. knocked; needs

    C. knock; calls for   D. knocking; needs

11. After two hours of hard fighting, the northern army won the _____.

    A. attack   B. force   C. war   D. battle

12. They would rather spend time _____ than _____ in the street.

    A. read; wander   B. reading; wandering

    C. is reading; to wander   D. reading; wander

13. He is out of work now but he gets a good _____ from his investment.

    A. wage   B. salary   C. earning   D. income

14. I wanted to go there by plane, but I hadn't enough money to pay for the _____.

    A. journey   B. travel   C. voyage   D. fly

15. Today CCTV offers a great _____ of programmes to meet the different needs and

    _____.

    A. variety; tastes   B. many; interests

    C. deal; likes   D. number; habits

答案：DDDBC BAABB ADDBA

You will never have what you like until you learn to like what you have.   —Goethe

欲得到你喜欢的东西，应先学会喜欢你已有的东西。

————歌德

Word List 39

warn [wɔːn] *vt.* 警告；预告

【用】1. **warn sb. of /about sth.** 警告某人提防某事：I have warned you of the dangerous dog. 我已经警告过你这条狗很危险。2. **warn sb. not to do sth.** 警告某人不要做某事：Mom warned little Tom not to go out alone during the night. 妈妈告诫小汤姆晚上不要一个人外出。3. **warn sb. against doing sth.** 警告某人不要做某事：He warned me against going there at night. 他告诫我夜里不要去那儿。

【衍】warning (*n.* 警告)

wash [wɔʃ] *v.* 洗涤，冲刷 *n.* 洗；洗的衣服

【例】*Washing* clothes is the last thing I want to do. 洗衣服是我最不愿意做的事情。

【考】1. **wash up** 洗手洗脸；洗盘子 2. **wash out** 冲掉；洗退色 3. **wash away** 冲走

【衍】washing (*n.* 洗涤物；冲走的东西)；washroom (*n.* 盥洗室)

waste [weist] *vt.* 浪费 *n.* 废弃物；粪便

【用】1. **waste +time/money +on...** (**doing...**) 浪费时间（金钱）于…（做…）：Don't waste your money on silly things. 不要把钱浪费在无聊的东西上。2. **It is a waste of time to do...** 做…纯属浪费时间：It is a waste of time to wait for him here. 在这里等他纯属浪费时间。

watch [wɔtʃ] *n.* 手表 *v.* 观察，观看

【用】**watch sb. do /doing sth.** 观看某人做某事：The students watched the teacher do the experiment. 学生们看老师做了实验。注意：当使用被动语态时，动词不定式符号to不能省略。上句可以改写为：The teacher was watched to do the experiment. 此处，see, hear, observe等动词也有类似用法。

【考】**watch out** 小心，注意

watermelon [ˈwɔːtəˌmelən] *n.* 西瓜

【记】组合词：water（水）+melon（瓜）→水分很足的瓜→西瓜

wave [weiv] *v.* 挥手；摇动 *n.* 波，波浪

【例】My mother was crying as I *waved* her goodbye. 我向母亲挥手告别时她哭了。// sound *wave* 声波//a 15-month *wave* of violence 一场持续了15个月的暴力运动

*wax [wæks] *n.* 蜡，蜡状物

【例】*Wax* dripped down the side of the candle. 蜡油从蜡烛的一边滴了下来。

way [wei] *n.* 道路，方法；作风

【用】the way（方式；方法）由定语从句修饰时，定语从句用that引导或者不用任何引导词：What surprised me was not what he said but the way he said it. 使我吃惊的不是他说的话，而是他说话的方式。

【考】1. **no way** 不可能，没门 2. **by the way** 顺便说一下 3. **on the way** 在途中 4. **in a way** 在某种程度上，稍稍 5. **all the way** 一直；从远道 6. **by way of** 经由 7. **in no way** 决不 8. **in the way** 妨碍，挡路

website *n.* （计算机）网站

【记】组合词：web（网）+site（地址）→网站

【例】log on the *website* 登录网站

weak [wiːk] *adj.* 虚弱的；差的

【例】With nothing left to burn, the fire became *weak* and finally died out. 什么烧的都没有了，火势越来越弱，最后熄灭了。

【衍】weakly（*adv.* 虚弱地，差地）；weakness（*n.* 弱点）

wealth [welθ] *n.* 财富

【记】健康（health）是最大的财富（wealth）

【例】This country's *wealth* comes from its oil. 这个国家的财富来自石油。

【衍】wealthy（*adj.* 富有的）

wear [weə] *v.* （wore, worn, wearing）穿，戴；磨损，使变旧

【例】He always *wears* green. 他总是穿着绿色的衣服。//John likes to *wear* long hair. 约翰喜欢留长发。

【考】1. **wear down** 磨损，损耗 2. **wear out** （经常用于被动语态be

worn out) 穿破；使累坏：We were worn out by this hard work. 这项艰苦的工作弄得我们筋疲力尽。

【衍】wearable (*adj.* 可穿的，耐磨的)；wearer (*n.* 穿戴者，佩带者)；worn* (*adj.* 用旧的，疲倦的)

---

weather [ˈweðə] *n.* 天气

【例】The *weather* was pretty bad. 天气糟糕透了。

***wedding** [ˈwediŋ] *n.* 婚礼，结婚

【记】结婚 (wedding) 了，就有了家，有一个人在家里等 (waiting) 你

【例】Have you been invited to their *wedding*? 他们邀请你参加婚礼了吗？

***weed** [wiːd] *n.* 野草，杂草

【例】There are lots of *weeds* in the garden. 院子里杂草丛生。

---

week [wiːk] *n.* 周，星期

【例】I didn't go to school last *week*. 上周我没有去上学。

【衍】weekday (*n.* 平日，工作日)；weekend (*n.* 周末)；weekly* (*adj.* 每周的，每周一次的)

---

weep [wiːp] *v.* (wept, wept, weeping) 哭泣，流泪

【记】联想记忆：能哭出来说明伤得还不够深 (deep)

【例】She *wept* bitter tears of disappointment. 她失望得痛哭流涕。

---

weigh [wei] *v.* 秤量；重

【例】The fish *weighs* 12 kilos. 这条鱼重12千克。

---

weight [weit] *n.* 重量

【例】They use new materials to reduce the *weight* of the car. 他们采用新的材料来减轻汽车的重量。

【考】1. lose weight 减肥 2. put on weight 长胖

---

welcome [ˈwelkəm] *n./vt./adj.* 欢迎

【考】1. welcome to... 欢迎来到… 2. You are welcome. 不客气。

【衍】unwelcome (*adj.* 不受欢迎的)

***welfare** [ˈwelfɛə] *n.* 福利，安宁，幸福

【例】They were concerned for the children's *welfare*. 他们关心儿童的福利。

---

well [wel] *adv.* 好，充分地 *adj.* 健康的 *int.* 好吧 *n.* 井

【用】as well as 也，又：It's great fun as well as a good start in survival training. 这既有趣，又是生存训练的良好开端。注意：as well as相当于一个连词, 连接两个主语时, 谓语动词要和其前面的主语保持一致: Tom, as well as Mary and Jane, is coming to party. 汤姆和玛丽与简一样也要去参加舞会。

【例】You look *well*. 你气色很好。//a *well*-known doctor 一位著名医生

【考】1. as well 也 2. **well off** 经济宽裕

west [west] *adj.* 西边的 *adv.* 在西方, 向西 *n.* 西部

【考】**in the west** 在西方

【衍】westward (s) * (*adv.* 向西, 朝西)

western [ˈwestən] *adj.* 西方的; 西部的

【例】Britain has allied itself with other *western* powers for trade and defence. 英国与西方其他强国结成了贸易和防御联盟。

wet [wet] *adj.* 湿的

【例】I went out in the rain and got *wet* through. 我冒雨出去, 结果被淋透了。

whale [weil;hweil] *n.* 鲸

what [wɔt;hwɔt] *pron./adj./conj.* 什么

【用】1. what可以引导主语从句、宾语从句和表语从句: What we can't get seems better than what we have. 我们得不到的似乎比我们拥有的更好。注意: what+to do相当于what引导的名词性从句: I don't know what to say. 我不知道说什么。2. what用于感叹句, 后接名词: What a beautiful park (it is)! 多美丽的公园啊! 注意: how用于感叹句后接形容词或副词: How beautiful (the park is)! 多美丽的公园啊!

whatever [wɔtˈevə;hwɔtˈevə] *conj./pron.* 无论什么

【用】whatever既可以引导名词性从句, 也可以引导让步状语从句, 引导让步状语从句时相当于no matter what。如: Whatever I do, I do it for you. (=No matter what I do, I do it for you.) 无论我做什么, 都是为了你。类似用法的词还有: whoever, whichever, whenever, wherever, however等。

【例】They eat *whatever* they can find. 他们找到什么就吃什么。

wheat [wiːt;hwiːt] *n.* 小麦

【记】联想记忆: wh(o) +eat→谁吃? →人人都要吃小麦

wheel [wiːl;hwiːl] *n.* 轮, 车轮

when [wen;hwen] *conj.* 什么时候；当…的时候 *adv.* 在那时

【用】1. when引导定语从句，表示先行词所指的时间，在定语从句中作连接副词：Do you remember the day when we met? 你记得我们相遇的那一天吗？注意：如果先行词所指的时间在定语从句中不起状语作用，就不用when：Do you remember the day that was the coldest so far? 你记得迄今为止最冷的那一天吗？2. when引导名词性从句：They didn't know when they would go. 他们不知道什么时候走。3. when + 非谓语动词，相当于when引导的名词性从句或状语从句：They didn't know when to go. 他们不知道什么时候走。// Generally speaking, when taken according to the directions, the drug has no side effect. 一般而言，如果按照说明服药，这种药没有副作用。

【例】It was raining *when* we arrived. 我们到的时候正在下雨。

whenever [wen'evə;hwen'evə] *conj.* 无论何时

【例】Wash the car *whenever* it's convenient for you. 你什么时候方便就什么时候把车洗了。

where [wɛə;hwɛə] *adv./conj.* 那儿，何处

【例】That is the small town *where* I used to work for years. 那是我曾经工作过多年的小镇。//There were dirty marks on her trousers *where* she had wiped her hands. 她的裤子上有几块擦手时留下的脏印。

wherever [ˌwɛər'evə;ˌhwɛər'evə] *conj.* 无论何处；任何地方

【例】I'll go *wherever* you want. 你想去哪儿，我就去哪儿。

whether ['weðə;'hweðər] *conj.* 是否

【记】注意不要和weather (*n.* 天气) 相混

【例】I'm not sure *whether* I have time this Sunday. 我不敢肯定这个周日是否有时间。

【辨】**whether, if**

whether和**if**都是连词，都可以表示"是否"之意，引导从句时二者常可互换，但下列情况时只能用**whether**，不能用**if**：1. 位于名词后引导同位语从句时；2. 位于句首引导主语从句时；3. 引导表语从句时；4. 位于介词之后时；5. 后接动词不定式时。6. 另外，常说**whether... or not**而不说**if... or not**。

which [witʃ;hwitʃ] *pron./conj.* 哪一个；哪一些

【用】which引导定语从句时，可以指代前面整句话的内容：The weather turned out to be very good, which was more than we could expect. 天气最后非常好，这大大超过了我们的预期。

whichever [witʃ'evə;hwitʃ'evə] *pron.* 不论哪个

【例】I'll give this cookie to *whichever* of you wants it. 你们谁要，我就把甜饼给谁。

while [wail;hwail] *conj.* 正当…的时候；然而 *n.* 一小会

【用】1. while引导时间状语从句，表示主句和从句的动作同时发生，从句动词必须是延续性的：While I was walking along the road, I found a bag lying on the ground. 我在街上走时看见地上有一个包。//—I'm going to the post office.—While you're there, can you get me some stamps? —我要去邮局。—你到邮局时帮我买些邮票好吗？2. while引导让步状语从句，相当于although：While I accept that he is not perfect, I do actually like the person. 尽管我接受他不完美的事实，但我的确喜欢他。3. while用作并列连词，表示前后两者的强烈对比：I don't like tomatoes, while Mary loves them. 我不喜欢吃西红柿，而玛丽非常喜欢。

【辨】while, when, as

while, when, as都可以引导时间状语从句。when和while都可以表示主句动作与从句动作同时发生，when常与一般时态连用，而while引导的从句必须是进行时态或延续性动词：While he stood there he saw two men enter the bar. 他站在那时，看见两个男人走进了酒吧。as可以表示两个动作同时进行，强调一种伴随关系：As it grew darker it became colder. 随着天色越来越暗，天气越来越冷。

while, but

这两个连词虽然在汉语中都可以翻译成"但是"，但是but是指逻辑上的转折关系，而while只是一种对比关系。如：I tried not to be angry with him, but I can't. 我试着不生他的气，但是我做不到。// Fred is very good at science, while his brother is absolutely hopeless. 弗莱德很擅长理科，而他的兄弟则绝对是无可救药。

whisper ['wispə;'hwispə] *n./v.* 低语，私语

【例】You should *whisper* when you're in the library. 在图书馆的时候，你应该轻声低语。

whistle ['wisl; 'hwisl] *n.* 口哨声；汽笛声 *v.* 鸣笛，吹口哨

【例】Bill *whistled* to get my attention. 比尔吹口哨想引起我的注意。

whisper

white [wait; hwait] *adj.* 白的 *n.* 白人

【考】**white lie** 无恶意的谎言

who [hu:] *pron./conj.* 谁

【例】You are the only person here *who* knows me. 你是这儿惟一认识我的人。//They haven't found out *who* did it. 他们还没找出是谁干的这件事。

whole [həul] *adj.* 完整的，所有的

【例】Mary did the *whole* job herself. 玛丽自己完成了所有的工作。

【考】**on the whole** 大体上，基本上 // **the whole life** 一生

whom [hu:m] *pron./conj.* 谁

【例】She was a woman *whom* I greatly respected. 她是一个我非常敬佩的女人。

whose [hu:z] *pron./conj.* 谁的

【用】whose引导定语从句，在从句中充当定语，表示所属关系：I have a good friend whose name is Liu Mei. 我有一个好朋友名叫刘梅。//Recently I bought an ancient Chinese vase, whose price was very reasonable. 最近我买了一个年代久远的陶瓷花瓶，价格非常公道。

why [wai; hwai] *adv./conj.* 为什么 *int.* (表示吃惊或满意) 哎呀！什么？

【用】1. why用于引导主语从句、表语从句和宾语从句：Why he shot her is a complete mystery. 他为什么枪杀了她完全是个谜。//This is why I left early. 这就是我早早离开的原因。//I don't know why he is late again. 我不知道他为什么又迟到了。2. 先行词是reason时用why引导定语从句：There are several reasons why we can't do that. 有几个原因使我们不能做那件事。

wide [waid] *adj.* 宽的，阔的

widespread ['waid'spred] *adj.* 分布广的

W

【记】组合词：wide（宽广的）+spread（传播，分布）→分布广的

*widow [ˈwidəu] n. 寡妇

【记】寡妇（widow）守在窗户（window）口等待不可能再回来的
丈夫

wild [waild] adj. 野生的

【衍】wildlife（n. 野生生物）

单元自测

1. Though _____ of danger, he still went skating on the thin ice.

   A. warned   B. to be warned   C. being warned   D. had been warned

2. What _____ time it is to listen to a speech having nothing to do with you!

   A. waste   B. wastes   C. a waste of   D. a waste for

3. _____ your step, or you might fall into the water.

   A. Care   B. Notice   C. See   D. Watch

4. _____ I can see what you mean, even though I don't share your point of view.

   A. In any way   B. By the way   C. In a way   D. In the way

5. He gained his _____ by printing _____ of famous writers.

   A. wealth; work   B. wealths; works   C. wealths; work   D. wealth; works

6. The swimmers were standing along the bank, _____ swimming suits.

   A. all of whom wearing   B. all wearing

   C. all wore   D. all of them wore

7. — _____.

   —Yes, a bit cold, though.

   A. Cold weather, isn't it?   B. Bad weather, don't you think?

   C. Hot weather, isn't it?   D. Nice day, isn't it?

8. The boss said he would _____ in mind one plan against the other to arrive at an answer.

   A. think   B. get   C. discuss   D. weigh

9. The foreigners were _____ by the students from our school.

   A. welcome   B. welcame   C. welcomed   D. welcoming

10. Miss Zhang didn't feel _____ last night, so she sent for a doctor.

   A. well   B. good   C. nice   D. glad

11. Although he knew little about the work done in the field of physics, he succeeded _____ other experienced experts failed.

A. which   B. that   C. what   D. where

12. It is generally considered unwise to give a child _____ he or she wants.

A. however   B. whatever   C. whichever   D. whenever

13. The film brought the hours back to me _____ I was taken good care of in that far-away village.

A. until   B. that   C. when   D. where

14. After the war, a new school building was put up _____ there had once been a theatre.

A. that   B. where   C. which   D. when

15. Many places are flooded by heavy rainfalls, so they can't walk _____ they like these days.

A. whatever   B. whichever   C. whenever   D. wherever

答案：ACDCD BDDCA DBCBD

Victory won't come to me unless I go to it.

—*Moore*

胜利不会向我走来，我必须自己走向胜利。

——穆尔

Word List 40

will ［wil］*aux. v.*（would）将要 *n.* 意志；遗嘱

【用】will作情态动词：1. 表示意愿或决心：I will do my best to help you. 我愿意尽力帮助你。2. 表示习惯或规律：Fish will die out of water. 鱼儿离开水就会死。3. 表示请求、建议或询问，此时would不指过去，只是语气更委婉：Would you like a drink? 你要不要来杯饮料？

【例】Maggie had the *will* to finish her degree in four years. 麦琪希望能在四年内取得学位。

willing ［wiliŋ］*adj.* 情愿的，乐意的

【用】**be willing to do...** 愿意做…：The gentleman is willing to pay for the bill. 绅士乐意买单。

win ［win］*v.*（won, won, winning）赢得，获胜

【例】*win* the game 赢得比赛//*win* the prize 获奖

【衍】winner（*n.* 获胜者）

wind ［wind］*n.* 风 *vt.*（wound, wound, winding）盘绕，旋转

【例】I *wound* the fishing line around the reel. 我把鱼线绕在卷轴上。

window ［'windəu］*n.* 窗户

windy ［'windi］*adj.* 多风的

【记】来自wind（风）+y（…的）→多风的

wine ［wain］*n.* 葡萄酒

【记】获胜（win）了喝酒（wine）庆祝

wing ［wiŋ］*n.* 机翼；翅膀

【记】容祖儿的一首歌《挥着（swing）翅膀（wing）的女孩》

***wipe** ［waip］*vt.* 擦；扫

【例】*Wipe* apple juice off your face. 把苹果汁从脸上擦掉。

wire ［'waiə］*n.* 电线

320

wisdom ['wizdəm] *n.* 智慧

【记】来自 wise（*adj.* 聪明的）→智慧

【例】I appreciated my advisor's *wisdom*. 我欣赏我顾问的智慧。

wise [waiz] *adj.* 聪明的，英明的，有见识的

wish [wiʃ] *n./v.* 祝愿；想要

【用】1. **wish to do** 希望做某事：How I wish to go there! 我好想去那儿啊！ 2. **wish+宾语从句**（虚拟语气），表示无法或难以实现的愿望：I wish I were as strong as Tom. 我希望能像汤姆一样健壮。// I wish that it would stop snowing. 我希望雪能停。

with [wið] *prep.* 与，伴随；有，以

【用】with+宾语+宾补，这个复合结构常用作状语或定语，该结构中的宾补可以是不定式、现在分词、过去分词、形容词、副词和介词短语。具体用法如下：1. **with+宾语+to do**：With two exams to worry about, I have to work really hard this weekend. 由于有两个考试，我这个周末不得不好好复习了。2. **with+宾语+doing**：In parts of Asia you must not sit with your feet pointing at another person. 在亚洲的某些地区，你坐的时候不可以将脚对着别人。3. **with+宾语+done**：It was a pity that the great writer died with his works unfinished. 很遗憾那位伟大的作家还未完成著作就去世了。4. **with+宾语+介词短语**：She saw a brook with red flowers and green grass on both sides. 她看到一条小溪，两岸长着红花绿草。

*withdraw [wið'drɔ:] *v.* (withdrew, withdrawn, withdrawing) 缩回，撤退

【例】John *withdrew* his suggestion when no one supported it. 当没有人支持时，约翰收回了他的建议。

【衍】withdrawn（*adj.* 内向的，孤僻的）

within [wi'ðin] *prep.* 在…内

【例】*Within* three months, the dieter had lost 15 pounds. 三个月里，节食者减去了15磅。

without [wi'ðaut] *prep.* 没有，不

【例】How long can you work *without* sleeping? 你能不睡觉连续工作多久？

*witness ['witnis] *v.* 目击，作证 *n.* 证人，目击者

【例】The police questioned the *witness* about the accident. 警察就事故向目击者询问。

wonder ['wʌndə] v. 想知道；对…感到惊讶 n. 奇迹

【用】**(It is) no wonder + (that)** 从句：难怪，怪不得：He hasn't slept at all for three days. It is no wonder he is tired out. 他已经三天没睡觉了，难怪他疲惫不堪。

【例】I *wonder* if I could ask you a few questions. 我能否问您几个问题？

wonderful ['wʌndəfl] adj. 极好的

【例】We had a *wonderful* time on vacation. 我们度假非常开心。

*****woolen** ['wulən] adj. 羊毛的，羊毛制的

【记】来自wool（羊毛）+en→羊毛的

【例】*woolen* gloves 羊毛手套

word [wə:d] n. 单词；言语；消息，音讯

【例】Danby left *word* with my secretary that he would call again in the afternoon. 戴比给我的秘书留下口信儿说下午再打电话。

【考】1. **in a word** 总之 2. **in other words** 换言之 3. **keep one's word** 遵守诺言 4. **have words with sb.** 与某人争吵 5. **have a word with sb.** 与某人谈话

work [wə:k] n. 工作；著作 v. 工作；运作；奏效

【考】1. **work out** 计算出；（事情）进展顺利或结果令人满意 2. **work on** 继续工作；影响 3. **work for...** 为…工作

【衍】worker（n. 工人）

worry ['wʌri] v. 担忧，烦恼 n. 烦恼，担忧

【用】**worry about...** 担心…：Many people worried about the existence of wildlife. 许多人担心野生动物的生存问题。

【衍】worried（adj. 担心的；烦恼的）

worth [wə:θ] adj. 值得的；价值…

【用】worth是表语形容词，主要用于1. **be worth doing** 值得做：The man isn't worth waiting for. 这个男人不值得等。2. **be worth+n.** 价值…：That necklace was worth five hundred francs at the most. 那条项链最多值500法郎。

【衍】worthwhile*（adj. 值得的）

*****worthy** ['wə:ði] adj. 值得的；相称的

【例】The place is *worthy* of a visit. 这地方值得参观。//a *worthy* name of the city 与这个城市相称的名字

would [wud] *modal v.* 将；愿；会 *aux. v.*（will的过去式）

【用】1. would作为情态动词，表示请求或邀请，常用于疑问句：Would you please count your change? 点一点找给你的钱好吗？2. would作为情态动词还可以表示过去的习惯：She would sit for hours doing nothing in the afternoon. 她总是在午后连续坐上几个小时，什么也不干。3. 作为助动词，构成虚拟语气。虚拟过去用 would（not）have done... 本来会（不会）做…：The ship would have sunk with all on board but for the efforts of the captain. 要是没有这位船长的努力，这艘船连同船上所有的人早就一块儿沉没了。虚拟现在和未来用would+do/be：If I had enough money, I would buy a car. 我如果有足够的钱就会买辆汽车。

*wrestle ['resl] *v.* 摔跤，格斗；斟酌

【例】The police officer *wrestled* the criminal to the ground. 警官将罪犯摔倒在地。

*wrinkle ['riŋkl] *n.* 皱纹

【记】眼睛一眨一眨（twinkle）都起皱纹（wrinkle）了

wrist [rist] *n.* 手腕，腕关节

【记】和fist（*n.* 拳头）一起记

write [rait] *v.*（wrote, written, writing）写

【考】1. **write out** 写出 2. **write to** 给…写信 3. **write down** 写下，记下

wrong [rɔŋ; rɔːŋ] *adj.* 错误的

【考】**go wrong** 走错路；发生故障

【辨】**wrong, false**

两者都有"错误的"之意。**wrong**主要偏向"不正确的"，"不合适的"或"不道德的"；而**false**则主要指"虚假的"或"伪造的"。

X-ray ['eks 'rei] *n.* X射线；X光

【例】The *X-ray* showed the boy's leg was broken. X光片显示出那个男孩的腿断了。

yard [jɑːd] *n.* 码；院子，场地

【例】Every morning, Tom and his sister have to clean their *yard*. 每天早晨，汤姆和他的姐姐都得打扫院子。

*yawn [jɔːn] *v.* 打呵欠

【记】躺在草地（lawn）上伸懒腰，打呵欠（yawn）

【例】I felt so sleepy that I couldn't stop *yawning*. 我太困了，不停地打呵欠。

*yell [jel] *vt.* 大叫，呼喊

【记】联想记忆：ye（看作yes）+ll（想像成高高举起的双臂）→高举双臂，高呼"Yes"。

【用】**yell at...** 向…大叫：He yelled at her to be careful. 他大声朝她叫，让她小心。

yet [jet] *adv.* 到目前为止；还；仍然

【用】用于否定句和疑问句（肯定句中用still）：No decision has yet been made. 还没有做出任何决定。//Have they arrived yet? 他们到了吗?

yoghurt [ˈjɔgət; ˈjəugərt] *n.* 酸乳酪

【例】I'd like two strawberry *yoghurts*. 我要两份草莓酸乳酪。

yummy [ˈjʌmi] *adj.* 美味的

【例】*yummy* flavours 怡人的香味

zebra [ˈziːbrə] *n.* 斑马

【例】*zebra* crossing 斑马线

zip [zip] *v.* 拉开/拉上拉链 *n.* 拉链

【例】a *zip* bag 带拉锁的包

*zipper [ˈzipə] *n.* 拉链

【例】The *zipper* on my coat has got stuck. 我外套上的拉链卡住了。

*zone [zəun] *n.* 区域；范围

【记】动感地带M-zone

【例】time *zone* 时区

*zoom [zuːm] *v.* 突然扩大，使猛增

【例】Overnight trading caused share prices to *zoom*. 隔夜交易使得股价直线上升。

单元自测

1. —Write to me when you get home.

— _____.

A. I must　　　B. I should　　　C. I will　　　D. I can

2. We _____ you a pleasant journey to Shanghai.

A. hope　　　B. wish　　　C. want　　　D. expect

3. There are many things whose misuse is dangerous, but it is hard to think of anything that can be compared _____ tobacco products.

    A. in   B. with   C. among   D. by

4. _____ the temperature falling rapidly, we couldn't go on with the experiment.

    A. Since   B. For   C. As   D. With

5. _____ came of his success in the singing competition abroad.

    A. Word   B. Words   C. A word   D. Some words

6. We're pleased to see that things have _____ all right.

    A. worked out   B. worked at

    C. got up   D. got in

7. Only one of these books is _____.

    A. worth to read   B. worth being read

    C. worth reading   D. worth of reading

8. I just did what I should do, nothing _____ praise.

    A. worth of   B. worth   C. worthy   D. worthy of

9. We used to work in the same office and we _____ have coffee together.

    A. would   B. should   C. which   D. might

10. Who can _____ me a ball-pen _____?

    A. save; to write   B. borrow; to be written

    C. spare; to write with   D. spend; writing with

11. Old as the car is, _____ it works quite well.

    A. but   B. yet   C. so   D. however

12. Both teams were in hard training; neither was _____ to lose the game.

    A. willing   B. reluctant   C. ready   D. hoping

13. —Mind your own business, OK?

    —Don't get me _____; I just want to help you.

    A. false   B. right   C. fault   D. wrong

14. —It is said that the math exam this time is really difficult! You know math is the last course I want to study.

    — _____; I'll help you with your math.

    A. That's OK   B. That's all right   C. Don't worry   D. That's fine

15. Do you know how many time _____ are there in our world?

    A. areas   B. zones   C. places   D. regions

答案: CBBDA ACDAC BADCB